Learning to Teach Science in the Secondary School

A companion to school experience

Second edition

**Edited by
Jenny Frost and Tony Turner**

RoutledgeFalmer
Taylor & Francis Group

LONDON AND NEW YORK

First published 2005
by RoutledgeFalmer
2 Park Square, Milton Park, Abingdon, Oxon OX14 4RN

Simultaneously published in the USA and Canada
by RoutledgeFalmer
270 Madison Ave, New York, NY 10016

RoutledgeFalmer is an imprint of the Taylor & Francis Group

Typeset in Bembo by
HWA Text and Data Management, Tunbridge Wells
Printed and bound in Great Britain by
TJ International Ltd, Padstow, Cornwall

British Library Cataloguing in Publication Data
A catalogue record for this book is available from the British Library

Library of Congress Cataloging in Publication Data
A catalog record for this book has been requested

ISBN 0–415–28780–4

Contents

Illustrations

FIGURES

TASKS

Contributors

Alastair Cuthbertson has taught science and physics for 24 years and lectured in science education at the Institute of Education, University of London for four years. He is currently Head of Science at Ivybridge Community College in Devon, a Specialist Sports College with Training School status. His interests include effective science teaching and management of science departments.

Jenny Frost is a senior lecturer in science education at the Institute of Education, University of London. She has many years experience of working on the initial teacher education course for secondary science teachers and working with the science mentors in London schools. Her interests include effective science teaching, the use of practical work in science, primary science, and encouraging teachers to adopt a research role to their teaching. She was co-author and editor of *Teaching Science* (Woburn Press) and author of *Creativity in Primary Science* (Open University Press). She taught science and physics originally in secondary schools in London and Ghana before joining the Institute of Education.

Christine Harrison is a science education lecturer at King's College, London and director of the assessment group. The main work of this group since 1998 has been working with teachers on formative assessment strategies at primary, secondary and tertiary phases. Christine taught science in secondary schools in and around London and part of her role at King's is working with trainees and school mentors on the PGCE course.

Ralph Levinson taught science at secondary schools in London and is now a lecturer in science education at the Institute of Education, University of London. Previous to working at the Institute he was at the Open University and University College, Northampton. He is the editor of *Teaching Science*, co-editor with Jeff Thomas of *Science Today* and co-editor with Michael Reiss of *Key Issues in Bioethics* all published by RoutledgeFalmer. He has written widely on science, science education and on socio-scientific issues. Some of his books for children and short stories have won national awards.

Katherine Little currently teaches science at a comprehensive school in Hampshire. Prior to training to be a teacher at the Institute of Education, University of London, she was awarded her doctorate in anthropology, researching the genetics and behaviour of Indian monkeys.

Ian Longman is a senior lecturer in education at the University of Brighton where he is science route leader on PGCE (Secondary), BA(Honours) Science Education and BA(Honours) Upper Primary/Lower Secondary Education courses. Prior to this he was head of a science department in a school in Brighton. This followed a three-year contract working as an LEA advisory teacher for science. He has also taught in science departments in comprehensive schools in Essex, Kent and East Sussex. He is currently chairman of the Surrey and Sussex Region of the Association for Science Education. He was involved with supporting schools in using *Nuffield Co-ordinated Sciences* and *Pathways Through Science* materials.

Jane Maloney is a lecturer in education at the Institute of Education, University of London where she is a PGCE science tutor. She has worked there part-time since 2001 while completing her doctoral thesis. Prior to coming to the Institute of Education, she worked part-time at King's College London as a PGCE tutor and as a teacher at the Royal Botanic Gardens, Kew. She worked for six years at Kingston University where she taught on BEd, PGCE and CPD courses and was the science team leader. She has taught in secondary schools for over 13 years as a biology teacher and was a head of year and health education co-ordinator.

Michael J. Reiss is professor of science education and head of the School of Mathematics, Science and Technology at the Institute of Education, University of London. After a Ph.D. and postdoctoral study in evolutionary biology and animal behaviour, he trained as a school teacher and taught in schools before returning to higher education in 1988. He is the author of a number of books including *Understanding Science Lessons: Five Years of Science Teaching* (Open University Press, 2000). He directs the Salters-Nuffield Advanced Biology Project, is the inaugural editor of the journal *Sex Education* and is currently a member of the UK government's Science Review Panel examining genetically modified crops. Michael Reiss is chief executive of the newly established Regional Science Learning Centre, London.

Pete Sorensen is a lecturer in science education and co-ordinator of the flexible PGCE route at the University of Nottingham. After teaching in schools in Oxfordshire and Ghana for eighteen years, with periods as a lecturer in science education at the University of Cape Coast and as Secretary of the Oxfordshire Teaching Associations, he moved into higher education at Canterbury Christ Church University College before taking up his current post. Pete jointly edited *Issues in Science Teaching* (RoutledgeFalmer, 2000) and is currently researching in initial teacher education, with a particular interest in flexible routes and peer learning.

Tony Turner was Senior Lecturer in Education at the Institute of Education, University of London (until retirement in September 2000). He is co-editor of *Starting to Teach in the Secondary School* (Routledge, 1997) and is preparing a second edition of that book. He is co-editor of *Learning to Teach in the Secondary School*, 3rd edn (Capel, Leask and Turner).

Bernadette Youens is a lecturer in science education at the School of Education, University of Nottingham where she teaches on the PGCE secondary course. She taught science in comprehensive schools in Nottinghamshire before moving into initial teacher education in 1998. Her current research interests include mentoring in initial teacher education and pupil perspectives on science and science teaching. She contributed the chapter 'External examinations and assessment' in the companion text *Learning to Teach in the Secondary School: A Companion to School Experience*, 3rd edn (RoutledgeFalmer, 2001).

Acknowledgements

Since the first edition of this book appeared in 1998 several significant changes have occurred in secondary education. A new science National Curriculum came into operation in 2000 and vocational courses in science have developed further. The lists of competences once expected of newly qualified teachers (NQTs) have been transformed into a more holistic set of Standards and new ways of achieving Qualified Teacher Status have emerged and grown. In addition, a new route for some student teachers has been introduced – the Fast Track – for graduates likely to move quickly up the education ladder. The induction has been consolidated and a set of criteria published for the first year of teaching and this book anticipates that new challenge.

One of us (TT) wishes to thank two members of the science staff of the School of Mathematics, Science and Technology, Institute of Education, University of London who took up the challenge of revising the first edition of this book, Jenny Frost and Ralph Levinson, and without whom the book would not have been written.

The editors wish to acknowledge the input of Ralph Levinson who contributed considerably to framing the structure of the book, to fleshing out the details as well as to his contribution of several chapters. We also acknowledge the contributions made by several members of staff of the Institute of Education and equally to colleagues in other Institutes of Higher Education and secondary schools who have contributed chapters. The editors, too, wish to thank Mike Vingoe, Head of the Faculty of Natural Science at Riddlesdown High School for providing discussion and material for Figure 7.3.2 and to Dr. Dibbs, Headteacher of the school for giving permission to use school material. We are grateful to Janet Maxwell for the sketches which make up Figure 6.2.1; and to Pam Bishop, formerly of the School of Education, University of Nottingham for permission to use the ideas which contribute to Figure 5.3.5. We should like to thank Ruth Frost for her help in checking and formatting the manuscript.

Finally we are indebted to Anna Clarkson and Jessica Simmons of RoutledgeFalmer for their professional advice, support and patience.

Abbreviations and acronyms

ACCAC	Awdurdod Cymhwysterau, Cwricwlwm ac Asesu Cymru (Qualifications, Curriculum and Assessment, Wales)
AEA	Advanced Extension Awards
AKSIS	Association for Science Education and King's College Science Investigations
ALIS+	Post 16 Information Service
APG	Autumn Package Guidance
AQA	Assessment and Qualifications Alliance (one of the three main awarding bodies)
A level	Advanced level (GCE)
AS	Advanced Subsidiary (GCE)
ASE	Association for Science Education
AVCE	Advanced Vocational Certificate of Education
BTEC	Business and Technical Education Council
CASE	Cognitive Acceleration in Science Education
CAT	Cognitive Abilities Test
CCEA	Council for Curriculum Examinations and Assessment (N. Ireland)
CEDP	Career Entry and Development Profile
CLEAPSS	Consortium of Local Education Authorities for the Provision of Science Services
CLISP	Children's Learning in Science Project
COSHH	Control of Substances Hazardous to Health Regulations
CPD	Continuing Professional Development
DES	Department of Education and Science
DfE	Department for Education
DfEE	Department for Education and Employment
DfES	Department for Education and Skills
EAL	English as an Additional Language

EDEXCEL	One of the three main awarding bodies
ESTA	Earth Science Teachers Association
GCE	General Certificate of Education
GCSE	General Certificate of Secondary Education
GTC	General Teaching Council
HEA	Health Education Authorities
HMI	Her Majesty's Inspectors
HoD	Head of Department
ICT	Information communications technology
IoB	Institute of Biology
IoP	Institute of Physics
KS1, 2, 3, 4	Key stages, 1, 2, 3 and 4
LEA	Local Education Authority
LSA	Learning Support Assistant
MIDYIS	Year 7–9 Information Service
NC	National Curriculum
NCC	National Curriculum Council
NVQ	National Vocational Qualification
NQF	National Qualifications Framework
NQT	Newly Qualified Teacher
OCR	Oxford Cambridge and Royal Society of Arts (one of the three main awarding bodies)
OFSTED	Office for Standards in Education
PANDA	Performance and Assessment Data
PGCE	Postgraduate Certificate of Education
POAE	Planning, Obtaining evidence, Analysing evidence, Evaluating evidence
PoS	Programmes of Study
PSHE	Personal Social and Health Education
QCA	Qualifications and Curriculum Authority
QTS	Qualified Teacher Status
RSC	Royal Society of Chemistry
RSPB	Royal Society for the Protection of Birds
SAT	Standard Assessment Test
SCAA	School Curriculum and Assessment Authority
SCITT	School Centred Initial Teacher Training
SEAC	Schools Examination and Assessment Council
SEN	Special Educational Needs
SENCo	Special Educational Needs Coordinator
SQA	Scottish Qualifications Authority
SRE	Sex and Relationship Education
SSR	School Science Review
TES	Times Educational Supplement
TGAT	Task Group on Assessment and Testing
TTA	Teacher Training Agency
VA	Value added
YELLIS	Year 10/11 Information Service

Introduction to the series

The second edition of *Learning to Teach Science in the Secondary School* is one of a series of books entitled *Learning to Teach {Subject} in the Secondary School* covering most subjects in secondary school curriculum. The books in the series support and complement *Learning to Teach in the Secondary School: A Companion to School Experience, 3rd edition* (Capel, Leask and Turner, 2001) which was first published in 1995. These books are designed for student teachers learning to teach on different types of initial teacher education courses and in different places. However, it is hoped that they will be equally useful to tutors and mentors in their work with student teachers. In 1997 a complementary book was published entitled *Starting to Teach in the Secondary School: A Companion for the Newly Qualified Teacher* (Capel, Leask and Turner, 1997). That second book was designed to support newly qualified teachers in their first post and covered aspects of teaching which are likely to be of concern in the first year of teaching. A completely revised and updated second edition of that book is to be published in 2004.

The information in the subject books does not repeat that in *Learning to Teach,* rather the content of that book is adapted and extended to address the needs of student teachers learning to teach a specific subject. In each of the subject books, therefore, reference is made to *Learning to Teach,* where appropriate. It is recommended that you have both books so that you can cross-refer when needed.

The positive feedback on *Learning to Teach,* particularly the way it has supported the learning of student teachers in their development into effective, reflective teachers, has encouraged us to retain the main features of that book in the subject series. Thus, the subject books are designed so that elements of appropriate theory introduce each topic or issue. Recent research into teaching and learning is incorporated into the presentation. The material is interwoven with tasks designed to help you identify key features of the topic or issue and apply this to your own practice.

Although the basic content of each subject book is similar, each book is designed to address the unique nature of each subject. The second edition of *Learning to Teach Science in the Secondary School* is a complete revision of the first edition with many new features and completely rewritten chapters. The second edition takes account of recent changes to National Curriculum science and to the way teachers are educated and the standards they must meet. The authors have introduced a new section addressing the wide knowledge background needed to teach science as well as retaining a modified section on the nature of science. The importance of language, communication skills and active learning are retained and strengthened.

We, as editors, have been pleased with the reception given to the first edition of the book and to the *Learning to Teach* series as a whole. Some subject books in the series have moved into their second edition and others are in preparation. We hope that, whatever initial teacher education programme you are following and wherever you may be situated, you find the second edition of this book supports your development towards becoming an effective, reflective teacher of science.

Susan Capel, Marilyn Leask and Tony Turner
April 2004

1 Learning to be a Science Teacher

Jenny Frost

INTRODUCTION – A DIVERSITY OF STARTING POINTS

People who come into science teaching do so from vastly different backgrounds, in terms of culture, age, educational experience, work experience, attitudes, levels of confidence, languages and religions. Science, along with mathematics, information communications technology (ICT), religious education (RE) and business studies, attracts people from more diverse ethnic backgrounds than other subjects. The age profile is wide with many people having worked in research, science-based industries, or finance before turning to teach science. Some come with teaching experience of say English as a foreign language, or science in schools where a teaching qualification was not required, or working as learning support assistants in local schools. Many have worked with young people in clubs and youth groups. Their educational experiences of science can vary widely, not only in the type of school they went to but the different teaching styles they experienced and the different resources to which they had access. The prominence given to practical work in UK schools can come as a surprise to many graduates from other European countries, from the Middle East, Africa and Asia. Qualifications vary considerably; there are those who came into science via vocational qualifications, possibly going to university for their first degrees in mid- to late-twenties, as opposed to others who went to higher education straight after school. Some have gone through access courses to gain entry to higher education. There is diversity also in studies at university, so that people with degrees as diverse as astrophysics, genetics, sports science and geology can all be training for the same job of 'science teacher'. Different religious beliefs may put creationists and evolutionists side by side as colleagues.

The diversity of backgrounds and perspectives has two important implications for your learning as a science teacher. The first is that people training together form an enormously valuable resource for each other. Different perspectives, different knowledge and different experiences can be useful in developing your own knowledge and also in challenging your own assumptions and preconceptions. The second is that each person makes their own personal journey in the process of learning to be a science teacher, because of the different starting points and the different modes of learning. They do, however, share similar experiences on the training courses. It is the reflection on, and discussion of, those experiences with colleagues which provide diverse and valuable ways of thinking about, and learning from, your experiences.

OBJECTIVES

By end of this chapter you should:

- be aware of factors which contribute to successful science teaching;
- know the features and demands of a course of initial teacher education in science;
- understand your personal responsibility for your own development;
- know the contribution this book may make to your development.

WHAT IS NEEDED TO BE A SCIENCE TEACHER?

Figure 1.1 provides an answer to this question in terms of the knowledge, skills, attitudes, values which are necessary to be a science teacher. You need knowledge of a range of science; the nature of science, pedagogical content knowledge, pupils' learning in science, resources useful for science and assessment strategies. Positive attitudes towards science and to your own professional development are essential. Your values determine your aims of education in general as well as of science education. Finally, awareness of your own learning processes is important. Figure 1.2 provides a different description of the learning you are to achieve, in that it relates to the school context in more detail.

Figure 1.1 has been used to structure this book, while Figure 1.2 has acted as a reminder of the contextual detail to be included. This book is written in conjunction with the generic book *Learning to Teach in the Secondary School* (Capel *et al.* 2001) and we assume readers have access to it. We have attempted not to repeat material in the generic book, although for clarity there is some overlap. Relevant references to the generic book are given in the 'further reading' at the end of each chapter or unit. Like the generic book there are tasks for you to do either on your own or in collaboration with mentors in schools, your tutor in higher education or your fellow students. There is the same mix of theory and practical advice, as theory is essential to interpret much of what you experience in your journey to becoming a science teacher. We have adopted the same convention of using 'pupils' when referring to people studying in schools, and 'students' for those learning to be a teacher, despite the fact that many people use 'students' for the former, and 'trainee teacher', 'beginning teacher' or 'student teacher' for the latter.

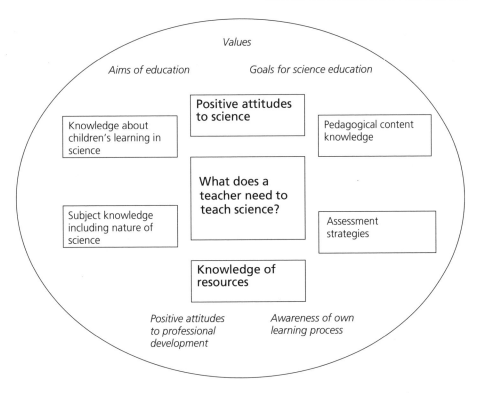

Values

Aims of education   *Goals for science education*

Positive attitudes to science

Knowledge about children's learning in science

Pedagogical content knowledge

What does a teacher need to teach science?

Subject knowledge including nature of science

Assessment strategies

Knowledge of resources

Positive attitudes to professional development   *Awareness of own learning process*

Figure 1.1 What does a teacher need to teach science?

Source: Glauert and Frost 1997: 129.

GUIDE TO THE CHAPTERS

You need positive attitudes to your own professional development, because ultimately you are in charge of your own learning. You are entering a profession which expects you to be engaged in continuing professional development. The training period is merely a start. In Unit 2.1 Jenny Frost and Bernadette Youens discuss how you can set up good working relationships with the people who will be supporting you in the training period, how to make the most of their expertise and the varied learning experiences which are provided and how to be responsible for your own learning. In Unit 2.2 Ian Longman helps you understand the context of the science departments in which you work. The sooner you understand the way departments are structured and know the people in them, the more likely you are to be able to benefit from the expertise which is there.

What are your goals for science education? Chapter 3, while giving you a background and understanding of the national curriculum in science in England, also asks you to address your own goals for science education, because it is these which determine the emphasis you put on your science teaching. We ask you to think about these at the start, so that as your knowledge and experience develop, you can reflect back on them. Your goals for science education cannot, however, stand apart from your own set of values and aims for education in general. Graham Haydon (in Capel *et al.* 2001) provides a helpful guide to

---

Students should:

- deploy a wide range of techniques in teaching *science* (which includes biology, chemistry, physics, astronomy, geology and scientific enquiry) effectively and safely to pupils in Y7, Y8 and Y9 and possibly Y10 and Y11;
- use similar techniques to teach their *specialist science* to pupils in Y10–11 and up to AS/A2 and Advanced VCE Level;
- *assess, record and report* pupil progress and achievement professionally;
- set about developing appropriate provision for students with *special educational needs* (SEN) and for students for whom *English is an additional language* (EAL) and those designated as gifted and talented (G and T);
- be aware of *health and safety* legislation and be reliably *safe* in the practical activities which they do themselves and which they ask pupils to do;
- make use of the results of *educational theory and research* which are relevant to the teaching of science;
- make use of *information and communications technology* for the teaching of science;
- appreciate the present situation and recent developments relating to the *science curriculum*, and its place in the *whole curriculum,* including the National Curriculum and its assessment framework;
- understand recent changes in the arrangements for education (in science and more generally) for example in England the proposals for the *14–19 curriculum*;
- *develop* their classroom observation skills progressively through the course;
- *evaluate their own practice* through different perspectives in order to extend and improve it;
- *map their developing skills* as a science teacher onto the national or other standards for their course. In England this is the DfES/TTA *Qualifying to Teach: Professional Standards for Qualified Teacher Status and Requirements for Initial Teacher Training* (DfES/TTA 2003a). The DfES requires students as well to prepare a Professional Development Portfolio (PDP) and Career Entry and Development Profile (CEDP) before starting their NQT year;
- enter into the process of becoming a teacher by engaging in *high quality enquiry.*

Figure 1.2 Objectives for a science teaching course

aims of education in general, along with tasks which help you articulate your own.

In the majority of schools in England science teachers are expected to be able to teach across the sciences to the 11–14 age group and possibly to the 14–16 age group. Confidence and competence are required therefore in your own knowledge of biology, chemistry, physics, geology and astronomy, the nature of science, social and technological applications and health education. Initially, this breadth of knowledge requirement is seen as one of the main 'hills' to climb when people start science teaching. Tutors provide workshops and sessions to help you develop knowledge in unfamiliar areas, but much of the learning is under your control. The need to teach parts of science, to explain it to pupils, provides a major motivation. It is important to have sound scientific knowledge as research shows that teachers with good subject knowledge encourage pupils to ask more questions and are more flexible in their teaching approaches. Units in Chapter 4 provide you with what we think of as 'maps' to the areas of science. They tell some of the 'big stories of science' so that when you are grappling with the detail for a particular lesson, you do not lose sight of the larger picture. Michael Reiss in Unit 4.1 explores ideas about the nature of science, from the perspectives of different writers, explaining why it is important for you to have your own understanding of the nature of science. In Unit 4.2, Katherine Little provides an insight into the living world at the macro levels of individual organisms and the communities in which they live, at the micro levels of the biochemistry of DNA, and at the theory level of how it all began. In Unit 4.3, Tony Turner describes 'recycling' as at the heart of chemistry and as the basis of the origin of life. Chemistry is reduced to two major stories, the 'microscopic' world of particles and the macroscopic world of materials and their behaviour. In Unit 4.4, Jenny Frost goes from a bag of crisps to the Big Bang theory of the Universe to provide an insight into the scope of physics. Finally, Tony Turner in Unit 4.5 outlines the processes in the Earth's crust which account for different rock formations, soils and earthquakes.

For you to have studied science for many years, and now to be turning to a career which still involves you in science, means that you have positive attitudes at least to some areas of science. It is rare for anyone, however, to be equally enthusiastic about all areas and you may now have to address parts which you disliked at school. As a professional you need to find ways of developing an interest and enthusiasm for sections which you did not like before, because your attitudes will have a profound effect on the pupils. The units in Chapter 4 may help.

We turn in Chapter 5 from knowledge of subject to knowledge of learners, learning and teaching. Ralph Levinson's account of progression in learning science (Unit 5.1) gives an account of what is known about pupils' learning. Much of your own learning will mirror the features of progression which he describes, so sensitivity to your own learning of science will provide insights into the learning processes which pupils might well go through. Students who read one of the classic texts on children's ideas in science (Driver *et al.* 1994) comment that the book is as much about their learning as it is about children's.

Ralph Levinson's unit ends by addressing what teachers can do to ensure that progression in learning occurs and takes the reader directly into the art of planning. Bernadette Youens develops this in Units 5.2 and 5.3 addressing medium- and long-term planning in Unit 5.2 and planning of individual lessons in Unit 5.3. The importance of being clear what learning you want to achieve is emphasised. The idea of pedagogic content knowledge emerges here, i.e. knowledge of how to turn your own understanding into explanations, analogies, and learning tasks which make sense to learners. It is further developed in Pete Sorensen's Unit 5.4 on teaching strategies and organising learning; the importance of attitudes of teachers is identified in his reports of classroom scenarios. This chapter on planning ends with Jenny Frost's Unit 5.5 on planning for practical work, made complex by organisational and safety issues, and by the fact that learners can be distracted from scientific ideas by the 'clutter of apparatus'.

Throughout the book there are references to resources for science teaching. Chapter 6 focuses on further resources, both inside the school (Unit 6.1) and outside school (Unit 6.2). The first part of Unit 6.1 focuses on the role of language in science learning and associated resources, the latter parts focus on the use of models and ICT. Unit 6.2 addresses legal responsibilities which teachers have when taking pupils off-site, alongside practical ideas for activities and their advantages.

In Chapter 7 we turn attention to assessment. Christine Harrison, in Unit 7.1, discusses the rationale and strategies for 'assessment for learning', i.e. assessment which is intrinsic to teaching and which provides both teachers and pupils with information on which they can act. Successive stages in teaching and learning are informed by such assessment. Summative assessment, the assessment at the end of a course, and particularly assessment leading to formal qualifications is the subject of Unit 7.2 by Jenny Frost and Alastair Cuthbertson. Finally, in Unit 7.3, Tony Turner identifies how results of summative assessment are reported and used in the publication of information about schools.

Chapter 8 returns to two areas which draw on skills and knowledge outside of what many people think of as mainstream science, i.e. science for citizenship and health education. In Unit 8.1 Ralph Levinson identifies concepts of 'rights', 'responsibilities' and 'ethics' which need to be part of the pedagogical armoury of science teachers and helpfully outlines classroom strategies. Jane Maloney explores the sensitivities which have to be appreciated in dealing with health and sex education in science lessons, with a reminder of the importance of liaising with other departments in the school. Her Unit, 8.2, prepares beginners for the possible pitfalls of teaching these topics.

Finally in Chapter 9 Ralph Levinson looks beyond the training year to life as a newly qualified teacher (NQT), and beyond. There is valuable advice about applying for jobs and the interview process. He adresses your continuing professional development during the NQT year when you still have considerable support. Different scenarios for career pathways beyond that bring us to the end of the book.

THE STUDENT TEACHER AS RESEARCHER

The most effective learners are those who engage with the task of becoming a teacher in a spirit of intellectual enquiry. We are expecting you to collect data systematically from classrooms, make sense of it, understand the implications for practice, change your practice and re-evaluate it. What you notice in other people's classrooms and your own will depend crucially on the theoretical perspectives which you have, so the intermingling of theory with practice is essential. The tasks are designed to help you enquire. There are many different types: information gathering; observing classrooms from different perspectives; trying out ideas in lessons; asking for targeted feedback; understanding other people's roles; using research evidence to alter your practice.

CONCLUSION

Whatever your background, becoming a teacher will involve an enormous change. A few weeks after the end of our course a couple of years ago, one of our students wrote to me saying: 'This has been the most amazing, tiring, yet exhilarating year of my life, I wouldn't have missed it for anything.' Learning to teach science may be the biggest challenge you have taken on yet. We hope the book goes some way to supporting your learning.

2 Becoming a Science Teacher

Although in Chapter 1 your learning on the course was described as your own personal journey, there are people designated to support that journey: your mentor in school, the science teachers whose classes you take, the technicians and your tutors in HE. Learning how to work successfully with these different people is crucial to your development.

Their support is important because training to be a science teacher is demanding emotionally, intellectually and physically. The emotional pressure arises from concerns many students have concerning their capacity to complete the year successfully, facing success as well as failure in teaching and managing a diversity of pupils. The intellectual demand arises from teaching across the sciences and learning to cope with different levels of achievements of pupils. The change of discipline from science to education, with its own theories and research base, is also challenging. Physically the course requires complete attention. Classrooms are busy places and you need to be alert to a variety of needs of your pupils. Managing pupils, encouraging some, controlling others, supporting the lower-achieving pupils, maintaining safety for all while promoting their learning is demanding. These tasks, coupled with the need to prepare several lessons daily and to try out new activities, make a teaching day extend far beyond its mythical '9–4' image.

By the end of the training period you have to reach the standards for Qualified Teacher Status (QTS) and responsibility for meeting those standards falls on you. Your mentors provide guidance, support and advice, important aspects of which involve helping you to undertake regular reviews of your progress. You are asked to analyse your practice, evaluate your lessons and learn from such reviews. Teachers, mentors and tutors watch you teach and provide feedback. You have to get used to being observed in this way, being written about and engaging in discussion with your mentor and others about your practice so that you learn from the experience.

Unit 2.1 offers guidance on how to take charge of your own learning, how to work with others and gain most value from the support, and how to take stock of your starting points. Unit 2.2 helps you understand the department as a whole, i.e. how it functions, what roles and responsibilities teachers and technicians have, and the policies it has developed. This is an important part of your introduction to science teaching.

Unit 2.1

Managing your Professional Development

Jenny Frost and Bernadette Youens

INTRODUCTION – BECOMING A TEACHER

Each year one or two potential students say at interview 'I am sure I shall be a good teacher when you have trained me', implying that learning to be a teacher is something done to students, thus denying their own role in the process. The majority, however, have already thought carefully about the nature of teaching, the characteristics of a teacher and have begun to identify the extent to which they believe they have the qualities to succeed. They have begun the process of taking responsibility for their own learning and are aware of the need to do so. This unit is aimed at helping you manage your own professional development from the varied experiences you will have on the course.

OBJECTIVES

By end of this unit you should:

- understand a model of professional development which helps you learn from experience;
- recognise strategies for using the Professional Standards for Qualified Teacher Status as an aid to learning;
- know how to work effectively with mentors;
- identify your starting points;
- appreciate the progressive complexity of learning experiences which will be an intrinsic part of your course.

During an initial teacher education course you have two types of professional base: the schools where you are 'on placement' and the higher education institution (HEI) where you are registered. In the schools you work as an individual student (or maybe as one of a pair of science students), alongside teachers and technicians. Early experiences in school involve observation of teachers and pupils, working with small groups of pupils, and team teaching. You gradually take over whole classes. One science teacher acts as your mentor and meets with you on a regular basis, with others also giving you advice. A professional studies programme allows you to learn about whole school issues which are not unique to science and in this you are likely to work with students of other subjects also in the school. In your other professional home, the HE institution, you are part of a bigger group of science students attending a highly structured programme of lectures, seminars, workshops and tutorials. Here you have access to a strong literature base in education. This second base provides you with a community of peers who share the ups and downs of learning to become a science teacher and from whom you can gain a perspective on your own particular experiences.

To make best use of the resources at these two professional homes, you need to understand the nature of professional learning, and the role not only of yourself but of the science teachers and tutors who work with you.

A MODEL OF PROFESSIONAL LEARNING

A useful model for professional learning is represented in Figure 2.1.1, i.e. the 'do–review–learn–apply' cycle (Watkins 1998). This cycle involves trying something out (the 'doing phase'), reviewing it, learning from the review and then applying the learning in a new situation. The 'doing' phase is not restricted to teaching in the classroom, but may include observing lessons, working with a tutor group, attending parents evenings, marking investigations, organising a science visit, being a participant in a mock interview.

Reviewing involves standing back, describing the event, analysing it from a particular perspective, comparing it with other situations and evaluating its significance. Research

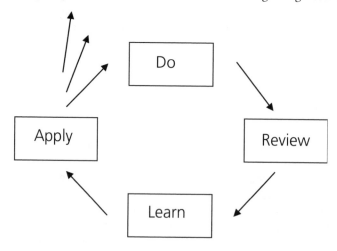

Figure 2.1.1 A model of active learning

shows that reviewing is most effective if done with another person, often a teacher in school, or your tutor. In the review other ideas are brought in, to make sense of what has happened, and to help identify general points which can be applied in another situation. It is in this phase that links are made to the more theoretical parts of the course, because these provide 'frameworks' for reviewing the event.

In the last phase you ask yourself the question 'what as a result of this would I do differently next time?' This leads to new goals and actions. You now return to the 'do' phase and go through the cycle again. This cycle will repeat itself throughout the course and hopefully throughout your professional life.

This cycle can be illustrated by two examples:

> Student A had prepared a lesson on micoprotein for a bright Y10 class. Her resources were well constructed and comprised: a worksheet with clear diagrams and information followed by questions which required pupils to interpret the information and apply scientific principles; clear diagrams of the fermenter on a data projector; cooked micoprotein for pupils to taste for 'acceptability'. In the review afterwards her perception was that she had talked for about a quarter of the lesson. Her observers' notes, however, identified that she had in fact talked for about three quarters of the lesson. She recognised that she felt under pressure to make sure that she told the pupils all the facts even though she knew this was not how pupils learned. Discussion focused on how she could provide pupils with more time when they were engaged in problems, which would in turn provide her with more information about their understanding. The discussion also focused on the personal courage she would need to 'let learners off the leash'. With her mentor she set her goals for the next lesson, to talk for no more than 50 per cent of the time, and to use the extra time to monitor pupils' achievements more thoroughly.

> Student B used a lot of questions especially at the start of a lesson, ostensibly to find out what pupils had learned. He was aware, however, that he was unable to do much with the answers other than give responses such as 'That's right' or 'No, does anyone else know the answer?' In discussion his tutor explained that his questioning had become 'ritualised IRF questioning' (Initiation by the teacher, Response from the pupil, followed by Feedback from the teacher). The pupils were playing the game of 'guess what is in the teacher's mind'. The questioning was contributing neither to the pupils' thinking, nor to the development of the subsequent lesson. The tutor opened up the discussion on questioning and gave him an easily accessible article to read about the nature of questioning. He planned to use questions in a more productive way, went back to observe how experienced teachers used questions and subsequently tried out new techniques.

Effective mentors will be able to support you in all the phases of the 'do–review–learn– apply' cycle. Figure 2.1.2 provides a guide to the sort of support which is known to be helpful. Obviously some people will be better at some parts than another. There may be teachers and technicians who are exceptionally good at helping you find resources and ideas for getting something done. Others may be much better at helping you to analyse what has happened. Your responsibility is to use the varying expertise of the people around you to best effect.

Mentors support action learners in the different phases of their learning in the following ways:

The 'Do' phase

They help students get the activity done by:
- supporting motivation;
- checking out practical details;
- smoothing communication with others.

The 'Review' phase

They help students review an experience by:
- encouraging students to make an account providing frameworks of questions to consider;
- making suggestions for comparisons and evaluations.

The 'Learn' phase

They help students to learn from experience
- bringing in useful ideas from a range of sources: reading, theories, others' views.

The 'Apply' phase

They provide students with tools to promote application by:
- giving support to the question of 'what would you do differently next time?'
- leading to action planning and goal setting.

Figure 2.1.2 Ways in which mentors can support an action learner

WORKING WITH 'THE STANDARDS'

Until 1992 in the UK, teacher training institutions set their own standards for qualified teacher status (QTS). From 1992, the Department for Education (DfE) described a set of *competences* which teachers needed in order to be effective, and required training institutions to ensure courses provided students with experiences to develop those competences (DfE 1992). In 1998, these were replaced by *standards*, comprising a long list of achievements which students had to reach to gain QTS (DfEE 1998). From September 2002, the standards were written in a more holistic way. These are the standards which are in place in England at the time of writing (DfES/TTA 2003a). Similar but not identical standards are in place in other countries within the UK.

The standards are divided into three main sections, with the third one divided into a further three subsections (see Figure 2.1.3.)

S1	Professional values and practice	S1.1–S1.8
S2	Knowledge and understanding	S2.1–S2.8
S3	Teaching	
	Planning expectations and targets	S3.1.1–S3.1.5
	Monitoring and assessment	S 3.2.1–S 3.2.7
	Teaching and classroom management	S 3.3.1–S 3.3.14

Figure 2.1.3 Categories for professional standards for qualified teacher status

Source: DfES/TTA 2003a.

There are three ways in which you are likely to be encouraged to use the standards:

- as an advance organiser;
- for personal profiling;
- as a vehicle for discussion with others.

Using standards as an advance organiser

The 42 separate statements of standards make you aware of the range of learning on the course and enable you to take stock of your individual starting point. The standards help you at various points in the course to recognise short-term goals and project forward to later targets; this will usually be done with mentors or tutors. This can guide you in planning your future learning and anticipate course components which occur later in the year.

Using standards for personal profiling

Using the standards to map the learning ahead goes hand in hand with reviewing progress. During your training you will be asked to produce *evidence* that you have achieved (or are beginning to achieve) the various standards. Lesson notes and evaluations, feedback from teachers on your lesson, mark books, reports and your own coursework count as evidence. Students often ask what counts as 'sufficient evidence'. Just as 'one swallow does not make a summer', one moment of success does not make a teacher. Some consistency and reliability over a range of contexts will be sought. Development is, in any case, a gradual process.

A necessary feature of this regular profiling and the need to provide evidence of progress necessitates keeping good documentation of your work. Students soon learn that multiple files are needed and that good administrative and oganisational skills are a necessary component of a teacher's repertoire.

Using standards as a vehicle for discussion

There is a need for a shared language with which to discuss educational problems. The detail in the standards helps to provide part of that language. Standards help to shape the programme you follow, they affect the way in which feedback to you is structured and the way you review your teaching. They are, however, not sufficient on their own as there are practical and theoretical ideas underpinning each standard. Take, for instance, standard S3.3.3 which requires you to be able to teach 'clearly structured lessons … which interest and motivate pupils … which make learning objectives clear to pupils … employ interactive teaching methods and collaborative group work … promote active and independent learning that enables pupils to think for themselves, and to plan and manage their own learning.' (DfES/TTA 2003a: 13). This opens an enormous agenda for you and the people working with you: What are objectives? What strategies are interactive and why are they effective for learning? What is collaborative group work, how is it set up, how is it managed, and how is learning achieved from it? When 'planning for learning' is something which you expect to do, what does it mean for pupils to plan and manage their own learning?

WHAT YOU CAN EXPECT FROM MENTORS AND TUTORS

Which people work most closely with you depends on the pattern of working in the HE institution where you are registered. It is likely that one HE science tutor has oversight of your progress during the year and acts as a personal tutor, and that one science teacher in the school acts as your school mentor. In addition there may be another teacher in the school (often a senior teacher) who has oversight of all the students there and who organises a professional studies programme. You work closely with science teachers whose classes you teach and these teachers give you guidance on your lessons and feedback on your teaching. They are involved in working with you on the 'do–review–learn–apply' cycle, as much as your main science mentor. You form working relationships with the technical teams in both the school and the HE institution.

School-based mentors organise the induction period in school, plan your timetable, support you as you move from observing classes, to working with small groups and then taking over whole classes. They ensure that you have class lists with appropriate information about particular pupils. They meet with you on a regular basis to discuss observations which you have made and your findings. They teach you more skills such as how to mark books, how to give constructive feedback, how to mark investigations etc. They discuss feedback you are receiving from other teachers, and your own evaluations, to help you identify targets in your next phase of development and ways of reaching those targets. They may well take an active interest in your coursework and reading. You must take a pro-active part in these meetings, going to them with the necessary documents and items you want to discuss.

Your HE tutor has responsibility for collating your experiences and monitoring your progress on the course as a whole and ensuring the components of the course add up to a coherent experience. Obviously your tutor contributes to the lecture, seminar and workshop programme. Tutors are involved in periodic profiling with students. When they visit schools, they spend considerable time talking with the mentors about the school programme as well as discussing your progress. They are likely to observe your teaching and to give feedback. The list of 'good practice' in Figure 2.1.4 gives the tenor of conversations you should anticipate with both your tutor and school mentor.

GOOD PRACTICE OCCURS WHEN:

- Students take an active role in the feedback sessions;
- Students are able to evaluate their own teaching;
- The lesson's aims or means of assessing pupil progress and achievement are used to structure feedback;
- Feedback is thorough, comprehensive and, where appropriate, diagnostic;
- There is a balance of praise, criticism and suggestions for alternative strategies;
- Points made in feedback are given an order of priority of importance, targeting three for immediate action;
- Students receive written comments on the lesson observed.

Figure 2.1.4 Good practice in giving and using feedback on teaching

Source: Adapted from Institute of Education, Universtity of London *PGCE Secondary Course Handbook, 2003–2004*, Section B: 58.

WHAT YOU BRING TO THE COURSE; REFLECTIONS ON YOUR STARTING POINT

You can start taking an active role in your own professional development by considering your own starting points. Three distinct aspects of this personal background are particularly important for teacher education and they all merit some early consideration:

- ideas about teaching;
- personal characteristics;
- subject knowledge.

Ideas about teaching

Your image of what teaching is about and the kind of teacher you want to become are powerful factors in teacher formation. You may also have thought about the way you want to be perceived by pupils. Make explicit the characteristics you associate with a good teacher by reflecting on your own experiences as a learner by undertaking Task 2.1.1.

The outcome of the first part of Task 2.1.1 is a list of features of a successful learning experience and of the qualities possessed by effective teachers seen from the perspective of individual learners. Science student teachers asked questions similar to those in Task 2.1.1 invariably generate a list, which includes the following attributes:

- knowledgeable and enthusiastic about science;
- approachable;
- know and treat pupils as individuals;
- ability to make science relevant to everyday life;
- able to explain scientific concepts and ideas clearly and logically;
- adopt a firm but fair and consistent approach;

Task 2.1.1
Reflections on your experiences of learning science

Think back to your own days at school and recall an educational experience, preferably in science, which you remember and value. Why was this a successful learning experience for you? List all the points which you remember as being distinctive about this experience. You may find it helpful to first think of the qualities of the particular teacher, followed by the nature of the learning activities.

With other science student teachers discuss and compare your responses to this task. Collate the positive features identified into a list of the qualities of a good teacher of science.

The second part of this task is to repeat the above exercise but this time focusing on an educational experience which failed to engage or motivate you. Once again compare and collate your responses with those of fellow students.

- patient;
- willing to give up their time to go over material;
- well-prepared.

This list is similar to the qualities identified by Year 8 pupils when they were asked to identify 'What makes a good teacher?' (Figure 2.1.5; also Capel *et al.* 2001, Unit 1.2).

One of the challenges of the PGCE year is to incorporate the qualities learners value into your work as a teacher. Task 2.1.2 helps you identify your starting point.

Personal characteristics

All students bring their own unique blend of personal characteristics but they also bring varying degrees of awareness of these characteristics. Learning to be a teacher has been described as 'Learning a new way to be yourself' (Black 1987) so some understanding of yourself is important. Standing before a class of lively expectant pupils tests personal confidence and resolve. Lively but reluctant pupils intensify this personal testing. The classroom presents a whole new set of challenges to personal composure, authority, leadership and capacity to build relationships.

Subject knowledge

Students have vast subject knowledge at the start of the course, although they vary in their confidence about this knowledge. The match between this knowledge and what is required for teaching is equally varied but possession of subject knowledge is a major positive contribution to your professional development from day one. Ideally this knowledge is accompanied by enthusiasm and a desire to learn. The latter is essential as the scope of what you have to teach encompasses chemistry, physics, biology, geology and astronomy. In Unit 3.1 we invite you to review your confidence in the subject matter needed for National Curriculum science.

Newman University
Library
Tel: 0121 476 1181 ext 1208

My Account 24/09/2018 15:10
XXXX4506

Item Title	Due Date
Learning to teach science in the secondary school : a companion to school ex	01/10/2018 23:59
Language and literacy in science education	01/10/2018 23:59
Teaching secondary physics	15/10/2018 23:59
Science learning, science teaching	15/10/2018 23:59

www.newman.ac.uk/library
library@newman.ac.uk

Descriptions by Year 8 pupils
A good teacher ...
is kind
is generous
listens to you
encourages you
has faith in you
keeps confidences
likes teaching children
likes teaching their subject
takes time to explain things
helps you when you are stuck
tells you how you are doing
allows you to have your say
doesn't give up on you
cares for your opinion
makes you feel clever
treats people equally
stands up for you
makes allowances
tells the truth
is forgiving

Figure 2.1.5 Qualities possessed by good teachers

Source: Hay McBer 2000: 1.

Task 2.1.2
Auditing your own starting
points

The range of qualities possessed by good science teachers may seem daunting at the start. You may already have many of these skills through the life experience you bring to teaching, but they may need adjusting to the classroom context. The generic qualities of good teachers can be categorised in three ways:

- The nature, temperament and personality of the person;
- Commitment to young people and the profession of teaching;
- Professional skills acquired through need and practice.

Use the lists generated above (Task 2.1.1 and Figure 2.1.5) to audit your personal qualities using these three categories in turn. What qualities do you need to acquire during school experience? In what ways do you expect your school experience to help you to develop these qualities and how?

Progressive challenges on the course

Throughout the book we have included tasks based on the model of professional development described at the start of the unit. There are things to be done such as observing teachers. Each task has a particular focus, indicated by the factors we want you to note or the questions which you have to address; these provide the start of analysis. You are encouraged to discuss the outcomes of the task with your mentor and often we ask you to consider the implications for your own practice. Some tasks are appropriate near the start of the course, others require a wider base of skills and knowledge before they can be tackled. You will find on whatever course you are on that the tasks become more sophisticated and complex as the training progresses. Tasks in this unit and in Unit 2.2 and Chapter 3 can certainly be done early in the course. Others such as planning and trying out discussion lessons in school will occur when you have more experience.

An important step in understanding how science lessons are planned and taught is to watch experienced teachers at work, to identify the strategies they adopt and the skills they use to generate learning experiences for pupils. It is a mistake to think of observation of teachers as something which you do only at the start of the course. It is equally important that you continue to observe other teachers once you have started teaching, because your own teaching experiences help you to focus on what to observe and you will notice subtle points which passed you by in your early observations. Observing other teachers should be an ongoing part of your development throughout this year.

For Task 2.1.3 we suggest you focus on one or two aspects of teaching as well as appreciating the general purpose and shape of the science lesson. We suggest just a few foci at this stage but clearly there are many possible points of interest you may wish to address or your mentor may suggest: e.g. starts and ends of lessons; questioning to elicit prior knowledge of the topic before teaching the main lesson; or the use of a motivating puzzle; managing time to maintain the pace of a lesson containing several activities; managing the transition between activities; managing movement of pupils or equipment; explaining e.g. a concept or a procedure. It is important that you concentrate only on one or two foci, to give you time to appreciate other events and to build experiences slowly rather than try to watch everything at once. Generic advice concerning classroom observation is given in Capel *et al.* 2001 (Unit 2.1 Reading classrooms).

Task 2.1.3
Watching science teachers –
teaching skills

With the prior agreement of the teacher arrange to observe a science lesson. Share with him the purposes of your observation and any particular focus you have (see suggested list above); if possible, arrange a short debriefing with him after the lesson. Use an observation schedule to help focus your observation; see, e.g. Figure 2.1.6. After the lesson make a list of questions to discuss with the teacher. Write a summary for yourself identifying the implications of your observation for your lesson planning and those practices which you might adopt.

Make notes about how the teacher accomplishes each of the tasks at the different phases of a lesson, and about what the pupils are doing.

1 Starting a lesson
- bringing in the class;
- settling and registration;
- opening up the topic;
  - checking prior knowledge;
  - explaining the purpose of work;
  - telling pupils what to do.

2 Equipment/resources
- location;
- working order;
- distribution;
- collecting in.

3 Main phase of lesson
- What is the class doing?
- What is the teacher doing?
- How does the teacher gain attention of class?
- How does the teacher move from one activity to the next?
- Are there problem pupils? How are they contained?

4 End
- timing;
- signal to stop/clear up?
- clear up/collect equipment?
- identifying/ draw out/summarising learning;
- setting homework;
- dismissing class.

Figure 2.1.6 Example of a guide for observing a lesson to understand phases of a lesson and management skills: see Task 2.1.3

You may feel at the start of the course that you are drawing extensively on other people's expertise and may wonder if you can give anything back to the school. You will find that schools welcome the questioning which comes from students, the different ideas which they bring in and the contribution they make to course development by the end of the year. The majority of students find that some of the resources which they have prepared for their own classes become part of the resources bank for the school.

SUMMARY

Given the unique starting points of students, the different experiences they have in their various placement schools, there is a premium on each student learning to plan and manage their own professional development. Understanding the 'do–review–learn–apply' cycle for professional learning makes it easier to seek appropriate help and to make best use of support and input from teachers and tutors.

Using standards as an advance organiser, for professional profiling and as a vehicle for discussion, contributes to professional development. Progress will be marked by an increasing sophistication of the analyses in which you engage and the move towards a time when you forget about what you are doing and focus entirely on the pupils' learning. This professional learning involves a complex mix of classroom experience and theoretical understanding. One without the other will not be productive.

Your tutors and mentors are important people in your professional life. Learn to make best use of the expertise which is available. Other science teachers, the technicians and fellow students will also be important resources.

Above all remember that you are in charge of your professional development. Your commitment to taking an active part in it is crucial to your success. Learning to teach will take a toll of your personal reserves; it takes stamina and persistence, it requires good administrative skills as well as skills and knowledge needed for the classroom; it will draw on your personal attributes of being able to deal with complex situations, of establishing authority and showing leadership. By the end of the training year you will be aware that you have learned 'a new way of being yourself' and will derive a great deal of professional satisfaction from this 'new you'.

FURTHER READING

Parkinson, J. (2002) *Reflective Teaching of Science 11–18*, London: Continuum. The chapter 'Learning to become an effective teacher' discusses the attributes of good teachers. It outlines issues of professional attitudes and responsibility including the need to review your practice regularly and suggests ways of doing this.

Wellington, J. (2000) *Teaching and Learning Secondary Science*, London: Routledge. Chapter 2 'Becoming a teacher' contains discussion of what the role of a science teacher might be and asks the student teacher to consider their own point of view. The chapter contains discussion of 'reflective practice' and the role of mentors in science teacher development.

Wragg, E.C. (1994) *An Introduction to Classroom Observation*, London: Routledge. This provides a review of how observers find ways of documenting what goes on in classrooms and explaining what those events mean about effective teaching and learning. Chapter 1, which gives the book its title, is a survey of what can be achieved and can be helpful in deciding how you might approach watching experienced teachers teach.

Unit 2.2

Working within a Science Department

Ian Longman

INTRODUCTION

While you are on school experience you become involved in working in a variety of teams, for example subject and pastoral teams. This unit helps you explore the ways in which the science team works in your placement school. The tasks should assist you in demonstrating the necessary professional values and practice required for the award of Qualified Teacher Status (QTS). If you have already spent some time in a primary school you should appreciate the difference between the curriculum structures in the primary school and your secondary school placement, reflecting the different organisation of the respective schools.

OBJECTIVES

By end of this unit you should be able to:

- recount how teachers are organised in a number of different teams within a school and know the meetings you are expected to attend;
- explain the structure of the science team and know the key responsibilities which individuals, both teachers and technicians, hold;
- form appropriate professional relationships as a student teacher with other members of the science team;
- appreciate the place of the science team within the workings of the whole school.

ORGANISATION

As part of their professional role teachers work in a number of different teams within a school. As well as subject teams, other teams are concerned with particular groups of pupils, for example Year groups or Houses, or certain parts of the curriculum such as PSHE and Citizenship, whilst others are responsible for other whole-school issues, for example inclusion. It is important for your professional development that you understand the organisation in which you are to work; see Task 2.2.1.

Task 2.2.1
School staff teams

Find out how the staff in your placement school is organised into teams. Many schools have a staff handbook which would contain this type of information. Some of these teams would focus on curriculum issues, others on the welfare of the pupils. Examples might include a Key Stage 3 strategy management group, year teams for form tutors and working parties for current initiatives. For each team where the science department is represented find out its main role in the running of the school, who is a member and how often it meets. For example, the Head of Department is probably a member of a committee with responsibility for the curriculum, another member of the department may link with a team considering the special educational needs of individual pupils, and so on. Ask your mentor or professional tutor which meetings it would be appropriate for you to attend and the dates of these during your block of school experience.

Traditionally, the curriculum in secondary schools has been divided up into discrete subject areas leading, unfairly, to the adage that 'Primary teachers teach pupils, secondary teachers teach subjects'. Normally this division of the curriculum is mirrored in the organisation of subject teams. Depending on the nature of the school, you may find yourself working within a faculty, for example 'Science and Technology', a science department or a distinct discipline team, for example a biology department. Factors affecting how subject groupings are organised stem from the ethos of the school and its philosophy, the choice of examination syllabuses, the number of pupils on roll, and the management structure of the school. For example, some schools have reorganised from the traditional, 'hierarchical' Headteacher – Deputy Headteacher(s) – Senior Teacher(s) – Heads of Department structure to a 'flatter' Headteacher – Assistant Headteachers – Faculty Managers system. For an example of the structure of a science faculty see Figure 2.2.1.

Figure 2.2.1 represents the structure of a science faculty in a school in the Midlands following reorganisation. Previously, there had been separate heads of biology and chemistry sections with the head of the physics section doubling as head of department in a co-ordinating role. This would have made the science department relatively top heavy in terms of managerial posts as well as encouraging the chemistry, physics and biology teachers to operate separately from each other. An OFSTED inspection recommended the move to a faculty structure, where posts of heads of separate departments were replaced by 'senior chemist/biology/physics' within a single large faculty. This particular example is not

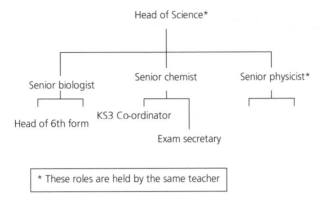

Figure 2.2.1 The structure of a science faculty

Task 2.2.2
The science staff team(s)

Find out from your mentor how the science team is structured. (This information may also be contained in a departmental handbook.) Try to relate this to factors in the school, as a whole, as discussed above. Have there been any changes in this structure and if so, why? It is useful to learn the subject specialisms of each science teacher and which classes they teach. In this way you know from whom to seek advice about subject matters or different groups of pupils.

---

untypical, with a physical scientist as Head of Department and other members of the team having senior roles in the management of the school.

The science team includes members of the technical staff who provide essential practical support in running the laboratories and often service visual aids and computing resources. To understand how important to teaching and learning are these members we suggest you spend a day working with them; see Task 2.2.3.

For the sake of simplicity this team of teaching and support staff is referred to as the 'science department' for the remainder of this chapter. You will find other adults working with teachers in the department in both planning and interacting with pupils. If their contribution is to be effective in supporting pupils' learning in your lessons then you need to find the time to plan this deployment together. Discuss the purpose and nature of the activities in which they are involved. Adults other than teachers could include teaching assistants working with whole classes, librarians supporting pupils' research, visiting speakers

f technicians

> With the help of your mentor arrange to work with members of the technical staff under their guidance for a day. Find out, by observation and discussion, the range of duties and responsibilities they have. They often have roles associated with health and safety, supporting teachers and pupils, as well as departmental administration and information systems, including the use of computers. Find out procedures for ordering equipment, learning materials and other resources for your lessons. You need to be able to practise science experiments well before a lesson. Find out how to get this organised and liaise appropriately with the technicians. Learn about access to computers including their availability, booking systems, particular passwords, technical support and so on. Explore the range of resources that are available to support your teaching. Learn how to book audio-visual equipment, for example video-cassette players, OHPs and data-projectors. In terms of accommodation you must know which rooms black out, which contain interactive whiteboards, and which contain (working!) fume cupboards.

and learning support assistants. The latter may be working with, for example, pupils with special educational needs, pupils for whom English is an additional language, Traveller children and pupils on catch-up programmes.

CHAINS OF MANAGEMENT

Heads of department (HoD) are usually 'middle managers' in the organisational structure of the school with resulting 'line' responsibility. This usually involves them in the appraisal of a selection of colleagues within the department as part of the school's performance management procedures. Just as schools are varied so too are science departments. Science departments are usually the largest curriculum area within a secondary school and many science teachers may have specific responsibilities delegated within a chain of management within the department. Some teachers may have responsibility for a specific science discipline, for example 'i/c chemistry'. Others may have responsibility for the curriculum for a particular age range of pupils, for example 'Key Stage 3 (KS3) Co-ordinator'. In a large department a number of teachers in addition to the HoD may have particular responsibilities for which they receive remuneration. These responsibilities are the subject of a job description and are often outlined in the science department handbook. In addition all teachers within the department are expected to share in the collective responsibility of ensuring its functioning on a day-to-day basis. You should not only understand the structure of teams in your school and department, but also the chains of management; see Task 2.2.4.

Heads of Department also act as 'subject leaders' in their school. In addition to the Standards for the award of Qualified Teacher Status (QTS) (DfES/TTA 2003a) the TTA has also produced National Standards for Subject Leaders. These do not have the same

Task 2.2.4
Management structures and responsibilities

This task is similar to Tasks 2.2.1 and 2.2.2, but here you are focusing on responsibilities and *chains of management*.

In science: Discuss with your mentor the structure and management chain of the science team, identifying individual teachers' responsibilities. Record this structure diagrammatically for your future use.

Whole school: Identify the levels of management between you (or a Newly Qualified Teacher (NQT)) and the Headteacher of your placement school. To whom would you turn if you needed advice outside your department?

status as the standards for QTS or Induction, i.e. they are not mandatory, but provide professional guidance based on how experienced and effective co-ordinators provide leadership in their subject(s) (TTA 1998: 3).

DEPARTMENTAL MEETINGS

In the drive to raise standards departments produce development plans which set out their priorities and how they aim to realise them within a whole-school context. The effectiveness of the department in improving the quality of learning for pupils depends in part upon how the plans are developed and agreed – the decision-making process – and the extent to which the agreed decisions are understood and implemented by the whole department.

Such decisions are discussed at departmental meetings where the quality of discussion is crucial to the effectiveness of the department. As a student teacher you are expected to attend departmental meetings in order to understand how departments function and to keep abreast of developments. The issues discussed are often varied, e.g. teaching and learning strategies, problems with curriculum continuity or problems associated with particular pupils.

In schools where there is extensive devolution of financial and policy control you may be surprised at the variety of decisions that need to be made by departments across the school year. These might include decisions about groupings of pupils, choice of examination syllabus, purchase of a published teaching scheme, the provision for pupils with special educational needs, choice of software, health and safety issues, educational visits and other contexts for out-of-classroom learning, homework policy, assessment procedures, professional development opportunities and so on. Departmental policies and much other information are often recorded in the department handbook. You need to be aware of the various policies in place so that you are able to conform to established expectations. For example, what rewards and sanctions for pupils does the department operate and how do these fit in with a whole-school policy on discipline? What are the procedures for communicating with parents?

Task 2.2.5
Science department policies

Departments have policies on a wide range of aspects of teaching, for example laboratory rules, discipline procedures, marking of science and literacy, health and safety including risk assessments, equal opportunities, homework, recording of assessments, reporting to parents/carers and so on. Consult the department handbook and other documents to become familiar with these policies. With the help of your mentor obtain the minutes of recent departmental meetings. Identify current areas of discussion and items of interest of which you would wish to know more. If an agenda for the next meeting is available read it and brief yourself about selected items.

MAKING THE MOST OF THE EXPERIENCE

As a student teacher on school experience you are in the role of 'trainee'. With the help of your mentor and other staff in the science department your priority is to be able to demonstrate the professional standards for the award for QTS. By becoming aware of the workings of the department and by adopting its policies and practices, as set out in the department handbook and elsewhere, you should make good progress in achieving Standard 1 (S1) 'Professional Values and Practice' (DfES/TTA 2003a: 7).

Meeting the demands of Standard 1 in this way would be true whatever subject department you worked in. However, there are specific issues related to science teaching that perhaps broaden your responsibilities further. Monk and Dillon (1995: 11–12) identified these four issues as safety, fieldwork, sex education and health education. You need to find out how, in the context of your school experience, these demands might impinge on your teaching. Perhaps this is a place in which to raise the effect on your teaching of diversity of pupils in our schools; how the different backgrounds, expectations, cultures and faiths impinge in particular on these four issues. You can find out more about these issues in other units in this book (Units 5.5, 6.2, 8.1 and 8.2), but in planning your lessons you need to be aware of and abide by legislation and any LEA and school guidance, policies and procedures that are relevant in these areas.

Whilst a major part of your placement involves planning, teaching and evaluating your lessons you also need to gain experiences of further aspects of working in a school. Find out to what extent you may be able to assist with extra–curricular activities such as a science club during your block of school experience. It is easy to become immersed in the physical confines of the science department, for example the laboratories, preparation room(s) and resource areas. In some schools members of the science department may have gained a reputation of being a clique, with rare appearances in the staff room. Do not fall into this trap. You need to gain a broader view of the corporate life of schools to which you can contribute and in which you can share responsibly (DfES/TTA 2003a: 7). In one school in which the author taught this whole-school approach to working was in part achieved by the virtual prohibition of departmental kettles and by providing tea or coffee in the staff room at break time.

EXPLORING OTHER DEPARTMENTS

Your block of school experience would be incomplete without an exploration of other departments. One example of where you can put this into practice is if the school open day/evening for parents of prospective pupils, usually held in the Autumn Term, occurs during your block of school experience. A notable feature of this event is the effort that goes into displays of pupils' work throughout the school. Certainly get involved with the planning and preparation of the science department's activities, but also negotiate with your mentor that you have time during the event to explore the work of pupils in other subject areas; see Task 2.2.6.

Task 2.2.6
Display

Look at the effectiveness of different types of display on show in other departments and consider how you could transfer the best practice, including examples of 3D work, to illustrate various scientific concepts in your laboratory in the future. This is important because a number of pupils have difficulties in interpreting and relating two-dimensional diagrams to real objects and structures. Incorporating three-dimensional modelling into science activities can promote learning. Make use of a digital camera to keep a record of the event for your files.

Find out who is responsible for the displays in the science area and how often they are changed. Displays are a means of valuing pupils' work. Discuss with your mentor whether space is available for displays of some of your classes' work and plan accordingly. Again take digital images for your portfolio of evidence.

During your blocks of school experience you will be observing a number of science lessons and focusing on a variety of professional issues. It is worth pointing out here the value of watching teachers other than science teachers at work. The different ways in which teachers approach their subject is illuminating and helpful in understanding how the same pupils respond to different contexts and teachers. You can often adopt similar strategies to widen the range of strategies which you use and to improve the effectiveness of your own science teaching.

SUMMARY

This unit has explored the workings of the team of teachers, technicians and other support staff who are responsible for the provision of the science curriculum. In most secondary schools this is the science department, but in some schools other organisational structures exist to teach the science curriculum.

Develop an awareness of the policies and procedures of the department and where you can find reference to these. There is often a department handbook which contains this and other essential information. As a student teacher you need to become familiar with your colleagues' expectations of you. You are expected to develop sound professional working relationships within this team and to check your development against the standards for your course. You also need to explore ways of contributing to the life of the school beyond the laboratory.

FURTHER READING

Billings, D. (1998) 'The role of technicians', in M. Ratcliffe (ed.) *ASE Guide to Secondary Science Education*, Hatfield: The Association for Science Education. This chapter is useful in exploring the variety of job functions which science technicians now undertake.

Dillon, J. (2000) 'Managing the science department', in M. Monk and J. Osborne (eds) *Good Practice in Science Teaching: What Research has to Say*, Buckingham: Open University Press. This chapter looks at what research tells us about effective management, particularly at departmental level.

Evans, M. (1998) 'Departmental management', in M. Ratcliffe (ed.) *ASE Guide to Secondary Science Education*, Hatfield: The Association for Science Education. Evans shows how departments can act as teams in responding to objectives.

3 The Science Curriculum

Jenny Frost

What is it about knowing science which you value for yourself? What is it about science which you value enough to pass on to the next generation? What are your aims for science education? Only you can answer these questions. You may want to jot down your initial thoughts on these questions now, before you continue to read.

This chapter starts with questions about your personal aims because a teacher's own perspective has a major influence on what constitutes a curriculum. Most of this chapter is about the National Curriculum in Science in England, which governs the 11–16 age range in secondary schools and the 5–11 age range in primary schools. It should enable you to recognise its characteristics, the aims and values embedded in it and be aware of the history of its development and likely changes in the future. You can make comparisons with your own ideas, and decide which of its aims and values coincide with yours.

There are only minor differences between the science curricula in Wales and Northern Ireland, so this will be applicable to people there. The chapter includes a short section on the science curriculum for pupils older than 16.

OBJECTIVES

By end of this chapter you should:

- be able to articulate your own aims of science education;
- be familiar with the aims, structure, content and key features of the National Curriculum Science;
- know in outline the related model of national assessment;
- begin to know how to use National Curriculum Science productively for planning teaching;
- be aware of the background to the development of the National Curriculum Science;
- know the determinants of the post-16 science curriculum.

NATIONAL CURRICULUM SCIENCE

Background

The national curriculum was defined as a set of ten subjects each with their own prescriptions when it was introduced in 1989. Science was one of those subjects. National Curriculum science (NC science) provides a framework for science teaching in all 'maintained' schools in England for students aged 5–16. It had a phased introduction into schools from 1989, such that by 1992 all students in the age range were following courses which were consistent with it. Since its inception in 1989, it has gone through three modifications (DES/WO 1989a; DES/WO 1991; DfE/WO 1995; DfEE/QCA 1999a) and will be modified again in 2006.

In the national curriculum as a whole, science was designated a 'core' subject alongside English and mathematics, and it retains that position today. Arguments for this status varied but included the need for more people in scientific and technical careers, the need for a scientifically literate population in an increasingly scientific and technical society, and the importance of passing on a major cultural determinant of the twentieth century. In the lead up to the national curriculum, there was pressure to make science not only compulsory up to the age of 16, but to allow it to take up 20 per cent of curriculum time for all 14–16 year olds (DES/WO 1985). This was resisted by some and certainly by the secretary of state for education at the time, who insisted there be a course which took only 12.5 per cent of curriculum time (DES/WO 1988b). This is why the programme of study for Key Stage 4 has two versions, one for 'double science' taking up 20 per cent of curriculum time and one for 'single science', taking up 10 per cent curriculum time. The national curriculum does not preclude schools offering what has become known as 'triple science' (i.e. biology, chemistry and physics taught as separate subjects) in the 14–16 age range. The minimum requirement is that pupils are taught single science.

A significant feature of the national curriculum was that science had to be taught in primary schools. There had been a steady increase in the number of primary schools teaching science prior to the introduction of the national curriculum, but from 1989 it became compulsory. Pupils now entering secondary school in Year 7 (Y7) have already had six years of science teaching. This has profound implications for the secondary curriculum.

The tasks in this chapter are based on the 1999 version of NC Science. This was published in two formats: as a separate document and as one section of a document which contained the specifications for all subjects. The page references refer to the former. If you are working from a more recent version, the tasks will still be valid and easily adapted.

THE PRINCIPLES AND PRACTICE IN THE DEVELOPMENT OF THE NATIONAL CURRICULUM

A curriculum model of steps and stages

When the national curriculum was introduced it brought with it a new vocabulary: 'programmes of study'; 'attainment targets'; 'levels'; the numbering of the school years from the entry to school at age 5, called Year 1 (Y1), to the end of compulsory education at age 16 (Y11) and the division of those years into four 'key stages': Key Stage 1 (KS1), Key Stage

2 (KS2), Key Stage 3 (KS3), Key Stage 4 (KS4). The model used for structuring the curriculum was one of 'steps' in scientific understanding, similar to the idea of grades used in learning to play a musical instrument. Learners would progress up these steps in their goal of reaching full understanding. The progressive steps are referred to as 'levels'. The criteria for achieving each level (eight levels plus a further one for 'exceptional attainment') are set out as a series of level descriptors for each of the four attainment targets, *Scientific Enquiry*; *Processes of Life*; *Materials and their Properties*; *Physical Processes*. Corresponding programmes of study specify what has to be taught. There are five programmes of study, one for each key stage except for KS4 where there are two, 'double science' and 'single science'.

This model is used to provide information about the levels at which pupils of different ages are likely to be working, and the expected level to be attained at the end of each key stage by the majority of pupils. The guidelines are shown in Figure 3.1.

The guidelines in Figure 3.1 do not cover Key Stage 4 (14–16 yr olds) even though the programmes of study cover this age range. Here expected achievement is defined via grades in General Certificate of Secondary Education (GCSE) examinations.

Breadth and balance in the science curriculum

Breadth and balance were two of the guiding principles of the national curriculum in science. *Breadth* involves including major ideas from across the sciences, technological applications, social consequences of science and something of the skills of being a scientist. *Balance* refers to giving equal importance to different branches of science, such that the curriculum could be the 'jumping off point' for study of any branch of science later, and equal consideration to acquisition of scientific knowledge and the understanding of the nature of science.

Some aspects of breadth and balance are easy to find, because each programme of study is divided into four clearly identified sections, SC1, scientific enquiry; SC2 processes of life; SC3 materials and their properties; SC4 physical processes. Other aspects require more searching. Social and technological issues, for instance, are interwoven in the detail of the programmes of study and in margin notes.

Range of levels within which the great majority of pupils are expected to work		Expected attainment for the majority of pupils at the end of the key stage	
Key Stage 1 (5–7 yr olds) (KS1)	1–3	at age 7, end of KS1	2
Key Stage 2 (7–11 yr olds) (KS2)	2–5	at age 11, end of KS2	4
Key Stage 3 (11–14 yr olds) (KS3)	3–7	at age 14, end of KS3	5/6

Figure 3.1   Expected attainment in each key stage in National Curriculum

**Task 3.1
Identifying breadth and
balance in NC science
(DfEE/QCA 1999a)**

Study the 'overview' in the margin notes at the *start* of each key stage in NC Science (1999 version), which give a summary of the overall aims of the key stage.

- What do they tell you about breadth and balance in the curriculum?
- How do they change from KS1 to KS4?
- Find the guidance on 'breadth of study' at the *end* of each programme of study.
- Again track how this guidance changes from KS1 to KS4.
- You will notice that the first part of each list refers to the contexts which should be used. List contexts which are suitable for the different key stages.

Historically this concern with breadth and balance was important. Prior to the introduction of the National Curriculum pupils had choice of subjects which they studied from the age of 14. As a result there was a higher proportion of boys selecting the physical sciences than girls and a higher proportion of girls selecting biology than boys. There were pupils who chose to study no science after the age of 14 and those who chose to study only one of the sciences. Science courses varied in the extent to which they included the teaching of investigational skills, with some including virtually nothing. There were only isolated examples of the nature of science being an intrinsic part of a course, although undoubtedly many teachers made some reference to it.

Equal opportunities

The science curriculum is for everyone; for those who like science and those who do not; for those who have a natural talent for it and those who do not. To write such a curriculum was an enormous challenge, and in fact the ability to make the science accessible relies not on what is written down, but on the way teachers mould the curriculum for different learners. In the 1980s when the curriculum was first written there was more concern about the gender imbalance than anything else, with concern that teachers should make the curriculum as appealing to girls as boys. That concern is still there, but thinking about equal opportunities goes much wider than gender. Task 3.2 draws your attention to the section on *Inclusion: providing effective learning opportunities for all pupils,* which has 'three principles for inclusion: A. Setting suitable learning challenges; B. Responding to pupils' diverse learning needs; and C. Overcoming potential barriers to learning and assessment for individuals and groups' (DfEE/QCA 1999a: 60–8).

Task 3.2
Thinking about 'Science for all'

Read the section on 'Inclusion: providing effective opportunities for all pupils' in NC Science (DfEE/QCA 1999a: 60–8).

- List the differences between pupils which are identified and addressed.
- Read through the advice on strategies which teachers can use which will be helpful to each category. Make a list of ten which will be most useful to you.

Links across the curriculum

Science does not stand on its own. As a science teacher you carry responsibility not only for helping pupils make connections between their science learning and other subjects, but also for contributing to their development in other subject areas. Links to English, mathematics and ICT are contained in the margin notes. You will need to look at the national curriculum documents in these three subjects to understand the significance of the notes. (See also 'Use of language across the curriculum', NC science (DfEE/QCA 1999a: 69), and 'Use of information and communications technology across the curriculum' on NC science (DfEE/QCA 1999a: 70).)

Linking to other subjects in the curriculum is one thing. Contributing to more general educational development is another. Through science you are expected to contribute to pupils' 'spiritual, moral, social and cultural development', to the development of their 'key skills' and to 'other aspects of the curriculum'. You may already have found the section 'Learning across the National Curriculum' on DfEE/QCA 1999a: 8–9, in the task above about 'breadth', but if not, read this section to appreciate the sheer scope of what you have to do as a science teacher.

Continuity in the curriculum

The curriculum is structured such that the programme of study of each key stage builds on what has been learned before, to prevent overlap of teaching and to provide opportunities for pupils to make advancement at successive stages. Such linking of the various parts is referred to as 'continuity'. Achieving continuity is not just a case of having a sensibly structured curriculum; it also requires teachers to link what they are teaching to what has been learned and experienced before and what is to come later.

A first step to fulfilling your role in continuity is to understand how continuity is achieved in NC science. Essentially there is a gradual transition from a predominance of simple, local, first-hand experience at KS1, to a widening of experiences and making generalisations at KS2, to explanations in early KS3, to using abstract ideas in explanations in later KS3, to much wider use of theory, models and mathematical reasoning at KS4. This is inevitably an over-simplified picture (pupils for instance at KS1 are engaged in giving explanations), but it provides a useful guide. Task 3.3 provides a short 'tracing continuity task' to enable you to appreciate how the curriculum is structured and, more importantly, what understanding the pupils are likely to bring to the secondary school.

Task 3.3
Tracking continuity in NC science

From the Programmes of Study track the teaching of each of the ideas listed below from KS1 to KS4:

- Ideas and evidence part of 'scientific enquiry'
- Considering evidence part of 'investigative skills'
- Photosynthesis
- Acids and alkalis
- Electromagnetism
- Rock cycle
- The Earth and its place in the Universe

You need to identify how the curriculum *changes*. Look *across* the different sections of the programmes of study; for instance, if pupils are to understand photosynthesis, they need to know some basic chemistry. Remember also that although genetics as such is not mentioned in KS1 and KS2 there are important things which are being learned about animals and plants which are essential background for the study of genetics later.

PROGRESSION

Progression is about pupils making progress. A well-structured curriculum will help but will not guarantee there is progression in learning. What is progression? What does making progress mean? Learning more information is not really progression although it may be a necessary precursor of progression. Progression is more concerned with being able to link information and use it in more complex situations, being able to deal with increased conceptual complexity and employ more advanced thinking skills. (See Unit 5.1 for a fuller discussion of progression.)

A description of how progression is conceived in the NC science can be gleaned from the level descriptors for each of the attainment targets. You need to appreciate the differences between one level and another because as a teacher you will have to provide the challenges and opportunities for pupils to develop skills of the subsequent levels.

Task 3.4 is similar to the previous one, except you are now tracking descriptions of progression through the level descriptors for each attainment target.

How were the level statements derived? In preparing the level statements the writers of the NC drew on the work of the Assessment of Performance Unit (APU) which had completed, between 1980 and 1984, large scale surveys of students' expertise in scientific concepts, in scientific investigations and in interpretation of data and graphs, at ages 11, 13 and 15 years (APU 1988a, 1988b, 1989). They also drew on the increasing evidence from research into children's ideas in science, much of which was drawn together subsequently by Driver *et al.* (1994). Development of graded assessments in science by some examination boards had already begun to develop a 'step' like model, with description of the achievements of different levels (Davis 1989). Their experiences as teachers was another influence. The

Task 3.4
Identifying progression in NC
Science (1999 version)

Using the level descriptors for the attainment targets (DfEE/QCA 1999a: 75–81).

1   Draw up tables to show the progression expected in:
     a)   ability 'to obtain and report evidence' (part of Attainment target 1);
     b)   the type of knowledge learned and the ways in which knowledge is used, in any one of the Attainment targets 2–4 (for instance you will find statements about understanding and using abstract scientific ideas in the higher levels only).
2   How would you describe the key differences between one level and another?

original set of statements of attainment were inevitably the 'best that could be done' at the time and like the programmes of study have evolved over time.

DEVELOPING FAMILIARITY WITH NC SCIENCE

As a science teacher you will be teaching the whole of the KS3 programme of study and much, if not all, of the KS4 programme, irrespective of your specialist science. Task 3.5 enables you to make a quick assessment of your strengths in different areas. Use the KS3 programme and the 'double science' programme for KS4, not the single science. The audit is, of course, not an end in itself. You need to develop your knowledge and confidence in, and more importantly, *enthusiasm* for all areas.

NC ASSESSMENT

Background

When the national curriculum was introduced in the Education Reform Act of 1988 (ERA 1988) it included national assessment. A group, the Task Group on Assessment and Testing (TGAT), was commissioned to develop a model of assessment which allowed monitoring of progress through the whole of schooling. TGAT proposed a 10 level model which described steps in understanding, producing a graph to show the broad range of levels of attainment at any one age and the 'average' attainment for end of key stages (DES/WO 1988a). This is the model which still exists today, although the number of levels has been reduced and the detailed descriptions of the original version have evolved into broader, less atomistic statements from those which occurred at first.

TGAT suggested that to meet the government's objective of having a system to allow national monitoring of standards, teachers would be in the best position to make the assessments. It proposed that teachers should report on achievement at the end of every key stage, with some tasks (Standard Assessment Tasks) being developed which would be used

This is a self-diagnosis exercise. Work from the National Curriculum, Science (DfEE/QCA 1999a). First, look at each section of the programme of study for Key Stage 3. Are you familiar with these topics and activities? If yes, ✔, or ? for unsure or X if mostly unfamiliar, in the table below. Then repeat the exercise for Key Stage 4 (double science).

The last row of the table is to record the levels of attainment in your own knowledge and understanding. Use the attainment target level descriptors on pp. 75–81 in the National Curriculum, Science for this task. Scientific enquiry, and breadth of study are summarised on the second sheet.

Section	Life processes and living things					Materials and their properties			Physical processes					
	1. Cells and cell function/ Cell activity	2. Humans as organisms	3. Green plants as organisms	4. Variation, classificat. Inheritance and evolution	5. Living things in their environment	1. Classifying materials	2. Changing materials	3. Patterns of behaviour	1. Electricity and magnetism	2. Forces and motion	3. Light and sound waves	4. The earth and beyond	5. Energy resources and energy transfer	6. Radio-activity
KS3 PoS: pp. 28–36 ✔ if familiar ? if unsure X if unfamiliar														
KS 4 PoS pp. 46–56 ✔ if familiar ? if unsure X if unfamiliar														
Attainment levels	AT2					AT3								
Which of the 8 levels are you happy with?														

Scientific enquiry should be taught through the contexts of the other attainment targets. Confidence in Sc1 will depend on the context in which you are working. Nevertheless, undertake a similar audit for this and for 'Breadth of Study'.

Section	Scientific enquiry		Breadth of study		
	1. Ideas and evidence in science	2. Investigative skills	Contexts for knowledge skills and understanding	Communication	Health and safety
KS3 PoS: pp. 28–29 ✔ if familiar ? if unsure X if unfamiliar					
KS4 PoS pp. 46–47 ✔ if familiar ? if unsure X if unfamiliar					
Attainment levels Which of the 8 levels are you happy with?			Levels are not applicable in this section		

te teachers' assessments, in order to give comparability across the country. These
d only be given to a 'sample' of students across the country.

tails of what happened to this initial model are beyond the scope of this book, but
on at the time of writing is that pencil and paper tests (Standard Assessment Tests,
SATs) are used to assess achievement in SC2–4, and in some aspects of SC1. These tests are
taken by all pupils at the end of KS2 and KS3. There is no national testing of science at KS1.
Teachers also make their own assessments of pupils at the end of these key stages. It is,
however, the results of the pencil and paper tests which are used in school 'performance
tables' (see Unit 7.3).

Becoming familiar with the levels

As a science teacher you not only have to be aware of the level descriptors, you also have to
use them, for both planning and assessment purposes. Through the progression exercise
(Task 3.4) you will be familiar with features of the level descriptors. Task 3.6 gives an
opportunity to use the levels, for judging the level at which a pupil is working.

Task 3.6
Matching pupils' statements to the NC levels

Part A
Place the following statements from pupils at the appropriate NC level
(see level descriptors for Attainment Target 3). Think about your reasons
and comment on the problems of levelling in this way.

1   'When water goes into the air it's called evaporation.'
2   'Evaporation is when puddles dry up and paint dries on walls and it
     happens quicker in warm weather.'
3   'Lakes dry up and our washing dries more quickly in hot weather
     because the particles of water at the surface have greater kinetic
     energy at higher temperatures.'

Part B
Select one piece of work from each of three very different pupils. Review
the work, and decide what evidence there is for a particular level. Discuss
your conclusions with your mentor, or another student teacher, to refine
your ideas. (Note that in practice a much wider range of evidence is used
to determine the level at which a pupil is working, but the task helps you
to become more familiar with the level descriptors).

PLANNING WITH THE NATIONAL CURRICULUM

The NC science remains the statutory framework which must be used as a basis for planning
for science in schools. The schools in which you work are likely to have detailed schemes of
work which have been devised to ensure that the work in Y7 builds on what students bring
from primary school, and work in Y8 and Y9 grow from these. These schemes of work are

often linked to some of the many curriculum resources and textbooks which have been published 'to match the NC'.

The Qualification and Curriculum Authority (QCA) has published schemes of work for KS1, 2 and 3, which are available on the internet in down-loadable format (www.standards.dfes.gov.uk). They are non-statutory; they are merely an example of how the science curriculum can be organised and taught. Some schools have, however, adopted these, with only minor modifications.

What is important to remember is that for all the guidance written down, planning by individual teachers is still essential. Schemes of work do not tell you how to teach, what to say, nor how to support students in drawing out the significance of the activities in which they are engaged.

KS3 STRATEGIES – TEACHER DEVELOPMENT FOR NC IMPLEMENTATION

In 2001/2 the government financed the gradual introduction of what it called the 'KS3 Strategies' to raise achievement, by strengthening teaching and learning across the curriculum for all 11–14 year olds. English and mathematics were the first subjects, followed by science, Teaching Foreign Languages (TFL) and Information and Communications Technology (ICT) in 2002/3. The reasons for this development were that there was deemed to be insufficient progress in Y7, with considerable replication of Y6 work, an increase in exclusions in Y8, a gender gap and underachievement, and in science, some disaffection with the subject by Y9.

The KS3 strategies are based on four principles:

- Expectations (targets);
- Progression (from KS2 to 3);
- Engagement (motivating approaches);
- Transformation (professional development).

'Expectations or targets' based on national curriculum assessment data, are that the majority of 14-year-olds will achieve level 5. Schools are expected to set themselves targets and strategies for improving what they do and what pupils achieve. Materials related to 'progression' help departments to identify the extent to which there is genuine progression from KS2 to KS3 (rather than repetition) and enhance it. 'Engagement' focuses on implementing motivating approaches for pupils, and 'professional development' focuses on supporting teachers in their professional development. Guidance for each subject is provided in what are called 'Frameworks' (see DfES 2002b, for the framework for teaching science in KS3). Subsequently considerable collections of good practice have been published and disseminated to schools and training institutions (see reference list and Units 5.4 and 6.1).

WORKING WITH THE NATIONAL CURRICULUM IN SCIENCE – SUCCESSES AND DIFFICULTIES

For 15 years teachers have worked with various versions of a national curriculum for science which describes what science everyone should learn from 5–16. This has brought considerable homogeneity to what science is taught across the country. What diversity there is comes from:

- teachers' different interpretations of the curriculum and their approaches;
- teachers' willingness not to be constrained by the curriculum and particularly by the assessments;
- choices between single and double science at KS4;
- choices between higher and lower tier papers at GCSE and SATs (see Unit 7.2).

In practice these choices are not large, and there is evidence that the form of NC science, despite progressive revisions through the four versions, does not suit all pupils equally well. An influential report, *Science Beyond 2000: A Set of Recommendations* (Millar and Osborne 1998), describes the successes and failures of the national curriculum in science, with strong recommendations on ways forward. In the short term it recommended the incorporation of teaching about the nature of science in SC1 and the removal of overlap between the key stages. These suggestions were implemented in the 1999 version of NC science. In the medium term, it recommended that more formal trialling of innovative approaches in science education at KS4 should be established.

One such innovation is a course called *21st Century Science*. A pilot project is under way and began trials in 81 schools in September 2003. At the heart is change at KS4, with the development of a very different 'single science' curriculum from the one which currently exists. It is different in two ways. First, it aims for scientific literacy for all, and thinks of learners as *consumers* of science not *producers* of science. It aims to enable people to engage with science in the contexts in which they meet it in everyday life and to engage in the debates which surround science. Second, it will be a core subject for *everyone*. There will then be *additional* science for those who want to study double science. The additional science has two formats, one which is vocationally oriented (additional science – applied), focusing on science as practised, and the other which contains more academic arguments for scientific ideas (additional science – general). Such a curriculum will need not only new forms of assessment but new teaching methods. For more information about the structure of the course go to its website www.21stcenturyscience.org/hom/. QCA has a webpage about the development of the new forms of assessment which will be necessary for this curriculum. You can access it, at the time of writing, at http://www.qca.org.uk/nq/framework/pilot_gcse_sciences.asp.

Changes to the KS4 NC science programme are not expected to be implemented until September 2006. KS4 science as a statutory requirement will have characteristics similar to the core of 21st Century Science, so the principle of compulsory core plus choice of optional additional science is accepted. What is being trialled for 21st Century Science are the teaching approaches and materials, not the model. (See *Changes to the Key Stage 4 Curriculum. Guidance for Implementation from September 2004*: 11–12, QCA website http://www.qca.org.uk).

POST-16 SCIENCE CURRICULUM

The post-16 curriculum in science is determined essentially by the combination of courses which the school/college elects to implement. The main courses in science post-16 are the General Certificate of Education (GCE) Advanced Subsidiary (AS) and Advanced (A) level courses in biology, chemistry and physics. In order to study these most schools and colleges require pupils to have gained at least a C grade in double science at GCSE at age 16. As over 50 per cent of the population gain such a grade, there is a potentially large pool of pupils, but applications for these courses have remained fairly stable over the last ten years (Nicolson and Holman 2003). There is no requirement that pupils should study all three sciences and in fact there is a growing trend towards mixed AS/A levels with pupils electing to study a mixture of arts, sciences and vocational qualifications. A few schools in England have switched from GCE AS and A level to the International Baccalaureate Diploma (see http://www.ibo.org/).

Other post-16 science courses include: AS level in 'Science for Public Understanding' a course which aims for scientific literacy; AS and A level in Science (as a single subject); a range of GCSE courses, and vocational courses such as the new Advanced Vocational Certificate of Education (AVCE). A fuller account of the various courses at post-16 is given in Unit 7.2 on public examinations.

YOUR OWN AIMS OF SCIENCE EDUCATION

Return now to your list of aims for science education. Do you think science is important to everyone? If you do, then what aspects should people be learning, given that most of us forget most of the detail if we are not using it routinely? When you have worked in school for some time, listened to different pupils grappling with the subject, some enjoying it, some finding it motivating, others finding it too challenging, come back to your aims and see if your views have changed.

SUMMARY

The national curriculum in science is characterised by breadth and balance. It covers all branches of science as well as the nature of science. It includes the link between science and technology and the role of science in environmental and health issues. It is designed to provide continuity from ages 5–16. Its introduction has provided coherence and comparability to science programmes in different schools throughout the country and has increased the number of pupils studying science to 16, because science was designated a core (and hence compulsory) subject. As a core subject it is examined in the Standard Assessment Tests at Key Stages 2 and 3 and hence has a high profile in schools' performance tables.

There are concerns that the curriculum in science is not engaging all pupils and that changes are needed. These changes focus on the need to develop scientific literacy and significant changes are expected to the KS4 science curriculum in 2006.

While the curriculum as written is defined and statutory, the curriculum as experienced by pupils is still strongly influenced by teachers and the way they teach. Your own aims for science education are important and in this chapter you have been strongly encouraged to articulate them.

FURTHER READING

Bennett, J. (2003) 'Context-based Approaches to the Teaching of Science', *Teaching and Learning Science. A Guide to Recent Research and its Applications*, London: Continuum, Chapter 5. This book gives an easy-to-read summary of research which has been done in science education and the implications for the classroom. This chapter addresses the research evidence for the effectiveness of the increased emphasis on linking science to contexts outside the classroom.

Chapman, B. (1991) 'The overselling of science education in the 1980s', *School Science Review*, 72(260): 47–63. There were, of course, a few critics of the enthusiasm for science in the 1970s and early 1980s. Bryan Chapman's paper is well argued and thought provoking even if you do not agree with his conclusions

Millar, R. and Osborne, J. (eds) (1998) *Beyond 2000: Science Education for the Future: A Report with Ten Recommendations*, London: King's College. You are strongly recommended to read this in full, not just the recommendations.

Nicolson, P. and Holman, J. (2003) 'National curriculum for science: looking back and looking forward', *School Science Review*, 85(311): 21–7. The successes of the national curriculum in science in terms of the numbers studying science up to 16, the relatively strong performance of UK pupils in international comparisons in science and the breadth of science studied are reviewed in the light of no increase in the number of pupils studying science at A level.

Osborne, J. and Collins, S. (2000) *Pupils' and Parents' Views of the School Science Curriculum*, London: King's College, London. This provides an insight into different pupils' and parents' reactions to the science curriculum, with many quotes from the people interviewed. Implications for the science curriculum are outlined in the last section. The following article was written from the data and may be more easily accessible than the project report.

Osborne, J. and Collins, S. (2001) 'Pupils' views of the role and value of the science curriculum: a focus-group study', *International Journal of Science Education*, 23(5): 441–68.

4 Getting to Grips with Science

The five units of this chapter on the nature of science (Unit 4.1), biology (Unit 4.2), chemistry (Unit 4.3), physics and astronomy (Unit 4.4), and Earth science (Unit 4.5), attempt to address two fundamental difficulties which science teachers face. The first difficulty is that they have to teach science topics with which they are unfamiliar, or which they did not like particularly when they were studying themselves. The second is that science is a 'content heavy' subject and it can be difficult to stand back from the detail and see how all the parts fit together. It is essential for science teachers to have some vision of what the bigger picture is. In fact, given the arguments for 21st Century Science (see Chapter 3), it may well be the bigger picture which becomes the more important one.

The units have been written by people who enjoy that area of science in the hope that their enjoyment can be shared. Do not expect text book knowledge; you cannot for instance capture the whole of biology in just 3,000 words. Each unit has further readings and websites to help you to explore further. There are sources which are useful for gaining an insight into, and enthusiasm for, the subject; others which are good explanatory sources; and finally, one or two which give good advice about the teaching of the particular area of science.

The majority of students find the exploration of areas of science which have been forgotten or perhaps never properly studied a source of immense personal satisfaction. In the process they often find they become sensitive to the particular difficulties which the different areas present and as a result are more aware of the challenges which their pupils face. For more detailed knowledge, textbooks are often the main source of information. We have not listed individual textbooks, of which there are many excellent ones. Explore several to find ones which you like. It is wise to select those with questions to try and with answers. Obviously, another route to developing your subject knowledge is to undertake assessment papers in them: a KS3 SATs paper, double science GCSE papers and GCE A level papers within your own specialism. However, this chapter is not about the detailed knowledge.

Unit 4.1

The Nature of Science

Michael Reiss

INTRODUCTION

In the UK, most university students of science are taught little explicitly about the nature of science. And yet the science National Curriculum in England requires pupils to be taught not only about investigative skills but also about ideas and evidence in science. Perhaps unsurprisingly, research evidence suggests that most pupils leave school with a somewhat lop-sided knowledge of this area of science.

This unit discusses what is meant by 'the nature of science' and goes on to consider how science is done. It looks at whether science always proceeds by the objective and rigorous testing of hypotheses, or whether there are other factors at play in deciding whether one scientific view comes to hold sway within the scientific community over alternatives.

Within schools, there are different views about the nature of science among both pupils and science teachers. These different views are important in terms of how people see scientific knowledge. Ways of getting at people's views of the nature of science are given below. It is hoped that these will be of interest and lead to richer teaching and learning in this area. This is important as it can be argued that long after pupils have forgotten much of the content of science that they are taught at schools, they will still hold a view as to how science is done and as to whether scientific knowledge is trustworthy or not.

WHAT DO WE MEAN BY THE NATURE OF SCIENCE?

The phrase 'the nature of science' is used as a shorthand for something like 'how science is done and what sorts of things scientists research'. It therefore contains two elements: the practice of doing science and the knowledge that results.

OBJECTIVES

By end of this chapter you should:

- distinguish between alternative understandings of how science is carried out;
- contrast science as undertaken by scientists and science as undertaken in school science lessons;
- help your pupils develop a deeper understanding of the nature of science.

WHAT DO SCIENTISTS STUDY?

It is difficult to come up with a definitive answer to the question 'What do scientists study?'. Certain things clearly fall under the domain of science – the nature of electricity, the arrangement of atoms into molecules and human physiology, to give three examples. However, what about the origin of the universe, the behaviour of people in society, decisions about whether we should build nuclear power plants or go for wind power, the appreciation of music and the nature of love, for example? Do these fall under the domain of science? A small number of scientists would argue 'yes' and the term *scientism* is used, pejoratively, to refer to the view that science can provide sufficient explanations for everything.

However, most people hold that science is but one form of knowledge and that other forms of knowledge complement science. This way of thinking means that the origin of the universe is also a philosophical or religious question – or simply unknowable; the behaviour of people in society requires knowledge of the social sciences (e.g. sociology) rather than only of the natural sciences; whether we should go for nuclear or wind power is partly a scientific issue but also requires an understanding of economics, risk and politics; the appreciation of music and the nature of love, while clearly having something to do with our perceptual apparatuses and our evolutionary history, cannot be reduced to science.

While historians tell us that what scientists study changes over time, there are reasonable consistencies:

- Science is concerned with the natural world and with certain elements of the manufactured world – so that, for example, the laws of gravity apply as much to artificial satellites as they do to planets and stars.
- Science is concerned with how things are rather than with how they should be. So there is a science of gunpowder and *in vitro* fertilisation without science telling us whether warfare and test-tube births are good or bad.

HOW IS SCIENCE DONE?

If it is difficult to come up with a definitive answer to the question 'What do scientists study?', it is even more difficult to come up with a clear-cut answer to the question 'How is science done?' Indeed, there is, and has been for many decades, active disagreement on this matter among academic historians, philosophers and sociologists of science. A useful point to start is with the views of Robert Merton and Karl Popper. In my experience, most working scientists have almost no interest in and know little about the philosophy and sociology of science. However, they do like the views of Merton and Popper once these are explained to them – though they generally think their arguments so obvious as not to need stating. The same working scientists are a great deal less keen on the views of Thomas Kuhn and others, to which we shall come in due course.

Robert Merton characterised science as open-minded, universalist, disinterested and communal (Merton 1973). For Merton, science is a group activity: even though certain scientists work on their own, all scientists contribute to a single body of knowledge accepted by the community of scientists. There are certain parallels here with art, literature and music. After all, Cézanne, Gaugin and van Gogh all contributed to post-impressionism. But while it makes no sense to try to combine their paintings, science is largely about combining the contributions of many different scientists to produce an overall coherent model of one aspect of reality. In this sense, science is disinterested; in *this* sense it is (or should be) impersonal.

Of course, individual scientists are passionate about their work and often slow to accept that their cherished ideas are wrong. But science itself is not persuaded by such partiality. While there may be controversy about whether the works of Bach or Mozart are the greater (and the question is pretty meaningless anyway), time invariably shows which of two alternative scientific theories is nearer the truth. For this reason, while scientists need to retain 'open mindedness', always being prepared to change their views in the light of new evidence or better explanatory theories, science itself advances over time. As a result, while some scientific knowledge ('frontier science') is contentious, much scientific knowledge can confidently be relied on: it is relatively certain.

Karl Popper emphasised the falsifiability of scientific theories (Popper 1934 [1972]). Unless you can imagine collecting data that would allow you to refute a theory, the theory isn't scientific. The same applies to scientific hypotheses. So the hypothesis 'All swans are white' is scientific because we can imagine finding a bird that is manifestly a swan (in terms of its appearance and behaviour) but is not white. Indeed this is precisely what happened when early white explorers returned from Australia with tales of black swans (Figure 4.1.1).

Popper's ideas easily give rise to a view of science in which knowledge steadily accumulates over time as new theories are proposed and new data collected to discriminate between conflicting theories. Much school experimentation in science is Popperian in essence: we see a rainbow and hypothesise that white light is split up into light of different colours as it is refracted through a transparent medium (water droplets); we test this by attempting to refract white light through a glass prism; we find the same colours of the rainbow are produced and our hypothesis is confirmed. Until some new evidence causes it to be falsified, we accept it.

There is much of value in the work of Thomas Merton and Karl Popper but most academics in the field would argue that there is more to the nature of science. We turn to the work of Thomas Kuhn (Kuhn 1970). Thomas Kuhn made a number of seminal contributions but he is most remembered nowadays by his argument that while the Popperian account of science holds well during periods of *normal science* when a single paradigm holds sway, such as the Ptolemaic model of the structure of the solar system (in which the Earth is at the centre) or the Newtonian understanding of motion and gravity, it breaks down when a scientific *crisis* occurs. At the time of such a crisis, a scientific revolution happens during

Figure 4.1.1 Black swans (*Cygnus atratus*) are native to Australia. Until they became known to people in the West the statement 'All swans are white' was thought to be true. Now we say that it is both falsifiable (i.e. capable of being falsified) and false. Karl Popper argued that scientific statements, hypotheses and theories all need to be falsifiable.

which a new paradigm, such as the Copernican model of the structure of the solar system or Einstein's theory of relativity, begins to replace the previously accepted paradigm. The central point is that the change of allegiance from scientists believing in one paradigm to their believing in another cannot, Kuhn argues, be fully explained by the Popperian account of falsifiability.

Kuhn likens the switch from one paradigm to another to a gestalt switch (when we suddenly see something in a new way) or even a religious conversion. As Alan Chalmers puts it:

> There will be no purely logical argument that demonstrates the superiority of one paradigm over another and that thereby compels a rational scientist to make the change. One reason why no such demonstration is possible is the fact that a variety of factors are involved in a scientist's judgment of the merits of a scientific theory. An individual scientist's decision will depend on the priority he or she gives to the various factors. The factors will include such things as simplicity, the connection with some pressing social need, the ability to solve some specified kind of problem, and so on. Thus one scientist might be attracted to the Copernican theory because of the simplicity of certain mathematical features of it. Another might be attracted to it because in it there is the possibility of calendar reform. A third might have been deterred from adopting the Copernican theory because of an involvement with terrestrial mechanics and an awareness of the problems that the Copernican theory posed for it.
>
> (Chalmers 1999: 115–16)

Kuhn also argued that scientific knowledge is validated by its acceptance in a community of scientists. Often scientists change their views as new evidence persuades them that a previously held theory is wrong. But sometimes they cling obstinately to cherished theories. In such cases, if these scientists are powerful (e.g. by controlling what papers get published in the most prestigious journals), scientific progress may be impeded – until the scientists in question retire or die!

In a chapter of this length there clearly isn't space to provide an account of many other views of how science is done but there is one philosopher of science whom you will either love or hate – Paul Feyerabend. In many ways Feyerabend anticipated the post-modernists with their suspicion of a single authoritative account of reality. His views are succinctly summed up in the title of his most famous book *Against Method* (Feyerabend, 1975/1988). Feyerabend is something of an intellectual anarchist (another of his books is called *Farewell to Reason*) and the best way to understand him is to read him rather than to read a summary of him. Here are a few quotes – to either whet your appetite or put you off for life:

> No theory ever agrees with all the *facts* in its domain, yet it is not always the theory that is to blame. Facts are constituted by older ideologies, and a clash between facts and theories may be proof of progress.
>
> (Feyerabend 1988: 39)

> the events, procedures and results that constitute the sciences have no common structure
>
> (Feyerabend 1988: 1)

> the success of 'science' cannot be used as an argument for treating as yet unsolved problems in a standardized way
>
> (Feyerabend 1988: 2)

> there can be many different kinds of science. People starting from different social backgrounds will approach the world in different ways and learn different things about it.
>
> (Feyerabend 1988: 3)

**Task 4.1.1
Getting pupils to consider the scope of science**

It is all too easy for pupils to take for granted that they get taught different 'things' in their different subjects in school. The aim of this task is to help pupils to become more aware of why there are certain things they study in science lessons as opposed to those studied in other lessons.

You can start by having a discussion with pupils about whether there are some things in science that they also learn about in other subjects (e.g. rocks in geography, muscles and breathing in PE, sound in music). Then get them, perhaps in pairs or small groups, to talk about the similarities and differences between what they get taught about in geography and what they get taught about in science. Pupils should end up appreciating that there are overlaps but that science is more interested in experiments, is more universal (so that most science is much the same in any country whereas geography is very interested in differences between countries) and has less to say about human action.

**Task 4.1.2
What is your view of the nature
of science?**

There have been a number of research instruments devised to enable a
person's views on the nature of science to be determined. Probably the
easiest for you to get hold of and use is that provided by two leading UK
science educators – Mick Nott and Jerry Wellington (Nott and Wellington
1993). If you quite enjoy reading questionnaires along the lines of 'Does
your partner find you boring?' in the backs of magazines while at the
dentist, this task is for you.

'REAL SCIENCE' COMPARED TO SCHOOL SCIENCE

There is much in the 5–16 science National Curriculum in England with which to be
pleased. However, one of the less successful areas is what is now (August 2003) called 'Scientific
enquiry'. For one thing, we don't do a very good job of getting children in school science
lessons to ask the sorts of questions that scientists actually ask or to ask the sorts of questions
that the rest of us ask and to which science can make a contribution. Instead, pupils are too
often restricted to uninteresting questions about the bouncing of squash balls or the dissolving
of sugar in what are misleadingly termed 'scientific investigations'.

The history of this part of the science curriculum (currently Sc1) since the first National
Curriculum Science Working Group, which published its report in 1987, has been analysed
by Jim Donnelly (2001). Donnelly argues convincingly that two conflicting understandings
of the nature of science can be detected in the battles of these years (and they have felt
much like battles to those participating in them). One is what Donnelly terms 'essentially
empiricist'; in other words, straightforwardly concerned with how factual data are collected
with which to test hypotheses. The other stresses social and cultural influences on science.
In the language of the first part of this unit, this is a contest between Popper and Kuhn
(Feyerabend does not get a look-in).

The reasons for this battle need not greatly concern us except in so far as the very
existence of the battle indicates the lack of consensus in this area among those responsible
for the science National Curriculum. This contrasts with many other parts of the science
National Curriculum. There is, for example, little controversy over the inclusion of food
chains, melting, and series circuits.

Much school science operates on the assumption that 'real science' only consists in doing
replicated laboratory experiments to test hypotheses. When I started teaching social biology
to 16–19 year-olds in England, the Examinations Board (it was in the mid-1980s, before
Awarding Bodies) that set the syllabus included a project. One of my students was a very fit
athlete who lived in Bahrain out of term time. He carried out on himself measurements of
such physiological variables as body temperatures and body mass just before and just after
completing a number of runs both in the UK and in Bahrain under very different
environmental conditions. Another student was interested to see whether a person's
astrological sign (determined by their birth date) correlated with their choice of school
subjects at advanced level (e.g. sciences versus arts) or with their personalities. Accordingly
she carried out a large survey of fellow students.

Both students had their projects scored at 0 per cent. Nor were these marks changed on appeal. I'm not claiming that either of these projects was the finest I have ever seen. But I am convinced that the marks they were given reflected too narrow an assumption in the examiners' minds about what constituted a valid piece of scientific enquiry (Reiss 1993).

Those who write science curricula and mark students' work are powerful determinants of what passes in school for 'real science'. A more valid approach to finding out what science actually consists of is to study what real scientists do. Careful ethnographic work on this only began in the 1970s – the classic book is Latour and Woolgar (1979). Much of this writing is rather difficult to read and it's much easier to read any really good biographical account of a scientist – though such biographies, in concentrating on individuals, do rather give rise to the 'great scientists' view of scientific progress.

The take-home message from the ethnographic work on science is that while scientific practice is partly characterised by the Mertonian and Popperian norms discussed above, there is plenty of support for Kuhn's views and even for Feyerabend's. For example, school accounts of the science often underplay the political realities of scientific research (not to mention the monotony of much of it). Nowadays, governments and companies are far more interested in funding work on genetic modification than research into moss reproduction. Actually, it's the exception that proves the rule. If your moss only lives in Antarctica, chances are you will get funding as many countries are keen to undertake research there so as to stake a territorial claim should the wilderness ever be exploited for natural reserves.

Task 4.1.3
Get pupils to research how science is done

There are a number of good books that deal with the history and practice of science at a level suitable for secondary science pupils (e.g. Solomon 1991; Ellis 1992; Hunt and Millar 2000; see also *Breakthrough* available from Peter Ellis at PREllis18@aol.com; the *Scientists Who Made History* series published by Hodder Wayland; the *Groundbreakers* series published by Heinemann and the *Science Web* Readers published by Nelson). Whether or not your pupils have access to such texts, get them to research using books in the school library or internet sources one example of the history and practice of science. For example, at KS4 you might get pupils to research one of the following:

- the theory of evolution;
- Rosalind Franklin's contribution to determining the structure of DNA;
- *in vitro* fertilisation;
- the Periodic Table;
- the history of glass;
- plate tectonics;
- the competition between dc and ac among domestic suppliers of electricity;
- the life and work of Galileo;
- the use of X-rays.

This exercise works best if pupils have a choice on what to work and have some opportunities to work collaboratively.

PUPIL'S VIEWS OF THE NATURE OF SCIENCE

In the UK, the most detailed research carried out on pupils' views on the nature of science dates from 1991 to 1993, i.e. in the early years of the National Curriculum. The work was carried out on 9, 12 and 16 year-olds in England and came up with the following findings (Driver *et al.* 1996):

- Pupils tend to see the purpose of science as providing solutions to technical problems rather than providing more powerful explanations.
- Pupils rarely appreciate that scientific explanations can involve postulating models. Even when they do, models are presumed to map onto events in the world in an unproblematic manner.
- Pupils rarely see science as a social enterprise. Scientists are seen as individuals working in isolation.
- Pupils have little awareness of the ways that society influences decisions about research agendas. The most common view is that scientists, through their personal altruism, choose to work on particular problems of concern to society.

One technique that has been used to examine how pupils see science is to ask them to draw a scientist (Figure 4.1.2). The drawings are then examined to see whether pupils tend to draw scientists as male or female, white or black, in laboratories or in other settings, etc. It has been suggested that the images produced are becoming less stereotypical, show less gender bias and are more realistic (Matthews 1996). However, a more recent study with a much larger sample size concluded that between 1990 and 1996 primary pupil perceptions did not change significantly (Newton and Newton 1998).

Task 4.1.4
Get pupils to do the 'draw a scientist' test

Get your pupils to do the 'draw a scientist test'. (This probably works better at KS3 than at KS4.) Explain to them before they start their drawings that this isn't a test in the sense of some people gaining more marks than others and that you aren't interested in the artistic quality of their drawings. Ensure they write their names on the back of the drawing (in case you want to analyse the results by gender, ethnicity, performance in science or something else that requires knowledge at the individual level).

Usually researchers get pupils to do this individually but you might decide that it would be interesting to get pupils to discuss in pairs what they are going to put in their drawings before they do them.

If you want to go beyond what most researchers do you might:

- require pupils to write a few paragraphs explaining why they drew what they drew;
- interview pupils about their drawings;
- try to untangle whether pupils are really drawing what they think scientists are like or whether they are drawing stereotypes or caricatures.

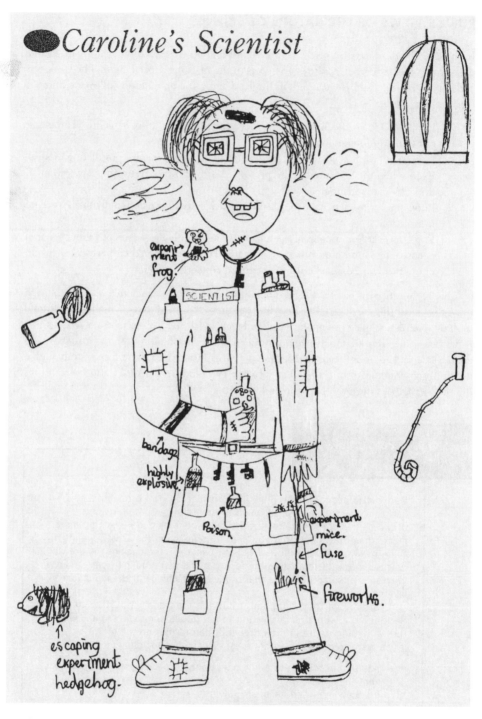

Figure 4.1.2 Caroline Allen's drawing of a scientist (Reproduced with permission from Caroline Allen)

SUMMARY

Science is concerned with the natural world, with certain elements of the manufactured world and with how things are rather than with how they should be.

The nature of science is a controversial area and there are several competing understandings of how scientific knowledge is produced. Robert Merton sees science as open-minded, universalist, disinterested and communal. For Karl Popper, the distinctive thing about science is that all its ideas are testable and so falsifiable. Thomas Kuhn goes beyond these views in seeing certain crucial episodes in the history of science as inexplicable within Mertonian and Popperian thinking. Kuhn stresses that when scientists switch from one way of seeing the world to another, i.e. as the paradigm changes, they do so for a variety of reasons not all of which are scientific in the narrow sense of the term.

Pupils generally have rather a limited understanding of the nature of science. The tasks presented here are intended to help deepen their understanding.

FURTHER READING

Chalmers, A.F. (1999) *What is this thing called Science?*, 3rd edn, Buckingham: Open University Press. An extremely clear and very widely read introductory textbook on the philosophy of science. If you want a readable account about any of the major questions on the nature of science, here is an excellent place to look.

Driver, R., Leach, J., Millar, R. and Scott, P. (1996) *Young People's Images of Science*, Buckingham: Open University Press. Written with great clarity by four of the UK's leading science educators, this book presents the findings of a major study into pupils' understandings of the nature of science. The study showed that the English school science curriculum resulted in only limited understanding in this area.

Kuhn, T.S. (1970) *The Structure of Scientific Revolutions*, 2nd edn, Chicago: University of Chicago Press. A classic in the history and philosophy of science. This is the book which undermined the straightforward Popperian view of science and convincingly argued for the importance of culture in the growth of scientific knowledge. Kuhn introduced the notion of paradigms in science.

Wolpert, L. (1992) *The Unnatural Nature of Science*, London: Faber & Faber. A book on the nature of science by a leading scientist. As the dust jacket puts it 'He explains … why philosophers and sociologists have made so little contribution to understanding science's true nature'! Wolpert argues that scientific ideas are counter-intuitive and that common sense often makes no sense at all.

Unit 4.2

Biology

Katherine Little

INTRODUCTION

The study of biology in schools is mainly concerned with only green plants and animals, meaning that there are only slightly more than a million organisms to come to terms with. However, because life on earth has a single origin, all living things share common characteristics – they respire, reproduce, respond to their surroundings, move, excrete waste, take in nutrients and grow. Therefore, by understanding some basic concepts, it is possible to extend and apply ideas to a wide range of organisms.

OBJECTIVES

By end of this unit you should be aware of:

- key concepts in biology;
- the distinctive features of living things;
- the role evolution plays in explaining how our living environment came to be as it is.

CELLS AND DNA

One of the most basic and important ideas in biology is that all living things are made of cells. So-called by Robert Hooke, after his first microscope observation of cork that resembled the regular, bare cells of monks, it has since been seen that far from empty, cells contain many components. Though contents of cells differ – from nerve cells to photosynthetic plant cells, muscle cells to sex cells – they all share fundamental constituents, including a nucleus, cell membrane, and cytoplasm.

The nucleus contains our chromosomes, along which a complete set of instructions for our lives are arranged as beads on a string in our genes, written in the four-letter code of DNA. Genes are translated into proteins, which are responsible for the functioning of a cell. Within an organism, different types of cells function differently because different genes are 'switched on'; between organisms there are differences in the forms, or alleles, of genes; for example, that which controls flower colour. When genes become so different between individuals that they give rise to sex cells that are incompatible, two different species are considered to exist. However, because of the common ancestry of living things, all living organisms share a wide range of cell reactions governed by the same genes. For example, we share 98 per cent of our DNA with chimps, our closest relative, but also share 60 per cent with mice.

DNA is copied faithfully during cell replication; depending upon the type of cell division, the daughter cells may be identical (mitosis), or genetically different (meiosis). In sexual reproduction the number of chromosomes is reduced by half in the gametes (the name given to male and female sex cells, either the sperm and egg, or contents of pollen and ovules). At fertilisation, the full number of chromosomes is restored, giving rise to an organism that has inherited half of its mother's and half of its father's genes. In this way, the genetic essence of an individual can be passed down through generations.

If the sole purpose of an organism's existence is to pass its genes to future generations, then the complexity of life shows the variety of ways in which this can be achieved. There are over 1.4 million named living species, with estimates of up to 10 times that still to be discovered (before they become extinct as a result of human activity). Of these, school biology concentrates upon the green plants of the world, and the animals, with great reference to human biology. Green plants and animals represent the two main groups of organisms. The first is able to produce its own source of food, whilst the second is dependent upon the first for its supply of nutrients.

PLANTS AS THE POWERHOUSES OF THE LIVING WORLD: PHOTOSYNTHESIS

Plants, often overlooked as inanimate and rather dull, are the powerhouses of the living world. Without the ability of green plants to capture the energy in sunlight, the carbon-based living world would rapidly cease to exist. This most amazing of chemical reactions, photosynthesis (literally, making with light), occurs in every green leaf. Simple molecules of carbon dioxide, from the air, and water, absorbed through the plant's roots, are combined in the leaf using the sun's energy captured by the green pigment chlorophyll to form glucose, a sugar built around six carbon atoms. The chemical energy in the glucose–oxygen system then becomes available for the plant, a producer, and any animal, a consumer, that might use that plant as a food source. Additionally, glucose can be polymerised into starch or glycogen for food storage, or cellulose for structural use in plant cell walls, or combined with other molecules to form amino acids, the building blocks of proteins, or fats and lipids. Proteins are structurally important, for example, skin and hair contain the protein keratin, and have a vital role as biological catalysts in their action as enzymes. Fats and lipids are the main constituent of cell membranes, and are also used for long-term food storage. Without photosynthesis to capture the sun's energy, there would be no glucose production, or its subsequent conversion into more complex biological molecules, and no atmospheric oxygen; hence it is true to say that the natural world is driven by sunlight.

SUPPLYING ENERGY: RESPIRATION

The majority of organisms respire aerobically, that is, they combine glucose with oxygen to create a supply of energy that can be used to drive cellular reactions. Carbon dioxide and water are produced as waste products. Anaerobic respiration can take place under extreme conditions when oxygen is less plentiful, but the amount of energy released is far less. In very small organisms oxygen and glucose needs can be met by simple diffusion of molecules from the external to the internal environment. However, as the size of organisms increases, the surface area to volume ratio is reduced, so not every cell will meet its requirements by diffusion. Large organisms have therefore evolved complex systems for the transport of vital molecules to the cells, and to remove potentially toxic waste products from them.

TRANSPORTATION OF MATERIAL

Both plants and animals use the process of mass transport to move large amounts of substances. Animals' transport systems are often typified by the example of the mammalian heart (demonstrating the often human-centred view of biology). In this system, the heart, a mechanical pump, moves the transport medium, blood, around the body in a system of arteries, capillaries and veins. These specialised vessels bring the blood's contents into close contact with every single cell, from where it is only a short distance for substances to diffuse into and out of cells. It is in this way that oxygen and nutrients are delivered to cells, and carbon dioxide, water and other waste products are removed.

Plants, being generally less active than animals, do not have such high energy requirements; their rate of respiration is therefore lower, and delivery and removal of molecules not as urgent. Nevertheless, plants do need to move glucose produced in their leaves to the rest of the plant, and must raise water from their roots to their photosynthesising leaves. Plants have two transport systems, xylem and phloem vessels. Xylem vessels can be thought of as long thin tubes that can stretch to the height of the tallest trees, through which it is believed water and minerals can move from the roots to the leaves by capillary action alone, no active energy-consuming transport process is needed and so xylem vessels are made of dead cells, containing no organelles. This process of water movement from the roots to the leaves is called transpiration, and its rate is governed by the rate of water loss from the leaves, either as it is used in photosynthesis or evaporates into the atmosphere. The second plant transport system is the phloem system. Phloem also is composed of tubes, but these tubes are living, and need to respire. The liquid moving in these tubes is far more concentrated than that in the xylem, being a solution of sugars being transported from the leaves to other parts of the plant, particularly the roots.

CHANGING LARGE MOLECULES TO SMALL ONES: DIGESTION

Whereas plants can build more complex organic molecules from their synthesised glucose and minerals absorbed from the soil, animals are dependent upon their diet to obtain many vital nutrients. However, food that is ingested is rarely in an appropriate form to be used by cells. It must first of all be digested, broken down mechanically and chemically into its constituent molecules. For example, the energy-rich starch molecule is too large to pass through a cell membrane, so must be digested into glucose subunits before absorption. This action is carried out by specific enzymes, amylase and maltase, which catalyse this breakdown. Even as the enzymes get to work, mechanical processes of chewing and churning will have begun the physical breakdown, giving the enzymes a greater surface area to act upon.

Surface area is a factor that affects many processes in the living world; so many are dependent on the diffusion of substances across membranes, and their rate is dependent on the surface area of membrane available. Thus, the rate of absorption of nutrients in the small intestine is maximised by the convolutions and foldings of the surface into villi and further into fingerlike microvilli; plants' absorption of minerals from the soil is aided by the fine projections of root hair cells from the finest of roots; gas exchange in organisms occurs in the spongy, air-rich mesophyll of leaves, across the surface of many-branched air sacs of the mammalian lungs, across the richly blood-supplied feathery gill surfaces of a fish.

CONTROLLING CONDITIONS: HOMEOSTASIS

To carry out the functions of life, organisms must strive to maintain constant internal environments, a process known as homeostasis. To consider a single factor, the water content of cells: if the water content of a cell becomes reduced, the cell will collapse; if the water content is too great, the cell will over-expand which may result in the membrane of the cell rupturing. The movement of water into and out of cells is governed by the concentration of solutes on either side of the membrane. In humans, two important osmotically active solutes are salt and glucose. If salt or glucose concentration is high in the blood stream, water will be drawn out of the cells causing them to dehydrate; this could occur through the ingestion of salty foods, or in the case of glucose, with the condition diabetes, where glucose is not effectively removed from the bloodstream. To moderate the extremes of solute content, and to eliminate metabolic waste, humans have kidneys that filter the blood to remove excess water and solutes. These complex filtration units use mechanisms of high pressure filtration to remove all particles below a certain size from the blood, then active transport and diffusion to return a correct balance of substances to the body. The final concentration of reabsorbed substances is governed by a hormone, a chemical messenger carried in the bloodstream, released from a gland in the brain, which affects the uptake of water in the kidney.

COMMUNICATION AND CONTROL: HORMONES AND THE NERVOUS SYSTEM

Many biological processes are governed by hormones, and their effects are often long lasting and wide-ranging. One dramatic hormone is adrenaline, released from glands on top of the kidneys, that elicits the increased heartbeat, raised breathing rate, dilated pupils and sweating palms of fear. Longer acting hormones include the sex hormones, testosterone, oestrogen and progesterone, released from the sex organs and responsible for growth and development of sexual characteristics and the development of gametes. The growth of plants is also governed by hormones, ably demonstrated by the use of hormone-rooting powder to stimulate root development in cuttings.

The action of hormones is in contrast to the nervous system of animals. Nerve cells carry electrical impulses at great speed to and from the central nervous system. These can elicit instantaneous reactions, in fractions of a second, between sensing and responding to a stimulus. For example, whereas plants will respond to light and grow towards it as a result of a certain hormone building up on one side of the stem and increasing cell permeability on one side, humans will respond to touching a hot object by immediately withdrawing their hand as a result of a rapid nerve impulse travelling to the brain from temperature receptors and a responding nerve impulse stimulating the muscles of the arm.

EVOLUTION AND GENETICS

The perfectly engineered solutions to problems of maintaining life presented here are the result of millions of years of successive minute changes in design, the designer being the pressures of the environment living creatures inhabit. In a world where resources are not infinite, it is not only other species with whom individuals compete, but also their peers. In a group, or population, of similar organisms, some will be better suited to the conditions and be able to produce more surviving offspring than those organisms struggling to survive. For example, in a field that is home to white rabbits and brown rabbits, white rabbits are more likely to be seen and eaten by foxes than their brown counterparts. Of the brown rabbits, those with long legs for fast running will escape the foxes. Eventually, the field will be home to only brown long-legged rabbits. Slight changes in species, generation after generation, have led to the living world we see today and continue to shape it. Evolution is dependent upon there being a diversity of genes within a species to begin with and the introduction of new beneficial genes by mutation. In the present day, when human activity is adversely affecting many habitats, organisms do not have the genes present in their populations that might enable future offspring to cope in some way with environmental disturbances. As they cannot adapt to their constantly changing habitats in one or few generations, they are becoming extinct.

One of the great milestones in the evolution of living things was the arrival of sexual reproduction. Reproduction is one of the seven defining characteristics of living things. The innate desire to propagate the small lengths of DNA that constitute our genes has driven the form and behaviour of much of the living world. A successful individual, in evolutionary terms, will pass on more copies of its genes than an unsuccessful one. However, to create mere copies of oneself, asexual reproduction, results in clones, or genetically identical individuals. A change in the environment would affect all of these; there is no genetic diversity that can be drawn upon to adapt to the changing environment. Sexual reproduction, through the combination of sex cells from male and females of the same species, results in offspring that are all genetically different. This re-assortment of the species' genes can relatively quickly produce more successful combinations of genes that may fare better in a new environment.

SUMMARY

From the elephant to the ant to the bacteria that live upon and within the ant, from the giant redwoods of California to the algae in a garden pond, all organisms are performing the processes of living things. They have arrived at a multitude of different ways in which to carry out these processes, remaining in the same place and producing their own food or moving around in search of nutrition; different methods of transporting substances throughout their systems; different mechanisms of sensing and responding to their environments. The diversity of life that is so overwhelming is the result of millions of years of evolution. From the initial single celled organisms have evolved the wealth of living things upon which David Attenborough has built his career. Biology provides answers for such questions as, 'Why are trees green?' 'How do fish breathe underwater?' 'Why do elephants have big ears?' 'Why are there two sexes?' 'What are we here for?' To study biology so enhances our appreciation of our own selves and of the world of which we are both an integral part and self-appointed guardians, that to disregard the discipline would be to go through life blind to the truly awe-inspiring nature of our unique planet.

Tasks 4.2.1 and 4.2.2 provide ideas for stimulating thinking and interest in the living world.

Task 4.2.1
Plants

- In late autumn, find a horse chestnut (conker) tree. On the ground underneath fallen chestnuts will be splitting their casings and a first tentative root reaching for the soil. Plant one in a pot to grow with you through your PGCE year and possibly till you draw your pension.
- For those less patient, grow cress seeds on a damp paper towel. Place them on the window-sill, and marvel at the tiny plants' ability to respond to sunlight.
- Always effective: stand a white carnation in a small depth of strong food dye, and leave it overnight. The dye will be transported in the xylem to the petals, where the intricate network of veins will be revealed. For added fun, split the stem and use different colours.
- Tie a clear polythene bag over a pot plant. After a few hours, droplets of water will start to collect on the inside. This is water that has been transported from the soil through the root hairs, into the xylem vessels and out through the leaves into the air. The process at work here is multiplied thousand-fold in taking water to the tops of the tallest trees.

Task 4.2.2
Our bodies

- A favourite: stand on your head and drink a glass of water through a straw. Why doesn't it run back out of your mouth? Peristalsis – waves of muscular contraction moving towards your stomach, regardless of gravity.
- Hold your breath. What caused you to breathe again? Not a need for oxygen, but an urge to rid the body of carbon dioxide. Whilst you do this, think of the abilities of some sea mammals to dive to depths of over 2 km for half an hour or more.
- In front of a mirror, cover one open eye with your hand. The other pupil will expand in response to the darkness experienced by the other pupil. Tiny muscles in the iris are constantly adjusting the size of the pupil in response to the light level. This represents a fraction of the stimuli from our environment to which our bodies are constantly reacting.
- Look at a flower. Look at a tree. Look at a snail. Look at birds in the sky. Aren't these the most amazing pictures you have ever seen? Created by a collection of light sensitive cells on your retina sending electrical signals to the back of the brain, these images enable us to appreciate the natural world.

FURTHER READING

Arthus-Bertrand, Y. (2002) *The Earth from the Air Postcard Book*, London: Thames & Hudson.

Attenborough, D. (1979) *Life on Earth: A Natural History*, Boston, MA: Little, Brown and Co.

Attenborough, D. (1995) *The Private Life of Plants: A Natural History of Plant Behaviour*, London: BBC Books.

Diamond, J. (1988) *The Rise and Fall of the Third Chimpanzee: How our Animal Heritage Affects the Way we Live*, London: Vintage.

Gonick, L. and Outwater, A. (1996) *Cartoon Guide to the Environment*, New York: Harper Information.

Gonick, L. and Wheelis, M. (1983) *Cartoon Guide to Genetics*, New York: HarperCollins Publishers.

Jones, S. (1995) *The Language of Genes: Solving the Mysteries of Our Genetic Past, Present, and Future*, New York: Doubleday Publishing.

Jones, S. (1999) *Almost Like a Whale: the Origin of Species Updated*, New York: Doubleday Publishing.

Reiss, M. (ed.) (2002) *Teaching Secondary Biology*, London: John Murray for the ASE.

Ridley, M. (1994) *The Red Queen, Sex and the Evolution of Human Nature*, New York: Macmillan.

Wilson, E.O. (1992) *The Diversity of Life*, New York: W.W. Norton and Co.

WEBSITES TO EXPLORE

Farabee, M.J. (2002) *Online Biology Book:* http://www.emc.maricopa.edu/faculty/farabee/ BIOBK/BioBookTOC.html – an online biology textbook, with more than everything you need to know.

Guardian Education, 'biological sciences': http://education.guardian.co.uk/higher/links – follow links to biological sciences.

Quill Graphics *Cells Alive*: http://www.cellsalive.com – lots of interactive diagrams of cells.

Unit 4.3

Chemistry

Tony Turner

In a sense human flesh is made of stardust. Every atom in the human body, excluding only the primordial hydrogen atoms, was fashioned in the stars that formed, grew old and exploded most violently before the Sun and the Earth came into being. The explosions scattered the heavier elements as a fine dust through space. By the time it made the Sun, the primordial gas of the Milky Way was sufficiently enriched with heavier elements for rocky planets like the Earth to form. And from the rocks, atoms escaped for eventual incorporation in living things.

(Calder 1977: 417-9)

Recycling is at the heart of chemistry. The 92 different types of atom which are known to occur in the Earth's crust and its atmosphere, group and regroup to form millions of different structures and hence millions of different substances. The sandstones, limestones, granites and clays of the Earth's crust, the soils of the surface, the water and minerals of the oceans, the air we breathe, the tissues of living things, and manufactured plastics, drugs and ceramics, are simply the result of different combinations of some of the 92 different atoms. Of course there are extraordinarily large numbers of each type of atom, 10^{23} carbon atoms in a 25 carat diamond; 10^{22} gold atoms in a wedding ring and 10^{21} oxygen atoms in a breath of air. Virtually nothing leaves or enters our planet, so every new material which is made, every new plant which grows has to be formed from material which is already in the 'Space ship Earth'.

OBJECTIVES

By end of this unit you should:

- have an appreciation of the scope of chemistry;
- be aware of how the microscopic story of particles illuminates the macroscopic phenomena of behaviour of materials.

PARTICLES AND PHENOMENA

Chemistry is about two stories: the macroscopic world of bulk materials, and the invisible particle world of atoms and molecules. They are different but consistent stories and are now so intertwined in our thinking about materials, that we often do not recognise when we are moving between the two. We must add to these stories the story of the flow of energy which accompanies the chemical reactions.

The macroscopic story can be fun, messy and very useful. What happens when different substances react together? Are there explosions as when hydrogen reacts rapidly with oxygen to form water, are there changes of colour as when lead nitrate and sodium iodide react, is there fizzing as when sodium bicarbonate is added to vinegar? What are the new substances which are formed and the old ones which have been deconstructed? What are the properties of the different substances? How can knowledge of chemical reactions be used to make new substances with properties which we want?

Chemistry grew out of alchemy which was first practised throughout India, China and the Middle East. The name 'alchemy' may be derived from the Arabic article 'al' and 'chimia', the ancient Greek name for Egypt, from which the word chemistry is derived. (Other words with Arabic roots include alcohol and algebra). Alchemy, which sought to make gold from base metals, provided an experimental basis for progress and identified important substances, such as acids. However its goal was false and the overthrow of alchemy was an essential step in the development of chemistry (Dixon 1989: 17).

What then is the other story – the story at particle level? It was Dalton in 1802 who suggested that elements were made of different identical particles which were of different masses. The idea of atoms goes back through Dalton (1802), to Democritus (fourth century BC), who was in turn influenced by earlier Egyptian science (Pappademos, 1983: 180). Mendeleyev's realisation of a pattern in the properties of different elements in 1869 led to the idea that perhaps there was some underlying mechanism which explained the pattern. It was not until the early twentieth century that the explanation was found to be linked to the fact that all atoms are made up of different numbers of only three even smaller particles. Each of the 92 different type of atoms has a different number of protons in its nucleus, one proton in hydrogen, two protons in helium, three in lithium, four in beryllium, five in boron, six in carbon and so on, up to uranium at 92. (Beyond that there are 10 to 15 larger very unstable atoms, formed in nuclear reactors.) The number of protons alone does not account for the relative masses of the atoms, but the addition of varying numbers of neutrons does. The shorthand labelling of elements is just a summary of this story. The label $^{12}C_6$ describes a carbon atom (symbol C) with six protons in the nucleus, and with an atomic mass of 12 made up of the mass of the six protons and the mass of a further six neutrons; $^{235}U_{92}$ symbolises a uranium atom of 92 protons and 143 neutrons.

The electrons which make up the rest of the atom are the most important components from the point of view of chemistry. These negatively charged particles, balancing the positive charge of the protons to make the atom electrically neutral, mostly determine the way atoms join together for the simple reason that they are the first thing another atom meets in a chemical reaction. (On the scale of the atom, electrons are 'miles away' from the nucleus, the radius of the atom being about 10^{-10} m and the radius of the nucleus about 10^{-15} m). Isotopes of the same element such as carbon-14 and carbon-12, ($^{14}C_6$ and $^{12}C_6$ respectively) therefore react chemically in much the same way, because they both have the same number of electrons. It happens in this particular example that while the chemistry is the same the heavier isotope is radioactive (i.e. a property related to the nucleus and not the electrons), which is useful in the dating of fossils (Brain 2003).

HOW ARE ATOMS HELD TOGETHER? BONDING OF PARTICLES

The story of the electrons enables us to answer questions such as: how do sodium and chlorine atoms bond together to form salt? How do carbon and oxygen atoms bond together to form carbon dioxide? How do the atoms of gold bond together in a wedding ring? There are three fundamental ways in which electrons link atoms: 'ionic bonds' making 'giant structures of ions'; 'covalent bonds'; and 'metallic bonds' forming 'giant structures of atoms'.

In ionic bonding, one or more electrons are transferred from one atom to another when a compound is formed. The resultant atoms are therefore charged positively and negatively, and are then called ions. The bond between ions is an electrostatic attractive force exerted in all directions, called an ionic bond. Substances bonded in this way are high melting point solids, e.g. sodium chloride. The structure of ionic solids is determined by the size and charge on the ions and the different ways they pack together to preserve electrical neutrality, forming the so-called 'giant structure of ions' of ionic compounds.

In covalent bonding neither atom becomes charged and discrete molecules are usually formed. An electron pair is shared between two atoms and is directional, i.e. lies between the two atoms. This feature is emphasised in a structural model of a substance – see Figure 4.3.1 and 4.3.2 in which a line represents a shared pair of electrons.

Covalent bonds also occur in some elements where two or more atoms of the same type form a molecule of the element as in bromine (Br_2) or sulphur (S_8). Compounds having covalent bonds include octane (C_8H_{18}) and glucose ($C_6H_{12}O_6$). Some molecules are very large, e.g. cellulose, a long chain of hundreds of glucose units. Cellulose is a polymer ('many

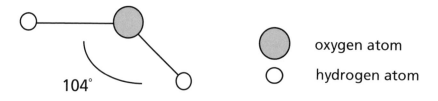

Figure 4.3.1   Structure of a water molecule: angle between O–H bonds 104°

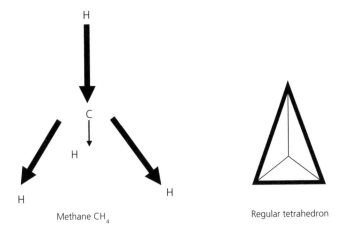

H

C

H

H   H

Methane CH₄   Regular tetrahedron

Figure 4.3.2   Directed bonds: the bonds between carbon and hydrogen in a methane molecule point towards the corners of a regular tetrahedron

parts') as are DNA, starch and Teflon. While the atoms *within* the molecule are tightly bonded, the links *between* the molecules are weaker, hence a molecular substance is a collection of many millions of molecules each loosely bound to each other. Molecular substances, therefore, melt more easily than do giant structures because the intermolecular forces are weaker than the forces between the ions in the giant structure. Some molecular substances are gases at room temperature such as hydrogen (H_2) and ammonia (NH_3).

The water molecule has an additional feature. The charge distribution between oxygen and hydrogen atoms is not even, the electrons being closer to the oxygen atom than the hydrogen atoms, so one end of the molecule is slightly negative and the other slightly positive. This uneven distribution accounts for some of the extraordinary properties of water, i.e. its ability to dissolve an enormous number of substances, its expansion on freezing, its being a liquid at room temperature. The solvent properties of water include dissolving many ionic substances, e.g. salt, or causing ionisation when it dissolves hydrogen chloride to make hydrochloric acid. Many other molecules show this property of uneven charge distribution; these type of chemical bonds are said to be polar.

Metallic bonding occurs in metals where the outer electrons are loosely held by the atoms but are not attached to any one atom. The atoms are held in a 'sea of electrons', maintaining overall neutral charge. Because of the free electrons, metals are good conductors of heat and electricity in the solid and liquid state. The resultant bond is called a 'metallic bond' and the solid is a 'giant structure of atoms'. Metals occur as elements, e.g. gold (Au) and as mixtures (alloys) such as brass (copper and tin).

Other 'giant structures of atoms' include diamond (C) and silica (SiO_2). In these examples the bonding is covalent, not metallic; both diamond and silica are poor electrical conductors. Graphite (C) is an exceptional substance being a good conductor of electricity but having substantial covalent bonding. Giant structures have high melting points because the bonding force is exerted in all directions throughout the structure.

There are some molecules which defy our attempt to give exact formulae. Two important life substances comprise large molecules with a metal atom. Haemoglobin in mammalian blood contains iron but there is no one formula to describe it. Chlorophyll comprises several closely related substances, including chlorophylls A and B both of which contain magnesium. In both haemoglobin and chlorophyll the metal atom is situated at the centre of a large organic molecule related to the porphyrins and bonded to nitrogen atoms (see Scifun 2003 website).

ENERGY RELEASED OR ABSORBED IN CHEMICAL REACTIONS

The story is not just about the particles and the forces which hold them together, but the energy which is involved in making or breaking the bonds between the atoms in a chemical reaction. When bonds are *broken* energy has to be supplied to pull the atoms apart (endothermic reactions). When bonds are *made* energy is released back into the environment (exothermic reactions). Sunlight, for instance, supplies the energy to break the hydrogen away from the oxygen in molecules of water, so that the hydrogen atoms can join with carbon dioxide molecules to make large molecules of glucose in photosynthesis. The energy released from the making of the glucose bonds is far less than the energy used in breaking the hydrogen–oxygen bonds, so the reaction is overall endothermic. Reactions where the making of bonds releases a lot of energy are often the most dramatic, hence our enjoyment of fireworks, bonfires, the thermite process and firing of hydrogen and oxygen rockets.

When discussing energy changes chemists talk of enthalpy rather than energy. Enthalpy is merely the energy change for a set number of particles in a particular reaction. If there is double the number of particles then there is double the energy change. The number chemists have chosen is the 'mole', which is called Avogadro's number, 6.27×10^{23}. A mole of carbon ($^{12}C_6$) atoms has a mass of 12 grams; a mole of nitrogen ($^{14}N_7$) atoms has a mass of 14 grams. When a mole of carbon atoms burns in oxygen, then 394 kilojoules (kJ) of energy are given out. If 6 grams of carbon were oxidised then 197 kJ would be given out. Equations like the one below describe the energy change when one mole of carbon is burned completely in oxygen. The negative sign is merely a convention, it means that the energy has been lost to the chemical system, although it might have warmed our hands and added to our system!

$$C + O_2 = CO_2 \qquad \Delta H = -394 \text{ kJ/mole.}$$

So by weighing it is possible to count atoms and know how many moles of substance you are dealing with. By looking up enthalpy tables it is possible to work out how much energy will be released by the amount of substance we are dealing with.

RATES OF REACTIONS

Even if reactions are possible the rate can vary from very slow, like the browning of an apple, or the oxidation of magnesium at room temperature, to very rapid such as the neutralisation of acids with alkalis. The rates at which chemical reactions occur can be altered, by finding ways of making the different atoms meet more often. Increasing the concentration of chemicals increases the rate of reaction because of the increased likelihood of particles meeting. Increasing the temperature usually increases the rate of reaction, because the faster moving particles meet other particles more often. Grinding solids into a powder increases surface area and exposes more atoms for a reaction.

Many reactions require an 'activation energy', that is extra energy to get the reaction to start. Once started, the reaction gives out enough energy to supply the activation energy to other atoms. Hence we have to generate enough heat from friction on the chemicals at the tip of a match to make them burn, and as they burn they produce an even higher temperature which provides the activation energy for the wood to oxidise. The first bit of wood to burn supplies the activation energy for the next bit of wood which then burns, and so on.

Reactions can be helped to go more quickly by the use of a catalyst. Catalysts provide an alternative pathway for a reaction, e.g. by allowing the formation of a temporary intermediate substance with a lower activation energy. Whichever pathway is used for a reaction the enthalpy change is the same. Common enzymes are catalysts and include those in the mouth and stomach juices, helping digestion.

ENTROPY

Chemists want to know whether or not a chemical change is possible before they attempt it. Enthalpy changes can be positive or negative and so knowing whether an intended change releases energy to the surroundings, or absorbs it, is not the answer.

The problem of knowing was overcome by realising that the total energy change of a reaction (enthalpy) is made up of two factors, the bond-breaking/bond-making part and a part related to the change in order/disorder (entropy) of the system. For example, when salt dissolves in water, ionic bonds are broken and new bonds made between the ions and the water molecules. In addition, ions in a salt crystal are in an ordered state whereas in salt water they are more randomly distributed, that is dissolving is accompanied by an increase in disorder. Left to themselves most changes move in the direction of disorder, i.e. increased entropy.

The value of this idea of changes in order was developed by the physicist Wilhard Gibbs in the nineteenth century. The difference between enthalpy and the energy factor involving the entropy term is the energy available to do work in a system, called 'free energy'. Free energy was later named Gibbs' Free Energy, and more recently Gibbs' Energy and it is this energy value that chemists use to determine whether a reaction is possible or not. Entropy does not feature in GCE A level specifications but is met at degree level. Some aspects of the map of chemistry in relation to matter, energy and change are shown in Figure 4.3.3.

LEARNING ABOUT THE MACROSCOPIC STORY AND THINKING ABOUT THE PARTICLE STORY

School chemistry lends itself to spectacular activities, occasionally with much heat, light and colour. Explosions are enjoyed by most pupils. Many chemists were attracted to chemistry by the element of fun and wonder. Making oxygen and burning things in it is exciting. By contrast, many important changes (to chemists and the curriculum) seem innocuous, e.g. neutralisation, dissolving, oxidation, and are often invisible without markers, e.g. litmus or a thermometer.

Practical chemistry often gives tangible results but the explanations of change use invisible particles and invoke hidden mechanisms. The switch between the particle story and the

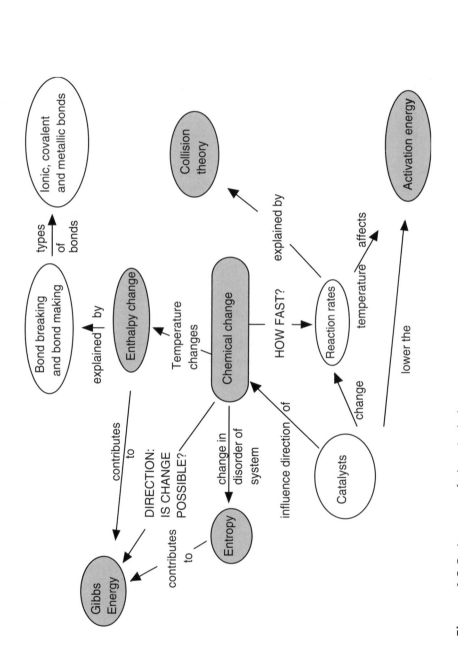

Figure 4.3.3 Aspects of chemical change

macroscopic story makes chemistry hard for many pupils, compounded by its early introduction in a pupil's exposure to the subject. You may find that pupils muddle the macroscopic and the microscopic stories such that they talk of water molecules melting when ice melts, instead of talking of them breaking apart so that they are free to move around and hence give an overall 'flowing' property to the bulk material, water.

You have to try and help pupils envisage the scale of the story you are telling. If atoms were the size of small marbles, a mole of them would cover the whole of the surface of the Earth 10 million times. Hence the number in those 10 million layers of marbles is the same number of atoms in an almond-sized lump of coal.

You may be able to help pupils understand the difference between the two stories by other images. Imagine being in a low-flying aircraft while watching people coming out of a football stadium. You would not see the individual people, and exactly how they move, but you will see the flow of the crowd like little rivers moving outwards from a large lake. The property of the crowd does not have the property of individuals within the crowd.

THE HISTORY OF CHEMISTRY

We have mentioned only in passing how the story at the particle level was unravelled. The stories are told well elsewhere and should be known by any science teacher; some of the important names are: Dalton, Lavoisier, Mendeleyev, Bohr, Rutherford, Chadwick, Bequerel, Thomson and the Braggs (father and son). These stories give an insight into how the detective work was done, what arguments were used, how careful measurement of reacting masses was a key to unravelling the story, alongside extraordinary feats of imagination. Some of these stories may be found in books listed at the end of this chapter.

The contexts are equally important for chemistry. Science teachers need to relate the knowledge of chemistry to how it is used and how new discoveries are made today. One of the major developments of the twentieth century was the unravelling of the structure of DNA from which has flowed the mapping of the human genome. The discovery depended on insight, imagination and much work on the part of many individuals. For example, the structure could not have been worked out without the use of X-ray crystallography pioneered and developed by the Braggs; or the discovery of the helical structure of proteins by Linus Pauling in the USA. Teasing out the structure itself depended on traditional chemical analysis and on the X-ray crystallographic studies of DNA by Maurice Wilkins and Rosalind Franklin in London. The final leap of imagination made by Francis Crick and James Watson has been told in print and film (Watson 1968) and is a story well worth telling your pupils. The discovery by Harry Kroto of new carbon species and the amazing carbon rings called buckyballs is another story worth telling (see Buckyballs, Diamond and Graphite 2003 in the Further reading section). See also Levi and Hodgkin in the Further reading section.

A major activity of chemists today is making new substances by recycling elements into new patterns. It is, however, the story of the world at the particle level which enables them to use computers to model new molecules. Their starting points are the properties of known molecules and knowledge of the bonds which hold them together. It is now routine to invent new molecules with predicted properties and structures and to make an assessment of the feasibility of synthesis and possible properties before a chemical ever reaches a test-tube.

SUMMARY

In telling the story of chemistry it is possible to see how it has illuminated our understanding of numerous processes in living things and has led to the specialised field of biochemistry. It also forms a bridge to the story more often associated with physics of what it is that holds all the particles within the atom together. It provides an insight into the world in which we now live where we take for granted that people make new materials, new drugs, purify our water, supply us with fuels and manufacture the fertilisers used to grow crops. Lastly, it provides the understanding to save our natural resources and undertake the recycling of waste products.

SOME RESOURCES FOR STORIES OF PAST CHEMISTS

Dixon, B. (1989) *The Science of Science*, London: Cassell.

Carey, J. (1995) *The Faber Book of Science*, London: Faber &Faber.

Daintith, J. and Gjertson, D. (eds) (1999) *Oxford Dictionary of Scientists*, Oxford: Oxford University Press.

Ronan, C. (1966) *The Ages of Science*, London: Harrap.

See also Porter and Ogilvie 2000, below.

FURTHER READING

Levi, P. (1995) 'The story of the carbon atom', in J. Carey, *The Faber Book of Science*, London: Faber & Faber, 338–44.

Hodgkin, D. (1988) 'Finding what's there', in L. Wolpert and A. Richards (eds) *A Passion for Science*, Oxford; Oxford University Press, 69–79. Reprinted as 'Seeing the atoms in crystals', in J. Carey (1995) *The Faber Book of Science*, London: Faber & Faber, 467–74.

Porter, R. and Ogilvie, M. (eds) (2000) *Dictionary of Scientific Biography*, Volumes I and II, Oxford: Helicon. A two-volume series which covers the historical development of science up to the present day. Separate discussions of each science including astronomy and earth sciences and in-depth biographies of scientists from the Greeks onwards.

McDuell, B. (ed.) (2000) *Teaching Secondary Chemistry*, London: John Murray for the ASE. One of a series of science books published for the ASE to support teachers teaching science especially for those teaching outside their specialist subject.

WEBSITES TO EXPLORE

Brain, M. (2003) *How Stuff Works: Carbon Dating*, available at http://www.howstuffworks.com/carbon-14.htm.

Buckyball, Diamond, and Graphite (2003) available at http://www.chem.wisc.edu/ ~newtrad/CurrRef/BDGTopic/BDGtext/BDGBucky.html.

Scifun (2003) *Chemical of the Week*, available at http://scifun.chem.wisc.edu/chemweek/ chlrphyl/chlrphyl.html.

Selected Classic Papers from the History of Chemistry (2003) available at http://webserver. lemoyne.edu/faculty/giunta/papers1.html#elem.

Useful resource for details of how important ideas were presented and the context in which they occurred.

Unit 4.4

Physics and Astronomy

Jenny Frost

INTRODUCTION

We had stopped for lunch, a late lunch as we had lost the route and been forced to do a fairly difficult scramble down steep rocks. We were still way up a mountain and the mist was thick. One of the group pulled out a bag of hermetically sealed crisps from her rucksack – it was blown up like a balloon. Nobody bothered to explain, but ate the crisps with the added satisfaction of knowing why the packet was like that.

THE SATISFACTION OF EXPLANATION

Nobody can quite explain why such little events can be so satisfying, but they are. Behind most of physics is a need to explain what the world is like, and what it is that makes things happen in the way they do. Physics has attempted to understand the 'rules' by which the universe works; the way in which matter holds together, how energy interacts with matter and how changes occur. There is a drive, perhaps for elegance or simplicity, to work with as few rules as possible, so that each rule has implications for a lot of phenomena. There are those who say people attracted to physics are those who have bad memories because they only have to learn a few rules!

OBJECTIVES

By end of this unit you should:

- be aware of the scope of physics and astronomy;
- have some insight into the ways of thinking and working characteristic of this area of science;
- be confident to explore the area further.

THE SCOPE OF PHYSICS

Physics covers an enormously wide variety of phenomena. The movement of stars and planets; the behaviour of light and heat, of sound, of electricity and magnetism; the discovery of less easily detectable phenomena such as radio waves, ultraviolet light, X-rays and radioactivity; the behaviour of the 'stuff' of which the world is made; the forces which exist and the way they determine what happens; and energy transfers which accompany change.

In size terms alone its scope is impressive, from the whole of the Universe down to the smallest of particles. On the scale of things, human beings are somewhere in the middle; the whole universe being a million trillion times larger than we are, and quarks (the particles of which protons and neutrons are made) being a trillion times smaller. So in both directions the story of physics has involved, and still involves, a lot of detective work, with people trying to *imagine* what the picture would be if only they were the appropriate size and with the appropriate detectors to 'see' everything. An important part of this imagining is to assume that the laws of physics are universal. (This was arguably one of Newton's major contributions in that he assumed the laws of physics applied 'out there' in the Solar system and beyond in the same way as they applied on Earth.) This imagining brings into existence a range of 'entities' – particles, current, voltage, gravity, electrons, density, power, energy, work, forces, which become not just end-points in their own right but the ingredients of other explanations.

THE 'BIG STORIES' OF PHYSICS

Many of the simpler 'cause and effect' physics stories which we help pupils to unravel in schools, especially in the lower secondary school, are parts of larger stories. As teachers we need acquaintance with these larger stories. I have selected eight to include here:

- We live on a hot rocky ball which is hurtling through space.
- We live in an expanding Universe.
- Matter is made of particles.
- Radioactivity.
- Radio waves and light waves are different facets of the same phenomenon.
- Fields.
- Change and energy transfer.
- The made world.

We live on a hot rocky ball which is hurtling through space

One of the stories must be an understanding of the place where we live. What appears to be a cool flat Earth is in fact a large spherical ball of rock, so intensely hot in the middle that much of the rock is molten. This rocky ball is spinning with a surface speed at the equator of 1,000 km/h and the whole thing is hurtling through space at 100,000 km/h as it orbits the Sun. It is covered with a thin layer of air confined to about the first 15 km from the surface, held there by the gravitational pull of the Earth. The material of the Earth stays together, it does not disintegrate into separate fragments. The Earth itself stays in orbit 'attached' to the Sun by an invisible 'thread' of gravity. The Earth with its companion, the Moon, is one of nine planets which are also orbiting the Sun. Some of the evidence for this story is its explanatory power, its ability to explain why we have day and night, why there are seasons, why we have eclipses of the Sun and Moon, and the phases of the Moon.

We live in an expanding Universe

The Earth, so large and important to us, turns out to be but a speck in an enormous Universe. Leaving our Solar System, there are four light years to the next star, and 100,000 light years to travel across our galaxy. Beyond that there are millions of other galaxies. Everything is moving away from everything else (detected by the red shift in the light from distant stars.) The Universe is finite, but with no edge. There is no one centre; every point is disappearing from every other point, irrespective of where you are standing.

How did it all begin? The story goes something like this. The Universe started with a Big Bang, which occurred in an extremely short space of time, far too short a time for much material to coalesce, so only small atoms were made, mostly hydrogen, a little helium and a lot of separate particles. Locally these coalesced and formed stars. The Earth formed not at the start of the Universe but at a later date, from an explosion of a star, which took place more slowly than the Big Bang and so allowed time for larger atoms to form from the coalescence of smaller ones.

Matter is made of particles

The particulate world of matter is another important story. Bernoulli (1738) imagined gases to be made of swarms of particles which moved according to Newton's laws of motion, hitting the sides of a container and bouncing off. Once he had imagined this he could explain the pressure of gases and the fact that gases are compressible. As gases get hotter the particles move more rapidly, and as they get cooler the particles slow down. Eventually they slow down enough to be unable to move far from nearby particles because of the forces holding them together, and then liquids are formed. As the temperature drops further they stay in the same position relative to neighbours and solids are formed.

Of course the question was, what were these particles? The outline of that story is told in Unit 4.3. Since the discovery, however, of what looked like the three fundamental particles (protons, neutrons and electrons), many more particles were found in cosmic radiation and in collisions in particle accelerators. By the 1960s over 200 particles had been discovered, more than the types of elements which Mendeleyev had to make sense of in his periodic table. The story of sorting them out is not unlike that of Mendeleyev's – i.e. looking for patterns in behaviour and for underlying explanations for the patterns. Another imagined world – this time of the quark, a particle more fundamental than the protons and neutrons, came into being. In fact all the 200 particles of the 1960s have been reduced to various combinations of 12 particles – 6 different quarks and 6 different leptons. The account sounds like the stuff of fairy tales, especially as the six quarks have been given whimsical names, as 'up', 'down', 'charmed', 'strange', 'top' and 'bottom'. Protons are made up of two up quarks and a down quark, and neutrons are made of two downs and an up. The question now is what is underneath these particles – are they manifestations of something even more fundamental. Is there yet more imagining to do?

Today, those working in astrophysics, studying the diffuse matter which exists in the rest of the Universe, in the stars, the galaxies, the interstellar regions, the black holes, share much of the same physics as those working in the field of fundamental particles. The rest of the Universe out there is like a large soup of fundamental particles, which are exchanging energy, coalescing or breaking up. It forms an extraterrestrial laboratory. It is a laboratory which of course we cannot control, but it can be watched by detecting the energy or particles which happen to come our way, and scientists can theorise from these scraps of information.

Radioactivity

The discovery of radioactivity was a crucial step in the discovery of the constituents of the atom. Here were materials which were ejecting what seemed to be bits of themselves (alpha, beta and gamma rays) into the outside world. We are now aware that some isotopes of different elements are unstable, and they throw out bits from the nucleus until they become a stable isotope. These isotopes can be made artificially, as in the case of cobalt-60, whose radiation is used to inhibit growth of tumours. Radioactivity is a statistical process; all the atoms do not decay at the same time; they have a 50 per cent chance of decaying in the time referred to as their 'half life'. Radioactivity can therefore be used as a timing device as in carbon-14 dating.

Radio waves and light waves are different facets of the same phenomenon

Light is representative of a family of radiation. Radio waves, infrared rays, light, ultraviolet rays, X-rays and gamma rays all turn out to be similar phenomena, namely electromagnetic waves generated by the movement of electric charge. The excitation of electrons in a heated filament produces light and the oscillation of an alternating current produces radio waves. For many purposes we think of them all as rays travelling out from a source until they bump into things, when they might be reflected, transmitted or absorbed. If they are reflected or transmitted they carry on travelling as light or radio waves or whatever. If they are absorbed they transfer their energy to the object they bumped into, which may get hotter or react in some other way. Obviously what counts as an obstacle varies for each radiation; skin, which reflects light, is transparent to X-rays.

This ray model does not work completely, and a wave model is necessary to explain how all of them can bend round corners or spread out when they go through very narrow gaps.

Fields

Fields are strange things; they are really 'areas of influence'. You will be familiar with magnetic fields: the areas around a magnet where the influence can be felt by another magnet or by magnetic material. The fascination which young children have with magnets is that they act at a distance. What is particularly intriguing is that both the objects (e.g. the two magnets) are affected the same way – they both feel the same force, although in opposite directions. It is a mutual effect. The same is true of electrostatic charge, and of course gravity. Each of us pulls on the Earth with the same force which it pulls on us, but in the opposite direction. If we jump off a table, while we are in 'mid air' and not touching the Earth, there is still the mutual attraction between us and the Earth. It was, in fact, Newton, who, disliking the idea of one thing at a distance influencing another (the Moon affecting the tides in the ocean, the Sun affecting the movement of the Earth), invented the idea of a gravitational 'field' which existed in space around all masses. Newton was not comfortable with this invention but we take for granted now magnetic fields around magnets, electric fields around charges and gravitational fields around masses.

Change and energy transfer

One of the most important stories in physics is that of energy transfer. It is an example of a story which drew together lots of diverse isolated stories. Any change in the world has to have an energy source of some sort. This may be a fuel which can be burned in oxygen, water which is high up which can run down gaining speed, a source of light such as the Sun, stretched or compressed springs which can go back to their original shape, chemicals which can react as in the case of batteries, or a temperature difference. In every case the energy available from any of these can be calculated. What is most extraordinary is that when any change has occurred (building materials lifted by an electrical motor on a crane onto the top of a building) the energy is not lost, but transferred to another part of the system. Here the building materials have gained some energy by being higher (and hence capable of falling down and gaining speed), some energy is dissipated as sound, and some energy goes to heating up the electric motor which as it cools dissipates it to the atmosphere. From a 'usefulness' point of view, only some of the energy remains, but from a total energy point of view, it can all be tracked.

The made world

It is easy to give an account of physics which makes it seem that the theoretical understanding of the world came first and the practical applications came afterwards. Technological development, however, is an intrinsic part of the story of physics both in the making of equipment for experiments and in a desire to change and control the environment in which we live. There is as much science in the design of the particle accelerator at CERN as there is in the study of the particle collisions which occur within it. Development of glass in Venice allowed the possibility of making airtight containers and was crucial to the development of knowledge about the behaviour of gases. Theories of thermodynamics developed hand in hand with the development of steam engines, used to drive pumps in mines and then engines for transport. Since 1945 development in radio technology and latterly space travel, have shifted astrophysics from optical astronomy to radio, microwave, and X-ray astronomy, revealing features of the Universe not previously known. Over the last two centuries and particularly at the early part of the 1900s many physicists were engaged in the technology of attaining low temperatures, hence opening up low temperature physics and a world of strange properties like superfluidity and superconductivity.

Ask pupils what they think are the main scientific advances of the last 100 years and it is technology which will dominate their answers: space travel; computers and iPods; mobile phones; cars; aeroplanes; surveillance equipment; surgical techniques; medical imaging; refrigerators; television; CD and DVD players … In thinking about physics it is as important to think about the made world as the world of abstractions.

STRANGENESS OF THE STORIES IN PHYSICS

There is a contradiction in physics. On the one hand when we get the hang of an explanation we recognise how 'logical' it is because all the pieces fit together 'obeying the rules, to make neat stories'. When gadgets work reliably, which most of them do for long periods at a time, we are aware of our mastery over the 'laws of physics' and the world seems an ordered place. On the other hand, the rules and the stories are not 'obvious' or 'common sense' and seem far removed from the everyday word 'logical'. It is not obvious that the table at which I am typing this is really made up mostly of empty space, and that the chair on which I am sitting and which I believe I am touching is really holding me at a distance by electrostatic forces between my molecules and those of the chair.

In engaging pupils in physics we have to help them engage with this contradiction. Perhaps just by recognising that the security of much of the knowledge we have about the way the world works is dependent on taking on board some fairly strange ideas, which are far from common sense, will provide us with a greater appreciation of what it is like to learn ideas in physics for the first time.

WAYS INTO THE PLEASURE OF PHYSICS

As a teacher you need to find a way of developing an empathy for physics, if you do not already have it. It may help to acknowledge what might be behind negative attitudes to physics. My own analysis is that there are four contributing factors: the belief that you have to be good at mathematics to understand physics; physics is about things rather than people; physics is associated with warfare; physics has some bizarre ideas.

It is a mistake to pretend that mathematics is not part of physics. Much of the modelling of the natural world in physics has been done by playing and thinking with mathematics. Maxwell's equations (1860–70) predicted electromagnetic waves from mathematical models long before such waves were transmitted by Hertz in 1886. Many learners, however, get into the mathematics far too soon and lose sight of the concepts and principles.

Although physics deals with things, the contexts in which it works relate to people. Try living a day without electricity to recognise the impact of this off-shoot of physics. The stories of the development of ideas are certainly human, and many of them are well documented (see further reading). If you are of a sporting nature, this may be your route into physics. Deep sea divers, for instance, have a good understanding of relative densities and buoyancy. Sky divers understand the drag effect of wind; bungee jumpers rely on the elasticity of rubber to provide gentle deceleration at the bottom of the jump.

War, or the threat of war, has provided, and still provides, contexts in which massive technological development has taken place; it is impossible to get away from it, although most of us would wish that talents were not used to destroy fellow human beings. But the off-shoots readily become part of everyday life. The global positioning systems (GPS) which the Americans developed for intelligence are used by shipping for locating where they are, and increasingly by car drivers trying to find a route they have not used previously.

The strange stories, while disconcerting at first, engage the imagination. There have been many occasions when the unthinkable had to be thought to make progress, such as in quantum theory and relativity. They are an essential part of physics.

You may find it helpful to talk to people who enjoy physics and ask them why. The answers I have received to such questions are of course varied. Some people enjoy the mathematical modelling. One girl could remember vividly the joy at understanding how an electric motor worked. Others report specific topics which they liked – cosmology and fundamental particles are two favourites. There are others who are intrigued by the engineering side of physics – the electrical and electronics topics, or making mechanical devices. Others have come to it through a study of sports science and begin to recognise how important physics is to our understanding of the human body. Some enjoy the absurdity of the stories within physics 'that object is not intrinsically green, it is only that it reflects the green light'. Some enjoy the general elegance of the arguments – that the parts seem to fit together well. Each comes with their own personal story about what drew them to physics.

SUMMARY

Any science teacher must find a way of appreciating physics and astronomy and finding intrigue at some level both for themselves and for the students they are teaching. There is no simple recipe. The Further reading and the tasks offer some possible starting points. Hunt always for the 'cause and effect', but be prepared, in some cases, to have to imagine some surprising entities to get at a 'cause'. Be prepared also for the fact that the 'cause and effect' chain, cannot go on for ever – you just have to say, at some point, 'that is the way of the world'.

I will end by returning to the bag of crisps. The air in the factory is denser than up the mountain (factories are not usually located high up). Air is left in the bag at packing to prevent crushing of crisps. The bag is made of material which will not allow air in or out (important, as the crisps can easily absorb moisture from the air and go soggy). Up the mountain the surrounding air is less dense so there are fewer air particles hitting the outside than the inside of the bag; hence the bag gets pushed out. Why the lower density of air up a mountain? The air particles are continuously pulled back down to Earth (gravitational pull) even though they keep bouncing back up.

**Task 4.4.1
Starting points –
in the home**

- Find all the mechanical 'machines' which you have at home, which enable you to do tasks you could not otherwise do (scissors; pliers; spanners; screw drivers; door handles; corkscrews …) and explain how they work.
- Have a look at a human skeleton and find all the levers in it.
- Extend your curiosity to other devices and use the website of 'how stuff works' for answers.

**Task 4.4.2
Starting points –
visits**

- Visit an iMac Cinema and watch *Space Station 3D*, which shows the space shuttle going to and from the Mir Space Station and the experiments on the space station.
- Visit Alton Towers (or the equivalent) and experience turning upside down without falling out – or stand and watch it and ponder how it works.
- Consider the imaging devices in your local hospital.

**Task 4.4.3
Starting points –
thinking and listening
tasks**

1 Listen to scientific programmes on radio about current developments. They are made for the 'general public', so provide a model of how to talk about new ideas, without losing the audience in detail.
2 Think up puzzling questions, they are the start of good physics

- Why does the Moon not fall down onto the Earth?
- Why can I beat eggs faster with a mechanical egg whisk than without?
- Where do the stars go during the day?
- Why is it difficult to turn corners on ice?
- Why do sprinters start their races from starting blocks?

FURTHER READING

Books concerned with learning and teaching physics and astronomy

Driver, R., Squires, A., Rushworth, P. and Wood-Robinson, V. (1994) *Making Sense of Secondary Science: Research into Children's Ideas*, London: Routledge. This provides an insight into learners' particular difficulties in thinking through the ideas in science. Select the physics and astronomy topics.

Sang, D. (ed.) (2000) *Teaching Secondary Physics*, London: John Murray for ASE. This book gives useful explanations of the physics of KS3 and KS4 as well as providing teaching strategies.

Science of Everyday Life, Everyday Phenomena and Technology

Brain, M. (2001) *How Stuff Works*, New York: Hungry Minds.

Brain, M. (2003) *More How Stuff Works*, New York: Hungry Minds. Easy to read collection of answers to a host of questions about technological inventions. See also his website: http://www.howstuffworks.com. Of the same genre.

Bloomfield, L.A. (1992) *How Things Work: The Physics of Everyday Life*, New York, Brisbane: Wiley and Son.

Fisher, L. (2003) *How to Dunk a Doughnut: The Science of Everyday Life*, London: Phoenix. (Try the chapter on levers – 'The Tao of Tools'.)

Morrison, P., Morrison, P. and the Office of Charles and Ray Eames (1982) *Powers of Ten*, New York: Freeman for the Scientific American Library. Accompanying video: Office of Charles and Ray Eames, 1977 *Powers of Ten*, IBM; available from Pyramid Films, PO Box 1048, Santa Monica, California. These are useful for understanding the scale of physics (see Task 4.4.3 above).

Naylor, J. (2002) *Out of the Blue. A 24-hour Skywatcher's Guide*, Cambridge: Cambridge University Press. A book which can be dipped into at any time you see something interesting in the sky – halos round the Sun and Moon; double rainbows … Explanations are given for them all.

Biographical texts

Daintith, J. and Gjertsen, D. (eds) (1999) *Oxford Dictionary of Scientists*, Oxford: Oxford University Press (1999).

Linenger, J.M. (2000) *Off the Planet: Surviving Five Perilous Months aboard the Space Station Mir*, New York: McGraw Hill. A contrasting account to that given by NASA in the film 'Space Station 3D'.

Macdonald, A. (2003) *Reading into Science: Physics*, Cheltenham: Nelson Thornes. This book, along with similar ones for biology and chemistry, was produced to support the Ideas and Evidence part of the National Curriculum. It contains short articles about development of science through both contemporary and historical case studies.

Porter, R. and Ogilvie, M. (2000) *The Hutchinson Dictionary of Scientific Biography*, Volumes I and II, Oxford: Helicon.

Sobel, D. (1996) *Longitude: The True Story of a Lone Genius who Solved the Greatest Scientific Problem of his Time*, London: Fourth Estate.

Books about physics written for a lay audience

Greene, B. (1999, re-issued 2003) *The Elegant Universe*, New York: Norton and Co.

Gribbon, J. (1992) *Q is for Quantum: An Encyclopeadia of Particle Physics*, New York: Simon & Schuster/Touchstone.

Narlikar, J.K. (1996) *The Lighter Side of Gravity*, Cambridge: Cambridge University Press.

WEBSITES TO EXPLORE

Brain, M. (2004) http://www.howstuffworks.com.

New Scientist, http://www.newscientist.com/lastword.

North American Space Agency, http://www.nasa.gov.

Google search engine www.google.com – this will provide you with a lot of information about almost any topic you wish to type in.

Unit 4.5

Earth Science

Tony Turner

INTRODUCTION

The Galapagos archipelago consists of volcanic islands moving slowly eastwards towards the western South American coast. The youngest islands to the west are about 700,000 years old and those towards the east over 3.5 million years old. These islands are the peaks of under sea volcanoes, over 7,000 m above the deepest part of the Pacific Ocean floor. Volcanic activity is associated with molten rock – magma – rising to the Earth's surface. Thus solid rock not only melts under appropriate conditions but also moves. Even stranger is the fact that rock below the surface is plastic, bending and folding under pressure. The appearance of volcanic activity on the Earth's surface has been well documented as have sites of earthquake activity (Earthquake Activity 2003). Until comparatively recently, however, understanding why some regions were active in these ways and others not was a puzzle.

Landscapes which characterise our localities reflect the properties of underlying rocks. South-eastern England is characterised by the presence of soft chalk hills (the Downs!) running westwards from Dover to Guildford before turning back eastwards to Eastbourne. Within this curve of chalk lie much older rocks such as the sandstone at Tunbridge Wells, beloved of rock climbers, as well as some heavy clay. Many questions arise: why is the older sandstone uncovered but elsewhere the younger chalk remains in place? Is this chalk connected to the chalk of Salisbury Plain or that comprising parts of the northern French coast? How did the remains of long-dead sea animals get into the chalk, well above sea level? Dinosaur footprints and their fossil eggs have been found in the chalk and in many other parts of world (Dinosaur Footprints and Eggs 2003). How could such events occur?

The development of Tectonic Plate Theory as recently as the 1960s (Wilson, J.T.) was the key to providing an explanation for the distribution, movement and relationships of land masses on the Earth's surface, the activity of volcanoes and earthquakes and the process of mountain building. This theory revived the 'continental drift' theory proposed by Wegener in the nineteenth century. Embedded in this theory is the story known as the 'rock cycle',

OBJECTIVES

By end of this unit you should:

- understand how the materials of the Earth undergo continuous change;
- be aware of the nature of the different layers of the Earth from the crust to the core;
- understand aspects of the Tectonic Plate theory and how it explains features of the Earth's crust.

THE ROCK CYCLE

Rocks on the surface and inside the Earth undergo continuous change (the phrase 'solid as a rock' needs qualification). As you go deeper into the Earth the temperature increases, largely due to radioactivity. Inside the Earth rocks melt, move and solidify; many come to the surface as magma or new rock. Over long periods of time surface rocks are eroded by the action of water, temperature changes and wind. The wind carries water and rock particles which erode other rocks. Eroded rocks are moved around by water and deposited elsewhere on the Earth's surface. Rock is recycled in these several ways on a massive scale now and in the past, see Figure 4.5.1.

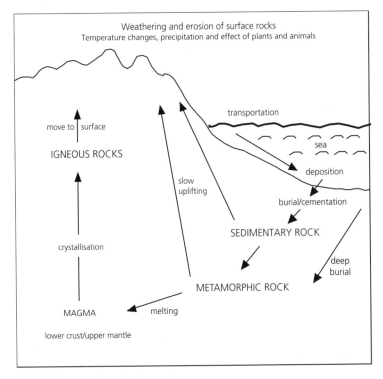

Figure 4.5.1 Some features of the rock cycle

Source: Adapted from McDuell 2000: 200.

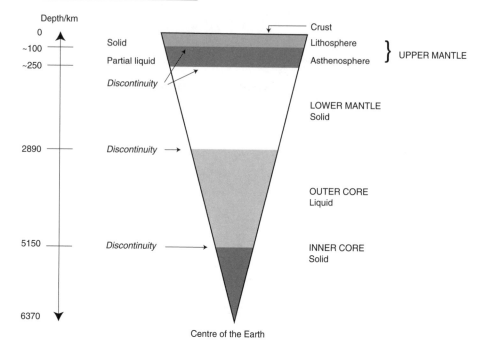

Figure 4.5.2 Segment cross-section of the Earth (adapted from King 2000: 60)

Evidence for the rock cycle comes from careful observation of the surface of the Earth, the analysis of rocks and minerals for chemical composition, physical appearance and fossil remains, from the study of the patterns of rock distribution across the surface, including the sea bed, and of the molten rock thrown up in volcanoes. The rock cycle is the story which makes sense of it all.

STRUCTURE OF THE EARTH

A large task facing geologists is to understand the state and composition of the Earth's interior without being able to go there. The deepest mine is 3.5 km deep while the radius of the Earth is approximately 6,000 km, so first-hand evidence is not available. Evidence about the interior of the Earth comes from seismic studies, the study of waves passing through the Earth, usually generated by earthquake activity. The different ways in which these waves pass through the Earth show evidence of solid or liquid phases and the boundaries between them. The picture of the Earth's interior that emerges is shown in Figure 4.5.2.

The Earth's crust and the lithosphere below are solid rock about 100 km thick, although the lithosphere (Greek *lithos* – rock) is largely igneous rock (see 'surface rocks', below). Beneath the crust is another layer, the asthenosphere (Greek *asthenes* – lack of strength) which is largely solid rock with some liquid (up to 10 per cent). The lithosphere and asthenosphere form the upper mantle. The solid lower mantle is about 2,500 km thick and sits above the liquid outer core. At the centre is the solid inner core.

How are earthquakes or controlled explosions used to give the picture in Figure 4.5.2?

Earthquakes release enormous amounts of energy, transmitted by waves. Waves can travel on the surface, which do a lot of damage, or pass through the body of the Earth. Body waves are transmitted through the Earth in two ways, either as primary waves (P) (longitudinal waves or 'push' waves) or secondary waves (S) (transverse or 'shake' waves). Using seismometers located around the Earth, the position, strength and time of arrival of the different body waves are recorded from which information about the Earth's interior is inferred.

P waves are transmitted by alternate compression and rarefaction of the material, just as sound is transmitted by compression and rarefaction, and can travel through solids, liquids and gases. The material, e.g. the rock, oscillates in the same direction as the wave travels. By contrast transverse (S) waves occur when the rock moves from side-to-side, i.e. at right angles to the direction of travel of the wave and are transmitted only through solids. The P waves travel faster (~5 km/sec) than S waves (~3 km/sec). Both S and P waves undergo reflection and refraction, like light waves.

Both P and S waves travel through the lithosphere indicating that it is solid; they pass more slowly through the athenosphere, indicating that there is some liquid present (one to ten per cent). Both P and S waves pass through the lower mantle, changing velocity at its boundary with the athenosphere indicating that the lower mantle is solid. S waves cannot, however, travel through liquids and this, coupled with other arguments, has been used to establish that the Earth's outer core is liquid and the inner core solid; see Figure 4.5.2. The motion of matter in the liquid outer core is believed to be the source of the Earth's magnetism.

Surface rocks

The Earth's crust contains thousands of different sorts of rocks. However, the oceanic crust is much thinner but more dense (~3.2 g/cm^3) than the continental crust (~2.7 g/cm^3) which is an important factor in discussing plate movement (see below).

Rocks are made up of minerals. Some rocks contain just one mineral, such as marble (calcite) or diamond (crystalline form of carbon); small amounts of impurities may change the appearance of the rock giving, for example, the decorative coloured marbles. Minerals often have characteristic features, such as a colour and regular crystal shape, for example quartz, diamond and many precious stones. Other minerals appear amorphous, such as opal and graphite. Many rocks are mixtures of minerals, such as granite, the constituents of which were formed by crystallisation from a liquid. Other mixed rocks arise from the way they were deposited, e.g. as sediments in rivers such as sandstone, mudstone and conglomerates.

In order to make some sense of the bewildering number of rocks they can be classified by origin. Igneous rocks are formed by molten rock, magma, cooling. If the magma cools slowly underground before being raised to the surface it contains larger crystals, e.g. granite, than if it cools quickly on the surface, as does basalt. Both rocks are made of interlocking crystals.

Most of Earth's rocks are sedimentary, formed by the erosion of other rocks and subsequent deposition. The eroded particles are carried by water and deposited on a river or sea bed (see the rock cycle, Figure 4.5.1). Characteristics of sedimentary rock include strata (the layering of successive types of sediment), often a cement holding together the particles, e.g. quartz bonded by calcite in some sandstone and sometimes, the presence of fossils, e.g. in limestone. Some sedimentary rocks are biological in origin, the product of deposition of dead animals, e.g. chalk.

A third type of rock is changed or metamorphic rock. Both igneous and sedimentary rocks change as conditions of temperature, pressure or chemical environment alter. Marble was once limestone, slate is altered mudstone and diamond metamorphosed graphite.

To identify a rock you need to know its location and the environment in which it was found, e.g. strata or the presence of fossils and, in addition, to examine its structure, type of crystals, size, etc. and to know its chemical composition and the constituent minerals. Other helpful factors include physical characteristics such as colour, density and hardness. Keys for identifying some common rocks are useful (McDuell 2000: 203) but have a limited application.

TECTONIC PLATE THEORY

The Tectonic Plate theory provides the basis for understanding how the Earth's features have come to be as they are, the mountains and trenches, volcanoes and earthquakes, continents and islands, faults and folds. The word 'tectonic' refers to the processes of building. The Earth's crust sits on the lithosphere; the crust and lithosphere are both solid and subject to forces from below. The lithosphere is a rigid layer divided into six major plates and a number of minor plates all of which diverge, converge or slide past each other. Figure 4.5.3 shows the large plates and many of the smaller plates and their boundaries. (Maps such as these may be found on the Internet; search using Google under plate tectonics, selecting the Google 'image' option.) Most plates move at about the same rate, about 2–3 cm per year, the rate at which your fingernails grow. Plate movements have given rise to the features of the Earth mentioned above and explain how continents move. At the plate boundaries earthquakes, volcanoes and mountains are formed and the mapping of sites of earthquakes and volcanic activity across the globe and the resulting patterns have contributed to the development of the Tectonic Plate Theory. Maps of earthquake and volcanic activity can be found on the Internet; see the advice above for Internet search. The plates move because the lithosphere sits on the asthenosphere, where the mantle is hotter and less rigid and the convection currents in this region 'carry the plates'.

The evidence for the Tectonic Plate theory comes from many sources including:

- the continents fitting together in a similar way to a jigsaw puzzle;
- the same rock sequences appearing in continents now separated by oceans;
- similar distribution of fossils appearing in continents now separated by oceans;
- alignment of magnetic particles in the ocean crust on either side of the mid-ocean ridges;
- pattern of distribution of volcanoes and earthquake zones on the Earth's surface.

Tectonic plates interact in different ways, including:

- at the mid-ocean ridges magma rises and solidifies and becomes part of the existing plates, a constructive plate boundary. The new material moves away from the ridge at equal rates on each side causing sea floor spreading. The mid-Atlantic ridge separates the Eurasian plate from the North American plate in the northern hemisphere. Iceland straddles that plate boundary and is one of the few places where you can see an active spreading ridge above sea level, such as at a place called Thingvellir, see Figure 4.5.3.
- When an oceanic plate meets a continental plate, the oceanic plate moves beneath the less dense continental plate, melts and becomes part of the mantle; this is a

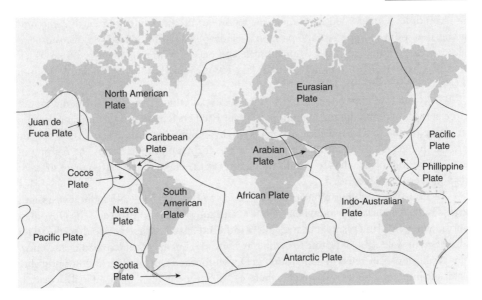

Figure 4.5.3 Map of the Earth showing plate boundaries

destructive boundary. Such regions have earthquakes and volcanoes; mountain ranges form, e.g. the Andes. In this case the Nazca plate is moving beneath the South American plate.

- When two continental plates collide, neither plate slides beneath the other but upheaval of the crust occurs to produce earthquakes and fold mountains, e.g. the Himalayas. This feature occurs on the boundary between the Eurasian plate and the Indo–Australia plate.

- If two plates try to slide past each other, the movement is restricted until the pressure overcomes the frictional forces. This situation produces sudden damaging earthquakes, e.g. along the San Andreas fault in California. Fault lines in rocks on the Earth's surface show evidence of past events.

- Sometimes the hot asthenosphere (Figure 4.5.2) finds a weak place in the lithosphere to allow magma to rise from beneath the ocean floor, sometimes forming an island in the sea, such as Surtsey, a volcanic island off Iceland which appeared in November 1963 (Iceland's Island of Fire, 2003). These events occur when an oceanic plate dips below another plate, producing a 'hot spot'. The Galapagos Islands were also formed in this way. As the plate on which they rest moves so one island moves away from the hotspot; later another island is formed above the hotspot and so a chain of volcanic islands is formed (for further information see Louie 2001). Other features of hotspots are the appearance of hot springs such as those found in Hot Springs National Park USA, Iceland and New Zealand.

TIME

The Earth is believed to be 4,600 million years old; mammals appeared about 65 million years ago and humans much later. Analogies help pupils understand this immensity of time, or 'deep time' (Gould 1988: 2). If one year represents the time since the Earth came into being, then humans appeared at 6 p.m. on 31 December (Webster 1987: 88). Erosion and sedimentation times are slow by human scale and need care in teaching, e.g. a 5 km thick rock may have taken ten million years to be laid down, a mean sedimentation rate of 0.5 mm a year (Webster 1987: 91).

Rocks and fossils are often referred to by the era in which they were formed. Eras are large periods of time, counted in millions of years. Each era is marked by significant changes in rock type and fossil population. An era is subdivided into periods characterised, too, by similar changes. The Precambrian era goes back to formation of the Earth. The naming of eras and periods often refers to significant features of the era or to the place where strata of that era were first recognised.

The Palaeozoic era (meaning *ancient life*) covers a time span 540–245 million years ago; includes the Cambrian period when there was an explosion of life forms and the Devonian period when first land plants appeared. The word Cambrian was first used to describe strata identified in Wales (the old name for which is Cambria) but are of widespread occurrence. The term 'Devonian' refers to rocks found in Devonshire and Cornwall including sandstone, slates and limestone, but they occur elsewhere, e.g. in Europe and N. America. Coal formation occurred in the late Palaeozoic era (360–286 million years ago), sometimes called the Carboniferous period.

Other eras include the Mesozoic (*middle life*) and Cenozoic (*recent life*). The Jurassic period (named after strata first described and dated in the Jura mountains in Germany) of the Mesozoic era was characterised by the evolution of large dinosaurs, followed by their extinction in the Cretaceous period (Latin *creta* for chalk) so called after chalk strata laid down at that time in southern England and north-west France.

DATING ROCKS AND FOSSILS

Two methods are used for dating materials, relative dating and radiometric dating both of which may be supported by fossil evidence. Relative dating identifies the order of geological events without assigning a date. Sedimentation studies predict that younger rocks lie above older rocks, the law of superposition. Faults and intrusions, lifting and folding complicate interpretations. Experience has given further guidance to sequencing rocks; for example, if a rock stratum has another material introduced into it, e.g. an intrusion of quartz, then the intrusion must be younger than the rocks of the main stratum.

Fossils are found in sedimentary rocks and are often unique to particular eras or periods of the Earth's history. They help to correlate rock sequences and interpret past environments. Some fossils are comparatively rare, e.g. of soft-bodied organisms and a record often incomplete. Shell invertebrate fossils from aquatic environments are most common.

Radiometric dating gives the age of a material by measuring the activity of the small amounts of a radioactive element in it. Radioactive decay occurs when an atom changes spontaneously into a different atom by giving off one or more particles from the nucleus. It is a random process; but since even a small mass of material contains millions of atoms you can calculate an average time for matter to decay. Half-life is one such average, the time taken for half the atoms to decay. The half-life of radioactive elements is known accurately.

Radiocarbon dating is used for materials up to 50,000 years old. Carbon exists naturally as two isotopes, carbon-12 (C^{12}) and carbon-14 (C^{14}) and the normal ratio of the two isotopes in atmospheric carbon dioxide is known. Only C^{14} is radioactive with a half-life of 5,730 years, decaying into nitrogen and releasing electrons (beta particles). When a plant makes food by photosynthesis it uses carbon dioxide containing both carbon isotopes. When the organism dies no further carbon is incorporated into the material. After many years the ratio of the two isotopes changes as C^{14} decays and the radioactivity of the material changes. The remains of plant, animal and products made from them can be dated by this method, e.g. pollen, bones, Turin Shroud.

Other radioactive systems can be used to date older materials. Some rocks, e.g. granite can be dated from their uranium content. Natural uranium contains uranium-238 which has a half life of 4.47 billion years and decays into a lead isotope (Wright and Patel 2000: 216–17).

SUMMARY

Earth science incorporates elements of the three major sciences and the relevant background may need to be taught before introducing some topics, e.g. evidence for the Plate Tectonic Theory or carbon dating methods. In this brief review a number of topics have been addressed but further elaboration will be necessary before teaching your pupils. Many texts carry this sort of information, e.g. Webster (1987) as does the Internet (Nevada Seismic Laboratory 2003); a useful Internet search tool is Google, as described above in the section Plate Tectonics. Experimental work to support Earth science teaching may be found in McDuell (2000) and Tuke (1991). The Earth Science Teachers Association (ESTA) provides resources, available from both ASE book sales and the Internet, as well as in-service training programmes.

FURTHER READING

Joint Earth Science Education Initiative. The first material produced by this group (a collaboration between IoP, IoB, RSC and ESTA) is an extensive and excellent set of resources for teaching the Earth sciences section of the National Curriculum in science. The package includes ideas for practical work, teacher demonstrations, worksheets and diagrams and a useful glossary of terms. It is available online and can be downloaded from http://www.jesei.org.

Jones, M., Jones, G. and Acaster, D. (1997) *Coordinated Science: Chemistry*, 2nd edn, Cambridge: Cambridge University Press. This book contains a useful section on the Earth and addresses several important geological principles, such as continental drift, plate tectonic theory and the structure of the Earth. There are sections on the three principal rock types and an illustrated section on geological time which may be especially helpful in teaching this idea. Although there are few pupil activities this text could be used by teachers seeking to consolidate their background knowledge.

McDuell, B. (ed.) (2000) *Teaching Secondary Chemistry*, London: John Murray for the Association for Science Education. There is a small section on Earth science which includes some useful suggestions for practical activities, for pupils as well as teacher demonstration, to illustrate the material of the National Curriculum in science.

WEBSITES TO EXPLORE

Association for Science Education, website http://www.ase.org/.

Earth Science Teachers Association (ESTA), Burlington House, Piccadilly, London WIV 0BN. Website http://www.esta-uk.org/.

ESTA Promotions, 4 Wyvern Gardens, Dore, Sheffield S17 3PR.

Louie, J. (2001) Plate tectonics: the cause of earthquakes; website http://www.seismo.unr.edu/ftp/pub/louie/class/100/plate-tectonics.html.

Nevada Seismic Laboratory (2003): About Earthquakes, website http://www.seismo.unr.edu/htdocs/abouteq.html.

5 Planning for Learning and Teaching Science

Being able to plan a lesson, a sequence of lessons or a whole course involves being able to construct, ahead of time, a set of events for yourself and 25 to 35 pupils. Learning to plan is an iterative process, where problems which arise as plans are put into action in the classroom, inform the planning process. There are guidelines which can be followed which help to minimise these problems. Nevertheless, you will find planning to be a time-consuming part of your work, and may not feel that you are planning with any degree of confidence until well into your course.

We have started with pupils' learning. Lessons may be entertaining, properly organised, with the pupils well disciplined, but if the pupils are not learning science then the lessons are not effective. An introduction to cognitive development in science provides guidelines on pupil progression in science as a basis for planning for individuals within a group and for assessing learning.

Your first lesson will seem 'a big event', such that it is easy to lose sight of the fact that individual lessons are only one tiny step in a long learning process. You must engage early on, therefore, with at least medium-term planning of whole topics so that you can recognise how ideas are built up step by step. The need to understand even longer-term plans quickly impinges on your work, because of the need to know what pupils have learned previously and what they will learn in later years. Good schemes of work in schools, and the National Curriculum in science, help you gain a long-term perspective and identify aims, objectives, learning outcomes, resources, learning activities, assessment opportunities and time allocations. There is a strong warning, however, of the dangers of imagining that well-developed schemes of work remove the need to plan. Unit 5.2 addresses principles of planning which apply across short-, medium- and long-term plans, while Unit 5.3 focuses on the detailed planning and evaluation of individual lessons.

Planning lessons involves ways of motivating pupils. Science may be interesting to you but not all adolescents are similarly enthused. An important phase of your development is identifying the ways in which effective teachers motivate, encourage and maintain the interest of a group of young people. At the centre of effective teaching is the willingness to listen to your pupils and to act on what you hear. Often a change of strategy is effective, not a change in learning outcome, because it allows different ways of engaging the interest of your pupils. Unit 5.3 explores a range of teaching strategies and the rationale for them.

The chapter ends with a unit on practical work. Practical work can be motivating for many pupils, and is an intrinsic part of school science, but it is time consuming, needs organisation and requires particular attention to safety. The planning of practical work involves an analysis of the purposes which it can serve in pupils' learning and an awareness of the teacher's role. Teachers need to plan the dialogue which will accompany practical work in as much detail as they plan for the distribution and collection of equipment.

While you need to plan lessons which respond to the curriculum in force and the examinations for which pupils are being prepared it is a process which draws on your *creativity* and *imagination*. Guidelines can be given but not recipes.

Unit 5.1

Planning for Progression in Science

Ralph Levinson

INTRODUCTION

What is unique to learning science is that the learner comes across strange ideas that defy experiences of everyday life and common sense. Invisible charges drift through wires, invisible forces hold matter together, the massive trunks of oak trees are made up of building blocks that come predominantly from the apparently immaterial air, balls moving upwards have only a downward force acting on them, the invisible products of a combustion engine have a greater mass than the petrol that is burned, electrical impulses constantly surge through our body. Electrons, atoms, cells, fields, neurones are the invisible or microscopic stuff of nature. Osmosis, entropy change, radiation are some of the processes that have to become real so that they have an explanatory power. Pupils can only start to understand these things if they are constructed on the back of experience and knowledge they already have.

Progression 'describes the personal journey an individual pupil makes in moving through the educational system' (Asoko and Squires 1998: 175). To understand how pupils' learning of science is structured you need to understand progression. But what is involved in this personal journey? Do pupils move from simple to more complex ideas? Is there a pattern in the way all pupils progress which might help us organise their learning more systematically? How personal is the journey – what is the role of teachers? This unit attempts to address these questions and to identify ways in which you can help pupils progress in their understanding of science.

OBJECTIVES

By end of this unit you should be:

- able to describe examples of progression;
- aware of the complexity of progression;
- able to start planning for progression;
- able to identify the kinds of activities that enable progression;
- able to differentiate between learning objectives and learning outcomes.

DESCRIBING PROGRESSION

Imagine a two-year-old at bath time playing with bath toys. Playing is hopefully a pleasurable experience for this infant although she is unlikely to make any distinction between toys which float and those which sink. Even if an adult intervenes and tries to draw the child's attention to these distinctions they are likely to go unremarked. When the child is a little older, say four or five, she starts to categorise objects by certain properties, such as shape, size, colour, soft and hard. She begins to notice that shells, coins and pebbles sink to the bottom of the bath but other objects like polystyrene toys don't, even if they are pushed down – they bob back up to the surface. This might prompt the child, possibly with the support of a helpful older person, to see what happens when a further range of objects are dropped into the water, all of which might be characterised as 'floaters' or 'sinkers'. Once the child has had a range of experiences and has been able to talk about them, she might be able to generalise that 'sinkers' have attributes different from those of 'floaters' and to predict what happens when an object is dropped in water. According to the experiences from which the child generalises, 'sinkers' might be heavy, hard, compact, lacking air. It does not matter at this stage whether these generalisations are correct or not, the point about generalisations is that there are exceptions which might prompt the child to re-think the basis of her reasoning. Contradictions, for example a hard heavy object like a boat that floats, might generate further trials either in the bathtub or, by this time, at primary school. The child might see what happens when she tries to submerge in water a bottle filled with air and then filled with water.

By this time the child's earlier generalisations are becoming refined, and through guided observations, the data collected is more directed. She begins to test certain things out, for example, to find out what happens when the bottle is half-filled with water. As well as being able to predict with some accuracy whether objects float or sink she might notice now that water seems able to 'push up' on an object. She develops a language, with support, where the scientific meanings are very specific, that an object *weighs* less in water than it does in air, that there are *forces* acting on the object, that the upward force acting on the object is called *upthrust*. She begins to test whether the same objects float or sink when placed in different liquids and ask why some objects which sink in fresh water float in salty water. To test her ideas she begins to make measurements, to use equipment to make the measurements (for example a measuring cylinder to find out the volume occupied by the object in water), to record her data, make inferences and test these inferences further.

Of course, we have looked at an idealised case. We have assumed that all the ideas follow on one from another, that the child does have baths in her early years! – and has bath toys (some only have showers or don't always have the time to play), and that there's a helpful older other person who intervenes appropriately and knows the right kinds of questions to ask. Some children may have very particular experiences, interest in boats for example from an early age, while others might not have seen natural watercourses. Whatever the circumstance of the child, the elaboration of one idea depends on an earlier idea. For example, a child cannot generalise about floating and sinking until she can recognise the difference and has thought about explanations for the differences. Children may go through these stages at different times and at different rates but the point is that all children go through the earlier stages. What we have described is progression, the child's developing ability to make increasing sense of the world, in this case floating and sinking. This developing ability can be mapped through a number of different routes:

- an increasing sophistication of explanations, from the everyday to using scientific explanations (these objects float while these sink to how ships float when they weigh thousands of tonnes);
- through moving from hands-on activities in familiar situations to applying ideas in less familiar contexts (observing things floating and sinking in a bath to testing ideas using laboratory equipment such as a measuring cylinder or 'Eureka' can);
- terminology becomes more precise and scientific ('water seems to be pushing on my hand' to 'water is exerting a force on my hand and my hand is exerting a force on the water');
- explanations move from qualitative to quantitative (these objects float, these objects float in liquids above a certain density);
- developing practical and mathematical skills to underpin understanding;
- development of procedural skills (making simple observations, planning experiments to test hypotheses, using models as ideas).

Further examples of progression are discussed in Unit 5.2: *Planning for Teaching and Learning* under 'Levels of Explanation'. Task 5.1.1 is an opportunity to map progression for another topic.

THEORISING PROGRESSION

From the previous section you would have a sense of progression of a moving forward from simple everyday ideas to more complex situations or to contexts requiring abstract concepts to explain them. Progression in all these situations may require the use of new scientific terminology and procedural concepts. But as a teacher you need to know how to enable and recognise this progression. Progression presupposes development, i.e. that, with maturity, the child can assimilate more experiences. Piaget produced the most widely-recognised explanation of cognitive development as development through a number of age-related stages. In these stages knowledge is actively generated as the learner explores her world. In the first years of life the child understands the world through her senses and moves on to begin to categorise and describe objects through their characteristics. These first stages are known as the sensory-motor and pre-operational stages respectively (see Burton 2001) and correspond to the child's playing followed by categorising and classifying as described for floating and sinking in the previous section.

**Task 5.1.1
Describing progression in
different topics**

Find another context or topic, for example photosynthesis, chemical reactions or light. Map the main stages in progression from Key Stage 1 to Key Stage 5, using about four main stages. For example, the more detailed account about floating and sinking above can be mapped:

Some objects float, others sink

↓

Light objects seem to float while heavy objects sink

↓

Objects denser than water sink, objects which are less dense float

↓

Whether objects float or sink depend on whether the force acting downwards is greater than the force acting upwards.

Two further stages were recognised by Piaget, the concrete operational and the formal operational. As the child moves from the stage of concrete operations to formal operations she moves from a manipulation (both mental and physical) of specific experience to generalising and to logical, mathematical reasoning about events not seen. For example, pupils working at the concrete operational stage may be able to measure the time period of a pendulum and show that it is dependent on the length of the pendulum, the longer the pendulum the slower the time period. If presented with the challenge of finding the effect of length and mass of the bob of a pendulum have on the time period, pupils unaided may not be able to separate and control the two variables until they are working at the stage of formal operations. Furthermore, until they have progressed to this higher stage they may not recognise the shortcomings of their approach and the validity, or otherwise, of their conclusions.

Piaget argued that children progress from one stage to the next as they encounter cognitive conflict and have to assimilate new explanatory models and more complex thinking. Although Donaldson has pointed to problems in Piaget's theory because research shows that children can manipulate more complex variables than Piaget originally supposed, the general point of sequential stages still holds (Donaldson 1978). Intelligible and fruitful learning experiences assist this progression (Posner *et al.* 1982), hence the teacher has to be aware of the appropriate point to present material and explanations which will advance understanding.

The picture so far is one of the child constructing knowledge of the world about her with occasional facilitation by the teacher. However, the child lives in, and partakes of, a social world in which she is interpreting diverse forms of communication, mainly through talk (Vygotsky 1978). The child, her peers and teachers generate meanings by interpreting what is said and co-construct new meanings together. The teacher, responding to detailed knowledge of the child's cognitive and social development, presents learning experiences which are beyond what the child already understands but gives enough support to move on to a 'higher rung of the ladder', a process teachers call 'scaffolding'; for further discussion of scaffolding see Burton 2001.

A third explanatory model is that of the child as information processor. The mind acts to transform the information it receives but care needs to be paid to the capacity of the processor at any one time. Information overload inhibits learning and too little information results in lack of stimulation. Knowledge of how much information the child can process is crucial to effective teaching and learning (Kempa 1992; Burton 2001).

All three models of learning come under what is broadly termed 'constructivist' theory, because the learners are seen as actively constructing their knowledge. In the UK there have been two particular developments in teaching related to progression in science based on constructivist theory, one is the Children's Learning in Science Project (CLISP) and the other is the Cognitive Acceleration in Science Project (CASE).

The Children's Learning in Science Project (CLISP) takes as its basic assumption that many children have conceptions about scientific phenomena that are different from the scientifically accepted explanations (Driver *et al.* 1994). Thus, for example, younger children and some older children think that when you add a substance to a beaker of water and the substance dissolves, the mass of the beaker and water stays the same, clearly contravening the principle of the conservation of mass. You can't see it so it's not there. Many examples of children's everyday thinking have been identified, and a few are given below:

- heavier objects fall faster than light ones;
- electric current is used up as it passes through a circuit;
- whales are fish;
- plants get all their food from the soil;
- when fossil fuels burn there is no product.

Research into children's conceptions about scientific phenomena began in the 1980s, largely influenced by research work in New Zealand (Osborne and Freyberg 1985). Since then, many articles have been written about children's explanations of events across the science curriculum. These explanations have been termed 'prior conceptions', 'misconceptions' or 'alternative frameworks' according to the disposition of the author. 'Prior conceptions' suggest that children have conceptions about nature before they are inducted into the accepted framework of science. 'Misconceptions' implies that children's ideas are often mistaken and need challenging and changing as they begin to understand correct scientific explanations. When children have 'alternative frameworks' the emphasis is that children have another way of explaining the world which is coherent to them and that science is another explanatory framework but there is no indication on their part that science is necessarily superior in its account of the world.

If children do have conceptions which do not accord with the accepted scientific explanation how can we help them to understand something that challenges their way of thinking, particularly when many scientific explanations are counter-intuitive? Under normal circumstances we don't see the gases produced when fuels burn so how can they be recognised as products? When an object rests on a table how can the table be pushing up with an equal and opposite force? A table is a static object which doesn't appear to be doing anything let alone exerting a force when an object is put on it. A whale lives in the sea and looks like a fish so it is a fish. Mammals are hairy and live on land. It just doesn't make sense to say a whale is a mammal.

The challenge for CLISP was to provide a strategy, based on constructivist principles, which allows teachers to support pupils through these transitions in their thinking. To plan the learning tasks it is important to know what ideas pupils do have and how dissimilar they are to the accepted scientific ideas. Much of this information can now be accessed from the literature but the starting point is to provide opportunities for pupils to make their own ideas explicit (Driver *et al*. 1985). Two stages are involved when children make their ideas explicit. The first is 'orientation' – setting the scene – where pupils are given stimulus material relating to the topic, recording what they already know. The next stage is to induce cognitive conflict by introducing students to discrepant events which may promote 'restructuring' of ideas. In doing so the teacher is promoting in the learner an awareness that there is a difference between their ideas and scientific ideas and that there is a strategy for bridging the difference. Socratic questioning can be used where the teacher helps pupils to identify inconsistencies in their thinking. The last stage is that pupils try out these new ideas in a variety of contexts involving 'application' of ideas and they finally 'review' what they have learned. This strategy is by no means watertight and teachers are often exasperated to learn that pupils repeat their original conceptions when there was every reason to suppose they had assimilated the new, scientific ideas. That is why these ideas are periodically revisited in different contexts. An example of this type of strategy is discussed in Task 5.1.2.

Task 5.1.2
Understanding conservation of matter

Context
Pupils are given a situation in which they are asked to choose between two possible explanations of an event; see Figure 5.1.1. In Figure 5.1.1 pupils have to decide whether the mass of the system changes or remains the same. This situation provides orientation by introducing a context and provides the second stage, elicitation, by asking questions. The third stage provides a situation where pupils are asked to carry out an activity which may challenge their preconceptions.

Your task
Go through this problem yourself identifying:

- concepts pupils might already hold (Driver *et al*. 1994; Driver *et al*. 1985);
- the scientifically acceptable conception;
- how the tasks might help restructure pupils' thinking about the topic;
- how you might run this activity in a Key Stage 3 classroom.

The CASE project has the aim of helping pupils to progress faster in their thinking skills by promoting cognitive conflict and through reflecting on their own thinking. The theoretical model for CASE is based on the learning theories of both Piaget and Vygotsky (see Burton 2001). As we have seen in Piaget's work, children move through a sequence of stages as their understanding about the world develops. In Piaget's model the child interacts with the

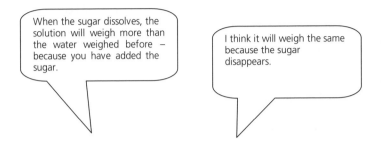

What do you think? How could you find out who is right?

Figure 5.1.1 An orientation exercise

environment where new stimuli are *assimilated* into the child's mental model. Where the child's cognitive structure has expanded so she becomes aware of discrepancies, there is cognitive conflict and the cognitive structure shifts to *accommodate* the new stimuli. The processes of *assimilation* and *accommodation* are intrinsic to Piaget's theory. For Vygotsky, the role of a peer or teacher (which he calls an 'other') is crucial in enabling a child to complete a task successfully. Here the teacher becomes a mediator in framing the task in such a way that the learner can make the necessary jump to success.

The CASE materials are based on the 'five pillar teaching model', which are stages in enabling progression (Adey *et al.* 2001). These pillars are listed below.

1   Concrete preparation: Pupils become familiar with the practical context of the task and the relevant terminology. The teacher and pupils develop a shared language through questioning and group work.

2   Cognitive conflict: Pupils are led towards observations which occasion surprise and do not meet their expectations. The conditions have to be right for cognitive conflict to occur. Some children may simply not be ready for it, very able children may be able to assimilate and accommodate new observations with relative ease.

3   Construction: The pupil actively puts bits of information together to build new knowledge and make it her own.

4   Metacognition: The pupil not only solves a problem but can articulate how it was solved and can therefore use their thinking skills much more flexibly.

5   Bridging: Pupils apply the skills they have learned to a variety of contexts. For examples of bridging strategies, see Shayer and Gamble (2001).

Activities across all five stages encourage children towards formal operational thinking through such characteristic reasoning programmes as classification, probability, control of variables, equilibrium, proportionality. The CASE Project is aimed at developing scientific reasoning skills. Although CASE uses content and context to realise its objectives the approach is not specifically designed to widen factual knowledge. Pupils may move more quickly through the Piagetian stages as a result of exposure to CASE activities but not all pupils may reach the level of formal operational thinking, or jump stages, such as from pre-operational thinking to formal operational thinking. Research shows that progress through CASE activities transfers across to progress in other subjects such as English and mathematics (Adey and Shayer 1994: 98–104).

As well as the main cognitive elements in progression, you should take into consideration other factors which may influence progression. Pupils:

- have different motivations;
- learn in different ways;
- learn at different rates;
- have had different experiences;
- have different language skills to help them;
- have different emotional responses to the topic.

PLANNING FOR PROGRESSION

To support progression in learning in all your pupils you should consider the following points:

1   What is it that you want the pupils to know, understand and do, i.e. to have learned, in this topic by the end of the course, module or lesson?
2   What is it that the pupils know, understand and can do at the start of the topic?
3   What sequence of learning activities will help pupils' progress from their present understanding to the objective?
4   How will you know when pupils have reached where you want them to go?

One way to think about planning for progression is to consider points 1 to 4 in turn.

1 What do you want pupils to learn? Learning objectives and outcomes

What you want pupils to have learned by the end of an activity, lesson or topic is known as the learning objective. An objective at Key Stage 3, for example, could be 'pupils understand that chemical reactions can either be exothermic or endothermic' or 'pupils know how flowers help a plant to reproduce'. But stating objectives in this way begs a further question: How do you, as the teacher, *know* when pupils have achieved these objectives? How can you *tell* a pupil knows or understands something?

To answer these questions, the pupils have to provide evidence of their understanding or knowledge. You need 'doing' words that describe this evidence, for example, 'sort these reactions into exothermic and endothermic', 'label the male and female parts of the flower', 'explain the differences between exothermic and endothermic reactions', 'draw what happens when pollen travels from one flower to another'. Statements like these are called learning outcomes, i.e. objectives that can be assessed. Outcomes contain terms like: *explain, design a poster, sort out, discuss, interpret, use the model to show (use the particle model to show the differences between solids and liquids)*. Finding out if pupils do understand the differences between exothermic and endothermic reactions, they could:

- describe what happens in terms of temperature change in exothermic and endothermic reactions;
- complete schematic diagrams showing where heat is being gained and lost;
- interpret data from an experiment to show that a reaction is exothermic or endothermic;

- identify the thermicity of a reaction from an energy diagram;
- suggest ways of finding out how exothermic or endothermic a reaction is.

Most outcomes and objectives will only be partly achieved. Pupil A may answer a homework question by describing an exothermic reaction as one that gives out heat and an endothermic reaction as one that takes in heat. Pupil B might respond 'Exothermic reactions such as the burning of a candle and the reaction of magnesium with acid lose heat to the surroundings. We can tell it is an exothermic reaction because the temperature of the surroundings rises as a result of the reaction. If we put a thermometer in the reaction mixture of magnesium and acid, the temperature rises until the reaction is complete ...' Clearly, pupil B has been able to meet the outcome more precisely than pupil A. You could therefore help pupil A to progress by giving a short exercise to help them identify instances of exothermic reactions and see if they can report what happens in terms of temperature change (see Unit 7.1 'Assessment for learning'). Pupil B can be superseded by pupil C who relates the temperature change to particle motion. Thus there are opportunities for progression within a particular outcome.

Some teachers identify several levels of learning outcomes to cater for different levels of achievement in the class. They might state their outcomes as follows:

- all pupils will be able to recall that heat is lost to the surroundings in exothermic reactions and that heat is gained from the surroundings in endothermic reactions;
- some pupils will be able to identify exothermic and endothermic reactions and to state what happens to the surrounding temperature;
- a few pupils will be able to translate energy diagrams into exothermic and endothermic reactions.

Task 5.1.3
Identifying three learning outcomes for one objective

Take the following objectives and break each one down into three outcomes, i.e. what all, some and a few pupils can do:

- plan an investigation to find out the best anti-acid remedy;
- understand that light can travel through a vacuum but sound cannot;
- know that habitats support a variety of plants and animals that are interdependent.

---

2 What is it that pupils know, understand and can do at the start of the topic?

To help pupils to meet learning objectives you must have some idea of where the pupils are starting from. There are at least two reasons for this. First, pupils may have done much of the topic before and may become bored going over old ground. Second, you may assume knowledge which the pupils don't have and if this is the case they may become quickly disaffected. Of course pupils won't all be starting from the same point so you need a means of finding out what pupils do and don't know before starting a topic. The list below gives guidance on how you can find the relevant information.

- Pupils ought to have covered something of the topic at Key Stages 1 and 2 if you are starting at Key Stage 3. Starting at Key Stage 4, there ought to have been some coverage at Key Stages 2 and 3. Find out from the national curriculum and the QCA schemes of work what they are likely to have covered.
- Ask more experienced teachers who can tell you about the kinds of things pupils know well and what gaps in knowledge to look out for.
- Acquaint yourself with the literature on children's ideas (Driver *et al.* 1994, Driver *et al.* 1985) so you can anticipate ideas pupils may bring to the topic.
- Use diagnostic tasks and starter activities to find out what pupils know. These activities can be given at the beginning of a topic. They should be:
  - short;
  - easy to administer;
  - engaging for the pupil;
  - able to give you the information you want;
  - quick to mark.

3 What sequence of learning activities helps pupils to progress from their present understanding to the next learning objective?

Starter activities and diagnostic tasks not only tell you what pupils already know and don't know, they also reveal a wide range of understandings within the classroom. The instruction and learning opportunities you give pupils within the lesson must then have two characteristics:

- offer sufficient challenge for all the pupils;
- allow the pupils to develop scientific ideas, skills, terminology etc. (this is likely to involve active instruction).

Whether you are teaching in a setted, streamed or mixed ability class there are always differences in knowledge and understanding, although the range of knowledge and understanding may be (but not necessarily) narrower in a streamed or setted class. Because all pupils are different there is a tendency to think that the best way out would be to give each pupil individualised work. This approach is clearly impossible and probably undesirable; pupils can learn from each other so devising activities for them which encourage discussion and exchange of ideas assists progression.

You need to ensure that you are starting from the appropriate level for those pupils who have clear misconceptions and that you are setting a sufficient challenge for those pupils who have clear understandings. Most departments have a bank of activities which you can adapt for your own purposes. You can support the lower attainers by giving them guided help. Suppose you ask pupils to explain how condensation appears on the outside of a cold flask (see Figure 5.1.2). Some pupils say that the water seeped through the bottle. You might want to help them by showing them a bottle containing water where condensate doesn't

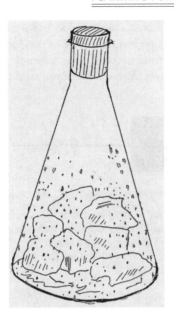

Ice inside the flask and the flask is fitted with a tight stopper.
Where does the water on the outside of the flask come from?

Figure 5.1.2 Presenting a puzzle: water condensing on a cold flask

appear on the outside of the bottle, or dyeing the ice red and demonstrating that the water
on the outside is colourless.

Don't expect pupils to accept immediately your explanations because you are challenging
beliefs they might hold quite strongly. When pupils come to realise that the explanations
they have held up to now contradict new explanations which they are beginning to own
intellectually, we call this situation cognitive conflict. Resolution of this cognitive conflict
can take some time and needs reinforcement; this is why you need to revisit concepts and
widen experience. Giving lower attainers experiences which help to reinforce the concept
is an important way to help them progress. For more advanced learners you need to ensure
that they have sufficient challenge while you are giving more time to others in the class.
This does not mean you give high achievers less time overall but at the crucial beginning
stages you are helping lower attainers in the fundamental understanding necessary to grasp
the main objective. Pupils are progressing through the topic but there are opportunities at
various stages for reinforcement for some pupils and extra challenge for others.

Teachers rightly want to ensure that all their pupils are challenged but it is important not
to be too ambitious and to devise too many activities. As a starting point, try the approaches
listed below.

- For each idea taught, devise three or four distinct activities, all of which underpin
  the understanding of the idea. For example, one activity might involve a short
  practical exercise such as finding out how quickly different liquids evaporate, another
  discussing a concept cartoon, a third answering questions on a short written piece
  and finally analysing a piece of data from a website.

- Devise an activity which all pupils can do but at different levels. For example, it might be answering questions on a piece of data, or a short extract from a video, where successive questions become more demanding.
- Ask pupils to plan an investigation where you set different demands.

Task 5.1.4
Planning differentiated investigations

If we take the example of evaporation, the following tasks could be set:

- find out the order in which these four liquids evaporate. You will need a measuring cylinder, stopwatch and evaporating basin. Start off with the same volume of each liquid;
- plan an experiment to show how surface area of a liquid influences the rate of evaporation;
- devise an experiment to find out if there is a relationship between particle size and rate of evaporation of a liquid.

Devise a set of similar graded investigations for the topic of seedling growth, electrical circuits or acids and bases.

---

4 How do you know when pupils have reached where you want them to go?

Pupils provide evidence of outcomes in the work they produce such as written exercises, drawings, analysis of practical work but much of pupils' understanding is ephemeral, captured quickly in off-the-cuff remarks or contributing something to a discussion when they are not aware of being watched. It is important for the progress of individual pupils that you are able to record the necessary information. While you cannot record the progress in a single lesson of each and every pupil, focus on a sample of three pupils for each lesson and make any notes on points that they appear to have understood or that they find difficulty with. An example of how you can do this is given in Figure 5.1.3. These notes should then be transferred to the register where you keep pupil records.

Self-assessment is another way in which pupils can keep a record of their own progress. When the teacher makes explicit to pupils the stages in their learning the pupils can check how well they have understood each stage. This helps both the pupils and the teacher. Helping the pupil to develop the skills needed for self-assessment is discussed in Unit 7.1.

SUMMARY

This unit has discussed the ways in which progression may be described and the theories that underpin such discussion. Children do not always progress in the same way and effective teaching has to maintain a balance between challenge and support, pitching the work at just the right level of demand to encourage participation and success. The keys to enabling progression are twofold: a sound knowledge of the topic in hand and a sound knowledge

CONTEXT: COMPARING THE RATES OF MARBLE CHIPS DISSOLVING IN ACID		
	Group 1 John, Paul and Mary	*Group 2* Laura, Pamjit and Anwar
Making predictions	Paul could with reasons. John and Mary struggled.	Laura/Pamjit, good predictions but not sure why.
Devising procedure	All gave good response, understood how to make test fair. John not sure why they are timing.	Laura and Pamjit OK. Anwar only understood when told.
Interpreting data	Paul, Mary OK. John – help needed to relate time to rate.	All OK – Anwar needed a little help.
Explaining results	Only Paul could link to greater surface area and more contact between particles.	Pamjit links to surface area and more particle contact.

Figure 5.1.3 Keeping notes of pupils' progress

Source: Adapted from SEAC 1991: 9.

and understanding of the pupils in your class. The first can be prepared for; the second develops over time, with increasing confidence and trust developing between you and your pupils. The main thrust of this chapter has focused on planning for progression and suggested the kinds of activities that you can try out in the classroom. The *Key Stage 3 Strategy for Science* (DfES 2002b) has many useful ideas which complement the material in this unit.

FURTHER READING

Harrison, C., Simon, S. and Watson, R. (2000) 'Progression and differentiation', in M. Monk and J. Osborne (eds) *Good Practice in Science Teaching: What Research Has to Say*, Buckingham: Open University Press. This examination of progression draws on research literature and helps the reader tease out several meanings of 'progression' which are appropriate to different contexts.

Jarman, R. (2000) 'Between the idea and the reality falls the shadow', in J. Sears and P. Sorensen (2000) *Issues in Science Teaching*, London: Routledge: RoutledgeFalmer. Ruth Jarman addresses continuity and progression across Key Stages 2 and 3 and raises important issues about acknowledging what prior learning pupils have and how that can be assessed and recognised.

Johnson, P. (2002) 'Progression in children's understanding of a "basic" particle theory: a longitudinal study', in S. Amos and R. Boohan (eds) *Teaching Science in Secondary Schools: A Reader*, London: RoutledgeFalmer for the Open University, 236–49. This is a report of a longitudinal study into secondary pupils' (aged 11–14) understanding of particle theory. Useful examples of strategies for discussing ideas with pupils and the types of understanding pupils display at different levels of progression are given.

Unit 5.2

Factors which Affect Planning

Bernadette Youens

INTRODUCTION

Planning is a 'nested' activity. The planning for a lesson is located in the planning for a topic, which is located in the planning for the year, which is located within the planning for a key stage and so on. In your training year you are closely involved in medium- and short-term planning (i.e. of topics and lessons) but you need an awareness of the long-term planning as well. This unit focuses on factors which you need to consider so that planning results in effective learning for the pupils.

OBJECTIVES

By end of this unit you should:

- be able to describe different levels of planning;
- be able to deconstruct schemes of work;
- be able to identify factors which contribute to planning;
- have sufficient understanding of the factors to be able to take them into account when planning.

LONG-, MEDIUM- AND SHORT-TERM PLANNING AND RELATIONSHIPS TO SCHEMES OF WORK

Planning is usually done as a joint, collaborative activity by a team of teachers in the preparation of schemes of work which are used by all members of the science staff. A scheme of work contains different levels of planning: the long term focusing on the whole of schooling and then on each key stage; medium-term planning for each year group showing the objectives for that year and listing topics to be taught; and short-term planning of individual lessons. Printed schemes of work are evidence that aspects of planning have been addressed by science departments. Figure 5.2.1 indicates what a reliable scheme of work is likely to cover.

Before you delve into the detail of a scheme of work, you need to be aware of the factors about yourself and your knowledge of pupils which contribute to your ability to plan well.

FACTORS WHICH CONTRIBUTE TO PLANNING

To be successful at planning effective lessons you will need to:

1   articulate your model of teaching and learning;
2   know the scheme of work and statutory science curriculum in force, and understand its aims;
3   understand how continuity is achieved in the science curriculum;
4   have sound personal scientific knowledge and understanding;
5   be able to transform science knowledge into effective teaching and learning activities, i.e. have pedagogic content knowledge;

A scheme of work should:

- cover the relevant National Curriculum or programme of study;
- meet externally set specifications related to public examinations;
- provide aims for science teaching at several levels (for the whole of pupils' schooling; for each key stage for each year; each topic);
- include objectives and learning outcomes (for topics and individual lessons);
- include assessment tasks to provide evidence for learning, especially at lesson level;
- suggest lesson and topic timings;
- suggest suitable activities and teaching techniques;
- draw attention to safety practice;
- offer strategies for differentiation;
- give references to prior knowledge you may anticipate, e.g. previous teaching of the topic;
- provide evidence of common misconceptions or learning difficulties associated with the topic;
- give opportunities for scientific enquiry and progression of enquiry skills;
- suggest homework activities;
- give references to books, resources and websites.

Figure 5.2.1 Features to be found in a scheme of work

6   know your pupils, classroom context and experience in school;

7   know something of your pupils' prior knowledge, understanding and mis-
     conceptions;

8   ensure progression in learning by monitoring understanding and achievement;

9   incorporate key skills into your teaching;

10   ensure safe working practices;

11   maintain a purposeful working environment in your classroom;

12   know the resources available;

13   plan individual lessons and units of work which fit the allocated time;

14   keep records of pupils' progress;

15   keep records of your own teaching and development.

1 Articulate your own model of teaching and learning

In Unit 2.1 we asked you to consider what sort of teacher you wanted to be, and what sort of learning you thought was both motivating and effective. Your ideas about teaching and learning are central to planning. If at one extreme, you believe that people learn by being told, then your planning will include a host of demonstrations, *power point* presentations, models, posters and there will be an emphasis on the good explanations you can give and on note taking. If you believe learners must be more actively engaged in their learning, then you will supplement the resources above with things such as puzzles and problems, and opportunities for pupil presentations. If in addition you believe in the value of learners monitoring their own learning, you will add self-assessment tasks. The dialogue which you plan to have in your classes will be different depending on your approach to teaching and learning.

2 Know the scheme of work and statutory science curriculum in force

You need to deconstruct a scheme of work to understand the thinking behind it. Just as planning is a 'nested activity' schemes of work are highly layered documents. Figure 5.2.2 provides an extract from a school's scheme of work, related to the foundation and higher tier courses for a topic on *maintenance of life* at Key Stage 4. This extract gives the lesson and topic timings and is consistent with the specification for the particular GCSE course the school is following.

Even from this tiny extract, it is possible to identify significant features. The foundation tier has three lesson (plant cells, water transport in plants, stimuli and receptor) which appear not to be taught to the higher tier. Perhaps these aspects are subsumed within other lessons for the higher tier. Homeostasis is on both lists with reference to regulation of body temperature and sugar level, but only in relation to the kidney in the higher tier. More time is spent on temperature regulation in the higher tier. From the fact that the courses are not in step, we can assume that the classes are taught separately. From this extract you cannot, of course, identify the underlying assumptions about teaching and learning, but these may be gleaned by looking at individual lessons or the overall aims of the course. Task 5.2.1 guides you to do a preliminary analysis of the scheme of work in your school.

Lesson no.	Foundation tier	Lesson no.	Higher tier
1	Plant cells	1 and 2	Photosynthesis
2–3	Photosynthesis	3	Factors affecting the rate of photosynthesis
4	Factors affecting the rate of photosynthesis	4	Photosynthesis and limiting factors
5	Photosynthesis and limiting factors	5	Plant growth and mineral ions
6	Plant growth and mineral ions	6–9	Osmosis and osmosis investigation
7–10	Osmosis and osmosis investigation	10	Active transport
11	Water transport in plants	11	Transpiration
12	Transpiration	12	Tropisms and plant hormones
13	Tropisms and plant hormones	13	Plant hormones and their uses
14	Plant hormones and their uses	14	The eye
15	The eye	15	Reflex actions
16	Stimuli and receptors	16	Homeostasis
17	Reflex actions	17	Hormones and blood sugar
18	Homeostasis	18–19	Function of the kidneys
19	Hormones and blood sugar	20–21	Temperature regulation
20	Temperature regulation	22–24	Smoking and disease; drugs and alcohol
21–24	Smoking and disease; drugs, and alcohol		

Figure 5.2.2 Extract from a school scheme of work for KS4

**Task 5.2.1
Understanding your
school's scheme of work**

- Examine your school's scheme of work, identifying which of the features listed in Figure 5.2.1 have been included*. Are there additional features?
- Does the department have an explicit (documented) view about what makes effective learning? You may find this in a departmental handbook rather than in the scheme of work itself.

*If your school does not have a detailed scheme of work, then download part of the KS3 from the QCA scheme (www.dfes.gov.uk).

---

3 Understand how continuity is achieved in the science curriculum

Continuity in a curriculum was discussed in Chapter 3 with reference to the science National Curriculum, which is built on a 'spiral' model, i.e. periodically the same topic is revisited and its scope and complexity widened and deepened. Similarly, a spiral model is found in the more detailed schemes of work which schools write. You need to be aware of where revisiting takes place, in both knowledge and understanding of scientific concepts and in

Task 5.2.2
Continuity in scientific content across an age group

1   Select one topic from your school's scheme of work. Identify how the topic develops over a period of time such as a year, or a longer phase of schooling (Key Stage) by showing how the concepts and knowledge broaden or deepen in complexity. Identify also the prior knowledge needed to start this topic. Make a table with four headings as follows;

- topic heading;
- when introduced;
- content covered – knowledge, concepts and skills;
- what pupils are expected to know, understand or do.

Summarise your findings identifying how continuity in the topic is made clear in the scheme of work. Identify changes in the complexity and understanding expected as the programme develops.

2   Repeat the exercise for enquiry skills (Sc1), selecting one, such as: the interplay between ideas and evidence in scientific enquiry; how to plan an enquiry; how to gain and present evidence; interpretation of data.

enquiry skills. Task 5.2.2 provides the opportunity to track continuity within your scheme of work.

4 Have sound personal scientific knowledge and understanding

It is impossible to plan sensibly, let alone teach, unless you have a clear understanding of the key ideas yourself, not only the ideas you are teaching at a particular time but how they link with ideas which come later, and ideas which were learned previously. One strategy which is helpful for summarising understanding of a topic is to draw concept maps. Examples of concept maps for four topics, the solar system, sound, hydrocarbons and genes are given in Figures 5.2.3–5.2.6. The first might be applicable for Y7, the second for Y8 or Y9, the third for Y11 topic and the fourth for a post-16 class.

5 Be able to transform science knowledge into effective teaching and learning activities, i.e. having pedagogic content knowledge

It is a common experience when starting to teach something for the first time to remark 'I thought I understood this topic until I began to teach it.' As well as properly understanding the science of the topic, additional knowledge and skills are needed. These include knowing ways of talking about a subject, having a bank of helpful stories to draw upon, knowing productive analogies, useful demonstrations, intriguing problems which help pupils sort out their ideas. Understanding the science and presenting it in ways that support learning is

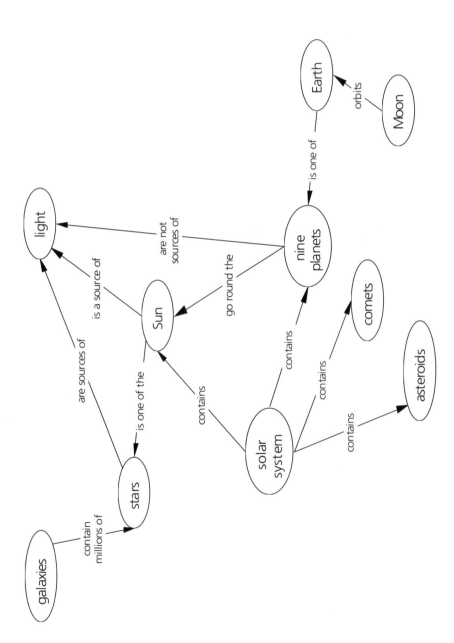

Figure 5.2.3 Concept map for the Solar System

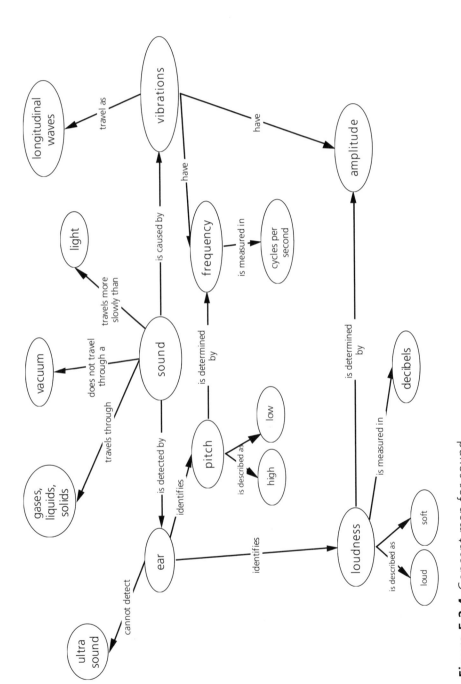

Figure 5.2.4 Concept map for sound

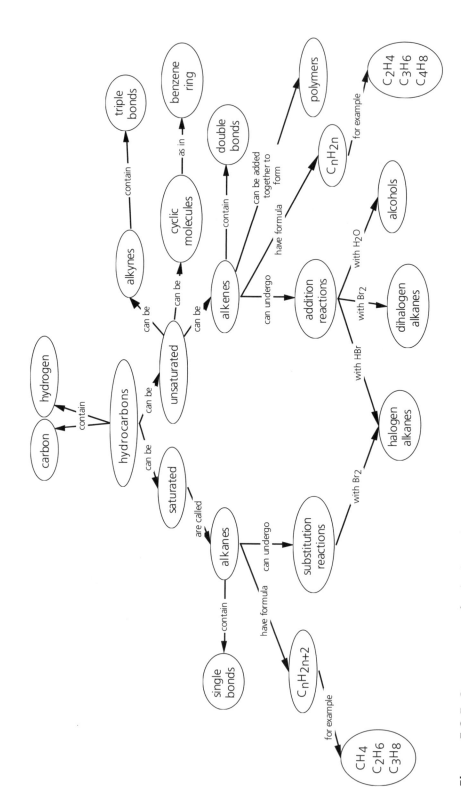

Figure 5.2.5 Concept map for hydrocarbons

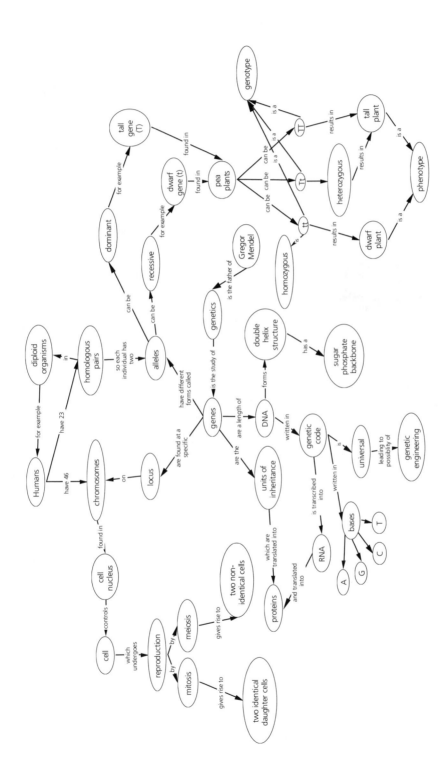

Figure 5.2.6 Concept map for genes

referred to as *pedagogic content knowledge*. Experienced teachers know how to select activities which help pupils practise new ideas and skills, and they know contexts which bridge pupils' prior experiences with the new understanding wanted. They also know when and how to intervene usefully when pupils don't understand a point. They seem to have 'up their sleeves' a range of ways of explaining a particular idea.

These resources for explanation include drawings 'Give me a piece of paper, and I'll sketch what you should be seeing …'; analogies 'imagine it is like …'; stories 'there was a soldier who had a hole blown in his stomach and while it was healing someone studied the effect of digestive juices …'; intriguing demonstrations 'I have here a hand warmer that you can buy in camping shops …'; bridging devices 'Imagine being pushed off a tall building on bathroom scales, the scales would not register any weight while you dropped …' 'Now these people in spacecrafts … they are also falling freely …'. Teachers rarely write these down. You will find that you develop some quite quickly in the act of explaining but you will develop a much larger store of such resources by listening and watching other teachers.

Task 5.2.3
Developing your personal teaching resources

Start a collection of resources and ideas to support your teaching. This collection might include examples of:

- useful demonstrations;
- helpful analogies to explain a concept;
- background information about scientists;
- bridging activities;
- stories about how an idea or new understanding developed.

Plan a file to collect these resources and a reference system for easy access. Be on the lookout for ideas when you are watching teachers.

Obviously, ideas or phenomena can be discussed at different levels of understanding and teachers need the flexibility to be able to move between them as appropriate. Figure 5.2.7 shows possible conversations you might have at different levels about the topic of levers, and Task 5.2.4 provides an opportunity for you to try this on other topics.

A fuller discussion of how teachers explain ideas in science can be found in Ogborn *et al.* (1996b).

'On a see-saw, the bigger person has to sit nearer the middle, the smaller one further out';

'The crowbar is like the lever … here's the pivot … here's where we put a force … this is the thing we are trying to move, it's much bigger and it is nearer the pivot …';

'If the other person were twice your weight you would have to sit twice as far out …';

'Force x distance is significant in turning, so it has been given its own name – moment of a force';

'Levers are force magnifiers … they enable you to exert a big force which you could not do on your own …';

'We can also look at levers in energy terms …' etc.

Figure 5.2.7 Different levels of explanation for levers

Task 5.2.4
Developing different levels of explanation

Select a topic or concept and develop a set of explanations which you might expect many pupils to know or understand at stages through primary and secondary school and post-16 (see Figure 5.2.7 for an example). For example:

* how water moves into and through a plant;
* the effect of temperature on the rate of a chemical reaction;
* how light travels through and between media;
* the path of the planets around the Sun.

6 Know your pupils, their experiences in school and classroom contexts

Pupils are individuals, yet you meet them first as a class and this perspective may dominate your early teaching. Later, increased personal confidence and better knowledge and understanding of the pupils allows you to work with them as individuals. The nature of the particular class to be taught is important to consider when planning, including the class size, age, gender balance, motivation, cultural diversity and spread of achievement. Pupils with special educational needs need to be considered when lesson planning, including working with support teachers. The physical environment also has an important impact upon the

of the learning experience. The laboratory setting, resources and facilities can all
bute to a positive learning environment, and hence encourage pupils to learn science.
A day spent shadowing a pupil helps you to understand what the school is like from a
pupil's perspective. It allows you to identify the varied contexts pupils experience as learners
and realise how their perspective is different from that of the teacher.

Task 5.2.5
The pupils' day – their
learning experiences

- Observe the school day from a pupil's perspective. Discuss the task
  with your mentor, clarifying the purposes of shadowing and setting
  up the practical arrangements. We suggest you follow a class and
  have one pupil in mind, but do not let the pupil know he or she is
  being observed. Find out from the class teacher the achievements of
  this pupil, including academic, extra-curricular and behavioural
  characteristics so that you have a framework in which to comment on
  the lessons you observe.
- Observe the different learning environments which the pupil meets:
  teaching styles, management styles, activities, conventions and
  expectations of different teachers; record how these factors appear to
  affect his or her motivation and achievement. Write a brief account of
  how the school day might be seen from the view of the learner and
  share the account with your mentor. What are the implications for
  your teaching, e.g. what factors need to be considered if your lessons
  are to take account of this learner's needs?

The SEN Code of Practice (DfES 2001) places responsibility on the classroom teacher
to identify pupils who may have specific learning difficulties, or who may be exceptionally
able, and to pass these findings on to the Special Educational Needs Coordinator (SENCo)
(see Capel *et al.* 2001: Unit 4.6). SENCos use a range of diagnostic tests to identify particular
needs. As a result of diagnosis increasing numbers of pupils have support teachers in lessons.
In your planning therefore as well as ensuring that your pupils with SEN or an Individual
Education Plan (IEP) are supported, you should decide how to work with the support
teachers in your class. Ideally, you need to share your lesson plans with them a day or two
before the lesson to ensure they can give appropriate help to the pupil(s) they support.

You can learn a lot about individual needs and the strategies which meet them by
arranging a discussion with your SENCo (see Task 5.2.6).

7 Know something of your pupils' prior knowledge, understanding and misconceptions

A crucial factor in helping pupils to learn science is what they already know and understand.
Pupils develop their own explanations of some phenomena through influences such as
reading, friends, relatives or science programmes on television and films. All pupils have

**Task 5.2.6
Learning about pupils
from SENCos**

Learn the following from the Special Educational Needs Coordinator in the school:

- Strategies which are helpful for a range of pupils with special needs, e.g.
  - gifted and talented pupils;
  - readers who have reading ages several years below their chronological ages;
  - pupils with English as an additional Language (EAL);
  - pupils with poor motor coordination.

- The *range* of needs of any one category, focusing particularly on how progress is monitored.

been taught science in primary school so you should expect a familiarity with some scientific phenomena, ideas and explanations when they transfer to secondary school. Finding pupils' starting points is dealt with in the second half of Unit 5.1, and again in Unit 7.1 on assessment for learning.

Another source of information about prior learning comes from primary schools. Your school scheme of work may well make reference to the knowledge that pupils bring from primary schools. Task 5.2.7 asks you to find out how your school builds on the knowledge and skills which pupils bring from primary school.

**Task 5.2.7
Continuity at primary–
secondary transfer in
science**

Inquire about how the transition between Key Stages 2 and 3 science is managed. Find out:

- the information regarding science achievement the school receives about pupils entering Year 7;
- how this information is shared and used;
- the links which exist between your science department and the local feeder schools and the nature of those links (one science teacher may have responsibility for liaison).

Summarise your findings by listing some implications for your planning for teaching Year 7 pupils.

8 Ensure progression in learning by monitoring understanding and achievement

Monitoring progression in learning is a complex task, but if done effectively it will enable you to recognise where you need to modify approaches for different learners. Opportunities for assessment need to be built in at the *planning* stage.

> ... assessment should not simply be a bolt-on addition at the end. Rather it should be an integral part of the education process, continually providing both 'feedback' and 'feedforward'.
>
> (DES/WO 1988a: par. 4)

Units 5.1, 5.3 and 7.1 address this in detail.

Careful monitoring of, and interest in, pupils' progress is important because when done well it has a profoundly positive effect on the relationships which you build with classes and individuals.

9 Incorporate key skills into your teaching

You need to consider how you plan development of key skills into your teaching, such as 'communication skills' and 'working with others'; see Chapter 3 'Common requirements of the NC'. Schemes of work typically give guidance on this, but it is easy to forget to include them explicitly in your planning.

10 Ensure safe working practices

Thinking about safety is both a professional and legal responsibility. Planning involves assessing risk of anything you do and taking the necessary precautions. Although safety procedures are written into schemes of work, you still have to make your own risk assessments. See Unit 5.5 for further guidance.

11 Maintain a purposeful working environment in your classroom

This focus involves ensuring that pupils know what they are supposed to be doing, that they have space to work, that the room looks as though you are ready for them, and that the behaviour of pupils allows everyone to learn. Think about the layout of the room, how groups are organised, whether you have sufficient work for pupils, and whether the work is of an adequate challenge. Ask yourself whether pupils will be gainfully occupied for the whole of the time.

To begin with, a great deal of your planning time goes on thinking about how to have everyone working quietly and contributing to the lesson. Task 5.2.8 gives guidance on how to learn about management strategies by watching experienced teachers at work. See also Unit 3.3 on 'Classroom management' in Capel *et al.* 2001; or for further guidance see the work of Cowley (2003).

Task 5.2.8
Observing management and organisation strategies

Arrange to observe one or more science teachers teaching. Over time, observe a range of classes and collect ideas about management strategies. Use the questions below to guide your observations.

- How do teachers settle a class?
- How do they ensure that everyone gets on task?
- How do they deal with minor disturbances?
- How do they deal with incidents of bad behaviour which could disrupt the class?
- What sanctions are used?

Discuss with your mentor the different strategies you observe in relation to the development of your own management skills.

12 Know the resources available

In Unit 2.2 you were encouraged to spend a day in the preparation room with the laboratory technicians, to learn about the way the technicians work and the resources which are available. Find out the availability of computers, interactive whiteboards, videos, data projectors, models, posters, and shared worksheets as well as laboratory equipment. Find out about photocopying facilities and how many photocopies you will be able to make. Task 5.2.9 provides you with a set of questions about resources:

Task 5.2.9
Finding resources

Questions to ask.

- What standard equipment is in laboratories?
- What equipment has to be ordered?
- Can any equipment be taken to any laboratory or are there constraints (too many stairs)?
- Do all rooms have blackout/fume cupboards?
- What models and posters are there? Are there places where posters can be put up?
- Are their chalkboards/flip charts/pen boards/projection screens in all laboratories?
- How do I book computers, video playback/data projectors?

Finally, think about resources which you could collect yourself, e.g. 'everyday' objects which would make good talking points, and begin to hoard!

13 Planning individual lessons and units of work which fit the allocated time

It is easy to view lessons one by one, especially when you start teaching. You need to recognise that each lesson is merely an episode in a longer sequence of learning, hence our emphasis on 'levels of planning'. Your planning must start from the longer episode, the unit or topic. Draw yourself a concept or mind map to show how ideas fit together, and then produce a flow chart to show the sequence in which you will teach before planning individual lessons. Keep in mind the time which has been allocated; if you have two hours per week for seven weeks, then all the teaching and assessment must be fitted into those 14 hours. Do not spend half the time on the first idea in the topic and then have to rush the rest.

14 Keep records of pupils' progress

Keeping records of pupils' progress is essential for good planning. This theme is returned to in Unit 7.1 on assessment for learning. Records of attendance, punctuality, what work has been handed in are necessary but not sufficient records. If you are marking to grades (A, B, C or marks out of ten) then record these also but these do not give you a lot of information about progress, nor what the particular strengths and weaknesses are. Keep comments on these as well. Discuss with several other teachers how they keep records (there are some ingenious and highly individualistic methods around). There may be a departmental policy about what records should be kept, particularly with respect to the NC levels.

Task 5.2.10
How do teachers keep records of pupil progress?

Find out how teachers keep records of progress:

- How are attendance and lateness recorded? How do teachers use this record to support learning?
- How is 'work completed' recorded?
- Are marks recorded? For all pieces of work? For selected pieces? What is the basis of the selection?
- How are areas of strength and weakness recorded?
- Are targets for pupils recorded?
- Are notes kept about topics which need revisiting for certain pupils?

---

15 Keep records of your own teaching and development

Keeping records of your own teaching and the development you are making are essential to allow you to review what has been taught, to collect the resources which you have used/ prepared and for you to monitor your own progress. Six months down the line early lesson plans will look naïve, which is evidence of progress. While in training you should evaluate all your lessons (see Unit 5.3). You may also find it useful to annotate lesson and topic plans so that when you turn to them again you can remember which parts need modifying and why. (See also Unit 2.1 for 'monitoring your own progress'.)

PLANNING SEQUENCES OF LESSONS WITHIN A UNIT OF WORK

If, despite what has been written above, you are not convinced of the importance of undertaking the planning of topics and sequences of lessons yourself, and think that the textbooks or the scheme of work have done all the planning for you, take heed of the comment below:

> Over reliance on unmodified schemes, however, leads to a lack of variety in lessons, to a slow pace, which takes insufficient account of pupils' capabilities and to missed opportunities to use local or topical illustration. Too many lessons centre on a double-page spread*, which comes to be regarded as a self-contained package of material, which expands, or contracts to fill the length of the available lesson.
>
> (OFSTED 2002: 12)
>
> ★ Refers to the practice where each lesson in a topic occupies two facing pages.

A scheme of work only provides you with a starting point for lesson planning. It is your responsibility not only to prepare lessons which reflect the departmental scheme of work but which also respond to the needs of your pupils. You should, with support, be able to draft a sequence of lessons on a topic and understand the rationale that underpins it.

Task 5.2.11
Planning a topic: developing a lesson sequence

Plan a set of lessons (in outline) for a topic, by identifying the sequence in which you plan to teach the several constituent elements. The topic should have between six to ten lessons, depending on the time available. We suggest you select one topic and address each of the following points in turn:

- identify the class for whom it is intended and time available (number of lessons);
- identify the content in the topic and draw a concept map to show the relationships between the knowledge and concepts to be addressed;
- write aims and objectives for the unit of work;
- draft a series of lesson outlines using the following headings:
  - titles to lessons; make sure the titles indicate the key ideas to be taught;
  - content to be covered and reference (to a scheme of work and National Curriculum)
  - the objectives of lessons*
  - learning outcome(s), say two to three per lesson*.

*Refer back to Unit 5.1 for definitions of objectives and learning outcomes.
Check objectives and learning outcomes for balance between knowledge, skills, understanding and attitudes. Finally, explain why you have chosen the sequence of lesson headings and indicate how the teaching sequence builds on previous teaching. Discuss the finished task with your mentor.

SUMMARY

Many factors have to be taken into account (we have listed 16) when planning lessons. Inevitably at the start students find they can focus on only a few but with experience they incorporate an increasing number. Guidance comes from teachers and mentors with whom they work, and progress comes from the experience of planning for real for different classes and evaluating the effectiveness of your planning. We turn now in Unit 5.3 to the more detailed planning of individual lessons.

FURTHER READING

Brooks, V. (2002) *Assessment in Secondary Schools*, Buckingham: Open University Press. This book provides a comprehensive coverage of assessment issues including an informative chapter on the relationship between planning and assessment.

Cowley, S. (2003) *Getting the Buggers to Behave 2*, 2nd edn, London: Continuum. This provides principles for establishing calm working environments in your classroom. Much of the guidance points to the need for good planning.

Ogborn, J., Kress, G., Martins, I. and McGillicuddy, K. (1996) *Explaining science in the Classroom*, Buckingham: Open University Press. This is a research report on studies of different teachers' explanations. It takes a linguistic approach and provides a fascinating insight into the nature of explanation. Short extracts are given in Amos and Boohan (2002), Chapters 4 and 13.

Parkinson, J. (2002) *Reflective Teaching of Science 11–18*, Bristol: Continuum Press. This book provides further discussions on both learning to become an effective science teacher and on planning for teaching.

Ratcliffe, M. (ed.)(1998) *ASE Guide to Secondary Science Education*, Cheltenham: Stanley Thornes. This is a useful handbook for all science teachers and includes chapters on lesson planning, continuity and progression.

Unit 5.3

Planning and Evaluating Lessons

Bernadette Youens

INTRODUCTION

Planning is about having a clear idea of what you want your pupils to learn and why this learning is important to your overall aims. It must address assessment strategies to check what has, and has not, been achieved and must respond to what pupils know and can do now, and to where you want to lead them. The ideas discussed in Units 5.1 and 5.2 provide the foundation for lesson planning. In this unit we consider how to plan individual lessons and show how the different components of planning, together with evaluation and reflection, form part of a cyclical process.

OBJECTIVES

By end of this unit you should be able to:

- identify the elements of a lesson;
- distinguish between objectives and learning outcomes;
- set achievable learning outcomes for pupils;
- understand that some objectives are difficult to assess;
- begin to plan activities and select resources to enable pupils to achieve the learning outcomes;
- address differences between pupils when planning lessons;
- begin to know how to assess pupils' learning with reference to lesson outcomes;
- understand the role of assessment in lesson evaluations;
- recognise the use of evaluations to inform future planning.

IDENTIFYING THE MAIN FEATURES OF A LESSON PLAN

In Units 2.1 and 2.2 opportunities were provided to observe science teachers and perhaps teachers of other subjects at work; you shadowed, too, a pupil for a day and worked with the science technical staff. These experiences, together with the factors discussed in Units 5.1 and 5.2, constitute a basis for planning your teaching. The next stage is to put these factors together to produce effective learning experiences for pupils. Good planning results in a well-structured, well-paced and well-resourced lesson which is appropriate for all the individuals in your particular class. Good planning reflects the nature of the class, the individuals within that class and of course the quality of the relationships that you have established. How you manage that lesson is dependent upon your personality and style of teaching.

You can learn about the structure of a single lesson by observing a lesson of an experienced teacher and analysing it in terms of its overall plan (see Task 5.3.1). Figure 5.3.1 gives a guide for such observations. In the left hand column are the main features of a lesson. The right hand column gives you questions to focus on when observing. If you have forgotten the differences between objectives and learning outcomes turn back to Unit 5.1.

**Task 5.3.1
Watching other science
teachers – lesson planning**

Negotiate with a teacher in your placement school to observe a lesson using questions in Figure 5.3.1 for guidance. Before the lesson talk with the teacher to establish the context of the lesson and the planned learning objectives and outcomes.

From your observations draft a lesson plan using the headings in the left hand column of Figure 5.3.1. Show the completed plan to the teacher and discuss how your inferred plan differs from his/her plan.

PLANNING THE MAIN FEATURES OF A LESSON – STAGE 1 – MAKING A START

There is a limit to what you can learn about planning by analysing another teacher's lesson until you have had a go at planning yourself. Once you have done that, you will of course benefit from watching other teachers again. To make a start on planning individual lessons, we suggest you think about:

- lesson content;
- subject knowledge and subject pedagogical knowledge;
- objectives and learning outcomes;
- learning activities and resources;
- assessment opportunities;
- management of pupils and resources;

- timing and pace;
- planning what you want to say;
- homework.

Main features of a lesson plan	Relevant questions
Lesson objectives	What are these? Are they shared with the pupils? How?
Learning outcomes	What are these? Are these also shared with the pupils? How?
Means of assessing the learning outcomes	How does the teacher get feedback on what pupils have learned? When does this occur – throughout the lesson or only at the end?
Phases of lessons Phase 1 – setting the scene	How does the teacher set the scene? How long does it take? Are there activities for the pupils?
Phase 2 – main and subsequent activities	What activities are used? How long do they take? What does the teacher do when pupils are working on their own?
Phase 3 – drawing ideas together – plenary	How are ideas drawn together? How does the teacher gain information that all the pupils have learned?
Phase 4 – clearing up, setting homework and dismissal	How long does clearing up take? Does the homework consolidate the learning from the lesson? Does the homework anticipate the next stage in the learning? How is the class dismissed?
Transitions between phases	How did the teacher manage the transitions between phases?
Resources	What resources were needed? How were they organised and managed?

Figure 5.3.1 Main features of a lesson plan and questions for observation (see Task 5.3.1)

Lesson content

The science content of a lesson is informed by statutory requirements, the departmental scheme of work as well as any relevant specification. Statutory requirements are often minimum requirements and your scheme of work may offer additional ideas or content. Make sure that you know what is to be learned in a lesson and remember that you have only an hour or so for any one lesson. You have to make efficient use of the time.

Your subject knowledge and your pedagogical content knowledge

Your subject knowledge must be secure in the subject of the lesson so that you can explain the science to your class in an accessible, relevant and informative manner. Make whatever notes you need, try out problems which you might set a class, make sure you can answer standard questions. It is important, too, that you know how that knowledge is linked within the whole topic so refer back to your concept map for the topic (see Unit 5.2). If you have not already done so at the topic planning stage refer to books such as Reiss (2000), McDuell (2000) and Sang (2000) to understand the level at which key ideas are to be treated at KS3 and KS4. You need to be able to transform your scientific knowledge into a form which pupils can understand and to select resources and activities to achieve this. If you are having difficulty explaining an idea, talk with colleagues in school and fellow students, or go to several books until you find explanations with which you are comfortable. Find teaching aids which will support your explanation.

Objectives and learning outcomes

You need to 'set challenging teaching and learning objectives which are relevant to all pupils in [your] classes' and that you 'use these teaching and learning objectives to plan lessons and sequences of lessons' (DfES/TTA 2003a: 10). Identify the objectives for the lesson, for example, 'pupils are to understand how the eye works' or 'pupils are to be acquainted with the Periodic Table'. Objectives may refer to skills and attitudes as well as to knowledge and understanding such as in 'pupils should be able to use a microscope accurately' or 'pupils should be able to work cooperatively on a joint research project' for skills, and 'pupils should show sensitivity towards living things' or 'pupils should respect other people's ideas in discussion' for attitudes. You might have aims for science education which include making pupils curious as well as knowledgeable, if so you may have objectives for your lesson such as 'pupils should show curiosity about the working of the eye.'

Learning outcomes, as explained in Unit 5.1, are *assessable* objectives and are written using *active verbs which refer to the pupils*. For example, for the objective that pupils should understand the working of the eye, you have to ask yourself the question 'How will I know they will understand?' You might decide that if pupils can:

- *label* a diagram of the eye;
- *explain* the functions of the different parts of the eye;
- *relate* the parts of the eye to the parts of a camera;

then they probably do understand the working of the eye. If you wish to add the objective about pupils being curious about the eye, your learning outcome might be that pupils should:

- *ask* questions about how the eye works.

It is good practice to share objectives with the class, so write them in language suited to your pupils. In the example above pupils should be told that by the end of the lesson, they will understand how the eye works. Most people argue that there is no need to share the more detailed learning outcomes, but there are no hard and fast rules. Writing lesson objectives and learning outcomes is not easy; Task 5.1.3 in Unit 5.1 gave practice in doing this.

Preparing activities and selecting resources

Designing appropriate activities to achieve your learning outcomes is one of the creative tasks of teaching. Ready made worksheets, commercial texts and other teachers are sources of ideas, but selection needs care and adaptation is often necessary. A variety of teaching and learning activities to develop a range of skills and cater for different learning styles is important.

> Although many science lessons are well planned and purposeful, and often include a single main activity of class practical work, some of the best lessons contain a variety of linked activities. This approach frequently helps develop pupils' understanding and caters for a range of learning styles.
>
> (OFSTED 2002: 13)

Unit 5.4 gives detailed guidance on teaching and learning strategies.

Designing, selecting and adapting activities is only the first step. Activities may look ideal but you must try them out to ensure that they achieve what you want and are manageable by you and the class. Work through the tasks yourself, e.g. complete the worksheet, carry out the web-based research task, perform the demonstration or class practical or make the poster. This will highlight potential difficulties, give a clearer picture of what you expect of your pupils and provide an estimate of how long activities might take.

Expect to be spoilt for choice as far as resources are concerned. For the lesson on the eye, for instance, you may have available a fluorescein eye (5 litre round bottomed flask full of water and fluorescein, with lenses stuck on the front which focus a beam of light on the other side), a demountable biological model of the eye; bulls' eyes which can be dissected; jelly lenses which focus differently when flattened a bit; a video of how the eye works; images of the eye from the internet; pictures and explanations in the pupils' books; ideas for pupils making their own model of an eye (tennis balls with holes cut on opposite sides, to hold a short focus lens and tracing paper). For practical activities carry out a risk assessment and record the outcomes of that assessment on your lesson plan (see Unit 5.5).

Assessment opportunities

Assessment opportunities are places during the lesson when the teacher is able to gain feedback from the pupils about the extent to which they understand the science being taught. From the example of the lesson on the eye above, a possible activity for the first outcome is to give the class a drawing of the eye and ask them to label it. You still have to decide whether you give pupils a drawing of the eye or they draw it themselves and whether a list of labels is given or pupils have to remember them. For the second outcome you have to decide whether they explain the working of the eye in writing or orally; whether they do it from memory or match functions to parts from a given list; or whether they correct a faulty account of the working of the eye. In a similar way you need to think of possible opportunities to assess all the learning outcomes. Both Units 5.4 and 7.1 give much fuller discussion of assessment strategies which you can use.

Task 5.3.3 provides an opportunity for you to watch for assessment opportunities in another teacher's lesson.

Task 5.3.2
Objectives and learning
outcomes: identifying
assessment opportunities

Observe a lesson taught by an experienced teacher in your school.

1   Before the lesson ask the teacher to share with you the:
  • objectives of the lesson;
  • learning outcomes.
2   Classify the objectives as knowledge, understanding, skills or attitudes
3   During the lesson, identify how each activity or learning opportunity contributed to achieving a stated objective.
4   List the opportunities taken by the teacher to get feedback about successful learning.
5   After the lesson ask the teacher to explain how successful each activity or learning experience was in contributing to the objectives, and to assess whether or not the pupils had achieved the learning outcomes and the evidence for that judgement.
6   Later, compare your notes on the lesson with the post-lesson discussion with the teacher and list implications for your lesson planning in terms of learning outcomes, choice of activity and lesson evaluation.

Management of pupils and resources

A key feature of successful lessons is good management, e.g. how to organise the movement of pupils or how to utilise the resources. For example, if you want your pupils close to you, during a plenary or a demonstration, where do you seat them and what instructions do you give about moving? If equipment is to be used by pupils, plan where it is to be placed and how it is distributed, e.g. by you or by selected pupils. Record these decisions on your plan. It is often in deciding about the management of pupils and resources that you make the final decisions about all the resources you need. Whatever resources you use, whether video, worksheets, overhead transparencies, practical activities, models, posters, computers etc., you have to think about the number which is available, as this determines the size of working groups. If pupils are to work in groups decide beforehand whether they are allowed their own choice in forming groups or whether you determine groups. Well in advance of the lesson, give your requisition list to technicians.

Timing and pace

Once you have selected activities and resources how do you package them into a well-structured, well-paced lesson? As Marland notes:

The pupil in a school is in a time-structured environment and expects that the component elements of the day should similarly be time-structured. There is no escape from this demand of a use of time, which is complete, intense and varied. The pupil is stimulated by a good use of time and bored and irritated by bad use.

(Marland 1993: 122)

By rehearsing the tasks yourself you have an idea how long each task or activity might take. You also need to judge how long it takes to change from one activity to another, i.e. the transitions between activities are events in their own right which have to be planned and timed. They may involve a change not only in task, but in focus, for the pupils and these have to be explained and orchestrated.

Each lesson needs a definite beginning and ending which introduces and summarises respectively the substantive content of the lesson (sometimes called 'starters' and 'plenaries'); these are elaborated in Unit 5.4. Leave sufficient time at the end of the lesson to review and consolidate learning and to link forward to the next lesson.

Planning what you say to pupils

Teachers spend a lot of time talking to pupils, including telling, explaining, describing, summarising, eliciting, as well as talking for management purposes. It is important to plan what you want to say. Do not rely on checking your knowledge and understanding in a book or scheme of work nor assume that the right words are 'in your head'. The process of writing out what you want to say clarifies key points for you. Think about each phase equally carefully; it is as important to plan what to say in the concluding part of the lesson as in the introduction and main phase. It may in fact be more important as ends of lessons are typically short of time.

When you are planning to introduce a new topic, your script should include what the topic covers, what pupils can expect to learn, how it links with what they have learned before and its relevance to their lives.

As well as planning and writing what to say, *practise* it either to a friend or to your mirror. Preparing in this detail is especially important when teaching a topic new to you. By rehearsing the ideas you want to share with your pupils you gain a better understanding of the material yourself. Further advice is given in *Teaching and Learning Strategies* (DfES 2002b: Section 5).

Homework

Most schools have a homework policy and you need to know what the policy is in your placement school and your departmental guidelines. You should know why homework is set and the learning outcomes you expect. Homework is a part of your lesson planning. Homework can be used to:

- consolidate learning;
- extend understanding;
- promote study skills;
- address differentiation issues;
- promote interest and intrinsic motivation;
- involve the home and parents in pupil development.

The purpose of the homework must be clear to the pupils. Homework should be timetabled into your lesson, an episode in the lesson plan (see below), so that you can explain the task and say when and where it is to be submitted. Outline the assessment criteria and provide information about your expectations. Check that your pupils can complete the task and that you are not making false assumptions about access to resources, e.g. books or the Internet.

If you expect pupils to treat homework seriously then you must set the example by sharing your expectations with them. Do not set homework orally just as the bell is to go; this practice sends a negative message to the pupils about its importance.

Keeping a written record of your plan

Only when your planning is complete do you summarise it in a written 'lesson plan'; see Figures 5.3.2a and 5.3.2b. There are many ways teachers summarise their lesson plans and no one way is best. Your training institution or placement school may provide you with a proforma for lesson planning.

A lesson plan should have a structure with which you are comfortable and space for notes you can consult as necessary during the lesson. The format may change as you gain confidence and acquire expertise. Use highlighter pens to remind you of particular issues, e.g. safety and management strategies. Figure 5.3.2a effectively gives a checklist of headings for a lesson plan summary and Figure 5.3.2b gives a summary of the action as the lesson progresses.

Checking lesson plans

Plans need checking and this may be achieved in many ways. Two ways are suggested below: using a list of questions to review the lesson and reviewing the lesson from the pupils' point of view.

Questions to ask yourself when checking a lesson plan

One way to check your plan is to ask yourself whether you have planned:

- how to greet the class and settle them;
- how to share the learning objectives and lesson outline with the pupils;
- a starter activity to engage the attention of the pupils;
- that pupils are actively engaged throughout the lesson, e.g. is there dead time while you organise books or equipment?
- how to talk to the class about a new topic and for how long;
- opportunities for pupils to discuss and assimilate new ideas;
- assessment opportunities;
- an activity for pupils to reflect on what they have learned;
- a plenary activity to reinforce the key learning points;
- how to anticipate the next lesson;

Name	Class	Topic
Date	Time	NC or other reference
Venue		e.g. PoS and level
Pupil with SEN...	EAL...........	Lesson no........ of ....lessons

Learning outcomes	Personal professional targets

Assessment opportunities and strategies	Prior knowledge
	Link to previous teaching

Key questions and important words

Learning issues to be addressed from previous lesson

Resources and their management, *e.g. named pupil to distribute tray of equipment per bench*

Risk assessment

Administration, *e.g. collect books from prep. room; hand back homework*

Homework, *e.g. details inlcuding assessment criteria*

Figure 5.3.2a Lesson plan summary: a checklist

Activity	Time	Pupil activity	Teacher activity	Resources
Episode 1				
Transition				
Episode 2				
Transition				
Episode 3				
Transition				
Episode 4				

Figure 5.3.2b A sample lesson plan summary: activities and timing

- homework and when it is to be handed in;
- how to praise pupils for the way they worked and set standards for next lesson.

You may wish to add to this list.

Checking lesson plans by thinking about the pupils' perspectives

Another way to check your plan is to visualise the whole lesson through from the pupils' perspective.

> The key to effective lesson planning is not the writing down but in the ability to think through a lesson in advance, as it were to preview rapidly the entire stretch of time.
>
> (Marland 1993:123)

To do this, think about 'What exactly will the pupils be doing at any moment?' How are you going to ensure that the pupils know exactly how you want them to complete a task? If, for example, you find that you have planned for the pupils to be listening to you for over 20 minutes, is this too long? Once you know your classes, this strategy can be particularly effective if you have one or more pupils in mind as you visualise the lesson. What is effective for those pupils may be effective for most pupils.

**Task 5.3.3
Checking a lesson plan
using two approaches**

- Review a newly prepared lesson plan using the two approaches described above, i.e. using a checklist of questions, or reviewing the lesson from the pupils' perspective. Modify your initial lesson plan as necessary.
- Which approach will be useful to your future planning, or should you use a combination of approaches?

Planning for differentiation

As you become more accustomed to planning lessons, you are able to focus on more difficult aspects of planning. These deal almost entirely with thinking about the learning of each individual and not just of the class as a whole. Planning for differentiation is about creating and adapting lessons so that they are suitable for all learners in the class. Recognising, and planning for, different levels of achievement are discussed in Unit 5.1, especially the task of setting differentiated learning outcomes (see Task 5.1.3). How to differentiate for different learning styles and different motivations is explored in Unit 5.4 along with the theories which underlie the recommended practice.

Other factors to take into account

As your teaching progresses other factors make demands on your planning. Figure 5.3.3 provides a list of such factors. It is important to recognise that you cannot address all of these all of the time. Incorporating one or more of these factors in your lesson plans widens your choice of objectives.

**Task 5.3.4
Lesson planning –
widening your aims**

Review one or more recent lesson plans using the ideas in Figure 5.3.3. Identify the extent to which you have addressed any of these factors and check your achievements against the standards for your course. Select one or more factors that you have not yet considered and plan ways to incorporate them in a future lesson(s). Plan and teach a lesson in which you have included one such factor and evaluate your lesson.

Monitor your inclusion of these wider aims and review your progress towards meeting the standards for your course.

- Individual Education Plans: are there pupils in the class with IEPs? Do my plans consider their needs?
- Additional adults: how many pupils have in-class learning support? Have I planned how to help teachers giving learning support?
- Learning styles: Have I varied the strategies I use in the lessons across the topic to address different learning styles? See above, 'Preparing activities', and Unit 5.4.
- Equal Opportunities: for example, are there opportunities in the lesson to use examples from different cultures? Is the content of the lesson relevant to the everyday experiences of the pupils in this class? Do boys and girls get an equal share of my attention?
- Cross-curricular links: are there any opportunities to make explicit links with work in maths, geography, Citizenship, Personal Social Moral Spiritual and Cultural (PSMSC) etc.?
- Literacy and numeracy: are there opportunities in the lesson to develop pupils' literacy and numeracy skills set out in the National Strategy?
- ICT: are there opportunities in the lesson to develop pupils' ICT skills. How can learning be enhanced by the use of ICT?

Figure 5.3.3 Additional factors to consider when planning science lessons

SETTING PROFESSIONAL DEVELOPMENT TARGETS

The lesson plan *proforma* has a place for your professional development targets. The objectives and learning outcomes discussed above refer to pupil outcomes. You have aims of your own about your development as a teacher. When you plan a lesson, in addition to setting learning outcomes for pupils, it is also important to remember to set objectives for yourself. These are sometimes referred to as professional development targets. Examples of targets might be to:

- *learn the names of five pupils*;
- question the whole class effectively, that is *'involve the whole class in answering questions by using true/false statement questions, and using true/false cards which everyone holds up'*;
- provide challenging work for a named pupil, i.e. *identify when the pupil has completed the main activity and provide her with an extension activity*;
- manage a whole class practical safely, *e.g. plan and give instructions about the safe use of chemicals in an activity, how to dispose of them after use and to get pupils to wash their hands afterwards*.

Professional development targets are important for your progress and should be specific and manageable. They should be shared with the person observing you, and you should ask for feedback on them specifically. Priorities will change as you progress. To begin with you are likely to focus on management issues, but you should find yourself moving to more sophisticated targets such as changing the style of your questioning to require higher order thinking skills, monitoring the achievements of six individuals in great detail, helping a class to assess their own learning.

LESSON EVALUATIONS

The process of evaluation is one key to making good progress as an effective classroom teacher. Throughout your training year you are expected to evaluate each lesson carefully, to record your evaluations and to file them along with your lesson plans.

Evaluations should respond to the professional development targets you set. They should be recorded the same day and a routine developed. It is of little benefit to you, and an ineffective use of your time and effort, to write up three weeks' worth of evaluations frantically before a meeting with your mentor or tutor. Lesson evaluations do not need lengthy prose; concise, well-focused bullet points can be more helpful. Figure 5.3.4 provides an example of a format that you might use. One effective strategy for managing this is to copy this format onto the back of the lesson planning summary sheet.

Evaluating your lesson must go beyond a 'good feeling'; whether pupils have learned anything is your 'litmus test'. Pupils may or may not have stayed on task, the practical may not have worked as planned and as a consequence you run out of time! Record facts such as these. Record your perceptions on the learning of the whole class, groups of pupils and individuals *with the evidence* you have or you expect to have (e.g. when you have marked homework). Identify and record which factors influenced the success, or otherwise, of the lesson. Review your professional development targets in a similar way to assessing learning outcomes.

Lesson evaluation is an important stage in planning and teaching but only if the issues identified by the process are used to inform future lesson planning and your own progress. Figure 5.3.5 summarises the position of evaluation in the lesson planning cycle, emphasising the importance of assessment and evaluation in the planning of teaching.

For further advice about evaluation see Capel *et al.* 2001, Unit 5.4: 279–81.

KEEPING RECORDS – TEACHING FILES

Keep written records of lesson plans and evaluations in a teaching file adhering to the guidelines of your own institution. Your files should typically include:

- a timetable of classes taught, including venue and name of class teacher;
- class lists, annotated to show special needs, disability, etc.;
- a chronological record of lessons taught, for each class;
- a chronological record of homework set;
- mark lists and other records of pupil progress;
- lesson plans including subject content notes and copies of resources used;
- your lesson evaluations;
- a record of all written observations of your lessons made by teachers, mentors and tutors.

Your file provides evidence of your teaching skills and progress in meeting the standards for QTS. Files form important professional documents. Student teachers frequently comment that they are expected to produce detailed lesson plans whereas qualified teachers do not appear to do so; experienced teachers have internalised many aspects of the planning process and therefore their plans will be much more succinct.

Class	Date	Time
Number of pupils	with SEN	with EAL
Topic	Lesson title	

Personal response
Record how you felt at the end of the lesson, what went well or less well

Learning outcomes
What did your pupils learn? Have the learning outcomes you set been met? What evidence have you gathered to make this judgement?

Next learning?
What should be taught?

Pupils
Identify those needing special attention (learning/behaviour)

Management and control
Identify achievements and issues to be addressed

Personal professional targets
Include skills of communication, explaining, organising, discipline, using resources, assessment. Cite evidence for your judgement. Record feedback by an observer

Personal targets for development
Short-term targets that you plan to use to inform your planning for the next lesson with this class

Figure 5.3.4 Example of an evaluation pro-forma

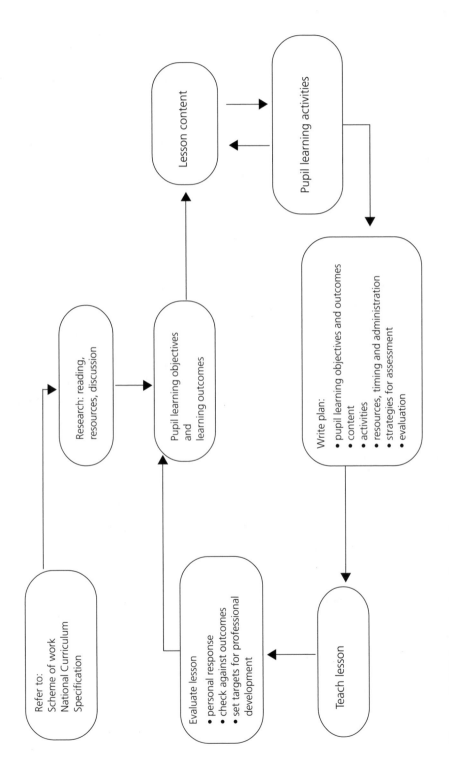

Figure 5.3.5 Lesson planning cycle

A word of caution

The model of lesson planning described above (i.e. starting with the objectives and working systematically through) is often referred to as a rational linear framework. *Planning is, in practice, a more untidy process because it is a creative process.* A mixture of past experience, available resources, including the scheme of work and the advice of other teachers, interact in a complex way to contribute to a lesson plan. Indeed, learning outcomes may crystallise towards the end as the plan is realised. Research evidence indicates that objectives-led planning is not used extensively by practising teachers, rather they use a non-linear model of planning in which activities are first selected followed by identifying the outcomes and with aims being set to explain the actions (John 1993). Do not attempt to fill in the proforma until the end of the planning process.

SUMMARY

Effective lesson planning is the key to successful teaching. The final lesson plan is the product of planning and the orderly simplicity of that document suggests that planning is a logical process. In practice, the interplay of many factors make planning a complex and creative process, summarised in the lesson planning cycle, Figure 5.3.5.

Although mandatory curricula or schemes of work provide a guide to the essential content of a lesson, the way you teach it and the pace of the lesson depends on what your pupils know and can do. Thus assessment and evaluation of your teaching are important aspects of planning. The cyclical nature of the process also highlights one of the most important qualities of a teacher, the ability to reflect critically on one's own practice and identify targets for future practice.

FURTHER READING

Parkinson, J. (2002) *Reflective Teaching of Science 11–18*, London: Continuum. An extensive chapter on 'planning your teaching' includes a section on writing lesson plans. Several types of proforma are given, explaining how they contribute to effective teaching and learning. A most useful text for the new teacher.

Ratcliffe, M. (ed.) (1998) *ASE Guide to Secondary Science Education*, Stanley Thornes. Contains advice on lesson planning, concept maps and developing schemes of work. The chapter on safety in the laboratory should be read by all intending science teachers.

Unit 5.4

Teaching Strategies and Organising Learning

Pete Sorensen

INTRODUCTION

'Miss, I'm bored!' 'Please don't give us any more to copy this lesson, Sir, we've written two sides already!' Most teachers have heard similar such cries over the years. You may even have uttered such comments yourself! At times criticism may be unfair but there are important lessons to be learnt from listening to pupils. Studies show that science is a very popular subject with pupils early in their school career but its popularity gradually declines. Worries about pupils' lack of interest and the implications for the future have resurfaced regularly over the past few years and recent parliamentary select committee reports have been very critical (House of Commons Science and Technology Committee 2002). Such reports have noted that many pupils perceive the science curriculum as of little relevance to them. Blame has also been attached to the teaching methods, which are often felt to be dull and uninspiring. Such assertions are in accord with some of the findings contained in the Elton Report (DES/WO 1989b), where studies focusing on behaviour and under-achievement often pointed to boredom as a factor, with poor planning, lack of match to pupils' needs and little variety in approaches used. The influential report *Beyond 2000: Science Education for the Future* (Millar and Osborne 1998) made similar points very strongly. In contrast to this gloomy picture, recent inspection reports show that the quality of science teaching is high in many lessons and the best lessons seen involve teachers who demonstrate enthusiasm, use a variety of different strategies linked to clear learning goals for the pupils and make lessons relevant to the pupils in their care (OFSTED 2000, 2002). Thus whilst the previous two chapters have focused on planning in general terms, here we look in more detail at the teaching strategies chosen and the manner in which these are implemented. These are crucial factors in gaining interest and maximising learning.

> ## OBJECTIVES
>
> By end of this unit you should:
>
> - be able to identify a variety of teaching strategies for use in science;
> - be able to select appropriate strategies to meet particular learning outcomes;
> - be aware of how different teaching strategies and teacher behaviour can influence the motivation and interest of different pupils;
> - be aware of ways of organising lessons to ensure that learning is maximised.

TEACHING STYLES

In Unit 5.3 of *Learning to Teach in the Secondary School*, teaching style is defined thus: teaching style = teacher behaviour + teaching strategy (Capel *et al.* 2001: 268). *Teacher behaviour* refers to the way that the teacher relates to the pupils. You may choose a very formal approach or a friendlier one; you may decide to use transmission modes of behaviour (e.g. to give instructions for a practical) or act more as a facilitator of learning (e.g. in class discussions). *Teaching strategy* concerns the actual choice and range of methods used. The teaching style (sometimes described as the 'teaching approach') chosen depends on particular views on how children learn (see Unit 5.1) and the intended learning outcomes for a particular lesson or topic.

Task 5.4.1
Analysing different
teaching approaches

Consider the three different approaches to teaching about corrosion outlined in Figure 5.4.1.

- List the strategies used by each teacher.
- Identify possible strengths and weaknesses associated with each approach.
- How would you characterise the overall approaches in each case?
- What differences in behaviour might be required of the teachers using each approach?
- How do these approaches impact upon the requirements for the organisation of learning?
- Which approach do you prefer and why?

The teaching approaches in Figure 5.4.1 roughly accord with the three broad bands of teaching styles described in Capel *et al.* (2001: 272) with the first 'closed', the second 'framed' and the third 'negotiated'. You may have judged one particular style to be more

Lesson 1

Four test tubes containing nails in different conditions present at start. Title: 'Corrosion' on board and diagram displayed on OHT. Class brought round front and teacher explains that each nail has been left for several weeks. Results explained to the class. Pupils return to seats and copy the diagrams and results from the board. Teacher explains nature of the processes taking place and dictates notes for the class to copy down. Class given some questions for homework as a preparation for a short test next lesson

Short test completed at start of lesson. Teacher goes over answers. Class given textbook showing results of corrosion experiments with different metals. Teacher explains results to group and writes notes on board to copy. Questions from book given to complete. Teacher concludes lesson by summarising work covered and relating to earlier work on the reactivity series. Second set of questions given for homework.

Homework questions discussed at start of lesson. Title 'methods of protecting against corrosion' given and slides of famous landmarks shown and discussed. Notes written on board for class to copy. Textbook with sections on 'factors that speed up/slow down corrosion' and 'uses of metals' discussed. Class asked to revise for test on corrosion next week as homework.

Past exam paper questions used for test. Last part of lesson used to discuss answers. Formal test signalled for end of year.

Lesson 2

Class given a brief introduction to the lesson, with an outline of the activities and objectives for the lesson. Worksheet distributed and discussed. This includes photographs of heavily corroded samples of 'iron' and others that have remained shiny and questions as prompts for suggesting hypotheses to explain differences. Class shown possible equipment that they might want to use and divided into small groups to suggest hypotheses and plan experiments. Plans shown to teacher and groups set up experiments to leave for next time. Class asked to complete plans for homework.

Short Q&A at start on last lesson. Objectives set. Group check nails. Changes noted. Teacher introduces idea of corrosion of different metals using video extract. Pupils set questions from book linking corrosion and the reactivity series. Lesson concludes with a Q&A to establish learning, and questions set for homework.

Pictures used for short Q&A at start, revising ideas covered so far. Nails checked. Teacher introduces set of nails left previously for longer period. Class discussion of findings. Pupils write conclusions based on class and teacher's results. Pupils' nails left set up to return to in 3 months time. Class set small group tasks to research 'factors that speed up/slow down corrosion' and 'uses of metals'. Class asked to research area for homework, to support posters for presentations.Class continue work on group tasks. Each group presents poster. Teacher summarises key points covered and pupils make notes. Q&A used to test understanding. Formal test to be given at end of year, with nails revisited part way through.

Lesson 3

Question on board: 'Why does Mr Turner's car have holes in?' Class brought round front. Discussion of question linked to title of 'corrosion'. Task set: 'investigate the factors that affect the corrosion of metals'. Class brainstorms possible factors and ideas to be investigated using flip chart. Class divided into small groups to investigate their chosen factors and prepare presentations. Some groups use the Internet; others decide to do a corrosion survey across the school; some opt for experiments. Class asked to gather information from home that might help, as their homework.

continued...

Teacher checks each group properly planned at start. Timings given. Support sheets provided to some pupils. Librarian and LSA work with groups who leave the classroom for surveys/research. Lesson finishes with group discussion of progress and further decisions on presentations. Some experiments shown to the whole class. Each pupil asked to write one thing they've learnt on posters stuck on wall by next time.

Posters on wall at start with 'things learnt'. Time limit set of first half of lesson to be ready to present. Teacher supports group preparation. 5 minute presentations given. Some involve rap, some posters, some plays, one a PowerPoint presentation. Teacher annotates flip chart from first lesson. Homework to prepare ready to teach others next time. Posters used to identify key areas for teaching: necessary factors; slowing/speeding up; nature of metal; link to uses all included.

Jigsaw activities used for pupils to teach each other the different aspects. Pupils asked to produce revision tools for their portfolio. Whole class concept map produced for display, updating flip chart. Some experiments left running. Signal that corrosion will be revisited later.

Figure 5.4.1   Three outline approaches to teaching the corrosion of metals

applicable to teaching specific aspects of the topic or particular pupils or classes and we consider these issues further within the chapter. However, whatever the approach there are other aspects of your behaviour that are crucial to gaining the interest of the pupils. Thus an enthusiastic teacher, using the 'closed' approach, might start: 'Now, everyone! Look at this nail! Underwater for 20 years and it still hasn't corroded! How can that be?' Compare this to a tired teacher, using the 'negotiated' approach: 'We're looking at corrosion over the next few lessons. You've done a bit of stuff on this before but we need to do some more. I know it's not very exciting but you need it for your exams. OK, let's brainstorm what you know to find out where the gaps are and together we can try and find a painless way to get the boring bits done'. I think you'd agree that the first teacher is more likely to gain the pupils' interest. However, many would argue that the *potential* to stimulate interest and meet individual needs is higher in the negotiated approach. We return to such aspects of behaviour later in the chapter. In the next section we focus on teaching strategies, looking in particular at the range of methods available, their relationship to learning outcomes and the importance of using a range of strategies in your teaching.

TEACHING STRATEGIES: THE NEED FOR VARIETY

There are a number of reasons why it is important to use a variety of strategies in teaching. These include the need to:

- meet a variety of learning outcomes;
- cater for pupils' different backgrounds and attributes, including preferred learning styles (drawing on evidence from learning theory and our knowledge of the brain) – see Capel *et al.* 2001: 245;
- motivate and interest pupils.

Let us consider the implications of each of these considerations for your practice.

1 Learning outcomes

There are many possible teaching methods that can be used in a lesson. Together these methods constitute the teaching strategy employed. Thus in seeking to teach the reactions of metals with acids, the teacher may choose to start with a demonstration, run a class practical in the main body of the lesson and conclude with a group discussion of the results and some note-taking. In deciding which methods to employ it is important to identify the desired learning outcomes first, as indicated earlier in Units 5.1, 5.2 and 5.3.

Task 5.4.2
Activities and learning outcomes

Figure 5.4.2 contains a list of activities used by student science teachers during their course. Add to this if you can think of other examples. Imagine that you have been asked to teach 'The Eye'. Pick out a few examples of activities that you judge may be suitable for meeting each of the following learning outcomes in turn:

- acquisition of knowledge of the names and functions of the different parts of the eye;
- the ability to research information about the function of different parts of the eye and use this to explain problems with sight;
- improved observational skills;
- the ability to work with other people;
- increased motivation to learning.

In each case explain why you have chosen the particular activities. Are any of them capable of being used to try and meet all five of these learning outcomes?

In completing Task 5.4.2 you may have noted that some:

- activities are better suited to meeting particular learning outcomes (e.g. 'practical work' to the improvement of observational skills);
- outcomes may be achieved just as well by different activities (e.g. knowledge of the parts of the eye may be equally well learnt through producing posters or writing notes);
- activities may only lead to superficial knowledge acquisition (e.g. recitation) whilst others may support deeper level understanding and the attainment of higher cognitive goals (e.g. discussion or thought experiments);
- outcomes *cannot* be met by certain activities (e.g. 'the ability to work with other people' through 'dictation').

This need to link methods carefully to learning outcomes is one reason why it is important for you to use a variety of strategies in your teaching.

1. Assessments   2. Brainstorming   3. Card sorting   4. Case studies
5. Classifying   6. Concept Cartoons   7. Concept maps   8. Creative writing
9. Critical incidents   10. Crosswords   11. DARTS   12. Data analysis
13. Data bases   14. Data logging   15. Debate   16. Demonstrations
17. Design tasks   18. Diaries   19. Dictation   20. Discussion
21. Displays   22. Drama   23. Drawing   24. Evaluation
25. Experimenting   26. Fieldwork   27. Film   28. Flow diagrams
29. Games   30. Group discussions   31. Inductive approaches
32. Interactive whiteboard   33. Internet searches   34. Interviews
35. Investigations   36. Jigsaw activities   37. Lectures   38. Mind maps
39. Modelling   40. Multimedia   41. Music   42. Note-taking
43. Observation   44. Paired work   45. Photography   46. Posters
47. Practical work   48. Presentations   49. Problem-solving   50. Projects
51. Quiz   52. Radio   53. Reading   54. Recitation   55. Records   56. Reports
57. Role play   58. Simulation   59. Slide   60. Spider diagrams
61. Spreadsheets   62. Survey   63. Tape work   64. Thought experiments
65. TV   66. Video   67. Visitors   68. Visits   69. Web-page development
70. Word searches   71. Workshops   72. Writing

Figure 5.4.2 Ways of learning: possible activities to use with pupils

2 Pupil differences, learning styles and cognitive development

In selecting teaching strategies it is also important to recognise the needs of the learners. Thus research indicates that people have a range of preferences in the way they use their senses to explore ideas and construct their views of the world. Here we consider two ways of looking at differences and their implications.

Visual, auditory and kinaesthetic learners (VAK)

Evidence suggests that learners may have preferences for either visual, auditory or kinaesthetic modes of learning. Visual learners prefer to learn through seeing and tend to set up visual images that help them to remember ideas. Auditory learners prefer listening and have a tendency to set up 'internal dialogues' to help develop their thinking and understanding. Kinaesthetic learners prefer to learn through doing, often remembering the feelings accompanying the tasks undertaken. On average studies have shown that roughly 29 per cent have a visual preference, 34 per cent auditory and 37 per cent kinaesthetic (Smith 1996). This 'VAK' model suggests that it is important to pay attention to the different preferences in selecting teaching strategies, otherwise some learners might lose out. Thus the bored pupils in a class may have reached this state due to a lack of opportunity to engage using their own preferred mode. The mode most often lacking is the kinaesthetic one. Thus specialist teachers, working with pupils manifesting poor behaviour in mainstream classrooms, have found that changing teaching strategies to incorporate kinaesthetic modes of learning can lead to significant improvements in behaviour.

Task 5.4.3
Learning modes

You have been asked to teach 'Cells' to a Year 7 group. Consider ways to introduce this topic that will help to ensure that pupils with each of the three preferred learning modes are engaged early in the first lesson.

Gardner's multiple intelligence model

The multiple intelligences model of Gardner (1993) is also helpful in examining ways to support learning. Thus Gardner has identified seven components of human intelligence and suggests that a given individual will have some intelligences more highly developed than others. Figure 5.4.3 includes brief descriptions of each intelligence and examples of activities that can be used in relation to each learning style. However, it is important to note that in selecting activities it is not being suggested that learners be allowed to work entirely in their preferred style or styles. Workers in the field argue that it is important to select activities that allow access to all of the multiple intelligences over time, as we often use groups of intelligences together to solve problems and develop thinking. In this way there are likely to be gains in each of the intelligences and learning is likely to be maximised (see Capel *et al.* 2001: Unit 4.3 for further consideration of multiple intelligences).

Task 5.4.4
Multiple intelligences

You have been asked to teach the topic 'Energy Resources' to Year 7, based on the QCA scheme of work (DfES/QCA 2003).

List possible methods that you could include in lessons under each of Gardner's multiple intelligence headings and link these to particular learning outcomes indicated in the Scheme of Work.

Is it possible to use all seven ways of learning to meet any one particular learning outcome? If so, explain how this could be done. If not, identify a learning outcome that can be met by most methods.

These ideas on learning styles and preferences point to the need to include variety in lessons in seeking to meet the needs of a range of pupils. Taken together with the constructivist arguments examined in Unit 5.1, there are clear implications for differentiation in the application of teaching strategies. The attendant organisational issues are discussed later in this chapter. However, it is important to include a further reference here to pupils with additional needs. Thus, for example, various forms of physical impairment

Intelligence	Description	Example activities
Linguistic	Adept with language	Word games, listening to stories
Mathematical-logical	Like organisation, logic and structure	Number work, problem solving and sequencing
Musical	Recognise rhythm and tunes, react to mood	Design raps to learn sequences
Visual-spatial	Good sense of direction, create mental images	Concept maps, multimedia presentations
Body-physical (kinaesthetic)	Good control of movement, like to use touch	Role play and practical work
Interpersonal	Relate well to others	Group work, collaborative learning
Intrapersonal	Strong self-knowledge, metacognitive approach	Learning diaries, reflective evaluations

Figure 5.4.3 Gardner's multiple intelligences

may make it difficult or impossible for some pupils to learn if a particular teaching strategy is used. In such cases it is also important that a variety of strategies are developed in order to meet such needs. However, it is important to be aware of the need to seek to remove barriers to the inclusion of pupils with particular needs when planning teaching strategies, as the National Curriculum makes clear (DfEE/QCA 1999a). Difficulties can be overcome with the right support or modifications to course materials, equipment or buildings. In science practical work this could include resizing and providing unbreakable apparatus (where sight impairment or dyspraxia is an issue), providing adjustable tables (for example, to assist wheelchair users) or supporting a pupils' upper arms (where pupils have weak muscular control) (Peterson *et al.* 2000). For the generic issues, Unit 4.6 of Capel *et al.* 2001 gives sources of support for helping to meet particular additional needs. At the same time it is important to stress that ICT can often help overcome difficulties (see Leask and Pachler 1999: Chapter 8). Thus, for example, computer simulations of experiments which allow variables to be manipulated can enable a pupil to 'carry out' an experiment where modifications to apparatus or other support cannot overcome the physical barriers to doing the experiment 'for real'.

3 Motivation and interest

Here we simply point out the importance of variety in maintaining interest and concentration. Psychological research shows that an individual's attention span on single tasks is limited, even when the motivation is there in the first place. You will all remember what the second half-hour of a one-hour lecture can feel like when the learners' position is entirely passive!

THE ORGANISATION OF LEARNING AND TEACHER BEHAVIOUR

Thus far we have concentrated mainly on teaching strategies. It is now important to bring in the second part of the teaching style equation mentioned at the start of the unit, that of teacher behaviour, and consider how strategies can be implemented. This factor is crucial if interest is to be generated and maintained and learning is to be organised in an effective manner. In considering the organisation of learning we focus first on (A) the different sections of a lesson, including transitions between sections, second on questioning (B), third on differentiation issues (C) and finally on 'awe and wonder'.

A Different sections of lessons

Starts of lessons

The starts of lessons are crucial (DfES 2002b: 44). It is here that expectations are established and the correct atmosphere for learning developed. Although this chapter does not focus on the organisation of the classroom *per se*, it is worth remembering that the learning environment itself is important, so the factors affecting lesson planning, discussed in Units 5.1 to 5.3, and the physical environment of the classroom (Capel *et al.* 2001: 59–60) are relevant here too.

There are a number of actions to consider at the start of lessons:

- Seek to create a positive learning environment through the way you greet pupils. This means being at the door and being positive in the way you interact on arrival.
- Share the purpose of the lesson, indicating how it links to previous lessons.
- Share the learning objectives or outcomes with the pupils. It is often a good idea to have these displayed somewhere in the room so they can be referred to at different points in the lesson.
- Use formative assessment strategies to establish prior learning (see Unit 7.1 for examples of these; also Units 5.2 and 5.3).
- Use techniques to help relax the class (e.g. closing eyes and focusing thoughts; repetition of instructions to relax at progressively lower and slower rates; breathing exercises). Share these explicitly with the class, explaining their purpose. This will be particularly important for groups unused to this sort of approach.
- Use music to help establish a positive working atmosphere. There is evidence that particular music (e.g. Mozart) supports preparedness for learning through activating different parts of the brain and different music can be used to stimulate specific learning atmospheres. However, take care! For some people background music can be irritating and it is best to avoid more recent popular music as this can provoke off-task discussion and argument.
- Use activities which require co-ordination of physical and mental activity, often called 'brain gym' (Dennison and Dennison 1989). A well-known example of this is 'rub a dub'. This involves rubbing the stomach with one hand (using a circular action) whilst patting the head with the other one. At intervals pupils can be asked to switch between: the stomach and head, the left and right hand and the direction of rotation of the hand. Activities such as this have been shown to help develop coordination and prepare pupils for learning.

It is obviously not possible or sensible to use all of the different techniques each time. However, establishing routines that include scene setting and short activities to generate interest is important.

2 Starter activities

Aspects of many of the activities included in Figure 5.4.2 can be drawn on to develop starter activities. A typical starter will last from five to ten minutes. The one chosen depends on a number of factors, such as the objectives of the lesson and the nature of the group. Examples of starters include:

- brain gym (for examples see Dennison and Dennison 1989);
- thought experiments – examples can be found in the CASE materials (Adey *et al.* 2001); for a discussion of some famous examples see Brown (1991);
- 'science in the news' items. Present an article or headline relevant to the topic and ask for opinions or explanations;
- controversial statements, present and start the lesson by taking sides;
- diagnostic tests using 'show me' strategies for answering questions (e.g. answers written on small white boards; yes/no cards; 'traffic light' cards to indicate confidence/agreement (red indicates no idea/wrong, amber some idea/maybe and green sure/right);
- short video clips, e.g. volcanic eruption; woman on chat show making her eyes pop out of their sockets!
- key word games, e.g. loop cards, word dominoes; see Key Stage 3 Science Strategy for details of these and other examples (DfES 2002b: 44).

Task 5.4.5
Starting a lesson:
identifying strategies

Observe the start of a number of lessons on teaching practice. Make a note of any useful techniques. Ask the pupils what they think of particular strategies and use their opinions to help inform your judgements. Build up a database of starter activities and use them to inform your own lesson planning. See also Task 5.4.4 concerning observing other teachers' lessons.

3 Main body of the lesson

The main section of the lesson can itself include a number of different parts which depend on the nature of the activities being included. However, even if there is one main activity, such as a practical, it is important to ensure that this is broken down into parts to help maintain pace and check on learning. Thus short plenaries within lessons, with a focus back to objectives, may often be important. Other approaches, such as jigsaw activities, simulations and role-play may contain more natural breaks; for details of the thinking behind such approaches, see Joyce *et al.* (1997); for some practical examples in science see Parkinson (2002, Chapter 5). For some pupils it is helpful to use activities that last for relatively short periods in order to help maintain concentration, keep on task and generate pace. If you have the expected learning outcomes displayed in the room you can refer individuals back to these without interrupting the main flow.

4 Ends of lessons

The end of a lesson is as important as the start. A typical plenary at the end of a lesson might also last from five to ten minutes. It is here that you can check whether or not learning outcomes have been met. You can also reinforce expectations, share achievement and set targets. Again, strategies that promote the active involvement of pupils are important. A whole range of activities may be included here as well, with a focus on determining the learning that has taken place. Examples include key word matches, sharing mnemonics, pupil presentations and concept map development. It is sometimes good to dismiss the class in parts according to their responses to questions on learning, especially prior to break or lunchtime when there is no risk in delaying the next lesson!

5 Transitions between phases

A crucial point of lessons is the transition between activities. There are two important aspects of transitions to consider: organisational issues and learning considerations.

Careful management and organisation of transitions is vital. To be effective in this respect it is important to establish clear routines and ensure that expectations are met. Aim to develop signals to use with your group. These could involve a clap, drum roll, loud bang, particular snatch of music or an announcement of 'statues!' Such techniques can also be used to introduce breaks in activity (e.g. for brain gym or relaxation exercises) when pupils seem to be drifting off task. This is often important in longer lessons. However such signals are used, there is also a need to give clear time warnings in advance of transitions, sometimes counting down ('five minutes left now!'; 'one more minute only!' etc), so pupils are prepared for the point when you want everyone to stop. Such time warnings may also be accompanied by organisational instructions, such as: 'turn Bunsens off now!', 'return equipment to trays and clear up the bench' or 'discuss results with your partner ready to share with the class'? These again help to ensure pupils are ready for the change of activity or focus.

The second aspect of transitions focuses on intended learning outcomes and is equally important. This concerns the need to ensure that the links between possible learning outcomes from one activity and learning targets in the next part of the lesson are made explicit to the pupils. If this is not done it is likely that many pupils may miss the point of the activities and simply remember what they *did* rather than what they were supposed to learn. It is also possible that they will not draw on earlier parts of the lesson appropriately in later tasks. The cues needed to help with this aspect of transition are provided by phrases such as: 'now we've got those two factors identified, we're going to find out why they're important', 'hold on to that idea, you are going to use it to try and solve the next problem' or 'keep those results in mind, we are going to see if they fit with Newton's ideas'. As mentioned earlier in the chapter, it is sometimes useful to focus back on any intended learning outcomes shared at the start of a lesson at key transitions.

B Questioning

One generic aspect of teaching that is important to cross-reference here is that of questioning. This is a vital part of many teaching strategies. It is particularly important in science if targets associated with higher level thinking are to be achieved, for example in the scientific enquiry strand of the National Curriculum.

Task 5.4.6
Types of questions
science teachers ask

Read the sections associated with questioning in Units 2.1 and 3.1 of Capel *et al.* 2001 and the article on the types of questions asked by science teachers (Koufetta-Menicou and Scaife 2000). Observe one or more questioning sequences used by teachers during your observations on teaching practice and classify the questions according to the categories identified by Koufetta-Menicou and Scaife. Draw up a questioning sequence of your own for use whilst teaching a scientific enquiry-based lesson. Ask your mentor to provide you with feedback about the sequence used.

C Differentiation

The need to differentiate in order to meet particular needs raises a number of issues in relation to the implementation of teaching strategies and the organisation of learning. Thus whilst most people using the term would accept that 'differentiation concerns how we manage the learning of individual pupils in order to maximise the progress each makes' (Chapman *et al.* 2000), there are differences in the models applied to support differentiation. One much used model of differentiation (Dickinson and Wright 1993) focuses on four aspects of differentiation that are in the hands of the classroom teacher:

- by resource – different resources may be selected to meet particular needs, e.g. tape/video/posters materials/texts/CD-ROM;
- by task – this could involve differentiating by the cognitive demand of the task given to particular pupils; see Unit 5.1. Alternatively, you could provide opportunities for the same content or learning outcomes to be achieved through different tasks, e.g. knowledge and understanding of the structure and function of parts of the ear through either making a poster, a DART activity, producing a model using plasticine/clay or making a video presentation;
- by support – using other adults/individual teacher/cooperative approaches;
- by response to outcomes – various forms of feedback may be used by the teacher or other response partners involved.

**Task 5.4.7
Differentiation
strategies**

During school experience keep a log of the differentiation strategies you observe being used by practising teachers. Where possible discuss these strategies with pupils and note their response. How effective are the strategies seen?

Keep a log of the differentiation strategies you make use of during the early part of your school experience and in the later part experiment with any strategies you've not already had the opportunity to trial. Ask experienced teachers to observe and give feedback. Again, seek to determine pupils' responses and use these to inform your future practice.

Apart from differentiation by outcome, it is perhaps differentiation by 'task demand' which has been most prevalent in schools. This often involves judgements being made about a student's innate 'ability' or 'intelligence'. However, theories of multiple intelligences, as opposed to 'general intelligence', and studies which have indicated that some of the main determinants of pupils' examination achievements are class, sex and ethnicity, have challenged the validity of differentiating (or grouping) on this basis. Thus Chapman *et al.* (2000) have highlighted the risks associated with teachers using the 'notion of ability as a major determinant for differentiation' and argue instead for differentiating by 'approach to learning', a form of differentiation which they have termed 'non-judgmental differentiation'. They suggest a six-stage model of learning which involves:

- *Right Frame of Mind:* involving the establishment of prior knowledge – including advance organisers, setting targets and creating a relaxed learning environment;
- *Getting the Facts:* involving the use of multi-sensory inputs, with choice for learners as their independence grows;
- *Exploration:* including individual/pair/small group activities with differentiation based on multiple intelligences;
- *Memorising:* using review techniques to support long-term memorisation;
- *Show You Know:* with opportunities for learners to demonstrate new knowledge and understanding through group and whole class activities;
- *Evaluation of Learning:* including reflection and discussion with peers and teacher, that is, metacognitive reflection (see later section, Metacognition).

Task 5.4.8 encourages you to use this model.

AWE AND WONDER

Awe and wonder cannot be taught but maybe they can be caught. How can you as a teacher convey a sense of the excitement of science to your pupils? This comes back to the enthusiastic teacher mentioned earlier. Is it really amazing (as well as counter-intuitive) that bulb after bulb can be placed in parallel and still shine as brightly as the previous one? Or is learning physics simply a list of equations to be learnt and calculations to de done?

Task 5.4.8
The six-stage learning model

Return to the six-stage learning model during your school placement, following completion of Task 5.4.7 above. Select a class with which you feel most comfortable. Identify the challenges and any barriers you perceive in implementing this model with the class. Evaluate the model in terms of your own teaching experience and observations. Do you think this is a good model for learning? If so, what changes to your practice would be needed to implement this with this class and how would you go about introducing them? If not, how would you modify the model to support the needs of particular groups of learners?

Can a dull grey rock really contain that shiny metal? Or is Earth science really boring? A tree – from thin air? Imagine journeying to Mars! On paper it's hard to convey the behavioural attributes of a teacher who is seeking to generate such feelings of wonder without sounding crass or resorting to multiple exclamation marks. Yes, generating awe and wonder does require using a variety of teaching strategies, including those which allow feelings to be expressed and shared. Yes, appropriate use of ICT can help. Yes, it is important to know about the pupils' needs. However, it is your behaviour as a role model that is most important of all. Without showing that you are interested, you stand little chance of gaining the interest of many pupils. This is especially important in motivating pupils at the start of lessons, as noted earlier in the unit. Many of us were motivated to become scientists by either the subject, or the teacher, or possibly both. Richard Feynman attributes the influence of his father to his way of looking at the world and gives an example of such an encounter:

> I was playing with what we called an express wagon. It had a ball in it and I pulled the wagon and I noticed something about the way the ball moved, so I went to my father and I said 'Say, Pop, I noticed something: when I pull the wagon the ball rolls to the back of the wagon and when I am pulling it along and I suddenly stop, the ball rolls to the front of the wagon.' and I says 'Why is that?' And he said 'That nobody knows … this tendency is called inertia but nobody knows why it is true'. That's a deep understanding, he doesn't give it a name, he knew the difference between giving it a name and knowing something. He went on 'If you look close you'll find the ball does not rush to the back of the wagon but it's the back of the wagon that you're pulling against the ball; that the ball stands still or as a matter of fact from the friction starts to move forward really and doesn't move back'.

(Feynman 2000: 4–5)

Feynman's father had no direct scientific training but appears to have had a sharp eye, an inquiring mind and a sense of wonder about the natural world.

METACOGNITION

In conclusion let us return to the learners. A number of theories of learning are referenced in this book. These have led us to suggest that it is important to share objectives with pupils at the beginning of lessons, start from what they already know and use a range of social constructivist methods to help promote their learning. However, a further point is raised here. There is growing evidence that when students are taught about how to learn, encouraged to think about their own learning and given choices about the strategies they use, then their learning is enhanced (see Units 5.1, 5.2 and 7.1). In terms of the focus of this chapter, this means going further than simply selecting and implementing particular teaching strategies. It also means sharing with pupils the *reasons* why you are using the strategies chosen and the way you are implementing them. It also means sometimes giving *them* the opportunity to work in ways they choose themselves (see Units 5.2, 5.3, 5.4, 6.1 and 7.1). You might like to look back now to Task 5.4.1 and the implications of ideas on metacognition for deciding between the three approaches outlined.

SUMMARY

In this chapter we have discussed different teaching strategies and the way that these can be used to achieve particular learning outcomes and meet the needs of different pupils. We have also considered the importance of teacher behaviour in generating interest and enthusiasm. The important stages of a lesson have been highlighted and strategies that can be employed to help maximise learning discussed. Models of differentiation have been considered and arguments presented in support of strategies involving differentiation by approach to learning. In employing such strategies it is suggested that you should seek to do these *with* pupils rather than *at* them.

FURTHER READING

DfES (2002b) *Key Stage 3 National Strategy: Framework for Teaching Science: Years 7, 8 and 9*, London: DfES.

DfES (2002c) *Key Stage 3 National Strategy for Science: Year 9 Booster Kit*, London: DfES, available at http://www.standards.dfes.gov.u.k/keystage3/respub/sc_y9boost. These, together with other materials from the National Science Strategy, provide many useful examples of teaching strategies.

Parkinson, J. (2002) *Reflective Teaching of Science 11–18*, London: Continuum. Chapters 5 and 6 contain details of a number of teaching and learning strategies, including a focus on the use of ICT in Science in Chapter 6.

For reading on specific strategies for teaching particular science concepts there are two series of publications available to support student teachers:

The ASE series, published by John Murray

McDuell, B. (2000) (ed.) *Teaching Secondary Chemistry*, London: John Murray for the ASE.

Reiss, M. (ed.) (1999) *Teaching Secondary Biology*, London: John Murray for the ASE.

Sang, D. (ed.) (2000) *Teaching Secondary Physics*, London: John Murray for the ASE.

Sang, D. and Wood-Robinson, V. (eds) (2002) *Teaching Secondary Scientific Enquiry*, London: John Murray for the ASE.

The Hodder & Stoughton series

Jerram, A. (2000) *Teaching Physics to KS4*, London: Hodder & Stoughton.

Wilson, E. (2000) *Teaching Chemistry to KS4*, London: Hodder & Stoughton.

Winterbottom, M. (2000) *Teaching Biology to KS4*, London: Hodder & Stoughton.

Unit 5.5

Planning for Practical Work

Jenny Frost

INTRODUCTION

In UK most science lessons take place in laboratories, which reflects a long-held assumption that practical work plays an essential part in helping pupils learn science. As a beginner to teaching your first task is to learn to run practical lessons effectively and safely. Pupils and equipment have to emerge undamaged. But pupils must also come away with increased confidence in their scientific skills and understanding, which come more from them discussing the significance of the practical work than just 'doing' it. Supporting such discussions is your second task.

OBJECTIVES

By end of this unit you should be able to:

- identify the various purposes of practical work;
- recognise the different roles of teachers in each type of practical work;
- organise practical work sensibly and safely in a laboratory;
- plan so that pupils engage with the thinking associated with practical work as well as the doing.

PUPILS' RESPONSE TO PRACTICAL WORK

Many pupils enjoy practical work (Nott and Wellington 1999) although there is evidence that boys are more enthusiastic about it than girls (Murphy 1991), that 11–13 year-olds enjoy it more than older pupils (Denny and Chennell 1986) and that higher achieving pupils often find it tedious and unnecessary (Woolnough and Allsop 1985). It is important therefore to think carefully about the purpose of any practical work which you provide and ensure that it is both motivating and worthwhile.

Facets which many pupils report as liking are:

- dramatic or unexpected events (the whizzes, bangs and intriguing puzzles of science);
- autonomy in working – often working for 20 minutes at a time on their own with limited intervention from a teacher;
- open-ended investigations where they can make their own decisions (Osborne and Collins 2000; Simon *et al.* 1992);
- working together – cooperative nature of working in pairs or groups;
- having a sense of achievement – 'getting the right result';
- handling materials and seeing things happen for themselves.

TYPES OF PRACTICAL WORK

The term 'practical work' is a generic term for a range of activities which make different demands on the skills of both teacher and pupils and which have different purposes. Various writers have provided classifications for practical work according to purpose. Here a three way classification adapted from Woolnough and Allsop (1985):

1   *Illustrative* practical work designed to illustrate particular scientific phenomena;
2   *Exercises* to develop practical skills and techniques;
3   *Investigative* practical work and problem solving in order to learn how to investigate and how to solve problems.

Practical activities are often wrongly called 'experiments'. Most practical work comprises well tried and tested activities where teachers know what will happen (and the pupils know that teachers know). This certainly applies to illustrative practical work and exercises and to some extent investigations.

Illustrative: demonstrations

Demonstrations by teachers frequently fall into the category of illustrative practical work. Consider two demonstrations which you are likely to do at KS3:

- The reaction of alkali metals (sodium, potassium, calcium) with water;
- Production of sparks from a van der Graaff generator, including making your hair stand on end by charging yourself up from the generator.

They are not experiments. They are carefully contrived events which allow teachers to bring phenomena into the classroom, as and when, they want. Without the specially prepared chemicals (highly reactive chemicals stored under oil) and a particular machine, such phenomena would be impossible to demonstrate.

The purpose of such demonstrations is to show *and explain* what happens. The practical event acts as a springboard for conversations about abstract ideas such as the relative reactivity of metals, the ability of metals to release hydrogen from water; high voltages breaking down the resistance of air; the repulsion of millions of negatively charged particles arranged along hair fibres.

To do a demonstration well, you first have to be able to make the event happen with confidence. Your own practical skills have to be well-honed, such that you do not have to worry about whether the demonstration will work when in front of the class. Plenty of practice beforehand is needed. Experienced teachers will be able to tell you of obvious pitfalls. A humid day can, for instance, make it difficult to build up charge on a generator; even the moisture from the breath of 30 pupils can affect how well the charge builds up.

Second, you need to ensure safety for pupils and yourself. The alkali metals demonstration requires a safety screen and goggles, and only small pieces of the metals should be used. Stock bottles of sodium and potassium must not be in reach of the class. The small van der Graaff generators used in schools are safe for teachers to charge themselves up, if standing on an insulated platform.

Third you need to be aware that much of the equipment can distract attention from the phenomenon itself. Pupils may recall the safety screen, rubber gloves, goggles, tweezers rather than the details of the small pieces of metals which fizzed; or the shiny globe on the van der Graaff generator and the whirring of the electric motor driving the belt, rather than the sparks. You need to keep pupils focused on the significant observations so that they ignore much of the bulky equipment.

Your fourth task, which is probably the most crucial, is to engage pupils in dialogue about what is happening, at the same time as doing the demonstration. For many beginners, this is the most difficult part. They find they have long pauses during the demonstration when they do not know what to say. Planning and practising your 'script' is as important as practising the demonstration itself.

The fifth skill is to take the class *beyond* what they can see, and to persuade them of the theoretical story which explains it. This has been described as 'putting meaning into matter' (Ogborn *et al.* 1996b: 16), making the invisible seem real, the abstract seem tangible and relating the abstract story to the real phenomenon which has just been observed. This requires the art of persuasion on the part of the teacher and the act of imagination on the part of pupils.

A well-executed demonstration looks effortless, so it is easy not to realise how difficult it is until you try to do one yourself. A good start is to watch an experienced teacher and analyse the various factors involved in organising and running a demonstration. Task 5.5.1 is designed to help you do this.

Task 5.5.1 draws attention to demonstrations not being isolated events, but parts of a learning sequence with events leading up to them and activities which follow. Follow-up activities must allow pupils to consolidate the key ideas, making sense of the science for themselves.

Seating arrangements are also important. Moving the class up is an art. An experienced teacher may say just 'come up for a demonstration' and an orderly arrangement occurs. When you take over, you say exactly the same, but the result may be a 'rugby scrum', with half the class sitting right up against the demonstration bench, leaning on their arms to get

Task 5.5.1
Observing a
demonstration

Watch a demonstration carefully and monitor both the teacher and pupils by using the schedule below. You may need to vary it according to the nature of the demonstration.

Pupil positions: Are the pupils seated or standing? How visible is the demonstration for all the pupils?

Safety: How is safety ensured?

Presentation by teacher: What introduction is given? Are pupils clear about the purpose of the demonstration? Handling of apparatus – is this confident and skilful?

What is the nature of the commentary which the teacher gives during the demonstration?

Pupils' engagement/response: Is interest aroused? Is interest maintained? Any expectancy/surprise?

Pupil participation: Are pupils spectators or participants? Are pupils active through: i) questions and answers? and/or ii) making observations/readings?

Place in lesson/topic: How does the demonstration fit the rest of the lesson/topic?

How is the demonstration followed up? Does the follow-up activity consolidate the learning? Did it require pupils to apply what they had learned? Did it have some other function?

What record of the demonstration did pupils make? Did the pupils take notes during the demonstration? Was there any guidance?

a better look, but completely blocking the view of the demonstration for those behind. Why the difference? It is merely that you have not established your routines and expectations with the class. So a sixth skill is to decide, and make explicit, how you want pupils to come up and where you want them to sit or stand.

By way of summary, Figure 5.5.1 provides a checklist to enable you to evaluate your planning and preparation for a demonstration.

Illustrative: whole-class practical work

Much of the practical work which pupils do for themselves is also illustrative. Teachers hand over to pupils the task of setting up apparatus so that pupils can demonstrate phenomena to themselves. There is a host of activities which we know can safely, and productively, be given to pupils to do. Burning different materials, displacement reactions, testing leaves for starch, measuring rates of cooling, measuring angles of reflection and

Guides for planning and preparing a demonstration. Have you done them all?

- Make a risk assessment and implement the necessary precautions.
- Practise the demonstration so that it runs smoothly.
- Decide what features of the phenomenon you want pupils to notice.
- Decide what explanations you want to build round the demonstration.
- Plan how to move the pupils to their positions for watching.
- Think how you will focus pupils' attention on the key events.
- Check there is a board nearby where you can sketch diagrams, put key words, write results.
- Plan the questions, or other conversation starters, which you will use during the demonstration.
- Plan how you will move from the phenomenon to the theories or concepts behind it. Think what theoretical entities you are bringing into play.
- Plan follow-up activities which involve pupils using their new knowledge.

Figure 5.5.1 Checklist for evaluating planning of a demonstration

refraction, looking at cells down a microscope, watching snails move across a glass surface, measuring pulse rate before and after activity, separating inks by chromatography form just a small selection of a long list.

A well-run practical lesson seems straightforward. Of course it is not. Watch an experienced teacher analytically to see the different facets of the job (Task 5.5.2).

Task 5.5.2
Observation of practical
lesson: teacher focus schedule

Setting the task: How do the pupils know what to do for the practical work? How do the pupils know why they are doing the practical work?

Safety: In what ways is this addressed? Are reminders necessary?

Pupil Organisation: Where do pupils sit during the explanation of the activity? Where are they during the practical work? How is the transition organised?

Apparatus/ materials: How and where are these assembled? How are they distributed? How and when is the clearing up done? How does the laboratory look at the end of the lesson?

Involvement with the pupils: What is the teacher doing while the pupils carry out practical work? What noise level is acceptable?

Interventions: Does the teacher have to stop the practical work for any reason? Note the reasons for the intervention.

Timing: What proportion of the lesson is used for practical work? Is this enough/too much?

Follow-up: How does the teacher use the pupils' results? How does the teacher deal with 'wrong results'? What happens in the rest of the lesson? Is it related to the practical work?

The last part of the schedule draws attention to the fact that pupils' results might not be as you hoped. For an amusing and thought-provoking account of how teachers deal with such critical incidents read Nott and Wellington (2002). Wrong results can be the basis of some excellent teaching about the importance of repeatability and of how to explain anomalous results. It is relatively easy, but unhelpful, just to ignore them.

Now turn your attention to the pupils. You will notice differences in their motivation and approach to practical work, their skills and understanding. Use the task below (5.5.3) on a different practical lesson to gain the pupils' perspectives.

Task 5.5.3
Observation of practical lesson: pupil focus schedule

Setting the task: How do pupils find out what to do? Did they read any instructions?

Safety: Do pupils observe safety instructions? Note safe practice and unsafe events. Does safety become an issue?

Purpose of practical: Is the purpose clear to pupils? Identify and note uncertainties. What do you think is the purpose of the practical work?

Apparatus/materials: Do pupils know where to get apparatus? Do pupils know how to use apparatus? Note problems they experience.

Pupil grouping: Do pupils in groups collaborate? Do boys/girls share equally in tasks? Are some pupils passive passengers? Do pupils stay on task? What off-task behaviour do you see?

Pupil conversations: What do pupils talk about during the activity? Is the 'on-task' talk about procedure or purpose?

Intervention: Do pupils seek teacher help? What for? Do pupils seek peer help? What for?

Timing: How much of the work do pupils complete?

Application: Do pupils obtain results? Are pupils able to interpret results? How are pupils engaged in consolidation? What writing do they do about the practical work?

These two observation tasks (5.5.2 and 5.5.3) have been put in the section on illustrative practical work. If, however, you are watching a different type of practical lesson, say an investigation, the observations will still be valid, but you need to link them to the ideas in that part of the text.

Just as in demonstration, teachers need to plan how to interact with pupils during the practical work. They have to keep an eye on skills and help pupils in difficulty. Teachers must use questions to help pupil notice key events: 'Are those bulbs the same or different?' 'Does it make any difference if you turn the battery round?' 'Are you getting as many bubbles as before?' 'What might the bubbles be?' 'Show me what it looks like – are you sure it is round and not rectangular?' Teachers also ask pupils to think about why something is happening 'Why do you think it makes no difference if the battery is turned round?' 'Why do you think the bulbs are the same, when they weren't in the other circuit?' 'What do you imagine is going on?' 'What made you sure the bubbles were hydrogen?' 'Where might they have come from?'

Practical exercises for the teaching of techniques and skills

Considerable time in science lessons is spent on teaching practical techniques such as lighting Bunsen burners, using pipettes and burettes, putting together clamp stands, heating a test-tube in a clamp stand without burning the rubber, streaking agar plates, using microscopes and hand lenses, reading and interpolating scales on a range of measuring instruments. Most of the necessary skills will be second nature to you and you may have to think hard how to explain them. Practise to make sure your own skills and knowledge are good so that you can show pupils what skilful handling of equipment entails. Make sure that enough time is allowed for pupils to practise new skills.

While sometimes you will have a whole lesson devoted to such a skill (e.g. how to use a microscope) it is more likely that such skills are taught as an intrinsic part of another lesson. Watch an experienced teacher to see how he/she monitors practical skills and provides help for those who are having difficulty in mastering them.

The microscope provides a convenient example of a difficulty common to all practical lessons, that of ensuring pupils observe what the teacher wants them to observe. It is rare for pupils, even when their microscopes are properly focused to observe the detail which an experienced teacher would. Teachers have to draw attention to significant features. 'Look in the centre of the slide, do you see cells which look like two little sausages? Now look to the left, can you see others? Now look at some of the other cells, can you see faint green dots inside them?' Where schools have icams key features can be discussed together before pupils return to microscopes to find them for themselves. Alternatives of sketches on the board, or illustrations in books can be equally effective. The more general point is that observations are dependent on the ideas you have in your head; the more you know about a subject the more you observe and register. Teachers play an important role in helping pupils identify and register significant observations.

Investigations and problem solving: scientific enquiry

Investigations and problem solving form the third category of practical work. Learning about science involves learning about how scientific knowledge is built up and how scientists collect and use evidence to support their ideas. Pupils not only have to know about this, they themselves have to be able to put this learning into practice by carrying out investigations, collecting evidence themselves, analysing it and evaluating the strength of it. This section therefore covers the practical work associated with investigations i.e. the second part of Sc 1, scientific enquiry. Investigations may at times come close to genuine 'experiments', but even here many which are used in schools have relatively well-known outcomes.

There are several different sorts of investigations which are undertaken in schools. The categories in Figure 5.5.2 are taken from a study by Watson *et al.* (1999: 62) of the different types done in schools.

Teaching investigation procedures

Investigations typically involve some or all of the steps shown in Figure 5.5.3. A mistake which was commonly made when investigations were first introduced, was to assume that

Type of investigation	Characteristics and examples
Classification or categorisation	Making or using keys to sort out rocks, leaves or a collection of invertebrates.
Pattern seeking	Questions such as: 'What plants withstand trampling?' 'What plants grow on the beach at different distances from the sea?' would lead to pattern finding. In these variables cannot be controlled, so cause and effect are difficult to determine. Correlation between one factor and another is, however, possible to identify. Such investigations presuppose that pupils have learned survey techniques, in tackling problems such as: 'What is the total number of species growing in this field?'
Fair tests	Fair tests form the most frequently found type of investigation. They require the control of variables, and the need to identify dependent and independent variables. They may be couched in terms of simple comparisons: 'Compare the insulating properties of five different materials'; 'Compare the tensile strength of different fibres'. They may be in the form of finding the effect of one factor on another: 'What is the effect of the number of layers on insulating properties?'; 'What is the effect of different temperatures on the rate of reproduction of yeast?'. Lastly they may be in the form of finding the factors which affect another factor as in: 'What are the factors which affect the rate at which an apple turns brown?'; 'What are the factors which determine resistivity of a metal?'
Investigating models	Here a concept/theory is tested out by modelling a situation, for instance: investigating the rate of water loss from different sized cubes of 'oasis' in order to explore the effect of surface area to volume ratio on transpiration in plants.
Exploring	These may involve recording something over time; the growth of a plant; the light levels in a building; temperature differences in different parts of a building. Decisions have to be made about how often and for how long the measurements are made.
Making things or developing systems	Testing the accuracy and reliability of a new instrument, e.g. a pulse rate meter; testing the accuracy of thermometers; designing a method of measuring wind speed; make a circuit which will ring a bell when it begins to rain.

Figure 5.5.2 Types of investigations

Source: For classification of investigations used here see Watson *et al*. 1999: 62.

pupils would learn how to investigate just by doing investigations. What has become evident is that much more systematic teaching of what has become known as 'procedural knowledge' is required. Ideas for relevant teaching strategies have now been published (e.g. Sang and Wood-Robinson 2002; Goldsworthy and Feasey 1997; Goldsworthy *et al.* 2002a, 2002b; Watson 2000). Figure 5.5.4 gives examples of a selection of such strategies. Just as science teachers have to explain scientific concepts such as gravity and homeostasis they have to explain investigational concepts, such as validity, reliability, significant differences, independent and dependent variables, controlled variables.

Planning (P)
- finding an area of interest which is ripe for investigation;
- researching to find what others have found before;
- formulating a question so that it can be investigated;
- making some sort of prediction of what would be the outcome;
- deciding what data are needed to answer the question;
- deciding how to collect the data, and ensuring that they are valid;
- deciding which variables are to be controlled, if any;
- deciding which variables are to be changed (the independent variable), if any;
- deciding which variable is to be measured (the dependent variable).

Obtaining evidence (O)
- identifying and assembling the necessary equipment and tools to obtain the data;
- doing trial runs, and ironing out the difficulties;
- deciding on appropriate recording charts and tables;
- obtaining and recording data;
- deciding when sufficient data have been collected.

Analysing evidence (A)
- deciding whether transferring the data from a table to a pie chart, graph, or box plot, will enable patterns to be seen;
- looking for patterns in the data;
- using the patterns as evidence to answer the question and drawing a conclusion.

Evaluating (E)
- evaluating the strength of the evidence, by considering the reliability of the collecting techniques, the factors which were difficult to control, the accuracy of the measuring instruments, mistakes which might have been made;
- finding a way of expressing the answer to the original question, which reflects both the findings and the level of certainty of the findings.

Communicating
- writing a report of the research.

Figure 5.5.3 Steps in investigations categorised under National Curriculum headings (POAE)

Ask pupils to sort a collection of questions into those which are scientific questions and those which are not.

Give pupils a set of scientific questions and different ways of investigating, and ask them to match the questions to the appropriate method.

Ask pupils to critique accounts of invalid methods. These don't have to be in written form – you can always demonstrate an unfair test and ask pupils to spot the mistakes.

Provide sets of data and consider what different graphing techniques would be appropriate.

Provide sets of data with different interpretations, and ask pupils which interpretation fits the data best.

Provide other pupils' accounts for pupils to mark to a set of criteria.

Figure 5.5.4   Examples of teaching strategies which can be used to teach procedural knowledge needed for investigations

What do pupils find difficult about investigations?

There is a growing body of research into how pupils approach investigations and what they find difficult. Five aspects are worthy of further comment:

- identifying dependent, independent and controlled variables;
- the type of dependent and independent variables;
- the number of independent variables;
- the analysis and evaluation stages;
- the degree of openness of the investigation.

'Variable' is often taken to mean something which *does* change as opposed to something which *might* change, so this causes difficulty in the first place. Then the so-called 'independent variable' is the one which the investigator changes (so in another sense this variable is not independent of the investigator, another source of confusion!) The dependent variable gets its name from being *potentially* dependent on the independent variable (e.g. the current in a circuit is dependent on the resistance of the circuit). Controlled variables are ones which the investigator deliberately keeps the same (e.g. the voltage across the circuit, in the previous example). To distinguish the independent and dependent variables they are often referred to as 'what I change' (the resistance) and 'what I observe or measure' (the current) respectively. If, of course, the independent variable is quantitative then some measurement is involved in determining the different values to use, so using 'what I measure' will not, in pupils' minds, automatically identify the dependent variable.

There are three types of variables: categoric, discrete and continuous. Categoric variables are single categories such as colour, type of material, and are described in words; discrete variables are ones which come in whole numbers such as number of legs, number of layers; continuous variables can have any numerical value within a range such as temperature, weight, height. Pupils find it easier to deal with categoric, than with discrete variables; continuous variables are the most difficult. The types of variable, of course, determine the types of graph which can be drawn; for instance, using categoric independent variables but numerical dependent variables leads to bar charts (as in: which shoe is the most difficult to pull over the floor?); continuous variables lead to line graphs (as in: how is the volume of hydrogen produced per minute affected by the size of current?). If, of course, both dependent and independent variables are categoric (i.e. in which trees are spiders and mites found?), then no graph can be drawn.

Increasing the number of variables to be considered also increases difficulty. Asking pupils to study the effect of, say, 'surface area' *and* 'temperature difference between an object and its surroundings' (two independent variables) on the 'rate of cooling' (one dependent variable) is far more difficult than studying just the effect of one of the independent variables, say, surface area. It is not just a matter of its taking longer to do; many pupils who have not reached formal operational thinking cannot follow the logic of holding one variable constant at one point (e.g. keeping the temperature constant while they study surface area) and then changing it at the next. It is also possible to have investigations where there is more than one dependent variable, such as in an investigation into 'which liquid is the most viscous and the most transparent?' Here pupils would have to test for viscosity and transparency separately.

When it comes to analysing data and drawing conclusions there are several problems which frequently occur: the first is that pupils find it difficult to decide which data can be used to answer their original question; second they report the results again when writing a conclusion without any interpretation, the third is that they report what they expected to happen not what happened. Teachers need to give guidance by showing pupils how to 'interrogate data' first by looking for patterns. Questions such as 'Which is the highest, which is the lowest number?' 'Are the numbers increasing, decreasing, staying the same, or do they seem to change randomly?' 'Is there any number which is vastly different from the others?' are useful to help pupils look carefully at numerical data. Where graphs have been plotted, again practice is needed in interpreting graphs (see Goldsworthy *et al.* 2000a and Sang and Wood-Robinson 2002 for further guidance). When it comes to drawing of conclusions, pupils find it very difficult to make the switch from the description of patterns in data to a more generalised statement. To some extent it is a matter of language conventions. Sang *et al.* provide an example of '*The more turns on a wire the stronger is the electromagnet. The higher the current the stronger is the magnet*' being turned into '*The strength of the electromagnet depends on the number of turns and the size of the current. Generally the higher the current …*' (Sang and Wood-Robinson 2002: 83). In some investigations where it was not possible to control variables, pupils will be looking for correlations between two variables rather than cause and effect (e.g. as in 'What is the effect of temperature on the population of daphnia in a pond?') and their conclusions have to be couched in appropriate language.

I have made a point of highlighting the difficulty of analysis of data, as it is all too easy to have a busy practical lesson, where the class has just managed to complete the practical activity and pupils have a table of results, when the bell goes to signal the end of the lesson. The immediate reaction can so easily be 'For homework analyse the results and draw a conclusion'. This is unhelpful as the pupils are being sent to do what for them may be the most difficult part, unsupported.

Evaluation is as difficult as analysis. Here pupils have to think about accuracy and reliability of data. To estimate errors pupils have to be able to identify: the accuracy with which any parameter is measured (thermometers cannot for instance be read to less than half a degree); whether any results have to be discarded and why; situations where it is difficult to judge an end-point (e.g. when a chemical has completely dissolved); whether it is sensible to average all results, etc. They have to decide on the validity of data. If they were carrying out a fair test, the data will not be valid if they were unable to control variables sufficiently well. In investigations which required using a sample (e.g. ecological investigations) they will have to decide whether the sample size was adequate. Evaluation needs as much guidance and support as analysis.

The degree of openness of the investigation is determined by decisions which are left to the pupils. One technique which is commonly used to support decision making is providing prompt sheets. These can be written as a series of questions to be addressed as a checklist or as a writing frame with spaces. These 'props' will increasingly be removed the further pupils progress up the school. By Y12 when pupils are undertaking large investigations for Advanced Level courses they will be working relatively independently with only minimal support.

At this point we close the discussion on different types of practical work and turn to two issues which apply to all types, namely questions of safety and questions of teacher–pupil dialogue.

SAFETY ISSUES – RISK ASSESSMENT IN SCIENCE

Risk assessment in the workplace was first introduced as a requirement of the Control of Substances Hazardous to Health (COSHH) Regulations in 1988. Since then requirements have been updated and extended, and you need to be aware of the type of risk assessment needed for activities you do in school.

Teachers have a professional and legal responsibility for the safety of pupils in their care. During your training year, you will have support from the department and from the class teacher in making appropriate judgements. Concerns about safety have persuaded some teachers to abandon otherwise interesting practical work. This is not necessary as there is still a range of practical activities which can be done if pupils are taught to handle equipment properly and follow the necessary precautions. The most vulnerable are those who have never been allowed to try anything.

You are required to make a risk assessment of *every* practical activity which you do. This is a *legal* requirement. As a beginner, work with an experienced teacher to make a risk assessment. After you have done one or two, with support, write them on your own but check them with the class teacher well in advance. It is no good doing this ten minutes before the lesson. There are five factors which you will need to take into account when you undertake a risk assessment;

1   Inherent danger of materials and equipment;
2   Your own personal confidence with the materials and equipment;
3   Skills of the pupils;
4   Behaviour of the class and your ability to control it;
5   Precautions which can be put in place.

1 Inherent danger of materials

Inherent dangers of materials and equipment are clearly documented. Your department should have the Hazcards available from CLEAPSS (2000). Study these for any practical activity you do, even apparently simple ones, like making crystals from copper sulphate solution. Once you have read them consider whether, in the light of your ability to handle the class, there is likely to be a problem. If there is, find an alternative way of teaching or gain help from the class teacher.

2 Your own personal confidence and knowledge

If you are confident in handling materials and equipment and can explain the reasons for various precautions, then you are likely to conduct the practical work safely (and incidentally pass this knowledge on to pupils). Ignorance has been known to lead students to respond 'kindly' to requests from pupils to 'put in a larger piece of sodium' only to put everyone at risk from an accident.

3 Skills of the pupils

Do take into account the skills of the pupils, and adapt accordingly. Independence which you give to older pupils who are used to working in the laboratories you may not give to younger ones, who are more likely to be clumsy with equipment which is new or complex.

4 Behaviour of the class

Behaviour is a key factor. Activities which would be safe with one class, will not be with another.

5 Precautions

Frequently met hazards and precautions are given in Figure 5.5.5. DO NOT TAKE THIS AS A DEFINITIVE LIST; it provides merely a starter list. Use the figure only as an initial guide, you must follow it up with more detailed reading, for example see 'Risk assessment in science for secondary schools' (Borrows 2002). Publications with model risk assessments are available for use in school. Teachers and technicians refer to these publications and you must be familiar with them. Task 5.5.4 helps you to explore the risk assessment publications at your school and make a risk assessment.

	Sources of danger	Typical precautions
Clutter in the laboratory	Bags, coats, stools in gangways between the benches.	Stools, bags underneath the benches; places for coats need to be allocated.
Heating substances	Spitting or spills of hot liquids or solids; hot tripods, test tubes etc.; inflammable liquids; hair in flame; pupils being unused to handling fire.	Goggles worn (over eyes and not on some other part of head); you as a role model; pupils learn to turn Bunsen off as soon as chemicals spit; stand when doing practical work; test tubes not pointing to anyone; long hair tied back; luminous flame when Bunsen not in use; anticipate a level of excitement, or anxiety, in Y7 with flames.
Electrical equipment	Little danger from batteries; low voltage units are safe as school is required to have them checked on regular basis.	Dry hands when using mains equipment; no naked terminals on high tension units (used further up school).
Acids and alkalis	Alkalis cling to surfaces such as the eye; both can burn clothes and skin if strength and molarity are high.	Goggles worn; low molarity solutions used in lower school; small quantities only available.
Other chemicals	Toxic chemicals; chemicals which cause stains; highly flammable chemicals.	Check toxicity; use small quantities; keep control on stock bottles; some reactions can only be done in a fume cupboard.
Glassware	Chipped or broken glassware.	Check all glassware; container for broken glass; teacher to clear breakages.
Biological material	Toxicity; infections from animals/animal parts; allergies; cultures of microbes.	Check toxicity of any plant material; cultures of microbes to be sealed – some cultures not permitted.
Sharp instruments	Scalpels, knives and pointers can easily cut the skin.	Restricted use; safety corks on the end.

Figure 5.5.5 Common hazards and precautions

Task 5.5.4
Making a risk assessment

- List the publications used for making risk assessments in your science department.
- Briefly note how risk assessments and warnings are included within:
  - science department policy,
  - schemes of work and lesson plans,
  - pupil worksheets and textbooks.

For a practical activity you observe, write out your own risk assessment in detail, stating where you obtained information about the nature of the hazards involved (e.g. Hazcards).

TEACHER–PUPIL DIALOGUES: HELPING PUPILS TO THINK AS WELL AS DO, IN PRACTICAL WORK

The importance of teacher–pupil dialogue in relation to practical work has already been stressed. The last task in this unit is a planning activity which will help you prepare for both monitoring of practical work and engaging in appropriate dialogue. There are two sheets: Figure 5.5.6a and Figure 5.5.6b, and their role in planning is explained in Task 5.5.5. By way of an example, the sheets have been completed for a simple Y7 activity on techniques of separation.

Task 5.5.5
Planning dialogues for practical work

For any practical activity which you are to do, complete section 1 (Figure 5.5.6a) by deciding the type of practical work and its purpose. Then break down the practical task into its separate parts (or actions) and list these in part 2a (do not confuse these with the parts of the lesson, focus just on the practical work). Complete column 2b, giving the scientific reasons for each of the steps in the practical work. In column 2c record the criteria for good performance for each step (i.e. think here what you would expect to see or hear if pupils are doing the task well).

Now create questions in column 3a (Figure 5.5.6b). Try to relate these to the reasons in column 2b, and then anticipate answers at two levels (record these in 3b). This planning enables you to prepare conversations you might have with pupils.

After the lesson evaluate the effect of this more detailed planning on your ability to notice the levels of skills your pupils have, the way they were thinking about the science and your ability to make effective use of your and the pupils' time.

Title of practical activity	*Purifying rock salt*	
1 Type of practical work (underline)		
a illustration		
b exercise		
c investigation		
d other		

Learning outcomes: *pupils should be able to carry out a procedure to purify rock salt, and to evaluate how successful the procedure has been.*

2a Actions	2b Reasons for actions	2c Criteria for good performance
Weigh rock salt.	*To enable calculations of how successful the student have been at removing salt.*	*Weigh accurately to one decimal place.*
Dissolve in approx. 50 cm³ of water.	*To separate the salt from the rock.*	*Dissolve the salt in an appropriate amount of water; stirring to ensure all has been dissolved.*
Filter mixture.	*To remove the rock from the solution.*	*Remove all the rock from the solution leaving a clear liquid. No spills. No prodding of the mixture in filter funnel.*
Weigh residue.	*To enable calculations of how much salt should have been removed.*	*Weigh accurately to one decimal place.*
Evaporate solution.	*To remove the water from, the solution to leave the salt behind.*	*No spills. Remove all of the water without losing the salt by its 'spitting' out of dish.*
Weigh salt left.	*To enable calculations of what percentage of salt was removed and to see how successful the pupils have been.*	*Weigh accurately to one decimal place.*

Figure 5.5.6a Planning for practical work, pupils' performance

Students who have used this planning sheet in the past have reported that they have had a much more explicit framework in their heads concerning both the doing and the thinking parts of the lesson. They were thus in a better position to notice what was occurring in the lessons and adapt accordingly. They also found that conversations which were started *before* the practical work, fed into discussions *during* the practical work, and in turn led smoothly to the discussion of results *afterwards*.

EVALUATING YOUR PLANNING OF PRACTICAL WORK

In order to pull together all the ideas in this unit to guide your planning, Figure 5.5.7 gives a checklist of questions to ask yourself to make sure you are fully ready for practical lessons.

Plan five questions you could ask (or alternatives to questions – e.g. 'tell me about ...') in order to engage pupils in conversations about the science involved in the practical work. Decide what responses you would want from your class.

3a Questions (or alternatives to questions)	3b Expected answers (at two different levels)
How much did your rock salt weigh?	• *About 3 grams.* • *2.9 grams*
Why do we weigh the rock salt? (and again for each of the other weighing procedures).	• *So we can tell how much we've got.* • *So we can calculate how much salt we should have got and how much we actually got.*
Why do we dissolve the rock salt in water?	• *To separate the rock and salt.* • *Because the salt dissolves but rock doesn't so we can separate them.*
Why do we filter the solution?	• *To remove the rock.* • *Because the dissolved salt can pass through filter paper but the rock can't.*
Why do we heat the solution?	• *To remove the water.* • *Because the water will evaporate but salt doesn't, so the salt will be left behind.*

Figure 5.5.6b Planning for practical work, teacher–pupil dialogue

SUMMARY

Practical work for up to 30 pupils requires a lot of organisation and attention to matters of safety. These factors will dominate your thinking when you first start using practical work. It is important, however, that you analyse the roles that practical work plays in learning of science and make the time spent as productive as possible. To do this, you need to decide whether you are using illustrative practical work, exercises or investigations. Planning discussions to have with students alongside planning what they will do will increase the chances of their learning from the practical work.

Summary of questions to check planning of a class practical lesson:

- Have I done the practical myself beforehand?
- What is the purpose of the activity? What are the learning outcomes which I want? How will I explain the purpose?
- Will the pupils work on their own, in pairs or a larger group?
- How much apparatus will I need? Does the school have enough? If not, this may mean altering group size.
- Have the laboratory technicians been given the list in sufficient time for them to prepare what I want?
- What are the associated risks?
- How will I distribute the equipment? Are there some items which I will distribute myself (for safety, or equity reasons)?
- How will I give instructions of what to do? Orally? By demonstration? By written instruction? By pictorial instruction?
- What decisions will I leave to the pupils?
- How will pupils record observations? Do they make a table for results, or do I give them one?
- What would be 'good performance' for this age group?
- What will I talk about with pupils while they are doing the practical work?
- How long do they need?
- How do I stop the practical work? How and when should pupils clear up? Can chemicals go down the sink? If not, where do they go?
- How do I ensure all the equipment has come in? How do I make a record of numbers of items at the start?
- Do I need to collect class results? If so, how and when?
- What is the science I want to draw out of it? How do I do that?
- How long will this take?
- Do pupils need to write a report of the activity?
- What follow-up activity is there which will enable pupils to consolidate their new knowledge by applying it?

Figure 5.5.7 Questions for evaluating planning of class practical work

FURTHER READING

Borrows, P. (2002) 'Risk assessment in science for secondary schools', in S. Amos and R. Boohan (eds) *Aspects of Teaching Secondary Science*, London: RoutledgeFalmer for the Open University, 84–94. Peter Borrows has written on matters of safety for many years, and provides a measured response to those who delight in telling you that is too dangerous ever to contemplate doing anything in school laboratories.

Lubben, F. and Millar, R. (1996) 'Children's ideas about the reliability of experimental data' *International Journal of Science Education*, 18(8): 955-68. This paper and the 1994 paper below are reports of some of the findings of the PACKS project (Procedural and Conceptual Knowledge in Science) which explored children's ideas about investigation procedures. They provide useful insights into children's thinking in investigations and their approaches to them.

Millar, R., Lubben, F., Gott, R. and Duggan, S. (1994) 'Investigating in the school science laboratory: conceptual and procedural knowledge and their influence on performance', *Research Papers in Education*, 9(2): 207–48.

Parkinson, J. (2004) *Improving Secondary Science Teaching*, London: RoutledgeFalmer, Chapter 9, 'Learning through practical work'. This book is written for serving teachers. Once you are confident in organising practical work you will find this is valuable to help you improve the learning which comes from practical work and understand relevant research evidence.

Wellington, J. (1998) *Practical Work in School Science: Which Way Now?* London: Routledge. This collection of articles provides a range of very different perspectives on school practical work. I would particularly recommend that you read the first two articles in the book (one by Jerry Wellington and one by Robin Millar) and then delve into any of the others which particularly interest you. One article which not only questions the role of practical work but gives alternatives is: Osborne, J. 'Science Education without a Laboratory?' (156–73).

AKSIS Project

Goldsworthy, A., Watson, R. and Wood-Robinson, V. (2000a) *Getting to Grips with Graphs: From Bar Charts to Lines of Best Fits*, Hatfield: ASE.

Goldsworthy, A., Watson, R. and Wood-Robinson, V. (2000b) *Developing Understanding in Scientific Inquiry*, Hatfield: ASE.

Watson, R., Goldsworthy, A. and Wood-Robinson, V. (2000) *Targetted Learning: Using Classroom Assessment for Learning*, Hatfield: ASE.

ASE Book

reference like this

Sang D. and Wood-Robinson V. (eds) (2002) *Teaching Secondary Scientific Enquiry*, London: John Murray for the ASE.

Collins Science Investigations Books 1, 2 & 3

Gott, R., Foulds, K., Jones, M., Johnson, P. and Roberts, R. (1997) *Science Investigations 1*, London: Collins Educational.

Gott, R., Foulds, K., Jones, M., Johnson, P. and Roberts, R. (1998) *Science Investigations 2*, London: Collins Educational.

Gott, R., Foulds, K., Roberts, R., Jones, M. and Johnson, P. (1999) *Science Investigations 3*, London: Collins Educational.

These three sets of resources have lots of information about teaching investigations.

6 Selecting and Using Resources

Finding resources is not so much a problem of availability as one of excess, which brings with it the problem of suitability and selection. There are, for example, good textbook resources available that address each year of schooling, each key stage and examination specification. The growth of resources on the Internet has been dramatic and materials suitable for a wide range of pupils are available.

We have interpreted 'resources' quite widely but focused on resources with which pupils can engage actively in the process of learning science. The first unit focuses initially on language resources, because of the important role language plays in the process of learning science. Language shapes the way we think and understand. Science has its own language and pupils need to gain access to it as a resource for their learning. Language extends beyond the written word to diagrams and texts. Scientific ideas are expressed also in models which can be a powerful learning tool especially for visual learners.

Unit 6.1 concludes with use of ICT in learning science. ICT resources constitute one of the most rapidly expanding categories of resources. They are often attractive and beguiling but must be evaluated for the extent to which they contribute to learning. Guidance is given on criteria for selection and use. Two requisites are, of course, essential: first reliable hardware and software and second your own skills in using them.

Unit 6.2 focuses on resources for science which are available outside the school, in the school grounds, in the locality or further afield. These resources help link science to the everyday world. The unit addresses the advantages and disadvantages of taking pupils outside and the wider range of management and organisational skills which are needed. Obviously there are issues of health and safety and risk assessments are as essential here as they are in practical work.

Both units draw attention to the need for you to select resources that meet the needs of your pupils and promote learning. If active learning is valued then a transmission model of teaching will not support that judgement. The way you select and use resources reflects both the model you have of learning and the role of the teacher in that model.

Unit 6.1

Resources – Language, Models and ICT

Jenny Frost

INTRODUCTION

'How do you teach the heart/cells/particle theory?' 'Have you got any good ideas for films, activities for pupils?' 'Any good animations/websites?' 'How do you explain …?' 'I know it myself but don't know where to start …' 'What are they likely to know already?' 'What models are there I could use?' 'Are there any useful posters?' 'What do pupils find difficult?'

Suitable resources are an important component of good teaching. Anyone new to teaching asks questions like those above when faced with teaching a new topic. With the advent of email groups, information about good resources are sought and shared more than any other aspect of teaching. Personal recommendation is important. First, it means that someone whom you know and can trust has tried out the resource and found it worked well. Second, there is such a wealth of resources available 'out there' that time for searching and evaluating is just not available. Experienced teachers, even those good at ferreting out resources, still rely very much on word of mouth recommendation from colleagues. Take the opportunity which your training year gives you for making and collecting resources. You are able to watch a lot of science lessons and hence see resources in action, and you have time to make resources which can be used another year. Once a resource works well, keep copies, make sets of cards and laminate them, retain good overhead transparencies etc.

LANGUAGE RESOURCES

Decisions about what to select, or how to construct resources, while partly made on pragmatic grounds, should also be influenced by theoretical perspectives, such as those concerned with cognitive development discussed in Unit 5.1, or those concerned with different pupil motivations and learning styles discussed in Unit 5.4. Here an additional theoretical perspective is provided based on the role of language in learning.

LEARNING SCIENCE IS LEARNING A NEW LANGUAGE

Learning science is about entering into a scientific discourse, and learning to share both the language and assumptions of those who are already familiar with the discourse. Every science teacher is invariably a teacher of language, because they are teaching pupils to write about science, read about science, talk about science and listen to other people talking about science. The role of language goes much deeper; because language acquisition is inextricably linked to formation of ideas. 'Thought requires language and language requires thought ... difficulty with language causes difficulty with reasoning' (Wellington and Osborne 2001: 6).

Some appreciation of the nature of the language and discourse conventions of science (not just the technical terms and their definitions) is necessary for understanding the nature of the learning involved and the relevant resources. Think first about the nouns which are used in science explanations. They have been classified in Figure 6.1.1 into three groups, naming words, process words and concept words.

The naming words are the simplest to acquire, because they relate mostly to objects which can be seen. It does not mean that these words will be learned quickly, because people take time to learn new names and use them routinely. Resources which are useful are of course the objects themselves, or models of them or photographs of them. Resources which help memorise the words are vocabulary lists, posters with drawings and words, exercises where words are matched to pictures, diagrams to be labelled from key words, and of course being in an environment where the words are routinely used. As pupils learn more about the different objects the naming words move towards the concept words. The word 'heart', for instance, moves from the label for one particular object, to a label for a

---

Naming words – nouns which give the names of objects which can be seen;

spiders, ants, thermometer, battery, ammeter, measuring cylinder, crude oil, coal, rust, metal, heart, eyes, chlorine, sodium …

Process words – nouns which refer to a process;

dissolving, life cycle, respiration, cooling, evaporation, energy transfer, heating, radiation, transpiration, germination, photosynthesis, osmosis, diffusion, chemical reactions, erosion, homeostasis, carbon cycle, Krebb's cycle, evolution, plate tectonics …

Concept words – nouns referring to abstract concepts;

electrons, atoms, ions, molecules, polymers, entropy, energy, density, force, pressure, acceleration, velocity, enzymes, species, habitat, community, population density …

Figure 6.1.1 Categories of nouns
Source: Adapted from Wellington and Osborne 2001: 22.

range of objects which pump blood, so that it can be used for things as widely different in size and shape as the heart of a cow and the heart of a daphnia.

The process words are ones which involve a sequence of events. Some refer to processes which occur in a relatively short space of time, such as dissolving or freezing, which can be demonstrated easily. Others take place over a long period, such as erosion. Some, such as evolution, not only take place over a long time, but also rely on a great deal of theoretical knowledge to understand them. Timelines, and diagrams with arrows, are used to represent many of the processes (see Figure 4.5.1 for an example).

For the concept words there is a need to make 'entities', such as atoms, energy, etc., seem real in the first place, and having done that to use them in explanations as if they were as real as the objects in the naming words list. Teachers have, for instance, to make the idea of an atom seem real and then use it in the explanation of differences between elements and compounds. They persuade pupils to imagine unseen entities 'I want you to imagine it is like this …', they use physical models to help make the 'imagining' more concrete. They use analogies: 'imagine electrons in a wire as a set of railway trucks all linked together …' They use simplifications to help pupils focus on the most important features 'Imagine your digestive system like a tube of Polos … a hole down the middle …'. This repertoire of analogies and models forms an important resource on which teachers can draw.

Words associated with investigations

To these words we must add words and phrases associated with investigations. A helpful list is given in the Key Stage 3 strategies folder in Appendix 3 (DfES 2002b: 73–5). Here is a short list to start: *accurate, average, pattern, anomalous result, correlation, data logger, line of best fit, reliability, survey, sampling, sufficient data, trial run* … (see Unit 5.5 for relevant resources for this area of the curriculum.)

Connecting words, verbs, adjectives

Science is about causal relationships, which have their own language conventions, particularly in the use of connecting words and phrases.

- '*Because* the lungs expand, the pressure goes down, *consequently* …'
- 'Carbon is not a metal, *but nevertheless*, it conducts …'

There is a vast array of verbs which are used to describe events:

- 'The liquid *effervesces*'
- 'The diode *emits* light'
- 'Copper *accumulates* on the anode …'
- 'Hydrogen *is liberated* at the cathode …'

There are adjectives and adjectival phrases …

- 'The decay of radioactive material is *random* …'
- 'The difference in the temperatures is *negligible* …'
- 'This is *comparable to* what happens in …
- This material is *translucent/transparent/opaque* …'

Almost none of these words is part of the everyday language of most pupils even though they are not solely scientific words. They can therefore act as a barrier to learning if a teacher is not aware of the difficulties they may cause.

Scientific words with everyday meanings

Science also uses many everyday words which are given a specialised meaning. 'Properties of materials' does not, for instance, mean 'the houses owned by the rolls of cloth'. Collect your own list of words which have both scientific and everyday meanings to add to this starter list: *plant, animal, energy, pressure, force, dense, material, features, property, characteristic, field, circuit, compound, power, current* …

Reflect on your own facility with such everyday/scientific words. You judge the meaning of a word from the context, and have no trouble in switching your meaning of, say, 'power', in a scientific context (joules per second) to its meaning in a political context. Think of words which pupils use quite easily in different contexts ('cool' for instance) and make explicit this use of the same word to mean different ideas, so that pupils become aware that it is not so odd to have the same word with different meanings.

For a fuller discussion of the different words used in science and difficulties which pupils have with them, see Wellington and Osborne (2001: 9–23). Either using the limited introduction I have given above on language, or the more detailed account in Wellington and Osborne, identify the scientific vocabulary and language conventions being used in different classes in your school (Task 6.1.1).

The discussion on language is important for several reasons:

- language is one of the most important resources for learning;
- the discussion raises awareness of the nature of language and discourse with which pupils are learning to engage;

Task 6.1.1
Listening to scientific language

1   When listening to a class record the vocabulary that is being used.
     Record in short bursts of say 5 minutes at a time, switching from
     listening to the teacher and then listening to the pupils.

     Words used by the teacher
     •   scientific nouns;
     •   scientific verbs;
     •   connecting words;
     •   scientific adjectives.

     Words used by the pupils
     •   scientific nouns;
     •   scientific verbs;
     •   connecting words;
     •   scientific adjectives.

2   Use the classification in Figure 6.1.1 to classify the nouns which have
     been used.
3   List any words which have both scientific and everyday meanings.
4   Make a comparison between the teacher's and the pupils' language.
5   If possible observe the same teacher with a class of a different age (if
     you can switch from Y7 to Y13, this would be ideal). Compare the
     language use of both pupils and teacher in the different classes.
6   Use the guide to progression in oral skills in Wellington and Osborne
     (2001: 39) to recognise the skills of the different age groups.

- it alerts teachers to the need to develop ways of introducing pupils to different language conventions which are central to a scientific discourse;
- it alerts teachers to the need for providing opportunities for pupils to learn and practise the language;
- it encourages teachers to be careful in their own use of language in writing for pupils, in asking pupils to write, in selecting reading for them and talking with them.

Central to many of the ideas for resources for science is that pupils must be *actively* involved in construction of their ideas through reading, talking and writing. The book on which I have drawn already, *Language and Literacy in Science Education* (Wellington and Osborne 2001), contains a rich variety of language-related tasks. What follows below is a guide to this resource.

RESOURCES FOR READING

Reading material which is used in science more often than not falls into one of the following categories:

- instructions (how to do a practical activity);
- structure text and pictures (explaining the structure of things);

- mechanism text and pictures (explaining how something works);
- process text and pictures (explaining a process);
- concept–principle (explaining a concept or principle);
- hypothesis–theory (explaining a hypothesis and a theory).

Pupils need considerable help in using different texts and learning to extract information from them. Pictures may need as much deciphering as words; pictures are as much about language as text. Tasks which constitute *active* reading come into two categories:

- deconstruction of a complete text;
- reconstruction of a broken text.

In both cases the reader has to do something with the text other than just read it. Deconstruction exercises might be:

- drawing a concept map or spider diagram to summarise a complex text;
- underlining key ideas;
- extracting specific information in response to questions;
- summarising a paragraph in one sentence;
- tabulating information;
- rewriting for a different audience.

Reconstruction exercises are ones created by presenting learners with text which has been broken up in some way. This may be:

- diagrams which have labels missing;
- texts with gaps in them;
- jumbled sentences which have to be re-ordered (e.g. instructions for a practical activity in the wrong order);
- a set of statements which have to be put together in a flow chart;
- sentences which have to be made up from separate elements;
- incomplete text where the last paragraph has been taken out and pupils have to predict what it will be.

All these activities are referred to as DARTs (Directed Activities Related to Text). They require pupils to go to texts with a specific purpose, and have much in common with good study techniques which you will have used for note making when extracting information from texts and for revision purposes when you are trying to discover what you understand.

Figure 6.1.2 provides a set of prompts to support pupils extracting information from the rock cycle flow chart in Figure 4.5.1.

While the texts available for science mostly conform to the types listed above, there are 'narrative' texts and newspapers which may form a resource for science teaching. 'Narrative' texts such as the popular science books written for the general public weave a science story round some narrative. Unlike standard science texts they rarely have diagrams or pictures, but tell the story in words. They may include the people involved (for instance the story of Harrison in his attempt to solve the longitude problem (Sobel, 1996)). While as they stand they may well be good 'readers' for those doing A level science, extracts can be used to set the scene for science lessons about particular scientists or discoveries or be the basis of a DART.

Newspaper reports are discussed as a resource in Unit 8.1 particularly for debates on social and ethical issues. Whether you are using them to stimulate debate, or for a source of

Study the picture of the rock cycle

1   What does precipitation mean?
2   What does cementation mean?
3   What is magma?
4   What are the names of the three main groups of rocks?
5   List three factors which cause weathering and erosion of rocks.
6   What is the difference between transportation and deposition?
7   How do rocks become buried?
8   How do rocks which are formed underground reach the surface?
9   Why do rocks melt when they get far under the surface?
10 Which rocks are formed by crystallisation?
11 Now write three paragraphs to explain the picture of the rock cycle.

Figure 6.1.2 Prompts to support 'reading' the flow chart in Figure 4.5.1

information, they need to be read actively, and lend themselves to deconstruction activities. It is difficult to provide generic questions for a newspaper article but the following provide a possible selection:

- Why does it seem to be a newsworthy item? Why has it been written now?
- What are the facts reported?
- What is the evidence on which the article is based?
- How was the evidence collected?
- What conclusions does the writer come to?
- What relevance does it have for you?
- Do the title and article convey the same message? (they often do not.)

Before you tackle Task 6.1.2, on creating your own DART, discuss with the teachers responsible for supporting pupils with special educational needs (SEN) and pupils for whom English is an additional language (EAL), what sort of texts, layouts and pictures are accessible to the age group you have in mind.

Task 6.1.2
Creating your own DART

1   Read pp. 45–62 of Wellington and Osborne 2001, and review their samples of DARTs.
2   Collect a range of DARTs which you have used, or seen used in school. What type of DARTs are they? Is there a range or are they all the same, e.g. text completion where words have been omitted?
3   Construct a new type of DART to be used in your next topic, in four forms, one for pupils with special educational needs, one for pupils who have limited English, one for middle-attaining pupils and one for the high achievers.
4   Discuss your DART with your science mentor, with the special needs coordinator in the school and the teacher responsible for pupils with EAL.

RESOURCES FOR DISCUSSION IN SCIENCE

Sorting out ideas through discussion is an important way of learning. Many DARTs can be, and most usually are, done as collaborative activities in pairs or small groups and hence become a resource for discussion.

Other ideas for generating discussion come from the research into children's ideas in science (e.g. in Driver *et al.* 1994). Alternative conceptions are presented and pupils have to discuss which ones are right. These come in several forms, concept cartoons, true/false tables, sets of cards to be sorted, or multiple choice questions.

Concept cartoons enable pupils to distance themselves from the speakers and to discuss why one idea might be better than another. The teacher may have to play the role of devil's advocate, to help start discussion, or may have to act as a support to help pupils marshal their arguments. Some cartoons (see Figure 5.1.1) can be followed up easily by a practical investigation while the one in Figure 6.1.3 cannot be. How the teacher follows it up depends on the class, the prior knowledge of the class, the facilities, the time available, the purpose for which the teacher used the cartoon in the first place. The teacher may provide the

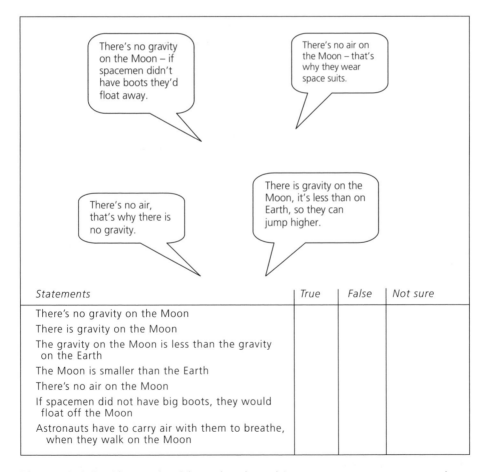

Figure 6.1.3 Alternative ideas developed into a concept cartoon and into a true/false table

explanation responding to the questions and puzzles which arose, hence resolving the apparent inconsistencies. See Naylor and Keogh (2000) for a collection of concept cartoons.

Another approach which encourages pupils to review evidence for different ideas (an important component of NCSc1) has been developed in a research project at King's College, London, in what is referred to as 'argumentation in science'. This involves pupils discussing evidence for supporting different ideas. Theories are presented along with evidence and pupils have to argue about which evidence best fits a particular theory. Four examples are given in Wellington and Osborne (2001: 92–4). Figure 6.1.4 shows the astronaut and Moon ideas developed into such a task. A fuller account of the thinking behind the project, further examples which could be used, and the associated pedagogy, are described in an article in *School Science Review* (Osborne *et al.* 2001). An inservice pack, including a video of argumentation being implemented in classrooms, is available from King's College, London (Osborne *et al.* 2004). Try Task 6.1.3 as part of your teaching.

See Unit 8.1 for running discussions on contentious social and ethical issues.

Interpretation of data is another source of discussion material. While we often associate this with the discussion of pupils' own results, there is value in having sets of data which have been generated elsewhere.

The oral activities considered so far have involved small group work or debates. Another useful oral exercise is presentation of ideas to the whole class. This can work well if pupils have researched different aspects of the same topic and then pooled ideas, e.g. you could have different groups researching different planets or researching the properties of different materials.

In pairs, study the evidence below about people walking on the Moon. One member 'adopts' theory 1 and one member adopts theory 2. What evidence supports your theory? Argue for your theory with your partner.

Evidence

- The Moon orbits the Earth.
- The Moon orbits the Sun.
- The Moon is smaller than the Earth.
- There is no air on the Moon.
- Astronauts who walked on the Moon carried air supplies with them.
- Astronauts jumped higher on the Moon than on the Earth.
- Astronauts wore space suits when they walked on the Moon.

Theory 1
The Moon does not have a gravitational pull.

Theory 2
The Moon does have a gravitational pull.

Figure 6.1.4 An argumentation task

WRITING FOR LEARNING SCIENCE

The act of writing is a form of discovery. It helps shape ideas. This should be one of, if not *the*, main reason pupils are asked to write – not just, as is so often said, 'so that you have

**Task 6.1.3
Planning a discussion
activity**

When you are familiar with the resources for group discussions plan a
lesson using one of the following as stimulus material for discussion:

- concept cartoons;
- competing theories;
- anomalous data;
- controversial issues.

where pupils draw on evidence to support their position within the
discussion. Evaluate the lesson, focusing on the learning outcomes gained
from the discussion activity.

something to revise from'. There are conventions of written language as there are of spoken
language. Writing in science is essentially non-fiction. The KS3 literacy strategy (DfES
2001) identified eight different types of non-fictional writing. These are listed in Figure
6.1.5.

Think back to your own school days and identify what sort of writing in science you
did. Which were the types you used most often? Now look at what is being done in your
present school (Task 6.1.4) to consider to which areas of non-fiction writing science lessons
contribute.

If pupils are to become competent in using the different writing modes they need
guidance in understanding the different conventions of each type of writing, support in
adopting them and opportunities for practising them. One such form of support comes in
what are known as 'writing frames'. Writing frames are documents which highlight the key

- **Information** – writing which describes how things are in a logical order.

- **Instruction** – writing which describes how a task should be carried out.

- **Explanation** – writing which explains the process involved or how things work.

- **Persuasion** – writing which argues for a particular point of view.

- **Recount** – writing which presents events in chronological order.

- **Discussion** – writing which presents different points of view.

- **Analysis** – writing which examines, for example, statements or data and makes
a reasoned response.

- **Evaluation** – writing which describes the strengths and weaknesses of, for
example, an experimental procedure.

Figure 6.1.5 Types of non-fiction writing identified in the KS3 literacy
strategy

Task 6.1.4
Identifying types of non-fiction
writing used in school science

- Which sort of writing (use the list in Figure 6.1.5) do you most commonly see in pupils' books?
- Identify the characteristics of the style in terms of tense and language used. The following article will be useful. Staples, R. and Heselden, R. (2001) 'Science teaching and literacy, part 1: Writing', *School Science Review*, 83 (303): 35–46.
- Create a writing task which fits any of the types which are missing.

features which have to be addressed. Many schools have them for investigations. Wellington and Osborne (2001: 69-74) offer four others, namely:

- a frame for supporting the writing of reports;
- a frame for writing explanations;
- a frame for writing up experiments;
- a frame to support an argument.

As well as thinking about the type of non-fictional writing, think carefully about the 'voice' in which you expect pupils to write. Progression to the transactional writing of science needs support. Figure 6.1.6 shows the sort of transition which pupils are expected to make as they progress up the school.

Provide pupils with different audiences for their writing. There is a tendency for science writing to be done for the teacher as an adjudicator. Do pupils ever write instructions for a younger child? Do they ever write a science newspaper or newsletter? Do they ever exchange their findings with people in another school or with people in another country? Do they prepare posters of projects which inform parents about the work they have been doing? Do they write collaborative posters? Are they ever asked to write in a genre more associated with fiction: write poems; imagine being a red blood cell and write about a day in your life; imagine what life would be like without electricity; write a story about being part of a space mission. Whatever you do, expect the transition from personal to transactional writing to be slow, but like any other learning, it can be helped if you make the learning explicit and do not expect it to happen on its own.

- Personal writing
  I ground up the rock salt. I poured water on it. I then filtered it. I then heated it and it dried up and salt was left behind.

- Transactional writing
  Salt can be extracted from rock salt by the successive processes of dissolving, filtration and evaporation.

Figure 6.1.6 Transition from personal to transactional scientific writing

LEARNING FROM MODELS

Models form another important resource for science teachers. Pupils can learn *from* models, but they need also to learn *about* models, because modelling is intrinsic to science. Models are not the real thing – but an aid to help focus on particular aspects of an object or phenomenon. Parkinson (2002) defines four types of models: *scale models*, such as biological models, of the eye, the ear, kidneys, human bodies; *analogue models*, such as atomic and molecular models, or a string of beads representing electrons in an electric current; *mathematical models* which allow people to manipulate a situation and find out what will happen if parameters are changed; and *theoretical models* which bring together a range of experiences and theories such as plate tectonics, the existence of quarks, the theory of evolution.

Encourage pupils to think about the limitations of the model, so that they become familiar with the function of models as an aid to thinking. With scale models, such as models of the eye and ear, this is relatively easy. It is helpful for instance for pupils to decide how big they think the real thing is. You will be surprised how many have images of the size of the middle and inner ear big enough to stretch across the whole of their heads. Analogue models have their limitations – light is sometimes modelled as a wave and sometimes as a particle. Mathematical models, so much a favourite of physics but used in all sciences, are always idealised cases. Pulley systems never in reality provide the mechanical advantage they theoretically should because the model fails to take account of the friction of the pulley wheels and the weight of the strings. Rabbits only approximately breed to an exponential law, even when there are sufficient resources available. Nevertheless, mathematical models form a powerful tool. Theoretical models are inevitably large generalisations of very complex processes, and incorporate a multitude of evidence and theorising. What is important here is to help pupils recognise the leap of imagination which has occurred in creating the models in the first place, and the arguments which go towards supporting the model.

Modelling as a means of learning

Model making can be a powerful learning tool. There are physical models, such as making a model of a biological cell (from a polythene bag and jelly), or of the digestive system (out of junk material), or of the structure of the Earth (out of different coloured plasticene) or of sedimentation, uplift and erosion (layers of plasticene, which can be bent and 'eroded'). Model making, like drawing, slows people down, and makes them think more carefully about the thing they are modelling. It often generates questions which can be answered from information sources. Modelling can be a 'pencil and paper' activity – such as 'design an animal which will survive in a particular habitat'.

Role play is a form of modelling and is useful for many of the 'process nouns' listed at the start because pupils can act out what is happening. Possible role plays of this type are listed in Figure 6.1.7. The role plays involve moving parts. The availability of animations on video or CD-ROM provide alternative resources, may not involve the same active participation of role plays.

Energy transfer in an electric circuit. A circle of pupils move round, collecting energy tokens from the battery and transferring them to the outside when they get to the bulb.

Diffusion of one gas into another. Pupils with two different coloured blindfolds. They start in two separate groups, but then are told to wander randomly in a confined space. Periodic views of the mixing which is occurring shows the progressive mixing and the eventual even distribution of the two colours.

Passage of the red cells round the body, collecting and releasing gases. Some pupils play the blood cells. One acts as the heart, one as the lungs and one as the body (you can elaborate this and have one for brain and head and one for rest of body, etc.). Tokens of carbon dioxide and oxygen are exchanged at appropriate places and the heart merely pushes them on in the right direction.

Figure 6.1.7 Suggestions of role plays to model different ideas and processes in science

ICT RESOURCES

The extensive use of ICT in schools is only realistic where there are good facilities and good technical support. Explore early on what hardware there is in school and what you have to do to book it for classes. You may find suites of computers in separate computer rooms or you may find one or two computers in each laboratory. Find out what presentation facilities there are such as data projectors and screens. Have interactive whiteboards been installed? Find out what software has been purchased for science and whether it has been installed on the schools' network or only on stand-alone computers.

Think about the purposes to which you will put ICT. Figure 6.1.8 gives such a summary of the main functions of computer systems in learning. It is adapted from a similar list in Rogers and Finlayson (2003).

Purpose	Details and resources
Information gathering	using Internet browsers and multimedia CD-ROMs
Practical work	using sensors, interfaces, data-logging software
Simulations	virtual experiments and visual aids, stimulating and helping explain phenomena
Data handling	spreadsheets and graphing software (e.g. Excel, Information Workshop), searching ready made databases
Use of mathematical models	exploring relationships, predicting and testing theories using packages such as Excel, Modellus
Communication	Word processing packages, *PowerPoint*, publishing, web authoring, digital capture of photographs and images

Figure 6.1.8 ICT learning activities in science

Information gathering

The rules discussed earlier in the unit for gathering information from texts apply equally well to information gathering from web sites and CD-ROMs. Pupils need a carefully constructed task to prevent them wandering vaguely through sites. They need specific questions, either ones you have generated or, better still, ones which they have generated themselves. Most sites are heavily text based, so select ones which are suitable for your particular class and for the particular learning objectives. Sites with few pictures, no animations, no means of interaction will not hold attention for long. Find sites and CD-ROMs which are easy to navigate, and which include video clips, good animations, search facilities and quizzes to test what has been learned. Check the level of interaction of the sites using as a simple guide:

- low interaction – browsing and reading only;
- medium interaction – with some tasks but only 'click and reveal';
- high interaction – tasks involve forms/multi-choice with answers, email access to authors;
- very high – communication, active participation.

Try sites and CD-ROMs yourself. If you find them difficult to use, then so will pupils. Always compare the use of a CD-ROM or website with a more traditional resource and decide whether using ICT will be more effective.

Practical work – data logging and control

Data logging involves replacing measuring devices, such as thermometers, by a sensor and replacing people recording results and drawing a graph, by a computer. In deciding to use data logging, therefore, you have to be convinced that there are real educational values to be gained from taking a sensor, computer with its relevant software, and interface unit (this connects between the sensor and the computer) into the laboratory instead of just, say, a simple thermometer with a pencil and paper. Data logging also covers devices called 'data loggers' which log (collect and store) data away from the computer. The data can be downloaded onto the computer at a later time. This can be useful, say, for recording temperature fluctuations over an extended period out in the field.

If schools have only one set of data logging equipment then it has to be used either for demonstration (where a big screen is necessary so everyone can see) or as a component of a circus of activities. Where there are class sets of lap top computers, sensors and interfaces, then the data logging can be done as a whole class activity.

There is a wide range of sensors now available, and a selection of the reasonably common ones are given below in Figure 6.1.9.

The guidance given about practical work in Unit 5.5 applies here, especially about trying it out beforehand. Find out, for instance, if your temperature sensors give the same readings as a conventional thermometer for temperature of boiling water, or the temperature of icy water. In fact, trialling data-logging equipment can form a useful investigation in its own right. I recently tried out a new pulsemeter which appeared to fluctuate wildly, giving apparent heart rates of anything from zero to over 200 pulses per minute, with intermittent periods when it would settle down and give plausible readings. As a result I devised an

Sensors	Examples of practical activities
temperature	exothermic and endothermic reactions; temperature changes over a day (inside a fridge, in a building, in a greenhouse, outside); investigating why some animals huddle in the winter;
light	investigating how fast photochromatic glasses change; monitoring light levels in different environments (field work); investigating light reflected from different materials;
sound	investigating the effects of different ear shapes on ability to collect sound; monitoring sound levels in the environment over a day;
pulse	investigating fluctuations in rest pulse rate; investigating how quickly pulse returns to normal after exercise
light gates (used as timing devices – and hence also velocity measurers)	measuring reaction times measuring velocity of trolleys on ramps
distance	distance–time graphs for moving objects (people, trolleys down ramps etc.)
voltage and current	investigating the voltage current relationships of resistors, thermistors, diodes etc. charging and discharging a capacitor
pressure	pressure change with depth of water pressure change with altitude (within tall buildings – take out on field trip in hilly country)
pH	investigating acidity in pond, stream, soilmonitoring acid–base reactions
oxygen	monitoring oxygen levels in a yeast culture to indicate microbial growth
position	investigating whether plants grow faster during the day than at night measuring distortion of elastic material monitoring the oscillations in a spring
weight (electronic balance)	monitoring rates of chemical reactions where gases are given off

Figure 6.1.9 List of commonly found sensors and examples of use in practical work

Note: Details of these (and other) activities are given in (Frost, 2002a, 2002b, 2002c).
See also his website (www.rogerfrost.com).

investigation into the limits of reliability of the pulsemeter, which led to interesting discussions of the fact that it was more reliable on some people than others, that for some people it worked better clipped to their ear, than to their finger (and vice versa), and that movement could upset it etc. In explaining these findings, we delved into many different aspects of science, including, of course, the design of the sensor.

There are three advantages in using data logging for learning science, namely:

- the simultaneous graphing offers the opportunity for discussion of what is happening *while* it is happening, and of identifying how the graph relates to the phenomenon, i.e. the phenomenon and the visual representation of the phenomenon are happening together;
- both fast and slow changes can be monitored which would be difficult or tedious if done manually;
- less time is spent on plotting graphs, which releases more time for interpretation of the graph, a skill which pupils find difficult.

Obviously none of these advantages will be gained if the software, computers or sensors are unreliable.

Control – problem solving

Another use of data logging is in control activities, such as in controlling the temperature of an environment or the light levels in a room. The advantage of doing some of this in science is the way it uses the same ideas as homeostatic control in the body. Pupils very often understand these ideas better from having to programme in relevant commands.

Simulations

Simulations cover virtual experiments such as making up electric circuits and finding out what happens, altering pressure and temperature in the Haber process, studying changes in a predator–prey relationship. They allow pupils to investigate a phenomenon, focusing on the conceptual understanding, without the clutter of reality slowing them down. They are interactive and provide feedback to pupils on what is happening. They must not be confused, however, with reality and unless pupils have experience of handling the appropriate equipment, and realising the messiness of connecting circuits, trying to alter the parameters on a chemical reaction, trying to find out about animal populations in the field, they will lose sight of what the simulation relates to. Simulations can also provide virtual experiences like journeys to the planets, or journeys through the blood system or models say of the human body or of molecules which can be manipulated in some way. Some simulations add 'conceptual labels' which you cannot see – for instance in showing the movement of a bouncing ball force and velocity arrows will be added so that it is possible to watch what is happening to these parameters as the ball moves.

Data-handling packages

Data-handling packages include spreadsheets like 'Excel' which handle only numeric data and packages like 'Information Workshop' which handle alphanumeric data as well as numeric data. If pupils have not learned what databases and data-handling packages are they need to prepare their own database and interrogate it, before they access external databases. Prepare relatively simple ones taking maybe only five or six fields. Try using data about themselves, selecting aspects which are not too sensitive (possible fields: hand span, arm length, size of foot, length of forearm, eye colour, hair colour). You can then use the software to draw bar charts and pie charts to review the alphanumeric data (e.g. distribution of people with different colour eyes); use search facilities to find those people, say, with blue eyes and large hands; correlation graphs to review whether people with long arms also have large hands; you can test the story that the size of your foot is the same as the length of your forearm etc. This ability to interrogate a database is important. This is where a lot of the discussion comes in and the time saved not having to draw all the charts and graphs can be used on interpretation.

A spreadsheet like Excel allows pupils to manipulate numerical data in two main ways. First, you can set it to do routine calculations by putting a formulae in (if you are measuring mass and volume, then you can set it to calculate density automatically in the next column). This can allow a whole class set of results to be processed and discussion can focus on the discrepancies or otherwise of the results – i.e. the reliability of them. Second it is possible to graph results, again if class sets are being collected, then it is possible to keep an eye on the graph which is building up.

Mathematical models

There are commercially available mathematical models, such as ones on the predator–prey relationship in ecology, or the breeding rate of rabbits in a limited environment. The only problem here is that pupils may not be aware of the model which is driving the software. It is helpful therefore if pupils can set up their own models, however simple, as they then know what the model is that they are experimenting with. Excel tends to be the simplest modelling tool. They could set up a model of the energy consumption in a house, with columns for 'appliance', 'wattage', 'time it is run', 'cost'. They can allocate a box for total cost over a week, another for budget which they must not exceed, and another for the difference between expenditure and budget. The model allows them to monitor their energy consumption against budget.

Communication facilities

Communication facilities do allow pupils the opportunity to prepare both colourful and imaginative presentations, whether for work which goes into their folders, or for posters. The use of clip art both by you and the pupils can add enormously to the appeal of material. The security which pupils have from knowing that they can easily experiment with writing by writing, reviewing and changing, encourages pupils to start writing. Remember that if you are using 'writing frames' these can be put onto the computers.

With the advent of interactive boards and data projectors in many schools, there is an increase in the use of power point presentations by teachers. The temptation at first is to put the lesson onto a power point presentation, like a lecture. This is a misuse of the medium. The best advice is to use power point for:

- images which you want to discuss with the class, including images which can be built up step by step;
- graphs to be interpreted;

- key points of tasks which pupils are to undertake (these can be left up as pupils are working);
- extension activities
- writing frames;
- short video clips, or digitised images from the BBC;
- key words;
- quizzes and other assessment tasks;
- homework tasks.

Most people find when they have the resources in this format at their fingertips, it can give a good structure to a lesson, which in turn adds pace to the work. It is important however to avoid gimmicks, too much pace and lazy activities which do not require pupils to think.

You will find much fuller guidance on the use of ICT resources in the June 2003 edition of *School Science Review* which was devoted almost entirely to ICT in science education (Wellington 2003). Roger Frost's books (no relation!) are an excellent resource of practical guidance on use of software and hardware (Frost 2002a, 2002b, 2002c, 2001).

Gradually the use of ICT is altering the way in which teachers and pupils interact. Where facilities are reliable, teachers are setting up websites of key resources for pupils, posting key readings and preparation for the following week for their classes especially their A level groups, and receiving and responding to homework on line. Your task in the first instance is to implement the use of ICT in a critical way. Task 6.1.5 enables you to do that.

Task 6.1.5
Using ICT for different purposes

During your school placements, ensure that you have used ICT for each of the purposes given in Figure 6.1.9. For each one, evaluate using the following questions.

- What challenges did you face in accessing the necessary hardware and software?
- What challenges did you face in allowing access by all pupils?
- Was the lesson enjoyed by pupils? Why? What evidence do you have?
- What learning was achieved? (relate to your learning outcomes). What evidence do you have?
- What were the benefits of using ICT over other resources?
- How would you modify the use of the computers and the particular programme next time?

SUMMARY

Science is a subject rich in language, images and models. A consideration of the role language plays in learning science determines the language resources which should be developed. Images are also important for both learning and communicating scientific ideas – so sources of images and animations need to be found. Textbooks provide many of the images which are needed but these are also available electronically. ICT resources in schools are becoming a more viable option with the increased reliability and availability of computers, school networks and suitable software. While they are modern and often engaging, they need to be evaluated to make sure they are an effective alternative for learning to other resources.

There are organisations which set up email groups amongst wider teaching communities and which provide commentary on resources. The most obvious one is the Association for Science Education (www.ase.org.uk), whose journals (*School Science Review* and *Education in Science*) provide information and evaluation of resources. The annual meeting of the ASE (held in early January) provides an excellent forum for browsing through an enormous range of resources. The Institute of Physics (www.iop.org), the Institute of Biology (www.iob.org) the Royal Society of Chemistry (www.rsc.org) and the Earth Science Teachers Association (ESTA) (www.esta-uk.org) also play a major role in developing resources for teachers. The awarding bodies prepare support material for the particular examinations (see Unit 7.2 on examinations for relevant websites). The DfES website (www.dfes.gov.uk) contains resources for teaching. BECTa (www.becta.org.uk) is the government's agency on the use of ICT in education and provides a guidance on ICT resources and training. It is worth spending time early in your training in browsing websites and locating the resources which will be particularly useful to you.

FURTHER READING

Amos, S. and Boohan, R. (2002) *Aspects of Teaching Secondary Science: Perspectives on Practice*, London: RoutledgeFalmer. This is an 'Open University Reader'. Of particular relevance for resources are: Section 1 'Talking about science'; Section 3 'Imagined worlds' (especially Chapters 12 and 13); Section 4 'Communicating science'.

DfES KS3 strategies – publications http://www.dfes.gov.uk. Find the resources which apply to science. The most useful ones are: *The Y9 Booster Pack* (2002); *Science for Pupils with Learning Difficulties; Working with Pupils with EAL; Effective Teaching and Learning of Different Topics* (Energy, Particles, Forces, Cells).

Frost, R. (2002a) *The IT in Secondary Science Book*, London: IT in Science.

Frost, R. (2002b) *Data Logging in Practice*, London: IT in Science.

Frost, R. (2002c) *Data Logging & Control*, London: IT in Science.

Frost, R. (2001) *Software for Teaching Science: A Critical Catalogue of Science Software*, London: IT in Science. The first three are particularly useful for ideas of how to use ICT in science teaching and how to set up equipment. They can be followed by a relative beginner. The fourth gives a useful guide to the software existing at the time, and criteria for judging software.

Leask, M. and Pachler, N. (eds) (1999) *Learning to Teach Using ICT in the Secondary School*, London: RoutledgeFalmer. This is an excellent guide to use of ICT, with practical advice from experts in the field and contact address and suggestions for further development.

Naylor, S. and Keogh, B. (2000) *Concept Cartoons in Science Education*, Sandbach: Millgate House Publishers. These concept cartoons covering a wide range of science topics provide an invaluable start for discussions.

Ogborn, J., Kress, G., Martins, I. and McGillicuddy, K. (1996b) *Explaining Science in the Classroom*, Buckingham: Open University Press. This is a report of a research project studying the nature of explanation. It identifies the richness of resources which science teachers use to explain science. Selected portions are reproduced as Chapters 4 and 13 in Amos and Boohan (2002) and these may form the best starting points.

Sutton, C. (1992) *Words, Science and Learning*, Buckingham: Open University Press. This is a study of the role of language in the creation of science, as well as in the learning of science. This is a delightful read.

Wellington, J. (special issue editor) (2003) 'ICT in science education', *School Science Review*, 84(309): 39–120. This is an up-to-date review of ICT in action with references to resources and associated pedagogy and rationale. There are ten articles on the use and evaluation of ICT for learning science.

Wellington, J. and Osborne, J. (2001) *Language and Literacy in Science Education*, Buckingham: Open University Press. The authors have brought together research from the last 40 years, on language in science education. They supply many examples of resources which can be adapted for your own lessons.

WEBSITES TO EXPLORE

For websites on particular topics a 'Google' search is often the most efficient way of finding them; search also the 'images' section of Google. The following websites are of organisations which make resources for teachers and will serve as a start for finding your particular favourites. See Unit 7.2 for the websites of the awarding bodies.

Science learning centres: http://www.sciencelearningcentres.org.uk. The government has funded nine science learning centres across the country, with one National Science Learning Centre in York. These centres will be operating from October 2004 (with the national one from 2005), and will be sources of information about resources for science teachers.

Association for Science Education: http://www.ase.org.uk. Note that the ASE made five CD-ROMs *AKA Science: Only Connect?*; *Can we: Should we?*; *Is there life?*; *Who Am I?*, during Science Year (2001). These contain a lot of resources for science teaching. Some of the material of these can be downloaded from their website. One of its most popular pages is Science upd8, which prepares science activities on a weekly basis which link with stories in the news (http://www.ase.org.uk/htm/teacher_zone/upd8/index.php).

Institute of Physics: http://www.iop.org. View the support which is given for education and the publications (Physics Education). There are also lists of demonstrations and information about the recently produced CD-ROM on the teaching of physics at KS3.

Institute of Biology: http://www.iob.org. This website has resources in term of publications (Samples of *The Journal of Biological Education* can be viewed on line) and support offered to teachers.

Royal Society of Chemistry: http://www.rsc.org. Many resources can be downloaded. It is easy to find publications for different age groups. Note they have recently produced materials to support the 'Ideas and Evidence' part of the National Curriculum.

Earth Science Teachers Association (ESTA) http: //www.esta–uk.org/. This website gives information about support for teachers, the publication *Teaching Earth Sciences* and support workshops.

Joint Earth Science Education Initiative www.jesei.org. The first material produced by this group (collaboration between IoP, IoB, RSC and ESTA) is an extensive set of resources for teaching the Earth sciences section of the NC science. Do download these; they are very useful.

Roger Frost's website: http://www.rogerfrost.com/. This provides information about his books, reviews of science software from several different companies, data from different experiments which can be used for data interpretation, and information about exhibitions and courses.

Exploring science for teachers (resources for teachers including classroom activities): http: //www.exploreteaching.com.

BBC Online – Education: http: //www.bbc.uk/education/home.

BBC2 and Open University: http: //www.open2.net/science/.

BBC Education – GCSE BITESIZE revision and tests: http: //ww.bbc.co.uk/education/gcsebitesize/.

BBC Online – Local Heroes-homepage: http: //www.bbc.co.uk/history/programmes/local_heroes.

BBC Online – Science – homepage: http: //www.bbc.co.uk/science/.

Becta: British Educational Technology and Communications Agency: http: //www.becta.org.uk. Ideas for use of ICT across the curriculum and within subjects.

Crosswords and other puzzles: http://www.discoveryschool.com.

National grid for learning. Information and links: http: //ngfl.gov.uk.

Science Learning Network: http: //www.sln.org.

Science on line resources for teachers. http: //www.scienceonline.co.uk.

Planet Science: http: //www.planet-science.com. Planet science was a continuation of 'Science Year'. It has now wound up but its website has useful resources on it. A weekly science letter is still sent out, with ideas for the week on it.

Unit 6.2

Beyond the Classroom

Tony Turner

INTRODUCTION

This unit encourages you to use out-of-classroom activities and resources in your science teaching and be alert to such opportunities.

Using the environment can give reality and purpose to science lessons, helping pupils to contextualise their world within school science. Science concepts make more sense when experienced, such as sampling plants in a habitat (adaptation), observing folding in rock strata or comparing the rod spacing in TV aerials. It may help pupils develop a sense of wonder about the world (Goodwin 2001). The beauty of a rainbow can be appreciated without scientific knowledge but enjoyment is enhanced when you can explain how it is formed. Such experiences contribute to the values dimension of the curriculum.

The Standards for teachers in training in England require you to be able to '... plan opportunities for pupils to learn in out-of-school contexts, such as school visits, museums, theatres, fieldwork and employment based settings ...' (TTA 2002) thus recognising the importance of contexts beyond the classroom to develop and broaden pupils' understanding.

OBJECTIVES

By end of this unit you should be:

- encouraged to widen your range of teaching strategies;
- convinced of the importance of relating science beyond the classroom to the science curriculum;
- aware of the range of resources which enable you to place science in interesting contexts, including fieldwork in the environment;
- able to plan and carry out some teaching outside;
- aware of the advantages of residential fieldwork for teaching science;
- alerted to the safety and legal factors when undertaking fieldwork.

OPPORTUNITIES

Why go beyond the classroom?

Many schools have activities in their Schemes of Work that can take pupils outside the classroom. These activities may be in lesson time, one-day excursions or residential fieldwork. Fieldwork encompasses investigations done outside, seeing the effects of science or technology on our lives and visiting a site of special interest such as a museum, building site or field centre. For example, the Salters–Horners physics course (Salters–Horners Advanced Physics, SHAP 2003) requires pupils, as part of AS coursework assessment, to visit a site of industrial and scientific importance and report on their visit.

Fieldwork can improve the teaching of all the sciences and helps raise awareness of the interaction of science and technology in the natural and made environment. By contrast, the extensive content of the science curriculum and its assessment requirements in England places constraints on teaching strategies (Leach 2002) and concern has been expressed about some decline in the use of field studies (Field Studies Council 2002; Lock and Tilling 2002).

Many schools have access in the classroom and laboratory to living material and the video and Internet bring excellent resources into the classroom. So why do fieldwork when it is, after all, more difficult to organise than laboratory work? Plants and animals in the wild do not perform to order and successful visits to many institutions depend on advance planning by visiting the site. The outcome of a special visit may depend also on the work of outside staff. Despite the added work and associated difficulties important benefits accrue.

The broad educational benefits of fieldwork include:

- promoting enthusiasm for science and the natural and made environment;
- encouraging a lifelong interest in some aspects of those environments;
- broadening understanding of how science and technology interact and are part of our lives;
- promoting awareness of issues around environmental damage and protection;
- revealing the impact of humans on the environment;

- developing positive attitudes towards the environment;
- encouraging speculation and discussion.

Fieldwork is necessary because it is, sometimes, the only way for pupils to experience some phenomena, e.g. the diversity of living things; the motion of the stars and planets; or the effects of pollution. The sedimentation patterns in the wall of a sand quarry carries a powerful visual image of geological time and unearthing a fossil in a sedimentary rock helps link observation to evolutionary theory. Fieldwork can relate abstract ideas to real life, e.g. help understand the forces acting in a suspension bridge (Oxlade 1996).

In relation to the science curriculum, fieldwork allows pupils to:

- increase their knowledge of science;
- improve their knowledge of their locality, e.g. local ecology, geology, industries, services such as communications, electricity and water supply;
- identify opportunities for inquiry;
- develop process skills, e.g. plan and practise inquiries and whole investigations; see Task 6.2.4;
- understand how numerical and other data are collected in the field;
- use data-logging equipment; see, e.g. Graham (2000) and Oldham (2003);
- work together;
- bring material from the environment into the school for further study and discussion;
- write reports of interest to them.

From a management point of view, pupils have greater freedom to talk and move outside the classroom. This enhanced freedom can be daunting to inexperienced teachers but can have a beneficial effect on behaviour and generate motivation. However, a successful trip needs to be carefully organised.

Task 6.2.1
Joining in a field trip or excursion

Discuss with your mentor opportunities for taking part in a school trip or excursion during your placement. If appropriate, offer to supervise one or more activities planned for the trip or, with support, plan an activity. Taking part in a science-based field trip would be ideal but taking part in an outdoor activity of another subject area is also beneficial.

Keep a record of how the trip was planned and carried out; the checklist in Figure 6.2.2 may help you. Collect your impressions of the pupils you worked with. The headings below may help you structure your perceptions:

- knowledge: what pupils knew about the subject before and what they gained from the task;
- understanding: could pupils explain what they were doing and why? Could pupils explain how the data, etc. they collected would help them meet the learning outcomes for the lesson?
- attitude: were pupils prepared to tackle the task; did they enjoy the experience and consider the activity worthwhile?

Working away from the classroom can involve using normal lesson time to work in the school grounds or nearby. More ambitious activities may require a half-day or whole-day visit. Occasionally, a residential field trip may be planned. We turn first to the use of regular classroom time, such as a timetabled double period.

FIELDWORK IN A DOUBLE PERIOD

Most schools have a playground, which is a source of habitats, materials and structures. Others have a playing field or access to open spaces. Planned carefully, part of a double period science lesson can be taught outside the classroom. Some activities are taught outside because they need space to be effective; other activities can only be taught outside. Ideas for activities and a discussion of associated planning are discussed below.

Activities

Collection of data; for example:

- measuring the length of a shadow as part of estimating Earth size (Ogborn *et al.* 1996a);
- identifying building materials (see below);
- estimating animal populations. Some pupils may regard small animals such as insects as insignificant, or be unaware of the diversity of insect populations or that some small animals are abundant and economically important, e.g. worms;
- reading instruments in a weather station. Helping pupils to connect physical measurements, such as pressure, humidity, etc. to the changing weather patterns and to national weather forecasting;
- sampling or comparing plant populations to show how plants respond to changing conditions;
- estimating the mass of wood in a tree as part of a study of the source of plant food and photosynthesis;
- sampling soils to relate e.g. differences in plant populations to soil profile;
- studying leaves to reveal variation in one plant, within a species or as part of a wider study of diversity;
- following a science trail to identify areas for study (Axon 2002; Borrows 1999; Foster 1989; Murphy and Murphy 2002a);
- studying lichen formation on headstones to relate, e.g. species preference for materials (Dove 1994).

Building materials and their properties

A useful exercise in a topic on 'properties and uses of materials' is to sketch a building and identify the construction materials used. By comparing a modern and older building, the origin and use of materials may be discussed and raise awareness of the advantages and drawbacks of different materials; see Figure 6.2.1. Local shops or offices may display interesting materials, e.g. marble cladding.

Some pupils may be reluctant to draw but sketching an object improves observation, promotes awareness and stimulates inquiry. The preparation of an outline sketch may help some pupils to get started. Carrying out the exercise yourself is an integral part of your planning and making photographic transparencies creates a useful resource.

Task 6.2.2
Planning a science trail

Explore the school buildings and grounds to identify sites of interest to include in a science trail that could be experienced by pupils within a double period. The stations should have a common focus. See the section on collection of data above.

Identify a topic or short sequence of lessons you expect to teach; or choose a topic of interest to yourself. Identify 4–6 stations that would provide interest and motivation and contribute to understanding of the topic. For each station identify the locality and what pupils are expected to look for and record. In addition:

- explain for yourself the science involved;
- prepare an explanation of the science for the pupils;
- link the pupil's experience to the topic and hence to the SoW or statutory curriculum.

Draft a record sheet for pupils to use on the trail. Discuss your notes and record sheet with your class teacher or mentor. Where possible try out the trail with a group of pupils or with your class. File for future use in planning a trail.

---

2 Demonstrating phenomena

Examples of activities that may benefit from working outside include:

- comparing the rate of evaporation at different sites;
- developing a timeline for the age of the universe (Murphy and Murphy 2002b);
- estimating the speed of sound (Rowell and Herbert 1987);
- erecting a water barometer (Rogers and Wenham 1978);
- modelling states of matter using pupils as molecules (Rogers and Wenham 1977);
- launching a water rocket!

3 Planning

Working outside the laboratory depends partly on your own attitude to teaching but also on departmental policy; some teachers encourage working outside, others are less enthusiastic. Find out from your school mentor what guidance is available in your department and across the school. As a teacher in training you cannot take a group of pupils outside on your own, the class teacher or another qualified person must be with you.

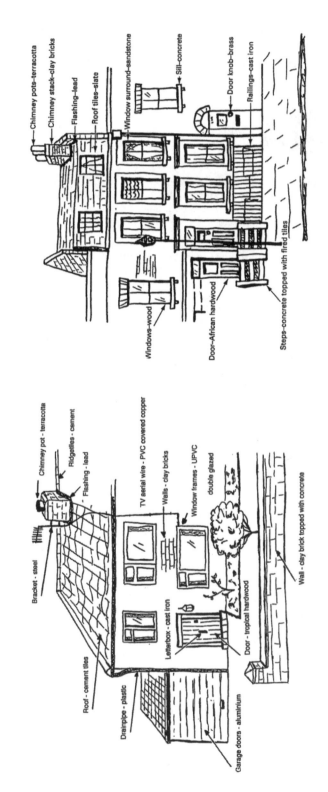

Figure 6.2.1 Sketch of a modern and an older building

Chimney pots-terracotta

Chimney stack-clay bricks

Flashing—lead

Roof tiles–slate

Window surround–sandstone

Sill–concrete

Door knob–brass

Railings–cast iron

Windows–wood

Door–African hardwood

Steps–concrete topped with fired tiles

Chimney pot - terracotta

Ridgetiles - cement

Flashing - lead

TV aerial wire - PVC covered copper

Walls - clay bricks

Window frames - UPVC double glazed

Bracket - steel

Letterbox - cast iron

Door - tropical hardwood

Wall - clay brick topped with concrete

Roof - cement tiles

Drainpipe - plastic

Garage doors - aluminium

Success depends on checking out in advance the proposed site. When planning your lesson consider factors such as the:

- length of a double period and what is possible;
- class size and your ability to supervise their activity safely;
- points to emphasise to ensure safe and sensible behaviour;
- suitability of sites for outside study;
- safety factors, e.g. road traffic, local ponds, unpleasant plants or pupils susceptible to hay fever;
- role of the regular class teacher in your activity.

Figure 6.2.2 may help you plan such an activity.

Aims

- What are the aims and learning outcomes of the activity?
- How does the activity fit in with the SoW and or the statutory curriculum?
- How are the aim(s) achieved by working outside?
- Are there guidelines for the activity in the SoW or elsewhere?

Legal and safety issues
Have you:

- discussed the proposal with your class teacher?
- carried out a risk assessment on the site?
- identified any special safety issues to be observed?
- planned your briefing to pupils to cover behavioural and safety issues?
- planned adequate supervision by you and the class teacher?
- checked that your pupils can work outside without risk, e.g. none have allergies?

Preparation and planning

- Try out the activity yourself and check that it can be carried out on the chosen site in the time available.
- Check that data obtained can be used to meet your aims and achieve your learning outcomes.
- Prepare briefing for pupils, including instructions and record sheets as well as safety and behavioural matters.
- Check the availability of equipment for the number of pupils in your class; discuss your requirements with technical staff.
- Plan how the equipment is to be distributed and returned.
- Check whether pupils need instruction about how to use the equipment you select.
- Plan timings for briefing, departure, work and return.
- Ensure that pupils know what to do with data on return to the classroom. Are the data to be followed up immediately or later?
- Where are the data to be kept between now and the next lesson?
- Plan, as needed, an appropriate homework task.

Figure 6.2.2 Checklist for planning a short outside activity

**Task 6.2.3
Planning investigations
outside the classroom**

Select a topic (unit of work) which you are going to teach or in which you
are interested, and which has the potential for working outside. Use your
chosen unit and identify opportunities for your pupils to carry out an
investigation outside the classroom which helps them to develop skills in
carrying out investigations. Choose one investigation and identify:

- a suitable task;
- the aims and key learning outcomes;
- the advantages of working outside;
- the investigative skills it promotes;
- how you expect to assess learning outcomes.

You may find it helpful to go to the Qualifications and Curriculum
Authority (QCA) website at http: //www.standards.dfes.gov.uk/schemes2/
secondary_science/ and look at Unit 9M on scientific investigations, as
there are ideas there for investigations which could be done outside.

GOING OFF-SITE

One-day excursions or residential courses allow activities which cannot be carried out in
double periods or in school. The new environment often stimulates motivation and greater
application. You may get to know your colleagues better and see pupils in a different light.

Student teachers are not expected to plan and organise a residential field trip. Be alert
to the opportunity to join a trip and offer to help with planning and preparation. Most
schools have a plan and checklist for fieldwork to which you should refer; see Task 6.2.4.

Sites of special interest

Many schools have contacts with field centres, sites of special interest, nature reserves, etc.
(Lubben *et al.* 2001). Examples include:

- a hands-on science centre (Wellington 2000);
- local or national museums (Griffin 2002);
- a neighbourhood industry, e.g. glass manufacturer;
- a weights and measures office;
- waste disposal, recycling and water treatment sites;
- building sites may offer interesting structures, e.g. cranes or deep drilling machines
  exposing a soil profile (Jennings 1986; Woolnough 1994: 88);
- waterways and bridges (Beckett 1986; Oxlade 1996).

Many field centres organise teaching programmes for groups of pupils or have a special
focus, such as the Royal Society for the Protection of Birds. Some organisations have
permanent or topical displays related to their special situation, e.g. iron making in the
Ironbridge Museum, Shropshire; Darwin's house at Downe, Kent or the Science Centre,

Planetarium and Arboretum at Jodrell Bank, Cheshire. See also Wellington 2000 in the Further reading section of this unit.

Sites of local interest may be known to school staff, the LEA science advisor or the regional Association for Science Education (ASE) network. Planning may be enhanced by using the proposed sites' 'website' (McKeon 2001).

Task 6.2.4
Planning a field trip

If the opportunity arises join in a field trip. Collect information about the enterprise, using the checklists below to guide you.

Educational aims – identify:
1   the purposes of the trip and links with the Scheme of Work;
2   the facilities at the field centre;
3   how fieldwork is to be followed up in school;
4   the contribution of fieldwork to preparation for public examinations;
5   the suitability of the field centre resources to the course.

Legal responsibilities – you should:
1   read the school (and LEA) regulations which apply to field trips;
2   identify how the Health and Safety at Work Act applies;
3   identify Risk Assessments for travel and fieldwork;
4   identify the responsibilities and rights of parents while their children are on residential courses;
5   know the agreement to which parents consent when they sanction a field trip for their child and how that consent is obtained;
6   know the adult–pupil ratio which applies to travel and working in the field;
7   know how insurance is effected for the trip;
8   know how pupils can be helped financially to attend the course.

Advance planning – find out:
1   how pupils are briefed and prepared for the trip, including the Country Code of Practice;
2   the equipment needed from the school and how that is identified, collected and delivered to the site;
3   who prepares the written course materials;
4   the domestic arrangements on course;
5   how to cost the trip and the parental contribution;
6   the transport arrangements.

Safety – obtain copies of documents which identify:
1   guidelines for working and behaving at the Field Centre;
2   special precautions/hazards associated with the particular field centre;
3   arrangements made for pupils and parents to contact each other in an emergency;
4   staff responsibilities, including responding to injured or unwell pupils.

Guidance on health and safety is given in DfES 1998, or Reiss 1999; see also the CLEAPSS web site.

What happens while you are away? Find out what should you do about your teaching responsibilities.

OTHER OPPORTUNITIES

People with knowledge or expertise

It is highly motivating for pupils to listen and talk to persons with special knowledge which links with the science curriculum. Outside speakers are particularly useful for controversial issues. Environmental safety officers can provide a useful link between health and hygiene and micro-organisms and decay, etc. Other sources of speakers include local industry, chambers of commerce, the health service and your local FE college and IHE. Many professional and learned societies provide speakers, e.g. Institute of Biology, Institute of Electrical Engineers and the Medical Research Council. Parents and governors of the school may be a source of expertise. Build a database of contact names and addresses (Harrison 1998).

Work experience

Many schools organise work experience for their pupils and local business and industry may provide you with useful links to the science curriculum. Your pupils may give personal insights into industrial processes by telling the class about their experiences. Talk to the work experience coordinator in your practice school.

Second-hand resources

Teachers traditionally substitute for first-hand experience by using books, posters, video, CD-ROM, simulations and the World Wide Web. The Science and Technology in Society resources are useful (ASE 1987, 1993 and 1999). The ASE publication *School Science Review* (SSR) carries articles about using the environment to teach science and has a regular feature called 'Science Web search'.

Some field centres undertake research and make experimental data available to schools, e.g. a database of a changing animal population. Such data can be used to develop pupils' skills of analysis and report writing. Find out what is available locally or on the web. Use your scheme of work to identify such opportunities. Look for opportunities for the school to take part in inquiries or surveys, e.g. reporting bird sightings in a particular period for the RSPB.

SUMMARY

The way teachers use the environment to teach science depends very much on attitudes and contexts. A tradition of going beyond the classroom encourages its continuation but absence of such practice can inhibit innovation. Whatever your circumstances there are often opportunities to go beyond the classroom in planning your lessons. Some schools promote inter-departmental field studies, e.g. geography and science and you should be alert to such opportunities (Oulton 1998).

What is possible depends on the local environment, your ability to identify opportunities and the support you get. In this chapter we have made suggestions of ways to go beyond the classroom and suggest you regularly monitor the publications of your professional associations for further ideas.

FURTHER READING

Braund, M. and Reiss, M. (2004) *Learning Science Outside the Classroom*, London: Routledge Falmer. A practical guide to using a wide range of informal, non-classroom based context for science education. Risk assessment and safety issues are addressed.

Department for Education and Skills (DfES) (1998) *Health and Safety of Pupils on Educational Visits: A Good Practice Guide*, London: DfES. Gives general guidance on a wide range and types of visits. There are sections on Risk assessment and web links to guidance given by the Health and Safety Executive. The document can be downloaded from web at www.dfee.gov.uk/h_s_ev.

Job, D., Day, C. and Smyth, T. (1999) *Beyond the Bike Sheds: Fresh Approaches to Fieldwork in the School Locality*, Sheffield: The Geographical Association. While this book is aimed at geography teachers, the discussion about approaches, strategies and purposes are relevant to science teachers. Examples of work are given in detail and include hydrology; weather and climate; energy; traffic surveys; food supply and movement and flora, indigenous and non-indigenous.

Reiss, M. (ed) (1999) *Teaching Secondary Biology*, London: John Murray for the ASE. An excellent resource addressing many important topics in the teaching of biology. Chapter 9 discusses ecology and provides valuable advice about using the environment and undertaking fieldwork.

Wellington, J. (2000) *Teaching and Learning Secondary Science: Contemporary Issues and Practical Approaches*, London: Routledge. Chapter 12 contains discussion on formal and informal learning and about using secondary sources in science lessons. There is an interesting and practical section on inter-active science centres.

7 Assessment in Science

This chapter describes and contrasts the professional purpose of assessment with the bureaucratic purpose of assessment. Professional assessment is that carried out by teachers to enhance learning and is known as 'formative assessment' or 'assessment for learning'. By contrast summative assessment, associated with certification and selection, is used to inform pupils of what they have achieved at the end of a course, as a means of selection for jobs or higher education, and as data in the published annual 'performance tables' of schools.

Assessing for learning is an essential aspect of teaching and has been a strong theme in earlier units on planning. Unit 7.1 focuses on this in more detail giving strategies which can be used and their underlying rationale. The unit is based on research and inservice work with teachers in which the writer has been engaged herself.

Another important role of the teacher is to prepare pupils for public examinations such as GCSE or the end of Key Stage assessments, both of which are summative assessments. Examination results are high stakes assessment; they provide individuals with a sense of achievement and influence future action. For similar reasons they are important to parents. Examination results affect the standing of the school locally and nationally and influence the popularity of the school to prospective parents. For these reasons, preparing pupils for examinations receives high priority in school. Unit 7.2 summarises the awarding system in science, and gives advice on the responsibilities which teachers carry for preparing pupils for examinations and for acting professionally in the marking of coursework.

Unit 7.3 addresses the emphasis and support given by government to raising standards through improving examination performance. Science, being a core subject, features prominently in performance tables and in calculations of the value which schools add to pupils' education.

Unit 7.1

Assessing for Learning

Christine Harrison

INTRODUCTION

Assessment in schools has three main purposes:

- to support learning;
- for review, transfer and certification;
- for informing on school improvement and accountability.

When people hear the word assessment, they generally think of the second purpose and see assessment as tests and examinations and for many, assessment is associated with stressful times either revising or waiting for results. At the present time, children in England face over 80 high stakes examinations or tests, the first within seven weeks of starting school. The burden of testing and the perceived need to keep written records of attainment

---

OBJECTIVES

By the end of this unit you should:

- recognise what assessment for learning looks like in the classroom;
- know some of the assessment strategies that support learning;
- begin to see how formative assessment fits alongside summative assessment;
- be aware of the importance of involving the learner in the assessment process.

to satisfy the second and third purposes of assessment has skewed how some teachers and some pupils think about assessment. Testing and the documentation of achievement have taken time and focus away from quality interactions between teacher and pupils and have undermined the role and importance of assessment for learning.

The word assessment derives from the Latin 'assidere', which means to sit beside, which sets a quite different hue to the meaning of the word from the feelings often experienced in the examination hall. While assessment does encompass summative examinations and may include tests intermittently, by far the main way that teachers need to use assessment is as a day-to-day tool in their classroom for monitoring learning and taking decisions about what to teach next. This more regular form of assessment is often called *assessment for learning*. This term was coined to distinguish it from assessment *of* learning; the difference being that the former informs the learning process while the latter provides a measure at a fixed point in the process. Assessment for learning can also be described as formative if the evidence from the assessment process is used to drive the next stage of teaching and learning. There is a body of firm evidence that formative assessment can raise standards (Black and Wiliam 1998) and so it is an area of your practice worthy of the time spent in developing it.

There are no simple recipes for developing formative practices and the many educational experiments that featured in the review of formative assessment *Inside the Black Box* showed a diversity of approaches (Black and Wiliam 1998). However, there were some features that arose in most, if not all, of the studies and these provide a starting point. Formative assessment, like all other ways to generate effective learning, requires pupils to be actively involved and so classrooms where pupils are encouraged to speak and do, rather than receive information, are more fruitful sites for formative assessment to function. Where teachers stick religiously to a transmission mode of teaching, where they focus on the subject matter that they have to teach, assessment becomes bolted-on at the end of a teaching sequence as a measure of how much knowledge has filtered through to the learner. In these circumstances it becomes increasingly difficult if not impossible to feed assessment evidence back into the teaching and learning process. A more effective approach is to embed the assessment into the teaching–learning cycle (Capel *et al.* 2001: 256) so that the pace and emphasis of the work can be matched to the needs of the learners.

For assessment to function formatively, teachers need to make teaching programmes flexible and responsive. This involves collecting evidence of how well pupils have understood part of a topic and refining future lesson plans to remediate any problems that have arisen or changing direction or pace if the class have mastered ideas quickly and so require more challenge in their learning. As new teachers, it is perhaps best to approach this lesson by lesson. If you use some assessment tool in one lesson to gather evidence then you have the opportunity to change your next lesson in response to that evidence. If you find out that Year 7 pupils can devise an experiment to demonstrate the differences between metal and non-metal objects and clearly can classify a range of materials into metals and non-metals, then there would be little gained from them doing that experiment in the next lesson. On the other hand, if you find that pupils keep referring to dissolving as 'the solid disappearing' this needs to be addressed in the next lesson to find out if it is simply slackness of language or a firmly held misconception of those learners. So the assessments and evaluations completed in one lesson modify future learning experiences. In time, as your confidence in the classroom grows you are able to accommodate formative assessment practices in a more proactive manner and deviate from your lesson plan as and when the learning needs demand such a course of action.

Assessment for learning increases teachers' understanding of their pupils and so helps teachers provide quality feedback to improve their learning. It also helps to develop classroom cultures where collaboration dominates competition and in which learning, rather than performance, is the goal. This is because pupils need to understand that the main emphasis of the work they do in classrooms is about improvement. One feature that appeared in several of the studies on formative assessment is the development of self-assessment strategies in the learners. One of the many tasks that you need to achieve through your teaching is helping pupils become self-regulating in their work so that eventually they become learners independent of the teacher. This is not an easy task as experienced teachers will inform you and needs a careful training programme for learners where they gradually come to hold a concept of quality about their work similar to the one that their teacher holds in her head. From the focused feedback that they get from their teachers, pupils can begin to grasp what quality means within their work and, acting on advice, can start to achieve it.

CLASSROOM ASSESSMENT

Assessment plays an important role in the teaching–learning cycle since it can both drive and modify the learning experience so that pupils' needs are catered for. It provides evidence for teachers about the way pupils understand and perform particular tasks; it also provides feedback to the learner on what they have achieved and how they might improve their work. Equipped with this evidence, teachers can plan the next stage of teaching more effectively and learners can begin to comprehend what they need to do to make progress. The role of the teacher is to create regular opportunities for assessment to occur. These opportunities can arise from a variety of sources including:

- classroom dialogue;
- class and homework activities;
- tests.

Each of these factors is addressed in turn below. These sources need to produce a rich source of data for teachers to make informed judgements that can then be fed back to the learner so that the pupil comes to understand both the concept of quality and the role of the assessment process in their learning. The focus needs to be on improvement and so the dialogue, activities and tests need to focus on establishing where a learner is in their learning and provide the detail of what they need to do next.

Classroom dialogue

To do this effectively, teachers need to create rich classroom dialogue where the quality of their questions encourages learners to reveal what they know and understand. If a class were asked to give a definition of friction, probably few children would attempt to answer. Rephrasing the question to explore pupils' ideas about friction might be done by a more open approach to questioning. For friction, this might be done with a question like 'Some people talk about friction as being the opposite of slipperiness. What do you think?' This opens up the possibility of learners discussing what they think they know and understand about friction and allows them to compare and build their understanding by both articulating their own thoughts and modifying these ideas in the light of what they hear from others. It is from these classroom dialogues that teachers can extract the evidence they need to judge whether specific children do, or do not, have conceptual understanding. This is because the question explores what is in children's minds rather than 'right answerism', where the questions being set have a fixed answer in the teacher's head that children have to guess at.

To encourage such discussions producing a rich source of evidence, teachers often try to leave several seconds thinking time before they take an answer. The time between a teacher asking a question and taking an answer is called 'wait time' (Rowe 1974) and, for many teachers in her study, this was shown to be less than one second. This is insufficient time for learners to think what they know and to put together an answer that they can articulate in class. Thinking time can be further enhanced, if it is a particularly challenging question, by asking learners to discuss their ideas with a partner or in groups because then their answers can be trialled, developed and modified before being offered in the public arena of the whole class. A further benefit from this approach is that there is pair or group responsibility for an answer which is less threatening for some learners. It also means that the classroom response is likely to be rich because the first ideas that the teacher selects can be added to, challenged or agreed with, by other pupils since the answers given can be compared with those that the pair or group discussed. So follow up questions such as, 'What might we add to Suzie's answer?' or 'How did Yagnesh's answer fit with Sally's idea?' broaden the discussion to involve more pupils answering and so enrich the evidence. This allows the teacher to make a more informed judgement about which steps to take next with the learning. However, to develop this approach the teacher needs flexibility and an ability to think on his feet. Such a demand requires careful planning and security in his knowledge of the topic.

Task 7.1.1
Observing and collecting questions

Begin work on this by observing experienced teachers working with their classes. Note down the questions that seem to prompt and promote dialogue and reflect on how the teacher handles the answers. Good teachers often manage questioning effectively without realising the skilled way in which they do this. It may be useful to ask them afterwards what they were trying to achieve with specific questions and how such questions have worked with other classes. Sort, sift and collect useful questions on different topics as well as collecting generic ones that you can use to develop and support classroom discourse.

Rich data can also be collected from classwork, homework activities and from tests, as long as the teacher plans for and supports learners by providing a means through which pupil understanding can be shown. Checking whether keywords are known or matching terms with definitions is only the beginning of the data collection that a teacher needs to do and caution needs to be applied because knowing a complex scientific word does not necessarily mean that a pupil has conceptual understanding in that area. Most pupils remember that green plants contain chlorophyll but this does not indicate that they realise that photosynthesis is an energy-transfer process that forms the main part of plant nutrition. Indeed, it could be that they know that chlorophyll is involved and may even be able to write out the correct equation but they mistakenly believe that photosynthesis is plant respiration. Many such misconceptions are well documented (Driver *et al.* 1994) and part of the teacher's role is to create activities where misconceptions can be revealed and challenged. The ways in which learners work with such activities again provides a rich source of evidence for assessment purposes.

Task 7.1.2
Developing your own questions

Start developing some questions of your own. 'What' and 'When' questions usually get descriptive answers that require only recall. 'Why' and 'How' questions require more thought. Use the stems below to think of questions that you might use in a specific science topic.

What is similar and what is different about ...?

Is it always true that ...?

How would you explain ...?

What is wrong with ...?

What does that tell you about ...?

CLASSWORK AND HOMEWORK ACTIVITIES

Different tasks set different demands for the learner and busy teachers are best advised to plan for assessment in those activities where the cognitive demands are high. Asking pupils to provide a written explanation of what they think would happen if a chemical was released that destroyed chlorophyll reveals far more of a learner's conceptual understanding than an activity where they describe the starch test. Similarly, setting work where pupils draw and explain what happens at the particle level when mercury expands in a thermometer gives more insight to understanding than asking pupils to copy drawings of the particle model idea for solids, liquids and gases from a textbook.

Many classwork and homework tasks involve noting keywords and descriptions, while some document the developing ideas in a particular topic and others record the method, data and conclusions of a particular practical activity that demonstrates a scientific idea. These are the building blocks that pupils need to construct their ideas and understanding of science. While it is important that a check is kept on these to ensure that a specific pupil has the building blocks in place, other types of classwork and homework provide better information about conceptual understanding and it is on these that teachers need to focus their assessments. Homework tasks in particular need careful planning to ensure that the product provides useful information about understanding.

Task 7.1.3
Planning for quality
feedback

1   Look through a sequence of lessons that you have taught or the scheme of work for a topic and decide which activities will produce work that needs checking and which will need more careful thought when marking in order to give quality feedback.
2   Decide what features of the activity, or product from the activity, suggest that more time should be devoted to giving detailed feedback.

TESTS

Tests are a quick and simple way of sampling learning and for both teacher and learner can be a good check that keywords and descriptions are known. Tests can be an effective way of monitoring factual knowledge but, in most cases, are less useful in assessing conceptual understanding. Thought needs to be given to the timing and frequency of tests; if given too late in the learning sequence, there is no time for remediation and improvement, and if set too often detract from the time available for learning.

RECORDING ASSESSMENT DATA

It might seem strange to look at recording assessment evidence at this point but this has implications for the way you approach marking and feedback. Most schools have policies that explain the purposes of marking pupil work and some system for marking and recording that provides coherence. The focus of this policy may be on reporting to parents and governors and suggest a summative evaluation that recognises accountability issues, as well as providing communication about individual pupil achievement on a specific piece of work. Other schools may have the primary aim of marking as a means of negotiating learning goals or targets with the pupil and seek to communicate progress rather than attainment in reports to parents. Yet other schools may do parts of both approaches and may have different approaches for different age groups of pupils. In order to understand the approach that you need to take in recording assessment evidence, you need to be clear about the policies for assessment and marking that exist in your school and how these play out in reality.

Decisions need to be taken about what to record in relation to a task that the learner has tried to do. Depending on the focus of the activity, you may want to record the processes that the learner used in completing the work (did they analyse data, make predictions or translate information into a different form?) or record attributes of the product they produced (was it a graph, table, drawing or prose?). Some teachers choose to record first attempts at a difficult piece of work as well as information on the final product because this gives them an idea of how pupils are responding to advice and moving forward with their learning. Other teachers choose to record data on finished products, and so use their mark book as a summative record.

**Task 7.1.4
Understanding your
school's assessment policy**

- Obtain a copy of your school's assessment/marking policy and any information that the science department produces on these issues.
- Read the documents carefully and check with your mentor any ambiguities, such as what 'marked regularly' means.
- Ask experienced teachers how they interpret the policies on a day-to-day basis and ask them to show you evidence of what they do in the pupils' work and in their mark books.
- Ensure that you know:
  - When and how to set and mark work for your classes.
  - How to store assessment evidence for your purposes and for the usual teacher of that class.
  - What the assessment evidence is used for.

The system of recording is complex and new teachers generally need several attempts at refining the process into a workable form. Most teachers use a mark book to record such data using coded systems to enable them to fit a large amount of information on one page. This allows them to record quickly but also gather an overview of the way individual learners are progressing. Again simple grades or marks can rarely provide sufficient information to provide the detail needed to generate an overview of achievement or progress. That is not to say that summative assessments should not be recorded as these provide indicators of overall progress. Tests or quizzes that are used in a formative fashion during the learning process rarely need recording but if the teacher does want to keep such information it is far better to record what the learner doesn't understand or cannot yet do, rather than the number of answers that they have got correct. This information helps the teacher devise more appropriate revision at a later stage.

FEEDBACK

Feedback has an essential part to play in the formative process. It provides the learner with the advice they need to promote their future learning. Quality rather than quantity is the key feature when giving pupils feedback on both oral and written work. The effort that many teachers devote to marking written tasks may be mis-directed. A numerical mark or grade does not tell pupils how to improve their work, so an opportunity to enhance their learning has been lost. This judgement is supported by a study that established that, whilst pupils' learning can be advanced by feedback through comments, the giving of marks or grades has a negative effect in that pupils ignore comments when marks or grades are also given (Butler 1988). Teachers are often surprised by Butler's study and yet it is easy to explain if you watch the way in which pupils in class respond to the marks/grades and comments in their books. Marks/grades are looked at and perhaps compared with peers but comments often get ignored and frequently go unread. So essential advice about improvement is unheeded in favour of being told week after week that you are B+.

The key to effective feedback is providing sufficient acknowledgment of what has been achieved alongside advice on what next steps to take. Some teachers use a technique called 'two stars and a wish' to achieve this in a concise but informative way. So a piece of work is assessed by noting two features that demonstrate the strength of the work or perhaps relate to an area that a specific pupil is currently targeting and then adding one aspect that might improve the piece. Learners can then begin to recognise for themselves what they have done well and understand where they need to put their efforts next. It also helps if the comment can be personally directed and written to encourage thinking. Examples might look like:

- 'James, you have provided clear diagrams and recognised which chemicals are elements and which are compounds. Can you give a general explanation of the difference between elements and compounds?'
- 'You have identified the anomalous results and commented on the accuracy of your experiment. What can you say about the sample size?'

Teachers also need to demonstrate to their learners that improvement is the main purpose of assessment and opportunities for pupils to follow up feedback comments should be planned as part of the overall learning process. A particularly valuable way of doing this is to devote some lesson time to redrafting one or two pieces of work, so that emphasis can be put on feedback for improvement within a supportive environment. This can change pupils' expectations about the purposes of classwork and homework as well as provide polished pieces of work that they can be proud of. Implementation of such practices can change the attitudes of both teachers and pupils to written work: the assessment of pupils' work will be seen as less as a competitive and summative judgement and more as a distinctive step in the process of learning.

While feedback benefits all pupils, it is particularly important that low attainers receive appropriate feedback, since they usually have greater difficulty than other learners in understanding the concept of quality that the teacher requires. The problem for the teacher is two-fold. First, they need to select the specific improvements that are needed and then to find the language to explain how the learner might approach the remediation work. However, it is only the learner that can close the gap between their current level and the new level that the teacher sets and so co-operation and a willingness to try are required. For some low attainers, feedback has been a painful experience where their shortcomings have been revealed and they have retired hurt from the learning process. Such learners often exhibit a type of behaviour that Dweck (1986) terms 'learned helplessness', where their self-esteem has been damaged by the assessment process and they are unwilling to engage in meaningful learning work. Teachers need to handle such learners carefully and find strategies to engage them once again with the learning process. In such a situation, marks seem to aggravate the problem and so this provides another reason for teachers using qualitative rather than quantitative data in their feedback to pupils.

Some schools have policies that require teachers to enter an achievement and an effort grade as a form of feedback. Effort is a difficult aspect to judge, especially where homework is concerned, and so quantity and neatness seem to be the criteria for judging this rather than time or concentration. Nevertheless, improvement in any of these factors may be a sign of progress and is to be remarked upon. While it is important to instill in learners that effort is needed if they wish to improve their work, effort grades detract from the message, if ill-judged.

Task 7.1.5
Providing constructive
feedback

Collect in a set of exercise books from a class that you teach.

1   Select three books; one from an average pupil, one from a high-attaining pupil and one from a low-attaining pupil.

2   Look through the work since the last time the books were marked. Decide which pieces of work need checking and which need more time to devise suitable feedback. This is likely to be one or two pieces at the most.

3   For the one or two pieces that require time spent on them, write down three objectives that you can see or had hoped the students would have achieved in this piece of work. Think also what you would hope this work to lead onto in the near future. These are the criteria for judging the work.

4   It may be helpful for you to produce what you would consider to be either an acceptable or a model example for the piece of work to help you recognise the quality required for the criteria to work in the context of the piece.

5   Think carefully about what you could write in each of the three student's books. A good tip is to use the idea of 'two stars and a wish'; two things you feel that they have done well and one feature that you had hoped would be there or could be there in the next step of their learning journey. Comments should encourage students to read them and act on them and hopefully think. It is important to try and avoid the use of 'but' in this type of feedback as it suggests shortcoming rather than an urge to improve. Examples might be:

  •   'The Haber process is well described and you have included the equation. Which variables affect the production of ammonia?'
  •   'Good examples of adaptation and features are clearly shown. Look again at the way you have described the process of adaptation and check it against the explanation in the textbook'.
  •   'You have provided clear circuit diagrams and correct examples for bulb brightness. Can you explain this in words as well as diagrammatically?'

Pupils can be helped to understand the detailed advice in feedback by involving them in whole-class activities where they become engaged in discussing the strengths and weaknesses in a specific example of a learner's work. This task models for them the self-assessment processes that they need to pay heed to as they create their own work. It helps them see the importance of focusing on the learning intentions and the success criteria as well as allowing them to focus on what needs to be done to improve a piece of work.

PEER- AND SELF-ASSESSMENT

Pupils need to be active participants in the assessment process rather than victims of testing. This can only be achieved if they develop the skills of self-assessment, understand their learning goal and can assess what they need to do to reach it (Sadler 1989). Self-assessment skills are not easy to develop but the first and probably most difficult task is to get pupils to think of their work in terms of a set of goals. In doing this they begin to develop an overview of that work so that it becomes possible for them to manage and control it for themselves and they become self-regulated learners.

In practice, peer-assessment turns out to be an important complement to self-assessment and a means by which the necessary skills can be developed. Peer-assessment allows pupils to begin to judge their own work by recognising similar or different qualities in the work of their peers. It is also uniquely valuable because pupils may accept, from one another, criticisms of their work which they would not take seriously if made by their teacher (Black *et al.* 2002) and is in a language and form that pupils themselves would naturally use and comprehend. However, self-assessment only happens if teachers help their pupils, particularly the low-attainers, to develop the skill. This process can take time and practice.

One way to practise self- and peer-assessment skills is to hold regular debriefing sessions towards the end of a lesson. A range of self-evaluation questions can be given which are linked to the learning intentions and success criteria for that lesson and pupils can be asked to voice what they feel they have achieved. Such questions might also ask 'Which parts of the lesson did you find easy and which parts difficult?' and discussions arising from this not only inform the teacher of areas they may need to return to but highlights for the pupils where they need to focus their attention for improvement.

One simple and effective idea is for pupils to self-assess completed pieces of work using 'traffic light' icons, labelling their work green, amber, or red according to their confidence levels with specific pieces of work. These labels serve as a simple means of communication of pupils' self-assessments. Pupils may then be asked to justify their judgements in a peer group, so linking peer- and self-assessment. This linkage can help in the development of the skills and the detachment needed for effective self-assessment.

Another approach is to ask pupils first to 'traffic-light' a piece of work, and then to indicate by hands up whether they put green, amber or red. The teacher can then reorganise the working groups so that the greens and ambers can pair up to deal with problems between them, whilst the red pupils can be helped by the teacher to deal with their deeper problems. For such peer-group work to succeed, many pupils need guidance about how to behave in groups, e.g. in listening to one another and taking turns, and how to judge quality, e.g. familiarising themselves with criteria. Techniques, such as the 'two stars and a wish' approach described in the feedback section can also be used in developing these behaviours particularly as they can be used to explore how the criteria for quality can be achieved within different pupils' work. Again peer-assessment through collaborative group work provides the vehicle through which self-assessment practices can develop.

Another approach which you could use as a supplement to one of the above ideas, or as an alternative way of developing self-assessment, is to spend time regularly asking pupils to reflect on their work. This might be done once a week for 15 minutes in class or as one of the homework tasks. Because pupils need help in recognising their learning, you might use summary cards like those in Figure 7.1.2.

Another variation might be asking them to judge where the easy and difficult parts come in pieces of work or topics so that they have keyed in where to focus their effort when it comes to revision.

Name ......Hannah S.................   Date ...Sept 30th.........

Two things I have learned in this lesson:

        Photosynthesis is the way plants make food from carbon
                        dioxide and water.

        Plants make starch and you can test for this with iodine.

A question I have:

        How does the plant make starch from a gas and a liquid?

Figure 7.1.1 Summary card

Name ....Hannah S.............   Date ...Nov 22nd.........

Things I found easy in this topic so far:

    That forces are measured in Newtons.

    That gravity makes things have weight.

    Using the forcemeter.

Things I found difficult in this topic so far:

    Drawing the pictures of where forces are acting.

    Understanding the experiment with the light gates.

Figure 7.1.2 Analysis card

The next step in helping pupils recognise their learning is by asking them to compare work done recently with that done earlier in the topic or earlier in the year, see Figure 7.1.3.

Once pupils have mastered these techniques then they are ready to negotiate targets for their learning, along with appropriate time frames and methods of self-monitoring to ensure they keep check on working towards their goal. All of these activities take time and effort to establish as working practice in the classroom and so need to be planned for as part of the unit of work.

Name ......Hannah S...........   Date....Dec 8th.........

I used to :

      Ask the teacher how to do the axes on my graph.

      Join plot to plot.

And now I can:

      Decide on the right scale for each axis.

      Know which variable goes on the horizontal and which on the vertical.

      Spot anomalous results.

      Draw the line of best fit.

Figure 7.1.3 Recognising learning card

ASSESSMENT OF INVESTIGATIVE WORK

Statutory assessment at the end of Key Stages 3 and 4 require teachers to make judgements about pupils' proficiency in scientific enquiry skills. Most schools have sorted out ways of complying with the rigour and demands that assessed coursework have placed on schools. What is less clear is how the teaching, learning and assessment issues interweave and lead up and feed into the system that the science department has devised. What is clear is that in both Key Stages there is a reasonable amount of time for assessment of investigative skills to feed into the teaching and learning cycle and so this aspect of the curriculum lends itself well to taking a formative approach to the development of enquiry skills.

The current model for assessment of enquiry skills identifies four skill areas: planning, obtaining evidence, analysing and evaluating (POAE). The AKSIS project (Watson *et al.* 2000) which was set up to investigate and develop teachers' approaches to investigative work in the classroom, found that pupils particularly require support in their analysis and evaluation skills during Key Stage 3 and that these skills can be enhanced through part investigations as well as full investigations.

Different investigations lend themselves to the development of particular skills. Such development might be achieved through utilising the analysis and learning recognition cards from a previous attempt at investigative work where a specific skill was being developed. A particular skill can also be enhanced by using samples of work by pupils who have previously performed the investigation and asking your current class to recognise how a specific skill is used within the context of this investigation. The criteria being explored might be decisions about appropriate sample sizes, or recognising anomalous results or finding the line of best fit on a graph. It is important that pupils realise the learning intentions when they are focusing on enquiry skills. It is also essential that the area that pupils are working on is made explicit to them and that they are able to identify what they need to do to achieve it.

Task 7.1.6
Assessing enquiry skills

1   Discuss with your mentor how enquiry skills are encouraged through the science scheme of work and how these are assessed for different year groups.
2   Select an area from the Programme of Study that appears fruitful for developing enquiry skills, such as rates of reaction, levers or photosynthesis.
3   Plan a lesson in which you can create an opportunity for the assessment of enquiry skills. Some useful prompts for planning include:

   •   Check what previous work pupils have done on enquiry skills and where their strengths and weaknesses lie.
   •   Decide which aspect of enquiry skills you will concentrate on.
   •   How will you inform pupils about the purpose of the lesson?
   •   How might pupils provide evidence relating to those enquiry skills?
   •   How will you make judgements about specific skills?
   •   How will you record the assessment evidence?
   •   Find out how the evidence might be converted into National Curriculum levels.
   •   Think through how you might best feedback to pupils about their achievement and next steps in improving enquiry skills.

SUMMARY

This unit has addressed the role of formative assessment in the science classroom and outlined ways of working which allows you to collect a rich source of assessment evidence about your pupils. Assessment prioritises classroom dialogue, written work and tests as sources for evidence of learning and understanding and suggests how each of these might be used to make judgements about the next steps in the teaching and learning. At this stage of your teaching career, it is essential that you try out and practise a range of assessment strategies and that you regularly discuss the implications of these on both teaching and learning with your mentor and peers.

This unit also highlights the pupil's role in assessment and offers ways into helping pupils develop self-assessment skills through a peer-assessment approach. Remember that setting up such practices in pupils who have not been encouraged in such behaviours is difficult and will take time and effort to achieve. When and how to move forward in this aspect of your teaching requires discussion and negotiation with the teachers in your teaching practice school.

FURTHER READING

Black, P. J. and Harrison, C. (2001) 'Feedback in questioning and marking: the science teacher's role in formative assessment', *School Science Review*, 82 (301): 55–61.

Black, P. J. and Harrison, C. (2001) 'Self- and peer-assessment and taking responsibility: the science pupil's role in formative assessment' *School Science Review*, 83 (302): 43–9.

Black, P. and Wiliam, D. (1998) *Inside the Black Box: Raising Standards Through Classroom Assessment*, London: King's College, School of Education.

Black, P., Harrison C., Lee, C., Marshall, B. and Wiliam, D. (2002) *Working Inside the Black Box: Assessment for Learning in the Classroom*, London: King's College, Department of Education and Professional Studies.

Black, P., Harrison, C. Lee, C. Marshall, B. and Wiliam, D. (2003) *Assessment for Learning: Putting it into Practice*, Buckingham: Open University Press.

Unit 7.2

Public Examinations

Alastair Cuthbertson and Jenny Frost

INTRODUCTION

Think back to your own experience of science examinations. Did you take all three subjects – biology, chemistry and physics – through to public examination level, as all pupils in maintained schools now do, or did you make choices between them? Which of your exams did justice, in your own view, to the course you had taken and the study you put in? How did you prepare and revise for them? Which patterns of study were helpful and which were not? Did you experience examinations where the testing was spread out over the course, as modular patterns in schools now do? Did you do coursework projects, and in what ways were the demands of these similar to, or different from, those you will make of your own pupils?

School examinations have experienced rapid change, alongside the curriculum changes, since the common 16+ General Certificate of Secondary Education (GCSE) arrangements replaced the dual system of General Certificate of Education, Ordinary Level (GCE O level) and the Certificate of Secondary Education (CSE), in 1986. Changes to GCSE science examinations have accommodated successive changes in National Curriculum science. Post-16 examinations and qualifications have also changed, with a vocational strand developing alongside more traditional general qualifications. Two of the main examinations in the post-16 age range are the General Certificate of Education Advanced Subsidiary level (GCE AS level) and GCE Advanced level (GCE A level) usually taken at the ages of 17 and 18 years respectively. The Advanced Vocational Certificate of Education (AVCE) is a recent addition. Viewing the 14 – 19 curriculum as a single continuum (DfES, 2002a, 2003c, 2003d) will occasion further changes in the qualifications available and the relationships between them.

In 2001, 88 per cent of pupils were entered for at least two GCSEs in science (the Double Award or for three separate subjects). In most schools, therefore, the results in science have a large impact for good or ill on the school's headline results, in particular the score for A*–C grades in five or more subjects. The publication of these figures in prospectuses and in local and national performance tables remains controversial but it has focused attention sharply on the factors contributing to the improvement of pupils' examination grades. Although significant, these factors are only one part of the larger picture to do with the quality of teaching and learning in science which shapes pupils' performance at the end of their courses.

OBJECTIVES

By the end of this unit you should:

- be familiar with the range of public science examinations taken in schools and with their main features;
- understand tiers of entry at GCSE and know what is involved in choosing the appropriate tier;
- recognise how GCSE science syllabuses differ;
- understand the implications of examination arrangements for the curriculum in Year 10 and above;
- understand the place of teacher assessment in science qualifications and know about the ways in which your own marking needs to be moderated;
- be aware of the changes which are pending with the development of a continuous curriculum for 14–19, and an associated national qualifications framework.

WHO SETS THE EXAMINATIONS?

There are currently three awarding bodies in England, one in Wales and one in Northern Ireland (they ceased to be called examination boards in the late 1990s). These bodies are responsible for creating and administering the examinations and assessments which are used by schools and post-16 colleges. The three English awarding bodies are AQA (Assessment and Qualifications Alliance), OCR (Oxford, Cambridge and Royal Society of Arts) and Edexcel (which has been renamed The London Partnership, but is still operating under Edexcel). They were formed from various amalgamations of *examining boards*, which were responsible for 'academic' examinations, and *awarding bodies* responsible for vocational qualifications. The current awarding bodies, therefore, produce specifications for assessment of general and vocational courses in a large number of subjects. They are funded by examination fees paid by schools and colleges.

The Qualifications and Curriculum Authority (QCA) is responsible for the criteria for each different examination, for the criteria for individual subjects and for monitoring standards across the awarding bodies. It was formed in 1997 from an amalgamation of NCVQ (National Council for Vocational Qualifications) and SCAA (Schools Curriculum and Assessment Authority). The comparable body in Wales is ACCAC (Awdurdod

Level	General	Vocational	Occupational (assessed in the workplace)
Level 5		BTEC Higher National Diploma (HND)	NVQ5
Level 4		BTEC Higher National Certificate (HNC)	NVQ4
Level 3	GCE A level (GCE AS is intermediate between GCSE and A level)	Advanced Vocational Certificate of Education (AVCE) BTEC National Certificates	NVQ3
Level 2	GCSE grades A*–C	GNVQ Intermediate	NVQ2
Level 1	GCSE grades D–G	GNVQ Foundation	NVQ1
Entry level	Entry level certificate		Entry

Figure 7.2.1 National Qualifications Framework

Cymhwysterau, Cwricwlwm ac Asesu Cymru – Qualifications, Curriculum and Assessment, Wales), and in Northern Ireland is CCEA (Council for Curriculum Examinations and Assessment). Scotland has the Scottish Qualifications Authority (SQA), but the pattern of examinations is different there.

QCA has developed a national qualifications framework in an attempt to both rationalise and show comparability between different qualifications. (See Figure 7.2.1 for a simplified version.)

WHAT SCIENCE EXAMINATIONS ARE AVAILABLE IN SCHOOLS?

The range of public examinations and qualifications available in science subjects and taken in schools is wide. Most are taken in National Curriculum based GCSEs (usually taken at age 16, at the end of compulsory education) and in separate subject GCE AS and A levels (usually taken at ages 17 and 18 respectively). Vocational science courses are on the increase, amongst them: GCSE Applied Science and AVCE Science.

In the following categories, the figures given are the numbers tested nationally in 2001, to the nearest hundred (www.qca.org.uk):

- GCSEs covering National Curriculum Science: Single Award (75100), Double Award (1,001,600), and Biology (56,000), Chemistry (47,000) and Physics (46,700) as separate subjects. Total entries 1,151,300.
- GCSEs in other science subjects, eg. Rural Science, Human Physiology and Health, Astronomy. The numbers are relatively small (18,000). GCSE Applied Science was introduced in 2002, so there are no figures for this. Similarly GCSE *21st Century Science* began a pilot in 2003.

- Entry Level Certificate in Science. This recognises achievement below GCSE grade G at the end of Key Stage 4, and allows pupils to achieve at National Curriculum levels 1, 2 and 3.
- AVCE, (science, double science) equivalent to 1 or 2 GCE A level passes. Take-up figures in 2002 were around 1400 and 1000 respectively.
- GCE A and AS levels in Biology, Chemistry and Physics. Take-up figures for the full A levels were around 52,400, 38,700 and 30,800 respectively.
- GCE A and AS levels in other science subjects, eg. Modular Science for a Single or Double Award; Science for Public Understanding; Environmental Science, Geology. Total take-up was around 4,300.
- GCE AEA (Advanced Extension Awards) in Biology, Chemistry and Physics. These are taken in addition to GCE A levels by a minority of high achieving pupils.

**Task 7.2.1
Examination courses in the department**

Make a table of science courses on offer in your school. Don't forget to include Year 12 (sixth form) one year courses, and possibly subjects taken in evening classes or a community programme. You may find closely related subjects taught in other departments, eg. electronics taught within the technology area.

For each examination course, list the:

- title;
- level of study and qualification to which it leads;
- awarding body (OCR; AQA; Edexcel);
- year group(s) studying it;
- number of pupils entered, analysed by tier of entry if possible;
- number of lessons (or time in hours) of study.

If there is a course with which you are unfamiliar, use the issues raised in this unit to prepare a set of questions, and ask the member of staff responsible if you can meet with him or her to find out more about it. You should also arrange to observe a class at work on the course, if possible.

UNDERSTANDING THE AWARD SPECIFICATION – GCSE SCIENCE(S)

Before GCSE, syllabuses were often quite short: a list of topics to be taught with details of the examination papers. The term 'syllabus' has been replaced by 'specification' a term used originally in occupational qualifications and in vocational courses, where it was necessary to specify what someone had to be able to do (in addition to material to be learned), in order to gain an award. If you have not already done so, look through the entire contents of the main GCSE specification booklet which governs your work with Key Stage 4 classes, to gain an overview of issues addressed. Gather the following items.

The school may be able to lend them or download them from the websites of the awarding bodies.

- The Specification
- The Guidance (or Support) Material booklet. This contains exemplar material for coursework tasks and their assessment.
- The Specimen Question Papers and answers, or (better) a set of recent past papers.
- A recent Examiner's Report, which gives information about how candidates tackled questions and where the main problems lay.

There are eight kinds of specifications according to their relationship to the Key Stage 4 Programmes of Study (POS) for Sc2 to Sc4 (see Figure 7.2.2). An awarding body will not permit pupils to be entered for more than one of these in any one round of examinations. The differences between them, along with grading arrangements and tiers of entry, are probably the most common queries which parents put to staff about GCSE science.

Subject	Specifications	Relation to KS4 NC PoS	Grades available
Science	Single Award	Includes KS4 PoS single science, but may go beyond	A*–G (see note 1)
	Double Award	Includes KS4 PoS double science, but may go beyond	A*A*–GG (see note 2)
Biology Chemistry Physics	Suite of exams, known as 'Triple Science'	Collectively cover at least KS4 NC double science, and may go substantially beyond.	A*–G A*–G A*–G (see note 3)
Applied Science	Single Award	Science content draws from the KS4 programme of study.	A*–G
	Double Award	Science content draws from the KS4 programme of study.	A*–G
21st Century Science	Single Award	Includes the proposed new NC PoS for single science (2006)	A*–G
	Double Award General	Consistent with the proposed new KS4 NC PoS for double science (2006)	A*A*–GG
	Double Award Applied	Consistent with the proposed new KS4 NC PoS for double science (2006)	A*A*–GG

Notes:
1. The single award science is intended to be of equal difficulty to the Double Award but is predominantly taken by lower achieving candidates (OFSTED 1995).
2. Double Award Science may provide additional information about candidates' relative performance on individual papers testing the biology, chemistry and physics components. This is known as the 'breakdown' of the grades.
3. There is no statutory requirement for pupils to take all three examinations of the 'triple science', even in maintained schools, although in practice they do. The minimum statutory requirement in maintained schools is to teach all of the Single Science POS.

Figure 7.2.2 GCSE Science courses and their relation to NC Science at KS4

Examination arrangements – linear, modular or staged

GCSE science specifications vary as to whether they are structured for linear, modular or staged assessments.

- Linear: The course is examined at the end of two years. This provides teachers with the opportunity to structure the course content as they wish providing that everything is covered by the end of the course.
- Modular: The course is structured into six modules for single science (12 for double science) and candidates take a module test at the end of each module. Marks for modules contribute to 30 per cent of the marks. Terminal papers are taken at the end of the two years and contribute to 50 per cent. This provides candidates with feedback on performance during the course and can make decisions about tier of entry (see below) easier.
- Staged: The Year 10 course is examined at the end of Year 10 and the Year 11 course is examined at the end of Year 11. This provides some flexibility over course structure within each year and some externally moderated feedback.

Tiers of entry – GCSE sciences

The standardised pattern is two tiers of entry: Foundation tier, with access to grades G–C, and Higher tier, with access to grades D–A*. There are separate written papers for each tier but the papers contain a proportion of common question material in the middle range of difficulty. This is one means by which examiners can check on the comparability of standards, especially at the C/D borderline, for the same grades awarded through taking different tiers. There has been a recent addition of a 'safety net' of grade E for candidates who narrowly miss a grade D on the higher tier paper. The GCSE certificate does not identify the tier of entry: a C grade is a C grade, whichever papers are taken.

Who enters for what tier?

In the case of some pupils it is difficult to decide on the appropriate tier for which to enter them. Difficulties arise in making decisions because on the one hand there are over-confident pupils (or ambitious parents) who press for entry to the Higher tier when their teacher's judgment is that they will do well to reach C. In this circumstance there is a danger that, tackling unsuccessfully the harder questions on the Higher tier papers, they will fall below the C and possibly even the D grade boundaries. On the other hand there are easy-going pupils (and uninterested parents) who are content with the prospect of a C to be gained by a comfortable route, despite the teacher's recognition of their potential to do better if they apply themselves to the task.

You should find out how science teachers approach the job of counselling and discussion with pupils and parents in these cases. If possible, attend a relevant parents' evening. Your science department may have an agreed entry policy. A lot depends on the timing and context of the information that is available during the course. Where module tests are taken, or a written paper at the end of Year 10, they provide externally validated feedback to pupils and parents before a final decision is taken over tier of entry in Year 11.

In selecting the specification you may have come across the label 'coordinated science' and 'Salters science'. The term 'coordinated' arose in the 1980s in contrast to 'integrated' science and separate science courses. Integrated science courses integrated material from physics, chemistry and biology within the topics taught. Coordinated courses separated physics, chemistry and biology so that the material could be taught by specialists but made appropriate links between them. Salters Science is the one course which retains something of an integrated nature by virtue of the fact that it starts from contexts.

Task 7.2.2
Analysing a GCSE science specification

Use the questions below to study a science specification, with its associated guidance. (Do not choose an Applied Science Course, which is dealt with in Task 7.2.4.)

- Is the content laid out by subject specialisms, or in shorter modules? Is there evidence of coordination, e.g. by cross-reference to other subjects or to other modules? If it is modular, how long are the modules? Are any of the modules integrated, i.e. drawing on more than one of Sc2–4?
- How is the content divided between the two tiers? Does it enable rapid identification of what needs teaching to whom?
- Is the content cross-referenced to the appropriate National Curriculum Programme of Study? Does referencing include investigative skills (Sc1.2) and ideas and evidence (Sc1.1), or are these left to the school to build in?
- Is the Foundation content an appropriate and manageable selection for low and middle ability pupils?
- Which items are additional to the POS? At the Higher tier especially, is the additional content for the more able suitable for those who may wish to go on to A level?
- What guidance is given for addressing cross-curricular themes: 'Spiritual, Moral, Ethical, Social and Cultural Issues'; 'Health, Safety and Environmental issues' 'citizenship' and 'key skills'?
- Is the content specified in detail or in outline? Is the depth of knowledge required made clear, and what pupils will be asked to do with their knowledge (e.g. recall facts, apply knowledge, describe functions, or explain reasons)?
- Are learning experiences or pupil activities suggested in the specification or in materials associated with it? Are different learning experiences suggested for Foundation and Higher work?
- What other forms of support, e.g. a textbook written for the course, inservice sessions for teachers, suitable CD-ROMs, or photocopiable masters for pupils or teachers, are available in the specification or its associated materials?

Using question papers to interpret specifications

The specification is the 'rule book' for a public examination, and equally importantly the question papers form the 'case law'. The question papers show the depth of treatment expected in teaching the course, and the relative emphasis given to different parts of the syllabus. You should therefore study them carefully at an early stage. Write out your own model answers, and if possible check them against a mark scheme. Make notes of the guidance that you will need to give pupils, especially when the time for revision comes round, in order to improve their ability to gain marks.

Task 7.2.3
Analysing question papers on a GCSE science specification

Using the same specification which you used in Task 7.2.2, complete a set of question papers and check against model answers. Then analyse the papers as follows:

- What are the main assessment objectives for the whole GCSE science specification? How are they broken down into sub-objectives?
- Which assessment objectives are examined by the written paper?
- Match the individual questions (or parts of questions) to the more detailed 'sub-objectives'? That is, try to separate the recall questions from the analysis and data interpretation questions, etc.
- How is 'ideas and evidence' tested?
- Are any aspects of investigations tested by the written paper – if so, what and how?

UNDERSTANDING THE AWARD SPECIFICATION FOR A VOCATIONAL COURSE – GCSE APPLIED SCIENCE

GCSE Applied Science courses started in 2002, with the first examinations in 2004. They have characteristics of vocational courses, focusing not only on knowing how science is used in the workplace but on learning the skills which would be useful for a science-based vocation.

The pattern of assessment is different from GCSE science(s). GCSE science has 80 per cent of the marks allocated by external papers, with 20 per cent allocated through teacher assessment of investigations. GCSE Applied Science has only a third of the marks allocated by external tests and two-thirds by portfolio. Portfolios of evidence include investigational work, with emphasis on scientific skills appropriate to science as used in the workplace rather than on skills related to the discovery or verification of scientific knowledge. Portfolios include pieces of work relating to other aspects of science as it is used at work such as Health and Safety issues.

Task 7.2.4
Understanding a vocational specification – GCSE Applied Science

Select a GCSE Applied Science specification from any one of the awarding bodies.

- What are the assessment objectives? How do they differ from the assessment objectives of GCSE Science courses?
- What aspects of Sc2–4 are included and how is the content organised?
- What 'vocational skills' are to be developed which would not be developed through the GCSE science course?
- What suggestions are made for incorporating a vocational context into the course?
- What implications does the vocational context have for the planning and organisation of teaching? (e.g. will teachers have to organise visits, work experience, outside speakers?)
- How many different items go into the portfolio?
- What guidance is given on marking the portfolio work?
- Are the criteria for the different grades clearly set out?
- Are the portfolios marked at the end of the course or at stages throughout the course?
- Are there 'tiers of entry' as there are for the GCSE Science?

UNDERSTANDING THE SPECIFICATION: SCIENCE GCE A AND AS LEVELS, AND ADVANCED EXTENSION AWARDS (AEA)

Advanced level GCE, first introduced in the 1950s, was conceived as a step towards higher education and admission to a degree programme. Typically pupils studied two, three or four A level subjects of their choice, over a period of two years, between the ages of 16 and 18. They were only allowed to embark on such courses if they had been reasonably successful in the previous examinations.

The structure of GCE A level in all subjects changed in 2000. The AS level, introduced originally in mid-1980s, changed from 'Advanced Supplementary', as difficult as A level but half the size in content and value, to 'Advanced Subsidiary', intended to examine the easier first half of an A level course, at an intermediate standard between GCSE and A level. A level specifications therefore come in two parts, AS with 40 per cent assessment weighting and A2 with 60 per cent weighting. As with GCSEs, modular structures have become popular and there are varied styles of content, organisation and patterns of examination. The purpose of AS is to allow pupils to have a wider curriculum in Year 12, by their taking say four or five AS levels in Year 12 and narrowing down to say 3 or 4 in Year 13.

There are choices between different specifications for each of biology, chemistry and physics. At the time of writing, each subject has a 'context led' course (Salters A level Chemistry examined by OCR; Salters–Horners A level physics examined by Edexcel; and Salters–Nuffield Biology examined by Edexcel). Physics has a new course in the form of Advancing Physics, sponsored by the Institute of Physics, and examined by OCR. There is a Nuffield Chemistry course examined by Edexcel. All three subjects have what might be regarded as more traditional syllabuses. In addition to these there are the AS and A level in: Science (rather like a 'balanced science' course at GSCE); Science for Public Understanding (AS only); Environmental Science; Geology.

Task 7.2.5
Analysing GCE AS and A level specifications for your specialism

- Select two specifications for your specialist subject (physics or chemistry or biology).
- Is the content the same?
- How is the content laid out? What are the similarities and differences between the two specifications?
- Is there any choice of content for the teacher/for the pupils?
- Are the assessment objectives the same?
- Complete a question paper and compare your answers with model answers.
- Are the questions set within some context? Does any one question draw from several areas of the content?
- What is the pattern of assessment? Are there open book examinations, reports of visits, investigation reports, etc? Is there a timed practical examination?
- What proportion is internally assessed?

GCE Advanced Extension Awards were first examined in 2002. They replace the special papers which were taken by high-attaining pupils in addition to their GCE A level papers. Only a small number of students take these papers, hence one awarding body is responsible for the examination on behalf of all others. CCEA is responsible for physics, AQA for the biology and chemistry papers. Specifications, specimen papers, past papers, and teacher guidance can be downloaded from the respective websites.

UNDERSTANDING THE SPECIFICATIONS: ADVANCED VOCATIONAL QUALIFICATIONS

Alongside GCSE and GCE A and AS level are the vocational qualifications, AVCE and BTEC (Business and Technical Education Council awards). These vocational qualifications need to be distinguished from workplace or occupational qualifications (NVQs) – National Vocational Qualifications. In the former the skills and knowledge are those which will be needed in workplace environments, the latter are those assessed in the workplace, by people already in employment, and they are competence based. The former will, however, involve visits to places of work and may also include some work experience.

You may come across the last remnants of GNVQ (General National Vocational Qualifications). GNVQs were introduced in the early 1990s and had three levels, Foundation, Intermediate and Advanced. Science GNVQ was commonly adopted at Intermediate level as an alternative to retaking GCSE in Year 12 and adopted by some schools as an alternative to GCSE in Year 10 and Year 11. (Intermediate GNVQ is equivalent to four GCSEs). Foundation GNVQ finished in 2003. Intermediate GNVQ will be phased out by 2005. Advanced GNVQ was replaced by the Advanced Vocational Certificate of Education (Advanced VCE or AVCE).

There are other qualifications closely tied to particular industries, such as BTEC Nationals in Applied Science, Sport and Exercise Science, Dental Technology, Pharmacy Services. There is sufficient difference between these and the various A level science courses that it is possible to study a science-related BTEC course alongside an A level science course, i.e. they are not 'prohibited combinations'.

Study an AVCE specification in the same way as the GCSE and A level specifications.

INTERNALLY AND EXTERNALLY ASSESSED COMPONENTS – COURSEWORK, PORTFOLIOS AND MODERATION

You will have realised from your study of the different specifications above that there is considerable variation in the scale and type of internally assessed components which are completed for different awards. In this section we turn to how and why such assessment is counted towards pupils' public examination results.

Some GCE A level syllabuses in science subjects introduced coursework projects as early as the 1960s. Since then coursework has slowly gained ground, either as an alternative to formal practical examinations of the traditional type or replacing them altogether. The argument runs that if pupils should be involved in observational and experimental science on a regular basis, then coursework is an appropriate way of giving status to that part of their work and of assessing it. Practical examinations have often been seen as too far removed from day-to-day practical science, and unduly limited in scope by the time and equipment that can be made available.

For similar reasons, coursework was established as integral to science GCSEs from the outset. In the early years of the GCSE, before the introduction of the National Curriculum, coursework assessment schemes varied in emphasis. 'Whole investigation' projects featured in only a few.

Now all GCSE science (single, double and 'triple' awards) have a common standard pattern of coursework, based on the National Curriculum model of experimental and investigative science comprising the four skill areas Planning, Obtaining, Analysing and Evaluating evidence (POAE). Specific lessons in Year 10 and Year 11 are often allocated to doing investigations for coursework. In addition, considerable time is spent throughout the course in learning and practising the component skills and knowledge. Evidence for achievement is judged almost entirely on the written account of investigations, although teacher observations of performance make some contribution. You will have realised that the assessment pattern for the applied science and the vocational courses is very different.

Examination rules and professional judgement

It is the job of the department's teaching team to end up with valid and reliable coursework marks to submit to Awarding Bodies. In the context of GCSE coursework: do the pupils' marks reward good experimental and investigative work that they have done for themselves, in line with the expectations of the syllabus and mark scheme? If they do, they are valid. Is the standard of marking fair and consistent across different pieces of coursework from any one pupil, and across different teachers' marking? This is the test of reliability. Both issues are addressed by the Awarding Body's rules, and both are also quite a professional challenge. The same issues are of course raised nationally concerning Teacher Assessment in Key Stages 1 to 3, A level and other courses.

Validity and 'authentication' of coursework

As with tasks of any kind, what pupils achieve in their coursework depends on what they are asked to do, how it is introduced to them and the help and support available to them whilst doing it. Choosing appropriate tasks in the first place is a challenge for teachers. If tasks are not suggested in the department's scheme of work, then see the guidance and exemplar material provided by the Awarding Body. Such material identifies suitable tasks as well as marked examples of pupils' coursework, including examples of tasks of varying difficulty.

The awarding bodies usually ask teachers to report the help given to pupils. 'Help' includes advice given to the class as a whole, for example through helpsheets. The teacher may also be required to make a note on pupils' scripts of help given to individuals. The Board should set out how to take such help into account in the marking of pupils' work. This requirement may lead to decisions taken within the school, or by the Awarding Body, about where and when coursework may be done, perhaps limiting some or even all of it to the classroom. They may also provide guidance about how and when to give credit for pupils' use of textbooks and other resources. Task 7.2.6 is concerned with the range of help and support that may be available to pupils.

Coursework can only remain credible and educationally productive if teachers act professionally in the way they conduct it. In general terms, the Awarding Bodies have encouraged teachers to provide positive opportunities for pupils to show what they can do. This means a careful balance between providing pupils with some freedom of choice and yet with an appropriate framework within which they can succeed, and between encouraging their resourcefulness and at the same time ensuring practicality and safety. These considerations place considerable demands on teachers' skill and professionalism.

Reliable marking and 'moderation' of work

Moderation is the process through which marks for coursework are brought in line with a common standard, thus making them reliable. 'Internal' moderation seeks to establish a common standard within the school. 'External' moderation makes the comparisons across schools and nationally.

Internal moderation may be carried out in various ways. In science, teachers generally aim to establish the correct standard of marking as early as possible, and at least before they mark the pieces of work which are likely to count towards the selected marks sent to the awarding body. Commonly, they look together at the Awarding Body's guidance and interpret it for their own circumstances; they may produce marking guidelines for particular coursework tasks, illustrating pupils' responses for different marks; they will exchange scripts,

Task 7.2.6
How can I help?

Find an opportunity to observe or teach a class tackling a coursework task for GCSE. You will need to ask questions about what came before the start of the coursework itself. You will also need to look at pupils' completed scripts and how they are marked. The following are all relevant to how pupils are helped with their work:

- How do previous lessons lead into the work? Has the class done similar work before? How similar, and how recently?
- Does the teacher remind pupils of what to do in general terms, e.g. 'choose a variable' or 'draw a line graph'? Or are they taken through the specifics of the topic, e.g. told which variable to choose or what axes and scales to use?
- Are the reminders oral or in writing, e.g. a worksheet, a helpsheet or a copy of the assessment points?
- Do pupils work on their own or in groups, either for the practical work only or for planning and writing up too?
- How does the teacher respond to questions from pupils? Is it treated like a practical examination or like a teaching lesson?
- Do pupils complete all the work in school, or are they allowed to take it home? Are they allowed to use family members and home computers as part of the resources available to them?
- How does the marking take account of any of these sources of help? Does the teacher annotate the script to show help given?

Compare your findings with other students. You may find considerable variations in practice. It has been said that: 'Marks should be given for how help is taken up, not taken away because help was given.' Do you agree, and how does this work for the different kinds of help you have seen?

mark them separately and then discuss them to resolve differences. The latter may be organised annually at a formal moderation meeting in the science department. Even when teachers have become familiar with applying the awarding body's criteria, any marks reported to pupils or their parents are provisional since they will still be subject to external moderation. Feedback to pupils is valuable especially if there will be future chances for them to improve their performance, but schools and departments may set their own rules about what feedback is allowed.

Task 7.2.7 provides you with an opportunity to experience moderation. You may be able to follow up this task by attending a moderation meeting in your science department. If not, you should repeat the exercise in collaboration with another student teacher and by exchanging groups of scripts from different tasks. It is considerably harder to decide on marks when you did not see the class do the practical work. This highlights the importance of knowing how the task was introduced and of annotating the pupils' work concerning the individual help given.

Early in the summer term each year, your science department works out the marks which represent pupils' best achievement according to the awarding body's rules. A number

Task 7.2.7
Internal moderation

Compare your own judgments in marking coursework with another teacher's judgments. If possible, do this first with the regular class teacher of a class you are working with and for a task you have seen them do.

Both the regular class teacher and yourself should mark the same scripts independently, without access to the other's marks. Mark at least three pupils' work, selected from the top, middle and lower ranges of achievement in the class. The first marker will need to annotate the script in line with the awarding body's guidance. Then compare the 'POAE' (Planning, Obtaining, Analysing, Evaluating) marks each of you has given; discuss the reasons for any differences and note how these are resolved.

of sample scripts are supplied to an external moderator appointed by the awarding body, selected from across the range of pupil achievement and from different classes and teachers. The moderator has the right to ask for additional scripts if necessary, so the department must keep all the pupils' scripts which contribute to their final marks until after the external moderation is completed. It is not uncommon for moderators to make adjustments to the school's marks, for example if the school's marking is too generous at one end of the achievement range. The adjustments are made to all pupils' marks from the school, even though based on a small sample. It is assumed that internal moderation beforehand makes this a sensible process. External moderators write a short report on their decisions, a copy of which is returned to the school.

PREPARING PUPILS FOR THEIR PUBLIC EXAMINATIONS

Schools and science departments pay increasing attention to preparing pupils for examinations. This is a task with several aspects:

- developing pupils' study skills for revision;
- teaching 'examination techniques' for answering questions effectively;
- providing specific resources to help revise course content;
- actively supporting pupils during the revision process;
- building up their confidence and motivation (most important of all).

General aspects of this preparation are addressed in Capel *et al.* (2001) Unit 6.2. Most schools make use of one or more of the published revision guides, often buying them in bulk and passing the discount on to their pupils. Revision guides are available which are exactly matched to each specification; pupils need not waste so much as a minute revising material on which they will not be examined! There are usually also accompanying Workbooks, though some schools channel pupils towards buying the Workbook from a different publisher, since otherwise revision can amount to no more than an undemanding copying exercise from the page in the Guide to the corresponding 'blanks' in the Workbook.

However, only a minority of pupils are likely to find Guides and Workbooks helpful; they require a text-based learning style (and a good deal of persistence). There are lots of ways to revise, just as there are lots of ways to learn. Different revision methods suit different learning styles. Teachers need to introduce the different techniques to pupils; using, for example, mind mapping, key fact summaries, problem-solving exercises, quizzes, paired testing and so on as well as practice examination questions. The KS3 Booster lesson materials (DfES 2002c, 2003d) are of course focused on KS3 content and were originally designed for pupils at the level 4/5 borderline, but they have proved useful for a wider range of pupils than this would suggest. Alongside the KS3 National Strategy training and packs, they have provided schools with many good models for revision as well as for learning that are now being successfully introduced for GCSE revision too. Software packages for revision are also popular with many pupils. They include on-line revision, for example the well-established BBC Bitesize, and reasonably priced CD based packages, some of which incorporate sophisticated tools for pupils to track their individual progress through the material. Similarly revision guides, and books of worked examples are available for GCE AS and A level courses.

Examination results play an important role alongside other 'performance indicators' by which a school is judged. Local Education Authorities (LEAs) and government agencies as well as schools themselves use a variety of such indicators to monitor school performance, including the results of Standard Assessment Tasks (SATs) and attendance statistics. How they are used is the subject of Unit 7.3.

PENDING CHANGES TO QUALIFICATIONS IN 14–19 AGE RANGE

Qualifications and examinations as currently construed are the result of the multiple histories of the diverse organisations involved. Successive rationalisations have occurred, the recent National Qualifications Framework being one, but the myriad of qualifications which still exists is confusing to many users. There are other concerns. While the majority of pupils gains GCSEs, a minority gains no qualifications and drop out believing they have failed. There is an overemphasis on written examinations at the expense of wider learning, skills and personal development.

Concerns such as these have provoked a wider debate about the curriculum and assessment in the 14–19 age range. The Government Green Paper *14–19 : Opportunity and Excellence* (DfES 2003c) was followed by the setting up of a Working Group on Reforming the 14–19 Curriculum and Assessment. The Working Group's interim report was published in February 2004 (DfES, 2004) and its final report will be published in June 2004. A multilevel diploma is proposed which allows for progression by a variety of routes, and has a 'core' of a breadth of skills.

As a teacher at the start of your teaching career, you need to be involved in the debates and aware that changes will occur. Whatever the changes, the skills which we have described in this chapter will stand you in good stead for whatever model of assessment is developed.

SUMMARY

Examination success is a highly visible and rewarding aspect of your teaching; good results are a source of professional satisfaction and pride. The annual set of GCSE, GCE AS and A level, and vocational qualifications results is one way in which individual teachers, subject departments and schools as a whole assess their performance, as well as an important basis on which they are judged, not least by their local communities.

As a science teacher you need to know your way around the specifications thoroughly, not only their subject content but their style, emphasis and organisation and crucially the patterns of assessment they use, through question papers, coursework and performance criteria. You have a particular professional responsibility for the fair and reliable marking of coursework. In addition, you will need to be aware of considerable variations in the provision which schools make for examination courses. For example, within one LEA the time given to teaching Double Award GCSE science courses in different schools varies between 3.5 and 7 hours per week. There are also wide variations in the provision of material resources, including books and whether pupils have suitable textbooks and access to the Internet available to use at home. Such considerations may be important to you when you are seeking your first post.

FURTHER READING

Capel, S., Leask, M. and Turner, T. (eds) (2001) *Learning to Teach in the Secondary School: A Companion to School Experience* 3rd edn, London and New York: RoutledgeFalmer, Unit 6.2.

Lambert, D. and Lines, D. (2000) *Understanding Assessment: Purposes, Perceptions and Practice*, London and New York; RoutledgeFalmer. This book provides a deeper guide into examination principles in the first half of the book. The second half is devoted to formative assessment, which will act as reading for Unit 7.1.

School Science Review, **85** (310). The September 2003 issue of *School Science Review* is devoted to the discussion of 14–19 science education and the changes in qualifications. It provides an insight into the debates and developments in the field and their impacts on qualifications.

Study carefully the guidance in the examination specifications and their associated publications for the science examinations in your placement schools. Become familiar with the examination papers and rules for assessing coursework. Read materials made available to pupils, both during the course and for revision purposes, and assess their strengths and weaknesses.

Unit 7.3

Reporting Progress and Accountability

Tony Turner

INTRODUCTION

While pupils use their grades in external examinations as evidence of personal achievement, LEAs, government agencies and the schools themselves use grades, along with other performance indicators such as attendance statistics and results of Standard Assessment Tests (SATs), to judge the effectiveness of the school. As a student working in a school you need to know how that school uses the information not only to judge its effectiveness but to improve it.

OBJECTIVES

By the end of this unit you should:

- understand the terms 'Benchmarking', 'Target Setting' and 'Value Added';
- know the current national benchmarks for science;
- know how these factors are used to monitor pupil progress;
- be aware how Value Added is estimated and reported;
- be alert to the requirements of report writing and parents evening.

MAKING COMPARISONS

There are three ways of measuring progress, one is to compare present performance with previous performance, and another is to compare present performance with the average performance of a much larger sample with similar characteristics and the last is to compare performance with a set target. In practice, schools use all methods; they look for trends over time in, for instance, their examination results, and compare these with national trends. The DfES provides schools with the analysis of their Performance and Assessment Data (PANDA) in the annual statistical report sent as part of the Autumn Package of Pupil Performance. This package contains information for 'benchmarking' 'target setting' and for judging 'value added'.

Benchmarking

A benchmark is a starting point, from which measurements can be made, and comes from the field of surveying, where it is literally a mark on a fixed place from which the surroundings can be measured. Figure 7.3.1 shows data which are used as two benchmarks in science, the proportion of pupils gaining A*–C in GCSE double science, and the percentage of pupils in England gaining level 5 in KS3 science SATs. Schools are compared with the national average to identify how much they exceed or undershoot the benchmark – a process referred to as 'benchmarking'.

Obviously schools vary enormously in intake; a highly selective school may have 100 per cent of pupils gaining these marks, whereas a school with a high proportion of pupils with SEN will be below the national average. The analysis of statistics has to take these, and a variety of other contextual features, into account.

Proportion (%) of pupils gaining level 5 and above in KS3 SATs, 1996–2003, judged by written test and by teacher assessment.

Year	96	97	98	99	00	01	02	03
% pupils (Test)	57	60	56	55	59	66	67	68
% Pupils (Teacher Assessment)		62	60	62	64	67	69	62

Proportion (%) of pupils gaining A*–C grades in GCSE Double Science, 1998–2003

Year	98	99	00	01	02	03
% pupils	49.7	49.7	50.6	51.2	52.0	53.8

Figure 7.3.1 Two benchmarks for science

Value Added

An important question for schools is 'What has the school done to improve the performance of its pupils?' (Stoll and Fink 1996:179); an approach known as finding 'Value Added'. The DfES uses a statistical model for determining the predicted outcomes in KS3 science tests, based on KS2 results, and of GCSE results based on KS3 science tests. Figure 7.3.2 is an example of such predictive information from the 2003 Autumn Package (for information about how numerical scores such as 26–28 are calculated from NC levels see the website, www.dfes.gov.uk/performance/).

The argument is that if a cohort's results match its predicted outcome then the school is adding the average value for schools nationally; if however the cohort does better than expected then the school is adding more value to that cohort's education than the national average, and if it does worse than expected, then it is adding less value.

Target setting

Target setting is a process of identifying future achievements, or goals, for an individual or group, to promote progression and raise the standard of their performance. Setting a suitable target for individuals involves factors such as their past achievement, prior indicators of potential, motivation and other personal circumstances. The target is a personal goal agreed between pupil and teacher. Obviously the statistical information on whole cohorts can be used to predict likely individual scores.

Target setting for a group aims to raise the standard of the group and the predicted outcomes given in the Autumn package are often used to form the basis of the target. Schools can choose other benchmarks in order to make fairer comparisons; see below. Target setting for the whole school, through subject departments, is a matter of judging what change can realistically be expected and planned for.

The DfES models form only one contribution to the analysis of past and predicted performance which most schools now undertake. Many use additional input data often incorporating the use of tests of cognitive ability, such as the Cognitive Assessment Tasks (CATs) produced and standardised by the National Foundation for Educational Research,

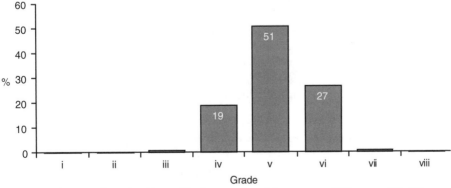

Figure 7.3.2 Predicted KS3 profile for pupils with average KS2 score 26–28.
Source: DfES/TTA Autumn Package Guidance, graph 3.2.5 see web addresses.
Key: i = level 1, ii = level 2, etc.

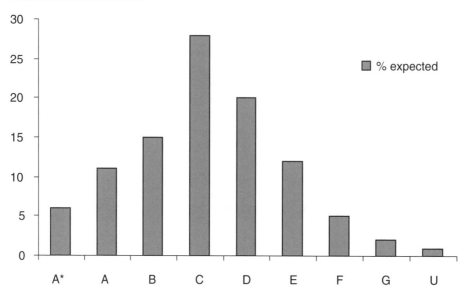

Figure 7.3.3 CAT: predicted profile of GCSE grades; Riddlesdown High School

the middle years information system (MidYIS), the year eleven information system (YELLIS) and the advanced level information system (ALIS). These provide baseline data about pupils early on entry into respective phases of schooling and predict or compare their eventual performance at KS3, GCSE and A level. (For details of CATs see NFER, www.nfer.ac.uk. For details of MidYIS, YELLIS and ALIS, go to the Curriculum, Evaluation and Management centre www.cemcentre.org). One of the reasons for using alternative information systems especially at the start of secondary schools is that the KS2 information is relatively undiscriminating with the majority in level 4 category.

Riddlesdown High School, Croydon, tested their Year 7 (295 pupils) in October 2001 using the CAT test. The test predicted that 60 per cent of pupils will achieve GCSE A*–C grades in science in 2005; see Figure 7.3.3.

In 2002, 71 per cent of Riddlesdown High School pupils achieved grades A*–C in science (up from 58 per cent in 1995) compared with the 2002 national average of 52 per cent (see Figure 7.3.1). If their GCSE science results follow past achievements, performance in 2005 may be greater than predicted, suggesting a positive Value Added component to teaching and learning. Alternatively the lower CAT predictions may reflect something about the nature of that Year 7 cohort, alerting staff to investigate the data closely, monitor pupils carefully and plan teaching accordingly.

PERFORMANCE TABLES FOR SCHOOLS IN ENGLAND

Schools share much of their performance data with parents via school brochures and annual reports; a limited amount is available automatically via the annual publication of Performance Tables. Up until recently these tables contained only the raw data of examination achievement in terms of percentages of pupils gaining different range of grades. In 2003 the percentage of pupils with SEN, both with and without statements was displayed alongside examination results.

The 2003 figures included the result of a pilot Value Added study which gave Value Added information about the sample of schools in the pilot. Details of how Value Added is calculated, how to read the tables, and the reliability and validity of the scores is available on the DfES website alongside the performance tables themselves (www.dfes.gov.uk/ performancetables). The hope is that Value Added answers will provide a fairer way of comparing school performance than tables based on data which ignores differences in pupil intake.

Task 7.3.1 What assessment data in science is available in your school and how is it used?

1   If possible borrow a copy of the PANDA report. You will find a wealth of data which compares science with other subjects, girls' performance with boys' and so on.
2   Find out from your mentor whether pupils' NC levels at KS2 in English, mathematics and science are collated by the secondary school. Are marks as well as levels known?
3   What predictive models are used (e.g. CATs, PANDA, Yellis etc.)?
4   How does the science department use the data from the predictions? (See the example of Riddlesdown above.)
5   What pupil assessment data is given to you as a class teacher? Discuss with your mentor how you should use it.

IMPROVING RATE OF PROGRESS IN SCIENCE

The investment in collection and interpretation of assessment data has led to considerable concern about the lack of progress between KS2 and KS3 (OFSTED 2001: commentary) and questions about the way assessment information is used in schools (OFSTED 2000:143). The National Strategy for KS3 Science (DfES 2000b) may improve this position but schools are also experimenting with a range of interventions. One such intervention is the Cognitive Acceleration in Science Education project (CASE) (see Unit 5.1). There is evidence that pupils following this intervention programme in Years 7 and 8 have shown, three years later, enhanced performances in GCSE English, mathematics and science (Shayer 1996). This interesting finding has been repeated over several years suggesting a real effect caused by the intervention programme. A recent paper interprets this effect in terms of 'Value Added' by CASE (Shayer 2002, see the web address). For further reading about this project and the scientific reasoning tasks used see Shayer and Adey 2002.

Find out from your mentor intervention strategies which are used in the school.

REPORTING TO PARENTS

Pupils and parents should be told about the way in which pupils are monitored and tested and what the results of testing mean, although not necessarily in the detail above. Your record keeping is central to this process. Reports to parents, whether written or oral, need to be concise and not overloaded with jargon (Capel *et al.* 2001, Chapter 6: 299–302).

Parents need to be aware of what is expected of their child and the evidence for it. Parents need to understand how the results of testing may affect the teaching group into which their child is placed, the GCSE course they are advised to follow or the tier of examination paper for which they are entered. Many parents simply want to know how their child is performing in relation to other pupils, locally and nationally and the grades to expect at examinations and map this onto career aspirations. Information, too, about their child's attitude to learning is valuable and how achievement reflects their effort.

There are two important reporting procedures, the written report and the face-to-face discussion at a parents evening.

The written report

Schools usually have a standardised way of reporting to parents and the format may include:

- commentary on achievement, effort and homework with a grading system ranging from very good to poor. Ensure you understand the criteria for points on the scale;
- level of achievement, using an internal scale of reporting together with links to National Curriculum Levels or GCSE grades. Ensure you understand these links;
- teacher commentary identifying pupil strengths and how to build on them. Also weaknesses and what the pupil needs to do to overcome them;
- a realistic statement of future progress and how the pupil can contribute to maintaining or improving on that diagnosis.

Parents need to be aware of any differences between the school's internal reporting procedure and that used nationally to avoid over optimism or undue pessimism.

Advice needs to identify future action or changes in behaviour. Attitudes, enthusiasm and enjoyment should feature in your report. See Haydn 2001: 297.

Meeting parents

Parents' evenings often take place after a written report has been sent home. Preparation for these events is the key to a successful meeting. Have available, including any written report, evidence about the:

- achievement of pupils at entry and subsequent performance, e.g. scores and grades;
- record of attendance, class work and homework to which you can refer (make sure information about other pupils is not visible);
- improvement seen or expected based on prior achievement;
- quality of work in class, written work, class tests, investigations;
- attitude to and interest in science.

Be prepared to give direction to focus on improvement, such as actions the pupil can take to improve, what work would look like when it is better and how parents can help with these developments.

Where curriculum choices are to be made, e.g. about tier of entry to GCSE, then you should have available information about:

- the choices on offer;
- how choice is made;
- consequences of choice for later study or career;
- how parents can help decision making.

Other curriculum choices may focus on selection between Single Science, Double Science or Separate Sciences; also the advantages and disadvantages of academic and vocational routes through GCSE, GNVQ and GCE A Level. Be prepared to give advice on study techniques and how to revise for examinations.

SUMMARY

National Standards have been rising nationally as judged by numbers of pupils achieving specified NC levels or gaining grade A*–C at science GCSE. Results by themselves do not tell us much about what we should expect from pupils; we have to take into account their prior achievements. Rising standards may signify improved teaching or learning or reflect a greater focus by the school on teaching to the test. Raised achievement, however, may be at the expense of enjoyment of and motivation for science.

Unease about the use of simple data in publishing national Performance Tables has led to different presentation of results by including data about pupils with Special Educational Needs. Value Added measures have drawn attention to the ways in which teachers motivate pupils to achievements above that expected from previous performance (Goldstein 2002).

Value Added is the outcome of comparing predicted performance of a pupil, or group of pupils, with actual performance. Schools use a variety of databases to calculate predicted performance, including those in *The Autumn Package of Guidance to Schools* (DfES/TTA 2003b) and CAT tests (NFER). However, the context in which pupils achieve may change. For example, there may be changes in the domestic or economic life of their family which can affect the way in which the pupil responds to school. Teachers need to continue to monitor the progress of pupils using all the information available to them, bearing in mind the needs of pupils.

An important task facing science teachers is the improvement of pupil performance during Key Stage 3. In the past, initial enthusiasm for science has declined towards the end of that stage and concerns over transfer between junior and secondary school continue (Jarman 2000). The KS3 Science Strategy in England (DfES 2002b) was initiated to address that problem; recent evaluation after two years has shown limited success (OFSTED 2003).

FURTHER READING

Goldstein, H. (2002) *League Tables and Schooling*, London Institute of Education, University of London (http:// www.ioe.ac.uk/hgpersonal/League-tables-and-schooling-P&S.pdf).

Goldstein discusses the limitations associated with ranking schools by test scores and the need for a Value Added component to be included. Examples of how this might be done are shown with reference to work of ALis+ and LEAs.

Richardson, C. (ed) (2002) *Assessing Gifted and Talented Children: World Class Tests,* London; Qualifications and Curriculum Authority. This provides a discussion and review of developments, by international authors, of ways to identify and teach talented pupils. Contains examples of tests in mathematics and problem solving and some early teaching material.

Saunders, L. (1998) *Value Added Measurement of School Effectiveness: An Overview,* Slough: NFER. This is a review of the effectiveness of Value Added in the late 1990s. Contains useful discussion of the meanings given to Value Added and the difficulties associated with its use.

8 The Broader Science Curriculum

The science curriculum is a vehicle for considerable cross-curricular work especially in literacy, numeracy and ICT (see Chapter 3). We focus here, however, on two other aspects of cross-curricular work, citizenship and health education. Both these areas use concepts such as rights, responsibilities, values and beliefs, drawn from disciplines other than mainstream science, and address issues of considerable personal and social sensitivity.

Citizenship was introduced as a discrete subject on the curriculum in 2000 and in many schools is taught separately. Nevertheless, science teachers are increasingly expected to be able to tackle a range of controversial issues both as an intrinsic component of science and as a contribution to citizenship education. Unit 8.1 provides sound advice on how to enable pupils to think through issues in a sophisticated way and on what roles the teacher can adopt.

Health education, and sex and relationship education have been part of the science curriculum for a long time, but like citizenship education they are not the sole responsibility of the science department. In both areas of the curriculum it is important to know how the responsibilities are distributed between departments. The issues related to teaching this area face science students early on in their training because it is very common for them to have to teach human reproduction to Year 7 classes as one of their first topics in school experience (this topic is typically placed in the second half of the winter term). Unit 8.2 gives guidance on how to work in this area to address legitimate questions from pupils without invading personal privacy.

Teaching social issues in citizenship, health education or sex and relationship education programmes through science should draw on the same teaching approaches and styles that you might use to teach any other aspect of science. There is, however, a further dimension to consider and that is one of values. Much science teaching may be said to be value free or at least the procedures and outcomes do not depend on a moral judgement. Many social issues discussed in this chapter carry with them a value judgement. Teachers have to balance knowledge against values, beliefs against evidence and be sensitive to the diversity of values held by the pupils, their families and cultures. A classroom which promotes respect for different points of view and takes into account the 'voice' of the pupil is one where the discussion of social issues is being taken seriously.

Unit 8.1

Science for Citizenship

Ralph Levinson

INTRODUCTION

You would be hard-pressed to watch, or listen to, any news programme or read any daily newspaper without finding a current contemporary scientific issue. There will be debates as to whether young children should be vaccinated, GM crop trials should go ahead, or new energy-saving technologies should be funded. Will the environmental costs of new developments for building dams or power stations be offset by the social advantages gained? What these issues have in common is that substantial sections of the population have differing views on what should be done, they all incorporate a social and/or ethical aspect, they are likely to affect us all in some way and they all have a scientific dimension. They relate to such contexts as rights and obligations, coverage by the media, community participation and the role of government.

We live in a complex, global and interdependent society. Individuals and groups experience conflicts which need resolution. We need to take opportunities to pool resources for everyone's benefit, to ensure that there is just and fair treatment for everyone. Accurate and well-directed information underpins a just and democratic society so we all have to learn to evaluate the media critically to access the information we need. Many of our social needs are mediated through political institutions which operate in a democratic society but which have to respond to constant pressure.

Changes in technology and scientific developments affect the nature of our society. What is the best way to vaccinate against certain diseases in both minimising the risks and the spread of the disease throughout the population? How do we ensure young people have a varied and balanced diet? How can we properly assess the risk from mobile phones when newspapers and mobile phone companies tell us completely different things? How should we behave responsibly towards each other with respect to the environment we live in? These are some of the issues that could be discussed within citizenship and science.

OBJECTIVES

By the end of this unit you should be able to:

- identify the opportunities for teaching citizenship through science;
- use a range of strategies to teach citizenship through science;
- locate appropriate resources;
- assess citizenship in science;
- draw on strategies for teaching controversial issues in science.

WHAT DOES TEACHING CITIZENSHIP THROUGH SCIENCE LOOK LIKE?

It may seem strange to teach citizenship through science. Concepts such as 'government', 'democracy', 'human rights' may not have formed part of the science lessons you experienced as a pupil. This is also true of more experienced science teachers so teaching citizenship is a new challenge to the science-teaching community generally. As has already been pointed out, you have only to be aware of issues in contemporary science to know that there is a connection to our roles as citizens.

But it is more than the terminology that seems strange. The concepts mentioned above incorporate a strong values dimension; they relate to preferences we have as individuals, communities, societies or nations. Although these values have a rational basis they have evolved in a particular social context and there may well be differences between individuals and societies as to the desirability and expression of these values. Moreover, concepts like 'democracy' are underpinned by more values: the values we put on listening to what others have to say, respecting other points of view, acknowledging that differences can be reconciled. All this seems to have an unreal relationship to the business of finding out the acidity of a variety of liquids or finding out which type of spring is the best at resisting being stretched.

Although the role of citizenship is clearest when teaching about 'issues' or the 'applications of science and technology' these values have a place in all science lessons. If pupils do not have an opportunity to explain their ideas, to discuss differences, say, over measurements, then we are in danger of not valuing what they have to say. The pupils will take a subliminal message from the way in which the lesson is being run. A classroom which promotes respect for different points of view and takes into account the 'voice' of the pupil is one where the nature of citizenship is being taken seriously.

Citizenship concepts and skills need to be made explicit so that when discussing a concept such as 'rights and responsibility' the teacher makes pupils aware of the term, its meaning and its broader use within the political world. Pupils learn about the term in a specific context but are then made aware of other contexts. One may have rights as to what fuel you choose to use but these rights might have to be circumscribed if they affect the rights of others to breathe fresh air. Pupils might be asked to think of other ways there might be rights issues, e.g. the right to clone and the right to free speech. They need to be made aware that these rights might come into conflict with the rights of other others and there are means to resolve this fairly. Similarly, issues to do with government in a school with regard to the local environment or school meals might point to broader governmental issues such as whether or not to raise taxes and whose voice is heard most clearly.

Teaching Citizenship through science should draw on the same teaching approaches and styles that you might use to teach any other aspect of science. In fact, what is good practice for teaching citizenship is good practice for teaching science. There are, however, skills and values made explicit in the citizenship curriculum that will have an effect on practice. For example, pupils should be taught about human rights and responsibilities, the importance of resolving conflict fairly, the world as a global community. To understand the concept of rights and responsibilities pupils need to be exposed to situations where they can experience their meaning.

WHERE DOES CITIZENSHIP AND SCIENCE APPEAR IN THE CURRICULUM?

Citizenship became a formal subject at Key Stages 3 and 4 on the National Curriculum in England in September 2002. While there are various models for organising the teaching of citizenship such as an individual subject or together with Personal Social and Health Education (PSHE), it is envisaged that knowledge and skills in citizenship can be taught through the science curriculum. There are three strands to the citizenship curriculum: social and moral responsibility, community involvement and political literacy. Through the programme of study pupils are taught about the knowledge and understanding about becoming an informed citizen, developing skills of enquiry and communication and developing skills of participation and responsible action. Together the strands and the knowledge, skills and understanding of citizenship form the warp and weft through which pupils learn about the political nature of the society in which they live.

Task 8.1.1
Becoming acquainted with the National Curriculum and citizenship through science

Read the Programmes of Study for Citizenship at Key Stages 3 and 4 together with the end of Key Stage descriptions DfEE/QCA (1999b). Identify any areas where citizenship could be taught through science. Look through the science curriculum at Key Stages 3 and 4 and identify any content that could be taught through citizenship.

In the Programmes of Study for Citizenship there are indications as to links with science. In NC Science at Key Stage 3 it is suggested that learning about 'the ways in which living things and the environment can be protected and the importance of sustainable development' (NC Sc 2/5a) will enhance knowledge and understanding of the 'world as a global community, and the political, economic, environmental and social implications of this …' (NC Citizenship: 1i). Pupils could look, for example, at deforestation in different parts of the world, its effect on the local fauna and the people who depend on the forest.

They could explore the economic impetus for deforestation and the political justifications used as well as the social effects both in terms of the beneficiaries and those who suffer from it. When studying food webs and food chains they could assess the effects from one change on a producer or a primary consumer and how these have ramifications beyond the organisms directly dependent on them.

Task 8.1.2
Linking citizenship to
science

There are links in the citizenship curriculum with science at Key Stage 4 in Sc2/4b and Sc2/5b. Suggest how that could link to 'the wider issues and challenges of global interdependence and responsibility, including sustainable development and Local Agenda 21'. Local Agenda 21 gives local authorities responsibility to improve sustainable development.

Although these links are suggested in the National Curriculum Science document, there are many different ways in which you can teach citizenship through science. Some examples are given below.

Pupil participation

- A school council could ask pupils if they were getting a varied and balanced diet from their school meals. They might think about ways in which they could canvas pupil opinion about school meals, how they would take pupils' views into account, what negotiations they would carry out.
- Pupils might be concerned about environmental effects, say, on birds visiting the school wildlife gardens. They could collect data and send letters to the local newspaper.
- Pupils might have devised toys or other machines that run on alternative energy sources, e.g. solar, wind, water pressure, etc. This may have been done in collaboration with a local engineers' group, e.g. Neighbourhood Engineers (see DfEE/QCA, 1999b Key Stage 3: Getting Involved: extending opportunities for pupil participation).

Developing skills of enquiry and communication

- Pupils could justify their personal opinions, for example, on whether their local environment is more polluted now than it was in the past. This could involve collecting information from the public records office and looking up relevant legislation such as the Clean Air Act.
- Pupils could analyse information on the effect of smoking (KS4: Double Science: Sc2/2q). This might mean using secondary data, e.g. on the relationships between

smoking habits and miscarriages and stillbirths. A useful discussion could be had on the nature of risk and the difficulty of reaching firm conclusions.

Knowledge and skills

- Pupils could explore the role of the media in society by examining science stories in the press, e.g. on cloning, polluting effects of vehicle exhausts, risks from vaccinations or mobile phones. They could ascertain what opinion the newspaper is taking and what facts the newspaper uses in justifying its opinion.
- Pupils perceive the world as a global community by looking at the producers and consumers of fossil fuels, the distribution of wealth and the effects on the environment.

Task 8.1.3
Citizenship and science in your practice school

Find out in your school where aspects of science in citizenship are taught. Are they taught:

- in citizenship as a dedicated subject?
- in PSHE?
- through out-of-school activities?
- within science lessons?

Why has the school adopted this particular form of curriculum organisation?

Look through your department's schemes of work. What opportunities can you identify for teaching citizenship in science lessons.

CASE STUDIES

In this section you can see how citizenship issues might be brought out in a science topic. We discuss two different areas of the science curriculum through the topic of immunisation and the debate over the safety of mobile phones.

Immunisation

Controversy over immunisation programmes has been a feature of public policy in the UK. There have been public vaccination programmes for many years and diseases such as diphtheria, polio and smallpox have been eradicated as a result of mass vaccination programmes. Where such diseases do flourish in the world it is generally due to a lack of the appropriate vaccine and/or a means of implementing a vaccination programme. Childhood diseases such as measles, mumps and rubella, which were common less than 30 years ago, are now very rare. The great majority of small children are vaccinated between 18 months and 3 years old against these diseases by a combined vaccination called MMR. In the early part of the twenty-first century controversy broke out in the UK because there was a report that cases of childhood autism were linked to MMR vaccinations. The government resisted any changes such as single injections although some parents' groups argued that these vaccinations put their children at risk of autism.

This disagreement could be built into a lesson on:

- the biology of immunisation and how the body builds up resistance after vaccination;
- people's rights and responsibilities;
- the nature of risk;
- the significance of the media in society.

Before addressing these issues pupils should have prior knowledge of what immunisation is, how it helps the body to resist disease and how immunisation reduces disease throughout society. A useful resource for introducing immunisation at Key Stage 3 is 'Jabs for James Phipps' in Solomon (1991) (see resources below).

Task 8.1.4
Rehearsing issues

Read through the short extract in Figure 8.1.1 on the debate on being vaccinated against measles, mumps and rubella. There are several questions you might want to reflect on yourself before presenting them to a class:

- Why is one parent against getting her child vaccinated?
- Are there other reasons against getting your child vaccinated?
- What arguments could you use to address the second parent's last point?

People can have the right to refuse to have their child vaccinated. This is a direct example of the way in which scientific discoveries have an impact on society, the effects of which raise moral questions.

In Task 8.1.4 one parent is expressing a right not to vaccinate a child. Rights, such as the refusal to have your child vaccinated, are something that you can claim, as one parent appears to be doing here, or something that is your due. However, with rights come responsibilities, and it is those responsibilities that the first parent is outlining. You have responsibilities not only to yourself and to your family but also to a wider society. Claiming your own right might well involve infringing the rights of others. It can be claimed that the second parent's action might infringe the rights of others to live in a society where there is a relatively low risk of contracting childhood diseases. This introduces the concept of risk; there is some kind of hazard associated with everything we do. Most of these we usually ignore without even realising there is a risk; however, in other areas such as vaccination programmes, a risk which is relatively small can be blown up out of all proportion while another much larger risk, which needs to be weighed against the first risk, is effectively ignored.

Two parents with babies are discussing whether to have their child immunised against catching measles, mumps and rubella, known as the MMR jab. Each parent has a different attitude towards the strong medical advice that immunisation is essential to protect the baby.

First parent (P1) We're taking April for her MMR jab tomorrow.

Second parent (P2) Oh, are you! We're not having Danny immunised, it is too risky.

P1   Yes, there is a risk but a very small one. April may have a bad reaction to the jab but the risk is low and that is better than getting the disease.

P2   Why take any risk? Very few babies get one of these diseases nowadays so the risk of getting measles, mumps or rubella is small.

P1   The reason the diseases have almost disappeared is that parents have immunised their children. If we don't continue to do this, the diseases may come back.

P2   Yes, that is true but most people do immunise their children so the risk of getting any of the diseases is small. It is not worth the risk of exposing Danny to any serious side effects of the MMR vaccine.

P1   I don't think we are risking very much. We have had health checks on both of us, as well as April, and looked at our family medical history and the risk is very small.

P2   We're not risking Danny. While other parents are having their babies immunised the risk of catching measles, mumps or rubella is small.

Source: adapted from 'Should we, Can we?' available on the Planet Science website at http://www.sycd.co.uk/can_we_should_we/immunisation/home.htm. Select 'What if everyone did that?'

Figure 8.1.1 Conversation about measles, mumps and rubella vaccine

Task 8.1.5
Influence of newspapers

Download newspaper articles about MMR from the resource 'Should we, Can we?' available on the Planet Science website at http://www.sycd.co.uk/can_we_should_we/immunisation/home.htm.
Select 'Come on Mr Blair, tell us!' and read the newspaper extracts. How do these extracts make the significance of the media apparent?

MOBILE PHONES

Recent debates have focused on dangers presented by mobile phones. It is argued that there might be a link between brain tumours and the microwave radiation produced by mobile phones and transmitters. The problem is that there is no clear evidence as to whether there is a serious health risk or not. Scientists working on behalf of mobile phone companies, for example, argue that microwave radiation is relatively safe compared with other forms of radiation and even with mild exercise. Other scientists, perhaps working in the Health Service, produce figures showing that there is a significantly greater risk of contracting brain cancer if you are a regular user of mobile phones than if you are not. Who is right? The answer is not clear. It also raises the important point that scientific evidence does not necessarily give us straightforward answers. How are non-experts supposed to interpret that information? Furthermore, there is the question of causality and distinguishing causation from correlation. If there is a greater frequency of brain cancer among mobile phone users it does not necessarily follow that use of mobile phones causes brain cancer.

Although there are now many good resources to help teachers address issues like immunisation and mobile phones it is by no means straightforward to teach them in the classroom taking into account that you are teaching both citizenship and science. One way forward is to use topics like immunisation and mobile phones as a context for addressing concepts both in science and citizenship. Thus, you might want to use a newspaper report on the dangers of mobile phones to look at the properties of microwave radiation, weighing up risk and evaluating the accuracy and reliability of data.

Effective teaching of citizenship in science involves the discussion of pupil ideas in the classroom. Many of these ideas are controversial and we discuss next the teaching of controversial issues.

Task 8.1.6
Addressing citizenship in a GCSE science specification

Awarding bodies have specifications for Education for Citizenship in Double Award for Science at GCSE (see Unit 7.2 for websites of the awarding bodies where you can find the specifications). Make brief notes of the ways in which you can address one of these ideas in your science teaching.

WHERE ARE CONTROVERSIAL ISSUES FOUND IN THE CURRICULUM?

A broader discussion on the teaching of controversial issues is found in the generic reader in Unit 4.5 (Capel *et al.* 2001: 215–17). The last version of the National Curriculum for England identified a number of areas which present opportunities for discussing controversial issues in science. At Key Stage 3 pupils 'think about the positive and negative effects of scientific and technological developments on the environment and in other contexts'; and 'they take account of others' views and understand why opinions may

At Key Stage 3 pupils should be taught about:
Sc2 (3a) ways in which living things and the environment can be protected, and the importance of sustainable development.
Sc3 (2i) the effects of burning fossil fuels on the environment and how these effects can be minimised.
Sc4 (5a) renewable and non-renewable resources.

At Key Stage 4 pupils should be taught about:
Sc2 (2k) control and promotion of fertility;   (4h) basic principles of cloning, selective breeding and genetic engineering;   (5c) importance of sustainable development.
Sc3 (2m) environmental consequences of the over-use of nitrogenous fertilisers;   (3r) use of enzymes in biotechnology.
Sc4 (3f) potential dangers of high frequency waves;   (4e) search for evidence of extra-terrestrial life;   (5b) economical use of energy, and the environmental implications of generating energy;   (6e) beneficial and harmful effects of ionising radiation.

Figure 8.1.2 Examples of controversial issues in Key Stages 3 and 4

differ' (DfEE/QCA, 1999a: 28). In Key Stage 4 this requirement includes a specific ethical component. In Sc1, pupils should be taught 'to consider the power and limitations of science in addressing social and environmental questions, including the kinds of questions science can and cannot answer, uncertainties in scientific knowledge, and the ethical issues involved' (DfEE/QCA, 1999a: KS4, Sc 1, d). In both Key Stages 3 and 4 pupils learn about knowledge, skills and understanding through a consideration of the benefits and drawbacks of scientific and technological developments. Pupils also learn how different groups have different views about the role of science. There is also mention in the National Curriculum about the role of controversy in scientific theories. While this has an important social aspect it is dealt with in Unit 4.1 on the Nature of Science.

There are no specific directions as to what topics lend themselves to consideration of controversial issues although some are more specific than others. See Figure 8.1.2 for examples.

Task 8.1.7
Building the idea of controversy into your teaching

From the Key Stage 3 or 4 Attainment Targets listed in Figure 8.1.2, develop a context, e.g. a story, for introducing the issue to a class at Key Stage 3 or 4.

WHAT IS KNOWN ABOUT THE TEACHING OF CONTROVERSIAL ISSUES IN SCIENCE?

Controversies arising from contemporary applications of science have often cropped up in the science classroom but there has rarely been systematic treatment of these issues in the science curriculum in the UK. In the 1960s various attempts were made to locate science in its social context and a movement grew up which had important influence in the UK, North America, Canada, Australia and New Zealand called STS (Science and Technology in Society). STS helped to frame science in its global context and was the inspiration behind resources such as SATIS (Association for Science Education 1987, 1993, 1999) providing ideas for teaching socio-scientific issues in the science classroom. These included ideas such as games, role-play, simulations and ideas for discussion (Solomon 1993). The introduction of the GCSE course, *21st Century Science* in September 2004 brings contexts for controversial issues into the core of the course such as 'Air Quality' and 'You and Your Genes'. At post-16 level there is an AS examination, Science for Public Understanding, which examines contemporary issues and ideas in science as a major part of the course (Millar 2000).

WHAT ARE THE CHALLENGES IN TEACHING CONTROVERSIAL ISSUES IN SCIENCE?

Teaching about core science concepts is very different from teaching about the controversial issues such as cloning. For example, consider teaching about the purpose of digestion and the processes such as chewing and enzyme action that support it. The teacher knows more than the pupils she teaches and introduces the relevant terminology where necessary. When pupils raise questions she is able to deal confidently with them. When teaching about cloning, however, questions arise that are normally outside the purview of a science teacher. 'Is it possible to clone humans?' 'Should there be a ban on cloning?' 'Should people be able to clone themselves if they want to?' 'Is cloning right?' 'How can we stop doctors cloning human beings?' If you look closely at these questions the answer does not necessarily involve a discussion of the scientific principles of cloning, i.e. nuclear transfer and implantation although it will include a discussion of evidence such as the difficulties of cloning. Addressing pupils' questions includes using terms such as 'ought' 'responsibility' 'rights' 'laws' 'policy' and so on and so forth. Recycling involves a consideration of such concepts as 'cost–benefit analysis'. Knowing the best way to dispose of nuclear waste depends on local issues as well as the nature of containment and the risk of contamination. Knowledge of terms such as 'half-life' and 'radiation intensity' helps pupils grasp the duration of the risk but are likely to contribute in only a small way to the range of information needed.

Not only are these ideas outside the usual discussions a science teacher might have in the classroom there are no necessarily right or wrong answers. Two people might have access to the same information but have completely different opinions. (Note that this situation may be very difficult for pupils to comprehend if science is taught as factual truth.) These positions might depend on the holders' basic values, their experiences in life, motives or their conceptions of right and wrong. For any teacher these issues are big challenges because pupils usually respond animatedly to these issues – sometimes because they hold very strong opinions, possibly with very little evidence to back them. It might be difficult for an inexperienced teacher to control discussion, to encourage children to listen carefully to each other or to staunch prejudice. In the very nature of contemporary issues up-to-date information may not be available for the teacher who might have to struggle on with little evidence at her fingertips.

But it would be wrong not to encourage pupils' curiosity about these issues. As a teacher you have a duty to help pupils to think properly about these issues, to pay attention to evidence, to be sceptical, to understand why some arguments hold more water than others. These considerations influence your approach to the topic. At the very least you have to ensure the class is well organised so that pupils know what dilemma they are meant to discuss and that everyone has an opportunity to speak and to listen. The teacher has to be sensitive to any difficulties. Importantly pupils should be encouraged to justify their opinions.

HOW ARE THESE ISSUES TAUGHT IN THE CLASSROOM?

Now is the point to look at the way you can teach these issues in the classroom. There are many strategies you can use but it is best to start by consideration of a focused dilemma. With younger pupils it is difficult to discuss broad areas of contention such as global warming, sustainability and nuclear power because the topic will go in all directions and be difficult to control. Focusing on a particular dilemma has a number of advantages such as:

- the class is clear about the specific question under consideration;
- the teacher has had the opportunity to think through some of the issues that may arise;
- the pupils can consider different aspects of the question in groups;
- the science concepts can be identified and fed in where necessary;
- resources that deal with the topic can be accessed in advance.

**Task 8.1.8
Controversial statements
which can be used as the
basis of discussion**

Below are some examples of controversial statements that might provoke discussion. Take one of these issues and talk through the arguments with a colleague. Think of them in terms of the numbered points at the end of this task.

- I think parents should be able to choose the characteristics of their babies, if the technology allows it.
- We should have a DNA sample of all citizens then when people commit a crime they can easily be identified. It'd be a safer world for all of us.
- Recycling is a waste of time, money and energy.
- I'm against the testing of genetically modified crops in the environment. We don't know what damage they might cause and it's best to play safe.
- We have no right to harm animals in any way even if it is at the expense of human health or progress.
- Nuclear energy is the safest, cleanest energy source and carries the least risk.
- I wouldn't give my child the MMR vaccine. There's too great a risk of developing autism.
- We should support gene therapy because it can eliminate many unpleasant illnesses.
- Experts disagree about the causes of global warming so I don't see why we should change the way we use fuels.
- Young people should be on the priority list as recipients for organ transplants.
- Schools should only provide a balanced, varied and healthy diet for school lunches.
- Anyone should be able to have babies through IVF.
- Wealthy countries should not export their poisonous waste to less well-off countries even though the latter might benefit economically.
- We should try and see no species become extinct but we should concentrate our energies on plants and animals that are useful to us.

1   What conclusion, if any, did you come to?
2   Why did you come to that conclusion?
3   What argument was more convincing than any other? What made it most convincing?
4   What science did you draw upon?

> Sharon: 'I just found out I'm a carrier for sickle cell anaemia.'
>
> Jane:'You ought to tell Rick since you're thinking of starting a family together.'
>
> Sharon:'But what if Rick turns out to be a carrier as well?'

Figure 8.1.3 A dilemma about sickle cell anaemia

A possible approach

To set up a focused dilemma it is best to give it a particular context. You could start off by referring to the example in Figure 8.1.3

Ask pupils to consider the following questions:

- What might happen if she did tell Rick?
- What might happen if she did not tell Rick?
- What is the right thing to do?

When preparing this type of discussion three important questions need to be considered. They are:

- What is it that pupils need to know before the discussion?
- What knowledge do they need during the discussion?
- How do you help pupils reach some kind of conclusion?

What pupils need to know before the discussion

There are two terms, 'carrier' and 'sickle cell anaemia', that may be unfamiliar to pupils but they need to understand them before a sensible discussion can begin. To understand the implications of the term 'carrier' pupils need to understand the terms 'gene', 'allele', 'chromosome', 'dominant–recessive' and how to construct a Mendelian diagram. They also need to know the symptoms of sickle cell anaemia, possibilities of treatment, effects on the sufferer and family and groups at risk. When pupils have some understanding of these terms the discussion can proceed with a suitable knowledge base. Once pupils take part the significance of the terms becomes clear to them as the discussion proceeds. However, you cannot assume this is the case and part of the role of the teacher is ensuring that pupils have sufficient understanding for the issue to be discussed.

Knowledge pupils need during a discussion

This is the most difficult aspect to deal with because you cannot always predict what pupils need to know. Most of the questions pupils ask are likely to be those for clarification but it is a good idea to have resources such as appropriate websites (see resources) and to ask other teachers who have run this type of discussion what questions pupils are likely to come up with. The main focus is on the emotional side of the problem and these features need to be dealt with sensitively. Find out if there are pupils in your class who have sickle cell anaemia or another genetic condition or if they have relatives who have the condition. Some pupils may prefer not to be present; on the other hand they may want to talk about their experiences. How this is handled depends on your relationship with the class but you should ensure that pupils listen sensitively to each other. Pupils may have questions they want to ask but not in the presence of their peers. Teachers sometimes employ the strategy of a question box where pupils can post questions anonymously. Answers to the questions are discussed generally in a following lesson.

How do you help pupils reach a conclusion?

Helping pupils make a decision does not mean you are telling pupils what to think. Sometimes a resolution is not possible but some means is needed to help pupils weigh one argument against another. One approach is the use of consequence mapping. Pupils are given a 'What if' question and consider the consequences by analysing a number of factors (Figure 8.1.4). After pupils have drawn their own consequence maps in groups the maps can be displayed on the walls together with the consequences. How do the maps compare? Do the pupils see the risks for each consequence as worth taking? What are their reasons?

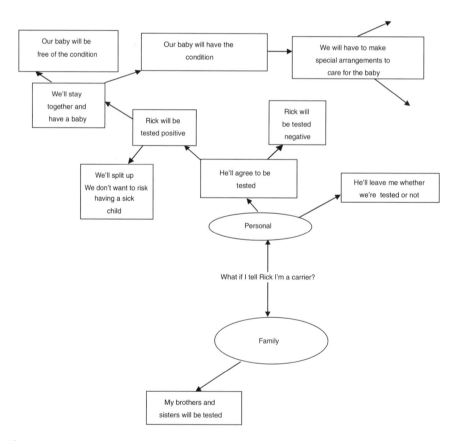

Figure 8.1.4 Consequences map

The consequence map is one way of thinking about ethical arguments: we look at the possible consequences of a particular action and decide on balance whether the action will broadly benefit people or not. This comes under the umbrella of an important ethical concept – utilitarianism – where an action is judged in terms of whether it makes people overall happier or not. However, there are other ways through which we can judge actions. Even though an action benefits people overall the motives behind it may be bad. A third way of looking at an action refers to the rules and core values which people hold dear. Embryo research promises enormous benefits in the eradication of certain genetic-based conditions. However, this kind of therapy involves creating an embryo to produce a line of stem cells where the embryo may be destroyed. Some people believe that the embryo is not a person and that this kind of research is acceptable because of the benefits that accrue to humanity. Others believe that it is fundamentally wrong to use embryos for research because once fertilisation has taken place there is life and life is sacrosanct. There are, of course, many different views on this issue but the point is that actions can be viewed as right or wrong regardless of consequences or motives.

While these different ways of judging an action are made known to pupils during their school career you may not be able to incorporate them within one topic. On the other hand, you should try and ensure that pupils are aware of the ways in which they are judging an action.

Task 8.1.9
Running a discussion

It is best not to be too ambitious at first. One good way to learn how to do this is to watch other teachers including, e.g. teachers of English, drama and history as well as science teachers. Try and observe discussions in PSHE lessons or citizenship lessons, if they are run separately. Observe:

- How the teacher presents the dilemma – does it come from the pupils? Does the teacher have a piece of information ready for discussion? Does she take an extract from a newspaper?
- How are the groups organised? Do the pupils have stimuli to provoke discussion? Does the grouping occur spontaneously or does the teacher allocate groups? Does the teacher allocate roles within the groups?
- What are the aims of the discussion? Are there expectations? How will the results of the discussion be presented?
- Do all the pupils contribute equally? What is the role of the teacher during discussion? What resources does she use? Are there silences? Are these uncomfortable? (We all need time to think quietly without feeling under pressure.)
- How does the teacher manage difficult viewpoints? Does she press for consensus? Does she try to highlight differences? How does she deal with dominant or 'opinionated' pupils? What level of noise is tolerated?
- How does the teacher deal with information which she doesn't know?
- What resources are used? How are they distributed? How much time in the lesson does the teacher talk? The pupils? Do the pupils seem content with what they are doing? Happy? Frustrated?

SOME GUIDELINES FOR DISCUSSION

To help plan a discussion lesson you should

- have an aim in mind;
- allocate a specific time;
- be very focused in the topic;
- use a stimulus such as a newspaper article;
- value contributions from all pupils;
- think of some anticipated comments and follow-up questions;
- not worry about failure; evaluate the lesson and learn from it.

Using newspaper articles

National newspapers, tabloid and broadsheet alike, often cover controversial issues in science. These can be a very productive source for debate and can be used to:

- identify the science and scientific terms in the article;
- find out what opinions are being presented;
- analyse the evidence that is being used to support or challenge the opinion.

Articles can be used as DARTS activities (see: Unit 6.1; Wellington and Osborne 2001; Capel et al. 2001, Unit 5.2). Ask the pupils to highlight the scientific terms and explain in their own words what they mean. They can then be asked to present the sentences on one side that support the argument and the sentences that oppose the main argument. See Task 8.1.5 which involves discussion of newspaper articles.

Task 8.1.10
Using newspapers to analyse a controversial scientific issue

Rehearse for yourself the use of newspaper articles for teaching. Cut out a couple of articles from the tabloid press. Look at the way scientific terminology is being used. Identify scientific terms for yourselves and check whether pupils at Key Stage 4 would have covered the science if you use these articles. In addition identify the

- facts the article draws upon;
- assumptions made in the article;
- doubts you have about the facts or the way they are presented;
- conclusion the writer draws from the facts;
- further information you need to come to an informed opinion.

What are the advantages and disadvantages of using newspapers as a learning resource?

Preparation

This type of lesson is likely to need more preparation than other lessons because the range of information needed is greater and you have to plan for pupils doing their own research on this topic.

**Task 8.1.11
Preparing to teach a
controversial issue**

When you are given your timetable:

- identify in the scheme of work where a controversial issue might be taught;
- identify the resources for teaching this issue that are available to you;
- ask other teachers in your department how they have taught this issue in the past, any pitfalls to be wary of;
- consult staff responsible for citizenship and PSHE (Personal, Health and Social Education) because they often have a lot of experience in dealing with controversial issues in the classroom. English and religious education teachers often have this experience.

TEACHING ABOUT CONTROVERSIAL ISSUES: THE TEACHER'S POSITION

Pupils sometimes hold a view, such as about abortion or animal experimentation, with deeply held convictions. Great care should be taken that such beliefs are dealt with sensitively and not held up to ridicule. When discussing controversial issues the role of the teacher is important because pupils may look up to the teacher as having authority and it is quite easy for the teacher to let slip a remark that sways their viewpoints. Teachers can take various roles such as a neutral chair or 'devil's advocate', each of which have their merits and disadvantages. A neutral approach may not be convincing to the pupils because they know the teacher has a point of view and they may select from the teacher's remarks only those parts that they want to hear. Having a balanced approach may not be feasible because the teacher simply cannot address every opinion thrown at her and counterbalance it. Making your opinions known may also court trouble because the teacher might be accused of indoctrination. In England and Wales, The Advisory Group on Citizenship (Crick Report) advocated a common sense approach so that in certain situations the teacher, when proposing a point of view that pupils have omitted to consider, might say that there are some viewpoints she would like to share with the class (QCA 1998). Here the tone of voice and timing can be crucial.

AVAILABLE RESOURCES

There are many sources of information to use for teaching controversial socio-scientific issues. Contemporary sources can be:

- specialist books from professional societies or interested parties;
- pamphlets;
- websites;
- broadsheets;
- tabloid newspapers;
- videos;
- audio;
- drama productions;
- films;
- science centres;
- discussion groups.

EVALUATING RESOURCES

Because areas of controversy are contemporary, teachers depend on information from external agencies which provide up-to-date information. That information will also represent the interests of the group. The challenge for the teacher is to have access to websites, pamphlets and books from a range of organisations with different perspectives. You need in advance to evaluate the material to be able to guide the pupils to analyse and evaluate the information appropriately.

> **Task 8.1.12**
> **Evaluating a resource**
>
> Access information from an organisation through a website or pamphlet about a specific issue.
>
> - What views does the organisation propound?
> - What might be the opposite viewpoint?
> - Are images used appropriately to support the message?
> - Do they give sources of their information?

SUMMARY

In this unit we have discussed the challenges facing teachers when dealing with controversial issues in science. While the challenges can seem formidable controversial issues, as well as being important in themselves, they often spark pupils' interest and, when handled well, help to enliven a topic. When starting out teaching make sure you give yourself the opportunity to see experienced teachers deal with these issues. Find out where there is the opportunity to teach a controversial issue by studying the schemes of work and identifying the lessons or parts of lessons. Plan the lesson well in advance. At first it is best to limit yourself to small focused topics and evaluate the progress you have made with them in the classroom.

FURTHER READING

Capel, S., Leask, M. and Turner, T. (eds) (2001) *Learning to Teach in the Secondary School: A Companion to School Experience*, 3rd edn, London and New York: RoutledgeFalmer. See Turner, T. (2001) Unit 4.5 'Moral development and values' and Turner, T. (2001) Unit 5.5 'Active learning'.

Fullick, P. and Ratcliffe, M. (eds) (1996) *Teaching Ethical Aspects of Science*, Southampton: Bassett Press.

Levinson, R. and Reiss, M. (eds) (2003) *Key Issues in Bioethics*, London: RoutledgeFalmer.

Ratcliffe, M. and Grace, M. (2003) *Science Education for Citizenship*, Maidenhead: Open University Press.

Sang, D. and Wood Robinson, V. (eds) (2002) *Teaching Secondary Scientific Enquiry*, London: John Murray for the ASE.

Solomon, J. (1991) *Exploring the Nature of Science (Key Stage 3)*, London: Nelson Blackie. (There is an excellent section on immunisation, 'Jabs for James Phipps').

WEBSITES TO EXPLORE

See also Further Reading

There are now many different websites that raise controversial issues in science. Among the best for secondary schools is: www.sycd.co.uk/can_we_should_we/startfil/home.htm which gives information in handling a number of issues in the context of Citizenship and Science.

Many issues can be accessed through websites associated with the Science Museum, The Wellcome Trust, Institute of Physics, Institute of Biology and The Royal Society of Chemistry. The BBC and *The Guardian* newspaper have excellent websites for accessing information on contemporary issues in science. Y-touring is a theatre company that presents dramas on contemporary biomedical issues for young people. They have a website to help teachers explore these issues; it is www.ytouring.org.uk.

For exploring science and citizenship in a global context, see: www.ase.org.uk/htm/ase_global/index1.php

Environment teachers' packs for Key Stage 3 can be downloaded from the Environment Agency website, see www.dfes.gov.uk/schemes

The QCA's website for sustainable development also contains useful resources: see www.nc.uk.net/esd

A very useful resource pack is: Pupil Researcher Initiative (2001) *Ideas and Evidence Resource Pack*, London: Collins Education. This contains information on mobile phones discussed in this chapter. There is also a CD-ROM associated with the pack.

Unit 8.2

Sex and Health Education

Jane Maloney

INTRODUCTION

Since the implementation of the National Curriculum in 1989 the role schools are expected to play in educating pupils about health issues has become more clearly defined. Guidance for the provision of sex education, in particular, has been provided through a series of publications provided by the National Curriculum Council (NCC 1990), the Department for Education (DfE 1993) and more recently by the Department for Education and Employment (DfEE 2000). The document titled *Sex and Relationship Education Guidance* (DfEE 2000) takes into account the revised National Curriculum science (DfEE/QCA 1999a) and the framework for Personal, Social and Health Education (PHSE) (DfEE 1999).

It is not necessary for you to be aware of the contents of these documents (although there are good ideas in them) but it is important for you, as a science teacher, to know how dynamic is the situation as regards sex education and be alert to any new guidance and changes in legislation that may affect your teaching.

Although this unit is about sex and health education, the main focus is on preparing you to teach sensitive issues in general and most teachers would agree that teaching pupils about sexual matters is one of the most sensitive issues on the science or any other curriculum. At least you can be assured of pupils' interest and cannot be accused of teaching a topic that is irrelevant to them in the future. In some ways the separation of 'sex education' from 'health education' is an artificial one, as part of a healthy life would include an understanding about sexual health. However, as sex education is subject to different constraints the two topics are discussed separately.

SEX AND RELATIONSHIP EDUCATION

State schools are legally required to have a Sex Education Policy. This policy should describe how sex education is provided within the school and who is responsible for providing it. Sex and Relationship Education (SRE) is defined as:

> … lifelong learning about physical, moral and emotional development. It is about the understanding of the importance of marriage for family life, stable and loving relationships, respect, love and care. It is also about the teaching of sex, sexuality, and sexual health.
>
> (DfEE 2000: 5)

The teaching of SRE cannot be taught entirely by the science department, but clearly some aspects of SRE can be provided within the science curriculum. This means that it is important to be clear about the responsibilities of different departments in the school. Such distinctions are important because aspects of SRE taught within the science and citizenship curriculum are under statutory order and those taught within the school's Personal, Health and Social Education PHSE are non-statutory. Here we focus on the responsibilities of the science department in the provision of SRE. However, it is important for science teachers to appreciate how their teaching relates to the teaching of PHSE and citizenship education so that pupils receive a coherent and coordinated SRE.

OBJECTIVES

By the end of this unit you should be able to:

- appreciate how science topics related to health education fit in with the whole school policy on SRE, PHSE and citizenship education;
- understand the legal aspects of health related matters and the teacher's responsibilities in teaching sex education;
- recognise your own concerns about teaching about sex and health education;
- identify teaching strategies that are more appropriate for teaching about sensitive issues in the science classroom;
- devise activities on health issues that develop literacy and numeracy skills.

THE NEED TO TEACH ABOUT SEXUAL HEALTH

The Department of Health (DoH) report on sexual health in England (DoH 2001) provides information that raises concerns about the effectiveness of sex education in schools today. Of course the responsibility for these issues does not lie solely with schools but it is worth considering what science teachers can do to improve young people's knowledge and understanding of sexual matters. Consider these points taken from the report:

- over a quarter of 14–15 year-olds think that the contraceptive pill gives them protection against infection;

- in 1999 most people questioned in a national study did not know what *Chlamydia* was;
- in 1999 there were nearly 174,000 abortions in England and Wales;
- England's teenage births are the highest in Western Europe.

(DoH 2001: 8)

Secondary school pupils do receive considerable information about aspects of human reproduction but research shows that this can result in 'patchy understanding' (Harrison 2000) and the DoH report would appear to support this view. Before we look at how we can improve the contribution of science teachers to developing a better understanding among young people we need to look at which health topics are taught in science.

Task 8.2.1
Health-related issues in the science curriculum

Examine the science curriculum and identify which health related issues are taught and when they are taught.
   Obtain copies of the science department's schemes of work for Key Stage 3 and the examination syllabus taught at Key Stage 4.

- What topics are related specifically to sex and health education?
- In which year group are these topics covered?
- Are any of the topics revisited as the pupils get older?
- What elements of SC1 Scientific Enquiry are relevant to the teaching of these topics?

This inquiry should help you to begin to appreciate what your responsibilities are, as a science teacher, for teaching aspects of sex and health education. Make a note of any topics you need to revise before you teach them. Note also any resources available in your school that you need to review to assess their suitability for your classes.

WHOLE-SCHOOL POLICY

Before you plan how you would approach teaching these topics you need to appreciate how the teaching of health-related issues in science lessons fits in with the school sex education policy. The guidance given to schools by the DfEE makes it clear that effective sex and relationship education is to be firmly rooted in the framework for PHSE. The aim of SRE is to equip pupils with skills, knowledge and understanding and in this respect it is much like any other part of the curriculum. However, health-related issues are often controversial and need sensitive handling at an individual and group level (Turner 2000). The topics have legal aspects not associated with other topics on the curriculum. For example, if you are teaching a Year 10 class about the hormonal control of fertility (National Curriculum reference KS4 Sc2, 2k), there is an expectation that pupils aged between 14 and 15 years old should not have first-hand experience of taking any control over their ability to conceive or not to conceive.

Your classes may well represent a wide range of particular and divergent views on contraception. Differences about sexual morality and religious views on sexual behaviour have to be taken into account unless we plan to teach pupils merely the biological facts about sex and reproduction. For a summary of the moral perspectives of six religious groups on aspects of sex education refer to Jennifer Harrison's *Sex Education in Secondary School* (Harrison 2000*)*.

Archard (2000) is quite clear that to teach pupils only about the biological facts is an unsatisfactory approach and he describes this as a form of sex education that merits the disparaging epithet of 'plumbing'. Teaching about the 'plumbing' is, however, part of a science teacher's responsibilities but we do need to understand how this fits in with the 'relationship' part of the SRE.

The most helpful guidance for you is to be well prepared, not just in your subject knowledge (as with any part of your science teaching) but also in the way you handle questions that are not appropriate for you to answer in a science lesson or questions you do not feel capable of answering. It is important therefore that you understand in which parts of the curriculum aspects of health and sex education are taught in your school.

Task 8.2.2
What is your school's policy for SRE?

This task requires you to liaise with teachers of other subjects with responsibility for health and sex education.

1   Obtain the school's documentation for these topics
  • sex education,
  • health education,
  • citizenship education,
  • PHSE.
2   Make a plan to show which topics are taught to which year groups in science, PHSE and/or citizenship lessons throughout the year.
  • Find out when science teachers teach about the physical and emotional changes that take place during adolescence (KS3 Sc2, 2 f);
  • Check when the pupils cover this topic in PHSE and/or citizenship.
3   Find out if there is one person with overall responsibility for co-ordinating these areas and check:
  • what guidance is on offer for a science teacher teaching sensitive issues;
  • if there is any team teaching or joint use of resources;
  • how the school ensures that the policies are kept up to date with current legislation.

This information helps you identify which aspects of the SRE and health education curricula come within the remit of the science department. It should also reassure you that even if you feel your teaching in science seems divorced from the discussion and reflection that pupils need to develop a fuller understanding of their sexual health, this need is being addressed elsewhere in the curriculum. It also gives you the confidence to avoid such discussion should you feel ill equipped to cope with this style of teaching in your class.

THE LEGAL ASPECTS

There are legal aspects about sex and the law of which you need to be aware. Below are those which are most pertinent to young people of secondary school age:

- the age a woman can consent to sexual intercourse is 16 in England and Scotland and 17 in Northern Ireland;
- a woman does not commit an offence if she has sexual intercourse under the age of 16 (17 in Northern Ireland);
- it is a felony for a man to have unlawful sexual intercourse with a girl under 13 years;
- it is an absolute offence (subject to the exceptions below) for a man to have unlawful sexual intercourse with a girl under 16 years;
- a man is not guilty of an offence because he has unlawful sexual intercourse with a girl under the age of 16, if he is under the age of 24 and has not previously been charged with an offence of this kind and had reasonable cause to believe the woman to be aged 16 or over;
- a boy aged 13 is not liable to prosecution for having sexual intercourse with a woman under 16, but he can be prosecuted for indecent assault;
- homosexual acts between men are legal provided that they are both 16 or over in England, Wales and Scotland (17 in Northern Ireland) and the act takes place in private;
- acts of lesbianism are legal provided that both women are over the age of consent and both consent to the act.

As legislation can change (the Sexual Offences Act was amended in 2000), you need to keep up to date with any changes in the law. For further information concerning sex and the law the Brook Advisory Centre website is very helpful. The inclusion of these aspects of the law in this unit is not to suggest that you should be teaching these items of legislation to your classes but to raise your awareness of their existence and to give you confidence should you be asked by your pupils about such issues.

LOCAL GOVERNMENT ACT (50/1) 1988, SECTION 28

One of the legal issues that has undermined teacher confidence in teaching about sex education is the Local Government Act (50/1) 1988, Section 28 (Harrison 2000). This clause states that:

> A local authority shall not (a) intentionally promote homosexuality or publish material with the intention of promoting homosexuality; (b) promote the teaching in any maintained school of the acceptability of homosexuality as a pretended family relationship by the publication of such material or otherwise.

Since sex education is the responsibility of the governing bodies of schools this act does not apply to schools (Reiss 2000). Nevertheless, it has left some teachers anxious about how they should approach the discussion of homosexuality. It is worth noting that the guidance provided by the DfEE (2000) is the following:

It is up to schools to make sure that the needs of all pupils are met in their programmes. Young people, whatever their developing sexuality, need to feel that sex and relationship education is relevant to them and sensitive to their needs. The Secretary of State for Education and Employment is clear that teachers should be able to deal honestly and sensitively with sexual orientation, answer appropriate questions and offer support. There should be no direct promotion of sexual orientation.

(DfEE 2000: 13)

Clearly, as a student teacher you would seek advice from your tutor in the department about the needs of any particular pupil who might relate to this issue. You also need to be clear how your teaching might expose your own views on such matters. It is important that you consider this point for all matters related to sex and health education.

Task 8.2.3
The need for ground rules

This task requires you to reflect on how much of your personal details you are willing to reveal to your class and to plan the 'ground rules' you expect your class to follow in your lessons.

1   Consider the implications of answering these pupils' questions.
    - Are you married?
    - Do you have a girl friend/boy friend?
    - Do you have children?
    - Do you smoke?
    - How much do you drink?
    - Have you ever taken drugs?
2   Consider which questions you would definitely not answer.
3   What does it imply to the pupils if you are prepared to answer some personal questions and yet not others?

Some of the answers to question 1 may be obvious to your pupils if you are an established teacher in a school; you may have your partner teaching in the school with you or your children may be friends of some of the pupils. However, pupils are unlikely to know personal details of a student teacher on school experience except that pupils will probably know if you smoke or not. It is really important that a smoker should consider how to answer such a question as pupils may feel uncomfortable being told about the hazards of cigarette smoking to their health by someone who is obviously ignoring the advice themselves.

TEACHING STRATEGIES

There is a range of teaching strategies you could adopt when teaching sex and health education but many science teachers avoid the more creative teaching methods recommended for this topic (Windale *et al.* 1995). There is no reason to leave the more innovative methods to PHSE/Citizenship teachers; science teachers need to select appropriate methods for the topic and age of the pupils.

Task 8.2.4
Developing ground rules

This task enables you to plan the ground rules to use with your classes. Although you probably want to ask your classes to suggest the rules themselves it is a good idea to have some idea of what you want beforehand. Consider this list and identify the rules that you think the pupils may suggest and the rules you may have to introduce yourself.

- We must listen to each other's opinions.
- We must respect different points of view.
- We must be able to change our minds.
- We should use the correct biological words whenever possible.
- We won't ask personal questions.

What other rules do you think should be added?

As so much of sex and health education involves pupils engaging in discussion and making decisions about their own personal life it can make lessons uncomfortable for them. To avoid pupils having to give details about their own life style or information that is too personal you can use techniques known as 'distancing techniques'.

DISTANCING TECHNIQUES

These techniques enable pupils to question and discuss topics that are of interest to them without having to disclose personal details. For example, they could watch a video where the characters act out a situation that raises questions that the class can discuss. The pupils can talk about the issues regarding the characters and at the same time raise issues that concern them.

Case studies with invented characters, theatre productions and role-plays are other examples of distancing techniques. Pupils are able to introduce issues into the discussions without exposing their own ignorance or experiences; they can explore the consequences of certain behaviours without indicating what they would do, or have done, themselves. Nevertheless, pupils need to be able to get the answers to specific questions which trouble them but how this is facilitated requires careful consideration. Imagine the possible scenario should a teacher invite pupils to ask *any* questions during a lesson. A common technique used to address pupils' queries is the 'Question Box' where pupils are allowed to write down any questions they have (without their names on) and place them in a box.

RESOURCES

There are a number of topics that come under the umbrella of 'health and sex education'. Some of these topics are controversial and/or the subject of ongoing research (Turner 2000). This means that you need access to up-to-date information from a range of resources. Materials and information can be obtained from a number of organisations which produce

**Task 8.2.5
The 'Question Box'
technique**

This task enables you to reflect on using the 'Question Box' technique and to consider how you would ensure its successful use in the classroom. Ideally you should be carrying out this activity with a class you teach. However, if you are not scheduled to teach this topic with one of your classes you can still obtain pupils' questions but you will have to agree with the teacher beforehand how the pupils' questions will be answered.

1   Negotiate with the science department to find a class where you can set up a 'Question Box' at the beginning of the topic on human reproduction. Alternatively, negotiate with the PHSE/citizenship coordinator to set up the box at the beginning of the topic sex education.

2   Explain the activity to the pupils and leave the box in a place that is accessible.

3   Empty the box and sort the questions out into these categories:
    a   Questions that should be answered in the science lessons and questions that you think would be addressed better in PHSE/ citizenship lessons (see Task 8.2.1).
    b   Questions that you don't know the answers to but do think should be answered (consider whether science or PHSE/ citizenship lessons).
    c   Questions you don't think are suitable to be answered in class.

4   Discuss with the class teacher how departments need to liaise with one another to answer pupils' questions posed in this way. How will you deal with questions in category b?

5   What resources are available in the school to help you answer questions in category c?

6   Consider how you would have dealt with all these questions had you opened the box and read the questions out for the first time in front of the class.

materials that help you design suitable activities for your classes and keep you advised of new developments. Among these organisations are:

• The Wellcome Trust;
• Institute of Biology;
• Department of Health;
• Health Education Authorities;
• television programmes for schools.

Some teachers adopt a technique known as the 'Graffiti board' where the pupils put forward words that they know are commonly used to describe the human reproductive parts and processes and these are written on the board. Then the correct terms are identified and pupils are subsequently expected to use these in lessons. You might feel that this is inappropriate for your school but it is important that we acknowledge that pupils are familiar with a rather different vocabulary from the one we would wish them to use in the classroom.

Task 8.2.6
Using resources in your school

This task provides you with a list of possible resources you could use in your lessons.

Obtain a copy of the QCA scheme of work for science Unit 7B (download this from the DfES website – see Further Reading).

- Look at the list of resources provided and see if your department has access to them.
- Does your department have other resources you could use?
- How many of these resources are used by the teachers?

When you look at text books and photocopiable materials study the language used and consider how many of these terms the pupils might be meeting for the first time, for example, *uterus, menstruation, ovulation, placenta, testis, scrotal sac*. Pupils may well have an understanding of the concepts but may not use these biological terms in their explanations.

However, we must ensure that the pupils can use the correct terminology and a way of helping pupils is to have clearly labelled diagrams readily available and to have key words on the board or around the room. As pupils become familiar with the new words it may help reduce their embarrassment and make them able to use the terms in the correct way. It also helps to reinforce the correct spellings of the words.

A typical activity used in school is to ask pupils to label the diagrams of the human reproductive systems, copying from a book or an overhead transparency, and then find out the function of each part. An alternative task could be to ask the children to describe or draw the shape and structure of each part first. In having to give such descriptions pupils will have to consider the relative size of the various parts, how many there are and where they are located in relation to each other. If pupils then find out the function of the parts it may help them to make associations between structure and function.

HEALTH EDUCATION

Ask pupils to draw a healthy person and they are likely to draw someone who has a big smile and looks happy. It appears that they appreciate that being healthy is not just about an absence of illness but is also about the state of mind and social well being of a person. Being healthy is about being confident to make informed decisions and being able to function within your own community. It is worth considering a little further what you mean by 'healthy'.

Task 8.2.7
What does 'being healthy' mean?

This task helps you clarify your thoughts on what being healthy means. It is also a useful introductory activity to use with your pupils as it engenders a lot of discussion, always a good start to a topic.

Indicate on the list of statements below whether you agree or disagree with each one.

Being healthy is....   *Agree   Disagree*
Enjoying being with people
Hardly ever taking medicine
Being able to run for a bus
Not smoking
Being the ideal weight
Being able to adapt to changes in my life
Eating the 'right foods'
Being able to touch my toes
Not being ill very often

If possible, share your decisions with other science teachers or trainee teachers. Can you suggest how your science teaching can promote the skills pupils need in order that they can choose a healthy life style for themselves?

Task 8.2.8
Devising activities for the classroom

This task requires you to devise an activity that develops pupils' literacy skills. Select a health topic taught in Key Stage 3 and devise an activity using one of the following tasks:

- Analysing teenage letters pages; what knowledge and attitudes are portrayed in the letters?
- Analysing two newspaper articles on the same topic; which one has the more detailed and accurate scientific content?
- Role-play – make a video of a discussion between two people of opposing views.
- Using ICT– make a PowerPoint presentation presenting alternative views.
- Write an article for a school magazine presenting an argument for and against an issue.

TEACHING ABOUT A BALANCED DIET, DRUGS AND ALCOHOL ABUSE

A key issue here for secondary teachers is that the work covered in these topics needs to *build on* that which pupils have covered at Key Stage 2. In the primary school they learn about the importance of an adequate and varied diet, the effects on the human body of tobacco, alcohol and other drugs. They may well have drawn posters to promote giving up smoking, drawn meals on paper plates that promote healthy eating and so the work at Key Stage 3 must take this into account.

An alternative approach to these topics can be used to promote literacy and numeracy skills that encourages them to draw on the knowledge they already have learned rather than just teaching it all over again.

The activities in Task 8.2.8 can also be used to introduce the concept of risk to health. Pupils need to understand how health risks can be affected by lifestyle choices. The story of Sir Richard Doll and how he established the link between smoking and cancer can be a good starting point to the topic.

Using data which helps pupils assess the risks to their health if they smoke, drink alcohol or take drugs (that are not medicines) make the topic more relevant to them and also involve them using numeracy skills. Key Stage 4 classes can use data to assess different levels of risk to their health if they drink alcohol or take drugs. Causes of death statistics for different age groups can be obtained from the Office for National Statistics. You may find it helpful to liaise with the mathematics department to find out when the pupils study probability so that they can appreciate how to estimate risk.

SUMMARY

Teaching pupils about keeping healthy is a topic that will, hopefully, always be a part of the science curriculum. However, the issues included under this title may change as can be seen if we look back at health education over the years. For example, teaching about the human immunodeficiency virus (HIV) will only be found on a school's curriculum from the 1980s.

So what changes can you look forward to in the future? The substances termed as commonly used drugs are likely to change as new drugs become available and the legal status of these drugs may also change. Links between certain diseases and diet may become more evident as more research is carried out. Evidence demonstrating the value of alternative medicines may become available.

Of course other aspects of the curriculum are not subject to such variation. The bodily changes at the onset of puberty are unlikely to alter (although the average age at which they begin may do so). The 'natural way' for conceiving a baby will not change although new techniques for promoting fertility may well be developed. What will be the status of human cloning? What diseases will be affecting the sexual health of the human population?

Our role as science teachers is to ensure that we keep abreast of these changes and work with other departments to develop the knowledge and skills of pupils in order that they can become informed and responsible citizens, able to understand issues of risk and to make decisions about their own lives, taking into account how these decisions affect other people.

FURTHER READING

Archard, D. (2000) *Sex Education* Impact No 7. London: Philosophy of Education Society of Great Britain.

Harrison, J. (2000) *Sex Education in Secondary Schools*, Buckingham: Open University Press.

Reiss, M. (2000) 'Sex Education', in Beck, J. and Earl, M. (eds) *Key Issues in Secondary Education*, London: Cassell.

DfEE (2000) *Sex and Relationship Guidance*, London: DfEE.

WEBSITES TO EXPLORE

Brook Advisory Centre website www.brook.org.uk

DfES web site www.dfes.gov.uk

Department of Health website www.doh.gov.uk

Office for National Statistics website www.statistics.gov.uk

9 Beyond Qualified Teacher Status – Becoming a Professional Teacher

Ralph Levinson

INTRODUCTION

The PGCE year is the launch pad of your teaching career. This chapter looks beyond attainment of Qualified Teacher Status (QTS) through the NQT year towards your further professional development. Although it addresses those on the PGCE route it is applicable to those entering teaching through other routes such as the Registered Teaching Programme or the Graduate Teacher Programme.

OBJECTIVES

By the end of this chapter you should be able to:

- list the essential requirements when applying for your first teaching post;
- identify the preparation necessary for your induction year;
- access information on opportunities are available beyond your induction year.

SELECTING THE SCHOOL FOR YOUR FIRST TEACHING POST

During your PGCE you are likely to scour the *Times Education Supplement* (TES) for teaching posts. As a science teacher, you may find many opportunities but these will vary depending on your subject specialism, where you want to live and the type of school in which you wish to teach.

At the present time those specialising in physics are most in demand, followed only a little way behind by chemists. If you can offer more than one specialist science subject up to GCSE this would increase your chances of employment. Those of you with joint or combined degrees or a general science background are likely to be at an advantage here. If you are a specialist biologist, for example, but have opted to put a lot of work into teaching physics at Key Stage 4 during your PGCE this experience stands you in good stead for your first post. It is helpful to remain open to teaching more than one specialist science subject at Key Stage 4, and possibly beyond. There are many opportunities to improve your knowledge, understanding and skills in teaching a subject that did not form a main part of your degree course, through in-service courses and distance-learning programmes. These courses are regularly advertised through the Association for Science Education (ASE), Local Education Authorities, leaflets to schools and websites of Higher Education Institutions (HEIs) and the professional societies.

Task 9.1
Identifying your potential

At this point jot down:

- the science subjects and extra-curricular interests that you can offer secondary schools now and the level to which you teach it;
- science subjects and any skills that you feel you can acquire through your induction year and with a little professional development;
- science subjects and skills that you would like to offer but you feel will take you some time to deploy with confidence.

For the first two bullet points carry out a web search starting with the ASE home page, www.ase.org.uk, to find out what Continuing Professional Development (CPD) opportunities are available.

The number of posts available varies in different parts of the country but as a rule of thumb there are more vacancies available in inner city areas. The reasons for this are manifold: the difficulties of buying a home in cities; the relatively large turnover in staff; perceived difficulties, often mistaken, of teaching in the inner city. Where there is a greater number of posts there is also a greater likelihood of promotion at an earlier stage of your career.

Most of you will opt to teach in the state sector but some may apply for jobs in independent schools. For your career development state schools have a lot to offer. Local Education Authorities and national structures for science teacher development are geared to the needs of science teachers in state schools. Some of the bigger independent schools can offer an attractive starting salary and impressive conditions of service giving both time and support for professional development. While most state schools cannot always match these conditions, you should remember that if you are well qualified you can negotiate with state schools a starting salary above the national pay structure and, whatever your qualifications, explore the many routes for professional development. Your union can also provide valuable information to address questions you have in applying for posts. All the major teaching unions offer free membership for teachers in their PGCE year and reduced rates during the induction year.

During your PGCE year your placement school might invite you to apply for a post. This should be taken as a reflection of the opinion the science department and the school has of your abilities but you should also stand back and think if this is the department and school you want. (Do not be concerned if you are not offered a post, there might not be one available!) For a new teacher it might seem ungracious to decline the offer particularly if there is a strong indication that you will get the job. You might have concerns that rejecting the post will prejudice your success in the teaching placement. No one will hold this against you, on the contrary they are likely to commend your independence of mind.

If this is your first placement school it is also the first school of which you have any knowledge at all. When applying for a job you should have been able to compare different schools from the perspective of the teacher. If you love working at the school, feel well supported by the staff, enjoy the facilities, are aware of a good career structure, plenty of opportunities for CPD and you generally have a good feel for the school then it is the right job for you. But it does make sense to have a look at another school before you apply for or accept a post.

APPLYING FOR A POST

By far the most common way of applying for a post is through an advertisement in a national newspaper, usually the *Times Education Supplement* (TES), but other routes are:

- through Local Education Authority (LEA) contacts such as LEA open evenings for new teachers;
- by writing directly to a school where you have special contacts or would particularly like to teach;
- by invitation (as mentioned before, in your placement school).

Schools send information with a job description which lists the criteria it wishes the candidate to satisfy. You must pay attention to the job description when writing your letter of application or filling in the application form. Usually the most important qualities are listed high up, with more peripheral needs down the list. Some institutions include essential and desirable qualities. All the points in the job description should be addressed in your letter of application. You could refer back to Task 9.1 to help you.

As an NQT, the main requirements are a good background in science, an enthusiasm for and competence in teaching science, and being a good teamworker. In addition, the school might be looking for someone:

- who can teach chemistry and physics up to GCSE or,
- with an interest in ecology and environmental science who will take responsibility for the science environmental area or,
- with a particular interest in teaching vocational science or,
- who can teach some mathematics or,
- who would be willing to take charge of the school rowing team.

These are examples of additional job requirements and there will be others. If these criteria are listed decide whether you have the necessary attributes to fulfil them. By making these specifications the school is inviting you to demonstrate your relevant background and you should take pains to point out how your experience qualifies you in particular. In your application give a concrete example of your experience. For example if they are asking for an interest in ecology:

- Do you have a background of ecology in your degree course?
- Have you taught ecology in your placement school? If so, how much and at what level?
- Most convincingly, have you taken an active part in projects or are you a member of a relevant local or national association, e.g. British Trust for Conservation Volunteers (BTCV).

Give enough information in your application form to generate interest so that these can be taken further in interviews. Avoid statements such as 'I have a great interest in teaching ecology' or 'I would find it a welcome challenge to teach maths' when you don't feel strongly about either statement. These general statements do not impress headteachers and heads of science but evidence and enthusiasm do. You are applying for an NQT post so primarily you want to put yourself over as a stimulating, enthusiastic teacher of science and the best way to do this is to exemplify just enough to whet the appetite.

Task 9.2
Do I fit in?

Figure 9.1 shows typical job descriptions. Tick those items where you definitely fit the criterion. Put a question mark against those where you are unsure and make a note about what you would need to do to tick it with confidence. Put a cross against those items where you have strong doubts about your ability. Do you feel confident about applying? How far do you fall short, if indeed you do, and do you think this is an obstacle to your application?

Remember to include those referees who can best support your applications. These are almost always the tutor at your HEI and your school mentor. An alternative could be your tutor at the college where you did your degree and a mentor, if for example, you are training by a less traditional route such as through a School Centred Initial Teacher Training (SCITT) course.

For more advice on completing an application form see the suggested reading list at the end of this chapter.

INTERVIEWING/VISITING THE SCHOOL/TEACHING A LESSON

If your application is successful you are shortlisted and invited to the school for a visit and interview. Should everything go well the school will offer you the job on the same day so be prepared to say whether you want the job or not (see later section, 'The Interview'). This means that you have to do your homework about the school in advance and prepare

Job description – School A (this was accompanied by additional information about the department, candidate specification, description of the school and an application form.)

Curriculum
- Teach integrated science across ability and 11–16 age range, and GCE phys/chem/bio.
- Keep abreast of NC requirements, NC tests and other educational initiatives.
- Teach the curriculum in accordance with Schemes of Work and the timetable.
- Contribute to development of teaching schemes, methods & resources.
- Stimulate interest in science – cross curricular and extra curricular activities.
- Promote aims of science dept.

Assessment
- Differentiate teaching and assessment.
- Prepare and mark work for students.
- Assess and record as specified by internal and statutory requirements.
- Meet needs of students on SEN register.

Communications
- Fulfil aims of school and contribute to its ethos.
- Participate in relevant directed time meetings and parents' evening.
- Meet statutory and school policy requirements.
- Cover lessons for absent colleagues when required.

Resources
- Maintain an appropriate learning environment.
- Produce and update stimulating displays.
- Use and develop IT as a tool to enhance learning in science.
- Be responsible for resources during lessons.
- Produce resources to supplement textbooks, within a team committed to share good practice;
- Comply with health and safety procedures.

Professional development
- Committed to furthering your own professional development, participating in appraisal and inservice training to optimise your performance as a teacher.

Administration
- Carry out administration as specified in handbooks, being mindful of the importance of teamwork.
- Responsible for carrying out designated school duties.

Pastoral
- Participate fully in a year team and undertake the role of a tutor as required.
- Be concerned with the welfare of pupils in your care.
- Help facilitate the extended and extra-curriculum opportunities for pupils.

Person specification – school B (Info' about the job and school were included)

The successful candidate is likely to be a person who:
- is a talented and successful classroom practitioner committed to raising achievement;
- is a graduate who is aware of current developments in the teaching of science in secondary schools;
- has good interpersonal and communication skills;
- is keen to initiate and innovate;
- has the drive and commitment to motivate pupils;
- has high standards and expectations of pupils and themselves;
- has a commitment to raising standards of achievement in science;
- is well informed on current developments in education and science teaching;
- is aware of the contribution science makes to the development of the whole child;
- will be able to make a contribution to the wider education of pupils at the school;
- is a confident user, both in the classroom and for administration, of a range of ICT applications;
- wishes to take part in development and training in order that they may seek promotion in the future.

Figure 9.1 Two job specifications

a list of things you want to look out for in advance. If the school has a website explore it fully. Examples of questions you may want to look out for in science are:

- Is there a collegiate feel to the department or do teachers tend to do their own thing? Are teachers friendly to you as well as to each other? Do the technicians and the teachers have a good relationship? Do you feel welcomed?
- What facilities are available? Are there sufficient technicians in each subject area?
- Is there an atmosphere of learning in the school?
- Are there contemporary posters on the walls? Is children's work displayed? Does it look fresh and interesting?
- How will you be supported during your NQT year?
- Will you have a dedicated laboratory or will you be moving round a lot?
- Is there good IT support? Do the computers look as if they are used?

Questions such as the number and type of courses taught and range of responsibilities within the department should be in the information the school sends to you. The response to the answers to the questions will depend on your preferences. For example, you may be the kind of person who likes to work in a quiet orderly atmosphere where the coffee mugs are nice and clean and you may not be too worried by a lack of congeniality. Or you might prioritise a friendly working atmosphere and not be concerned that half the sinks in the chemistry laboratory seem to be out of use. There is no unique answer to these questions but you do need to think about the working conditions you prefer.

Although you have a list of questions, the head of science might address these anyway when you go on your visit. Avoid asking question which have already been addressed. Asking unnecessary questions does not make a good impression. The head of science is likely to give you the chance to raise any queries you have. Do not have a long list but ask one or two well-pointed questions and push gently if you need more information. The head of science is best qualified to answer questions about your role within the department and who will support you during your NQT year. She cannot answer questions about how much you can expect to be paid. Questions about pay and overall NQT support are best answered by the head teacher and a senior curriculum teacher respectively. Candidates should have a substantial part of the day to look around the school, talk to staff and technicians and senior teachers. If no time is allocated to look around the school and department you should ask in advance of the visit to be shown around.

TEACHING A LESSON

Many schools invite candidates to teach a lesson to a group of pupils on the day of your interview. You are told the topic, what pupils have already learned in the topic, the age of the group and the facilities available to you. Understandably this seems a demanding task but your prospective employers are trying to find out:

- Do you look as if you can remain confident in front of a class?
- Can you explain the topic confidently and at the appropriate level?
- Do you show signs of an imaginative approach to teaching?
- Are you adequately prepared?

Schools usually give you a few days notice so leave time to prepare and gather good ideas. Below are three examples of activities given recently to candidates:

- A 20-minute lesson on energy transfer to Y7;
- A 10-minute episode on plant reproduction to Y9;
- A lesson lasting 50 minutes on reflection and refraction of light to Y9.

Do not be too ambitious, it is much better to teach part of a concept or skill well and clearly than a huge amount badly. Once you have a topic, jot down:

- the main idea you want to put across;
- one learning outcome;
- a short starter activity which is interesting;
- two different tasks which address the learning outcome;
- a simple direct resource to be used;
- a short plenary activity.

Rather than ask the school for lots of equipment, try and prepare some of your own resources. A 3D model, a simple and effective demonstration or a well-crafted worksheet offering opportunities for discussion would be welcome. Coming in with a good, simple resource suggests creativity and independence. On no account should you take in a video which takes up most of the teaching time and limits any interaction or opportunity for explanation.

You should expect to teach a well-behaved and reasonably responsive class unless you create discipline problems through your own lack of preparation. If the class is undisciplined with its usual teacher then the school is either looking for a miracle-worker (which you might be and therefore this is the school for the challenge you crave) or it has unrealistic expectations, which should tell you all you need to know about what you can expect during your induction year.

The interview

Just as you can prepare questions for your visit you should anticipate questions for your interview. There are a number of sources that will give you information about the kinds of questions to expect and appropriate ways to behave but you will almost certainly be asked to:

- describe and analyse an effective science lesson you have taught;
- discuss areas that you feel you need to develop;
- explain how you acted in response to a poor lesson you taught.

There is no right or wrong response, but keep to the point. If asked to describe a good or weak lesson don't give a blow-by-blow account. Give a brief summary of the topic and the challenges, outline how you dealt with them and how well you think your strategies worked. Think through your strengths and areas you need to develop because this will alert your induction tutor. Be realistic about these qualities; people will be suspicious if you feel you are strong in everything, equally don't run yourself down, the latter is a common feature of pre-service teachers. A response such as 'I'm hopeless at managing difficult children' will effectively show you the door whereas 'I have found it difficult to keep the class settled in the last five minutes of the lesson but I have gathered together a range of plenary activities such as … which are starting to do the trick' will demonstrate that you are both introspective and proactive.

At the end of the interview candidates are asked: 'If you were offered the post would you be prepared to accept it?' Your answer to this question is important because it will not reflect well on you if you change your mind. Before you go into the interview you should have been informed of contractual arrangements if you were offered the post, broad terms of conditions and salary. There are, however, financial inducements for retention and recruitment and some points for extra skills and these should be mentioned in the information you receive beforehand. If there is anything you are unsure about you should either clear this up before the interview or be prepared to ask at this point. For good reasons young pre-service teachers are wary of mentioning salary before a panel at an interview and the panel should be sensitive to this. If you would like to take the post but there are points about recruitment and retention that you want to clarify you should say that you would be delighted to accept the post but there is a query you have about salary that you would like to discuss before giving a definite answer. Either the headteacher will outline what is on offer directly and leave you to decide whether you are happy with this or not or she will offer to discuss it with you after the interviews are over. The usual procedure is that candidates are asked to wait until the interviews are over or phoned at home the same day so there should be time available for this.

If you like the school and the terms offered you should accept unreservedly. If you have decided before the interview that you do not like the school and cannot see yourself teaching there you should mention to the headteacher or her personal assistant that you are withdrawing and you will then be free to go on good terms. If you are interviewed and still feel that you would not accept the job you must say so. It will not be held against you. (Note that the headteacher might ask why you rejected the post. While your answer should be truthful it should not be blunt to the point of rudeness.) If you say 'I accept the job' you have made an oral contract of agreement and if you change your mind the school is entitled to feel aggrieved with your behaviour. While the school is unlikely to take any legal action against you they could inform the local authority and it would then be unlikely that other local schools in the LEA would interview you. You must be clear and honest.

You genuinely may not be sure if you want to accept the job and feel you need to talk things over, possibly with a partner, or just have a little longer to think things through. Most headteachers will allow you to ponder your decision overnight and respond the next day. They will often ask you to discuss any reservations with them. Again, headteachers respect courtesy and honesty.

PREPARING FOR THE INDUCTION YEAR

You complete a *Career Entry and Development Profile* (CEDP) with the help of your tutor, towards the end of your course as preparation for your induction year. You have to list four areas of strength, four areas for development and write a general statement about your expectations in the NQT year. During your PGCE year you will have collected a portfolio of evidence, demonstrating how you have progressed in your teaching, and in thinking through your teaching, throughout the year. This portfolio is an important document which you should maintain during your induction year and beyond. What goes in your portfolio will depend on you and the requirements of your training institution (see Capel *et al.* 2001, Unit 8.2). This portfolio is a reference source in compiling your CEDP.

The information in your CEDP is far more than a list of strengths and supposed weaknesses. Planning your professional development is about using your strengths and developing those aspects of your teaching which would best underpin these strengths. Professional development should also address those areas in which you have had less experience. Areas for development do not mean weaknesses. They might include one area which builds on your strengths. For example, if you have listed use of ICT in science as one of your strengths you might want to identify an aspect of ICT, such as datalogging, you would like to develop specifically during your NQT year, perhaps devising teacher-friendly materials to support specific lessons in data capture and interpretation.

Most science NQTs find that by the time they have attained Qualified Teacher Status (QTS) they have had relatively little experience doing one or more of the following:

- running and assessing a science investigation for Sc1;
- marking and moderating coursework for national examinations;
- deploying datalogging or computer simulations in the classroom;
- differentiating sufficiently for SEN students;
- using formative assessment effectively;
- engaging in broad areas of pastoral work;
- teaching examination classes;
- running field trips;
- teaching whole classes at AS/A2 level.

The items above are only examples and none may apply to you. But they reflect the fact that the PGCE year is only 36 weeks long and, while you may have done a little of all of these, you feel more experience in one or more of these areas would make you a more rounded teacher and help you to meet the standards at the end of your NQT year (Teacher Training Agency 2002).

Another area for development might specifically support the way you see your career going and can be incorporated in an area for development and in your general statement. Three case studies illustrate this point.

> Tamsin had been offered a post at her first placement school where she had become fully involved in out-of-school activities. She saw her future in the pastoral role rather than as a science specialist. Science would be her main subject area but she aspired to be a head of year and eventually responsible for pastoral provision within a school. In one of her areas for development and in her statement she included increasing her understanding of specialist pastoral responsibilities and requesting any CPD training days to support these skills.

> Julie had a degree in geology and her school had informally asked her to develop aspects of Earth science across the curriculum. Developing a GCSE and GCE A-level in geology was also an aspiration of hers. One of Julie's areas of develoment was to extend her teaching of Earth science and, in her general statement, to attend days for professional development run, for example, by the Earth Science Teacher Association (ESTA).

> Paul was a fast-track student who was likely to become a head of department

within the next few years. He saw a number of areas for development. Chemistry was his specialist subject and he felt he still needed to improve his understanding of physics. He therefore wanted to pay special attention to this during his NQT year, concentrating on teaching physics at Key Stage 3 and continuing the good work he had done in his PGCE year by taking a course for non-specialist teachers of physics. As a potential manager he also wanted to see how managers operated within the school and had put this down as another area of development.

Many NQTs still feel nervous about classroom management even though they have had a successful PGCE year. As you have recognised during your pre-service year, developing good classroom management techniques is very much a matter of experience and any school worth their salt in supporting NQTs will take this into consideration. You should discuss this carefully with your tutor but your CEDP should reflect how you see your career developing even though you will still have uncertainties about classroom discipline at this time. By all means refer to classroom management but try and identify an aspect of management in which you feel you will need particular support.

YOUR INDUCTION YEAR

So you have QTS and secured your first teaching post. Check possible starting dates for employment. Some schools offer a contract to NQTs from the July of their PGCE year. There are real advantages in taking up this offer. You will be paid not only from the beginning of July to the summer vacation but over the holidays as well. It also gives you a chance to prepare for your induction year free from a busy teaching timetable because pupils in years 11 and 13 will have completed their examinations and several classes will be out on school trips. It gives you a chance to get to know your way around the school and become more fully acquainted with your colleagues and the pupils. While this is a golden opportunity no harm is done if you do not accept it. Not all schools offer this early start anyway and you may also feel you have had a strenuous PGCE year and want a long break before you start as an NQT. This is a perfectly reasonable option and you may relish your last long vacation free of responsibilities from work.

We move on now to your NQT year. You are in a salaried post with all the advantages and security that offers. But this is not the end of your education as a teacher, it is in fact only just beginning and through your induction year you have one more hurdle to cross because you must fulfil the induction standards for your career to continue (Induction standards for Newly Qualified Teachers in England, online). There are many good sources to explain what you should expect during your induction year including regular support and briefing from a dedicated mentor. The responsibilities of both you and your mentor regarding the induction year are discussed further in the generic reader (Capel *et al.* 2001, Unit 8.2). Early in the year you discuss with your mentor an individual development plan based on your CEDP. Your progress will be monitored at intervals throughout the year and towards the end of the year you will review with your mentor and the headteacher how much progress you have made on the statements in your CEDP. By this point in your first year you should have a good indication that you are now ready to be confirmed as a fully qualified teacher.

During your NQT year you should expect to attend a number of dedicated in-service courses. Some of these courses will be organised by the school or local education authority, others in HEIs and still others by professional organisations such as the ASE (see below).

BEYOND NQT

As we mentioned earlier your growth as a teacher continues throughout your career. One typical route is teacher of science and chemistry > head of chemistry > responsible for Key Stage 3 science > head of science > senior teacher responsible for curriculum > deputy head teacher. This is an example of progression and the route you choose has to suit your own circumstances and make teaching a fulfilling and important part of your life. There are wonderful experienced science teachers who prefer the higher proportion of their time to be in the classroom rather than in administration. You can, for example, apply for Advanced Skills Teacher Status (AST). Even then you might feel that you love teaching your subject with as few extraneous responsibilities or application forms as possible and do not want to apply for AST. It cannot be overstated that the happiest teachers are those who love what they do, have time to relax and enjoy themselves and are content with their responsibilities regardless of salary.

COURSES

There are many openings which allow you to reflect on and interrogate your own teaching practice through post-graduate courses in academic institutions and there may be grants available to research an aspect of your teaching. Research needs to be supported by an academic member of staff in an HEI, and is likely to be part of a Masters degree or form the basis of a doctorate. Recent examples of research questions tackled by MA students are:

- How do teachers' interaction with pupils during practical work help to clarify the underlying concepts?
- What formative marking procedures are most effective in supporting understanding of science concepts with SEN pupils?
- How is the Learning Support Assistant (LSA) deployed in the science classroom and how can the LSA's role be most effective to support learning?
- How can discussion be promoted in the science classroom at Key Stage 3?

Diploma, certificate and Masters' courses are open to practising teachers at many higher education institutions usually as a part-time course extending over two years; many Masters' courses can now be completed through a distance-learning route. Schools or local authorities do not usually fund such studies but there are exceptions. Scouting around for available funding may well pay dividends. The traditional Masters' courses involve a largely taught component plus a research-based dissertation. You can follow a Masters' course comprising all modules in science education or you can make up your course in a number of different areas, for example, psychology of education, science education, policy studies, museum education. Prospectuses or websites of HEIs provide you with all the information you need about Masters' courses. Many courses are advertised in the educational press including the *Times Educational Supplement* (TES) and *The Guardian Education Section*.

Master of Teaching (MTcg) courses are open to NQTs and those who have only been teaching a few years. These courses are strongly linked to your professional development needs and involve a considerable element of online discussion with peers. This is a very worthwhile way of attaining a highly rated professional qualification.

Doctoral courses are also available in two forms: a doctorate of Education and a doctorate of philosophy. The former contains a substantial taught component as well as a research element whereas a PhD or DPhil is entirely research-based. Although a PhD and DPhil are supported by taught courses aimed at supporting your research these latter elements are not examined. Studying for a doctorate is an enormous commitment and you should only consider starting once you have been teaching for at least three years. It is based on an extended piece of research. You will need some time off work to write up your thesis but the dividends are enormous if it is strongly linked to a particular interest, for example in assessment of science, the teaching of physics or educational management. A full-time doctorate normally takes three to four years but doing it part-time, the more usual route nowadays, will take five to seven years.

PROFESSIONAL ORGANISATIONS

Like other professions, teaching has its own professional body, the General Teaching Council (GTC). The functions of the GTC can be accessed from its website (www.gtce.org.uk). There is, however, a professional organisation for science teachers, the Association for Science Education (ASE), already mentioned above. The ASE is the biggest subject teachers' organisation in the country and is an enormous asset in supporting and developing your subject teaching. Each year in early January the ASE holds its annual meeting which includes many talks on diverse aspects of science and science education, seminars, demonstrations, stands, shows, workshops, visits, film and theatre performances. There are also regular regional ASE meetings. In joining the ASE as a secondary teacher you receive the quarterly journal *School Science Review* which contains informed articles by teachers and educationalists on teaching and learning science, book reviews and many practical tips. *Education in Science* also comes out quarterly and contains articles on policy and contemporary issues in science education.

The three organisations for the main subject areas in science, the Institute of Biology (IoB), the Royal Society of Chemistry (RSC) and the Institute of Physics (IoP) have their own educational sections and also run many stimulating activities and produce their own educational journals which contain invaluable contemporary information; their websites are listed in the references. Education officers are also employed by some large industrial companies and organisations such as the Royal Society, the Association of the British Pharmaceutical Industry and the Engineering Council.

DOES A PGCE QUALIFY ME ONLY FOR TEACHING?

Success on the PGCE course results in QTS; however, there are employment possibilities offered by the PGCE that go beyond the teaching profession. This comes with a strong rider: it is only after you have completed your induction year and a few years more that these other careers in science education become a reality. Indeed their realisation depends on your ability to become an effective science teacher. Examples of careers linked to science education include:

- local authority science adviser or science inspector;
- freelance consultant in, for example, running in-service courses;
- education officer or adviser for professional bodies or institutions. These include such organisations as the Association for Science Education, the Royal Society, the British Association for the Advancement of Science, the Royal Society of Chemistry, the Institute of Physics, the Institute of Biology, voluntary organisations, large chemical and pharmaceutical companies, engineering companies, biomedical and medical charities such as the Wellcome Trust. Government organisations such as the DfES and non-governmental organisations such as the QCA and associated bodies also employ specialists in science education;
- education officers and educators at science centres and science museums;
- writing science books and textbooks;
- educational media including TV specialising in science education;
- research in science education and teacher education.

These reflect some of the main opportunities but in a rapidly changing world new opportunities are likely to arise while others dwindle so it is mainly a matter of keeping up to date and your eyes open. All these bodies serve teachers and students, and it is generally committed and experienced teachers with a wide range of interests who wish for a change who are likely to be the best candidates for these posts.

SUMMARY

This chapter has focused on the opportunities that face you as you progress from a pre-service teacher to an experienced professional, a route which opens out a vast range of possibilities. You need to be aware of the practice and accompanying documentation that supports a successful career as well as taking advantage of the courses that contribute to your progress as a successful science teacher.

FURTHER READING

Capel, S., Heilbronn, R., Leask, M. and Turner, T. (in press) *Starting to Teach in the Secondary School: A Companion for the NQT*, London: RoutledgeFalmer. This text is a thoroughly revised text of the edition first published in 1998. It covers many of the issues faced by NQTs of all subjects and provides help and advice about settling into a new department and school, managing time and pressure and meeting the standards for confirming Qualified Teacher Status. It contains a strong theoretical dimension about teaching and learning and is evidence based, supported by research evidence.

Holmes, E (2003) *The Newly Qualified Teacher's Handbook*, London and Sterling, VA: Kogan Page. A basic handbook which contains concise and practical advice on your induction year as well as information about applying for jobs and joining a school.

Parkinson, J. (2004) *Improving Secondary Science Teaching,* London: RoutledgeFalmer. A book for experienced teachers but may provide stimulation and opportunities for reflection for NQTs who are progressing well.

Wallace, J. and Louden, W. (2002) *Dilemmas of Science Teaching: Perspectives on Problems of Practice,* London: RoutledgeFalmer. A series of Case Studies addressing issues which face science teachers in the classroom. The dilemmas raised by the studies are discussed by experienced practitioners providing a theoretical foundation for the discourse. The individual studies may provide good material for mentor–NQT discussion or alternatively provide the new teacher with a chance to read in more depth about a particular issue facing him.

ORGANISATIONS

Association for Science Education (ASE)

The ASE is the first organisation to which a newly qualified science teacher might turn for help and advice. As well as publications, regular meetings nationally and locally it provides inservice courses for Continuing Professional Development (CPD). A recent innovation is the production of CD-ROMs providing resources for teaching. Their website is listed in the references.

National and Regional Science Learning Centres

These are new developments supported by central government in England to develop and improve science teaching. They are designed to support science teachers and contribute to their CPD. You should identify your nearest centre and find out what support is available. They are online and their website is listed under 'science learning centres'.

References

Adey, P. and Shayer, M. (1994) *Really Raising Standards*, London: Routledge, 98–107.

Adey, P, Shayer, M. and Yates, C. (2001) *Thinking Science: The Materials of the CASE Project* (3rd edn), London: Thomas Nelson and Sons.

APU (Assessment of Performance Unit) (Russell, T.) (1988a) *National Assessment: Science at Age 11, A Review of APU Survey Findings 1980–84*, London: HMSO.

—— (Archenhold, F.) (1988b) *National Assessment: Science at Age 15, A Review of APU Survey Findings 1980–84*, London: HMSO.

—— (Schofiled, B.) (1989) *National Assessment: Science at Age 13, A Review of APU Survey Findings 1980–84*, London: HMSO.

Archard, D. (2000) *Sex Education* Impact No 7. London: Philosophy of Education Society of Great Britain.

Asoko, H. and Squires, A. (1998) 'Progression and Continuity', in Ratcliffe, M. (ed.) *ASE Guide to Secondary Science Education*, Cheltenham: Stanley Thornes, 175–82.

ASE (Association for Science Education) (1987a) *SATIS (16–19)*, London: John Murray.

—— (1993) *SATIS 8–14*, London: John Murray.

—— (1999) *SATIS 14–16*, London: John Murray

Axon, C. (2002) 'The Bath scientific heritage trail' *The British Council Science Education Newsletter* (156, May), 4–5. Online. Available HTTP: http://www.ba-west.org.uk (accessed 12 February 2004).

Beckett, L. (1986) 'Bridges', in A. Jennings (ed.) *Science in the Locality*, Cambridge: Cambridge University Press.

Black, P. (1987) 'Deciding to Teach', *Steam: ICI Science Teachers' Magazine*, 8.

Black, P. and Wiliam, D. (1998) *Inside the Black Box: Raising Standards Through Classroom Assessment*, London: King's College, School of Education.

Black, P., Harrison C., Lee, C., Marshall, B. and Wiliam, D. (2002) *Working Inside the Black Box: Assessment for Learning in the Classroom*, London: King's College, Department of Education and Professional Studies.

Borrows, P. (1999) 'Chemistry trails', *Education in Chemistry*, **6**, 158–9.

—— (2002) 'Risk assessment in science for secondary schools', in S. Amos and R. Boohan (eds) *Aspects of Teaching Secondary Science*, London: RoutledgFalmer for the Open University, 84–94.

Brain, M. (2003) *More How Stuff Works*, New York: Hungry Minds.

Brown, J.R. (1991) *Laboratory of the Mind: Thought Experiments in the Natural Sciences*, London: Routledge.

Burton, D. (2001) 'Ways pupils learn', in S. Capel, M. Leask, M. and T. Turner (eds) *Learning to Teach in the Secondary School: A Companion to School Experience*, 3rd edn, London: RoutledgeFalmer.

Butler, R. (1988) 'Enhancing and undermining intrinsic motivation; the effects of task-involving and ego-involving evaluation on interest and performance', *British Journal of Educational Psychology*, **58**, 1–14.

Calder, N. (1977) *The Key to the Universe: A Report on the New Physics*, London: British Broadcasting Corporation. Reprinted in Carey, J. (ed.) (1995) *The Faber Book of Science*, London: Faber & Faber.

Capel, S., Leask, M. and Turner, T. (eds) (2001) *Learning to Teach in the Secondary School: A Companion to School Experience*, 3rd edn, London: RoutledgeFalmer.

Capel, S., Heilbronn, R., Leask, M. and Turner, T. (eds) (2004) *Starting to Teach in the Secondary School: A Companion for the NQT*, London: RoutledgeFalmer.

Chalmers, A.F. (1999) *What is This Thing Called Science?*, 3rd edn, Buckingham: Open University Press.

Chapman, J., Hamer, P. and Sears, J. (2000) 'Non-judgemental differentiation: teaching and learning styles for the future', in J. Sears and P. and Sorensen (eds) *Issues in Science Teaching*, London: RoutledgeFalmer.

CLEAPSS (2000) *Hazcards*, Brunel University, London: Consortium of Local Education Authorities School Science Service (CLEAPSS).

Cowley, S. (2003) *Getting the Buggers to Behave 2*, 2nd edn, London: Continuum.

Davis, B.C. (1989) *GASP: Graded Assessment in Science Project*, London: Hutchinson.

Dennison, P.E. and Dennison, G.E. (1989) *Brain Gym (Teachers Edition)*, Edu-Kinesthetics. Online. Available HTTP: http://www.braingym.com/html/our_products.html (accessed 12 February 2004).

Denny, M. and Chennell, F. (1986) 'Science Practicals; what do pupils think?', *European Journal of Science Education*, **8** (3), 325–36.

DES/WO (Department for Education and Science/Welsh Office) (1985) *Science 5–16: A Statement of Policy*, London: HMSO.

—— (1988a) *National Curriculum Task Group on Assessment and Testing (TGAT Report)*, London: DES.

—— (1988b) *Science for ages 5–16. Proposals of the Secretary of State for Education and Science and the Secretary of State for Wales*, London: HMSO (August).

—— (1989a) *Science in the National Curriculum*, London: HMSO.

—— (1989b) *Discipline in Schools. Report of the Committee of Enquiry, chaired by Lord Elton*, London: HMSO.

—— (1991) *Science in the National Curriculum*, London: HMSO.

DfE (Department for Education) (1992) *Initial Teacher Training (Secondary Phase) Circular 9/92*, London: DfE.

—— (1993) *Education Act 1993: Sex Education in Schools. Circular 5/94*, London: DfE.

DfE/WO (Department for Education and Welsh Office) (1995) *Science in the National Curriculum*, London: HMSO.

DfEE (Department for Education and Employment) (1998) *Circular 4/98 Standards for Award of Qualified Teacher Status*, London: HMSO.

—— (1999) *The National Curriculum for England Non-statutory Frameworks for Personal, Social and Health Education and Citizenship at Key Stages 1 and 2; Personal, Social and Health Education at Key Stages 3 and 4*, London: DfEE and QCA.

—— (2000) *Sex and Relationship Guidance*, London: DfEE.

DfEE/QCA (Department for Education and Employment/Qualifications and Curriculum Authority) (1999a) *The National Curriculum for England: Science*, London: DfEE and QCA.

—— (1999b) *Citizenship: The National Curriculum for England Key: Stages 3 and 4*, London: DfEE and QCA.

DfES (Department for Education and Skills) (1998) *Health and Safety of pupils on Educational Visits: A Good Practice Guide*, London: DfES.

—— (2001) *Special Educational Needs: Code of Practice*, Nottingham: DfES Publications.

—— (2002a) *14–19: Extending Opportunity and Raising Standards* (Green Paper), London: DfES Publications. Online. Available HTTP: http://www.dfes.gov.uk/14–19/ (accessed 12 February 2004).

—— (2002b) *Key Stage 3 National Strategy. Framework for Teaching Science: Years 7, 8 and 9*, London: DfES. Online. Available HTTP: http://www.standards.dfes.gov.uk/schemes2/secondary_science/ (accessed 12 February 2004).

—— (2002c) *Key stage 3 National Strategy. Framework for Teaching Science: Year 9 Booster Kit: Science*, London: DfES.

—— (2002d) *Year 9 Booster Kit: Science*, DfES ref: 012/2002. Online. Available HTTP: http://www.standards.dfes.gov.uk/keystage3/publications (accessed 12 February 2004).

—— (2003a) *Secondary School Performance Tables 2002: Key Stage 2 to Key Stage 3, Value Added Measure*. Online. Available HTTP: http://www.scalbyschool.org.uk/about/tables/default.asp (accessed 10 February 2004).

—— (2003b) *Teaching Resources, Science*. Online. Available HTTP: http://www.teachernet.gov.uk/teachingandlearning/resourcematerials/ks3/ (accessed 12 February 2004); search 'science'.

—— (2003c) *14–19: Opportunity and Excellence*. London: DfES Publications. Online. Available HTTP: http:// www.dfes.gov.uk/14–19/ (accessed 12 February 2004).

—— (2003d) *Annexes to 14 – 19: Opportunity and Excellence*, London: DfES Publications; see DfES 2003a.

—— (2004) *14–19 Curriculum and Qualifications Reform: Interim Report of the Working Group on 14–19 Reform* London: DfES. Online. Available HTTP: http://www.14–19reform.gov.uk.

DfES/TTA (Department for Education and Skills/Teacher Training Agency) (2003a) *Qualifying to teach: Professional Standards for Qualified Teacher Status and Requirements for Initial Teacher Training*, London: Teacher Training Agency.

—— (2003b) *The Autumn Package 2003 Guidance*. Online. Available HTTP: http:// www.standards.dfes.gov.uk/performance (accessed 10 February 2004).

DfES/QCA (Department for Education and Skills and Qualification and Curriculum Authority) (2003) *QCA Schemes of Work: Science at Key Stage 3*, London: DfES and QCA. Available HTTP:http://www standards.dfes.gov.uk.

Diamond, J. (1988) *The Rise and Fall of the Third Chimpanzee: How our Animal Heritage Affects the Way we Live*, London: Vintage.

Dickinson, C. and Wright, J. (1993) *Differentiation: a Practical Handbook of Classroom Strategies*, Coventry: NCET.

Dixon, B. (1989) *The Science of Science*, London: Cassell.

DOH (Department of Health) (2001) *The National Strategy for Sexual Health and HIV*, London: DoH.

DOH (Department of Health) Online. Available HTTP: http:// www.doh.gov.uk.

Donaldson, M. (1978) *Children's Minds*, Glasgow: Fontana.

Donnelly, J. (2001) 'Contested terrain or unified project? The nature of science in the National Curriculum for England and Wales', *International Journal of Science Education*, **23**: 181–95.

Dove, J. (1994) 'Headstones, local churches and Sc3', *School Science Review* **75** (272, March), 43–50.

Driver, R., Guesne, E. and Tinberghien, A. (1985) *Children's Ideas in Science*, Buckingham: Open University Press.

Driver, R., Squires, A., Rushworth, P. and Wood-Robinson, V. (1994) *Making Sense of Secondary Science: Research into Children's Ideas*, London: Routledge.

Driver, R., Leach, J., Millar, R. and Scott, P. (1996) *Young People's Images of Science*, Buckingham: Open University Press.

Dweck, C. S. (1986) 'Motivational processes affect learning' *American Psychologist (Special Issue: Psychological science and education)*, **41** (10), 1040–8.

Ellis, P. (1992) *Science Changes!*, Hemel Hempstead: Simon and Schuster.

ERA (1998) *Education Reform Act*, 29 July 1988, London: HMSO.

Feyerabend, P. (1975/1988) *Against Method*, revised edn, London: Verso.

Feynman, R. P. (2000) *The Pleasure of Finding Things Out*, London: Penguin Books.

Frost, R. (2001) *Software for Teaching Science: A Critical Catalogue of Science Software*, London: IT in Science.

—— (2002a) *The IT in Secondary Science Book*, London: IT in Science.

—— (2002b) *Datalogging in Practice*, London: IT in Science.

—— (2002c) *Datalogging & Control*, London: IT in Science.

Gardner, M. (1993) *Frames of Mind: The Theory of Multiple Intelligences*, London: Falmer.

Glauert, E. and Frost, J. (1997) 'Pedagogy in Primary Science', *Publication of the 3rd Summer Conference for Teacher Education in Primary Science: Developing the Right Kind of Teacher*, Durham: School of Education, University of Durham: 94–103.

Goldstein, H. (2002) *League Tables and Schooling*, London Institute of Education, University of London. Online. Available HTTP: http://www.ioe.ac.uk/hgpersonal/League-tables-and-schooling-P&S.pdf (accessed 10 February 2004).

Goldsworthy, A. and Feasey, R. (1997) *Making Sense of Primary Science Investigations*, 2nd edn revised by S. Ball, Hatfield: ASE.

Goldsworthy, A., Watson, R. and Wood-Robinson, V. (2000a) *Investigations: Getting to Grips with Graphs*, Hatfield: ASE.

—— (2000b) *Investigations: Developing Understanding in Scientific Enquiry*, Hatfield: ASE.

Goodwin, A. (2001) 'Wonder in science teaching and learning: an update' *School Science Review*, **83** (302, September), 69–73.

Gould, S. (1988) *Time's Arrow, Time's Cycle*, London: Pelican Books.

Graham, B. (2000) 'Interactive environments' *School Science Review*, **82** (299, December), 33–6.

Griffin, J. (2002) 'Look! no hands! Practical science experiences in museums', in S. Amos and R. Boohan (eds) *Teaching Science in Secondary Schools: A Reader*, London: Routledge Falmer.

Harrison, B. (1998) 'Industrial links, purposes and practices', in M. Ratcliffe (ed.) *ASE Guide to Secondary Science Education*, Cheltenham: Stanley Thornes.

Harrison, J. (2000) *Sex Education in Secondary Schools,* Buckingham: Open University Press.

Hay McBer (2000) *Research into Teacher Effectiveness: A Model of Teacher Effectiveness*, London: DfEE.

Haydn, T. (2001) 'Assessment and Accountability', in S. Capel, M. Leask, M. and T. Turner (eds) (2001) *Learning to Teach in the Secondary School: A Companion to School Experience*, 3rd edn, London: RoutledgeFalmer.

Haydon, G. (2001) 'Aims of education', in S. Capel, M. Leask, M. and T. Turner (eds) *Learning to Teach in the Secondary School: A Companion to School Experience*, 3rd edn, London: RoutledgeFalmer.

House of Commons Science and Technology Committee (2002) *Science education from 14–19*, London: HMSO. Online. Available HTTP: http://www.parliament.the-stationery-office.co.uk/pa/cm200102/cmselect/cmsctech/508/50801.htm (accessed 12 February 2004).

Hunt, A. and Millar, R. (eds) (2000) *AS Science for Public Understanding*, Oxford: Heinemann.

Institute of Education, University of London *PGCE Secondary Handbook 2003–2004*, Section B: 58, (Internal document) London: Institute of Education, University of London.

International Baccalaureate http://www.ibo.org.

Jarman, R. (2000) 'Between the idea and the reality falls the shadow: provision for primary–secondary science curricular continuity', in J. Sears and P. Sorensen (eds) *Issues in Science Teaching*, London: RoutledgeFalmer.

Jennings, A. (1986) *Science in the Locality*, Cambridge: Cambridge University Press.

John, P. (1993) *Lesson Planning for Teachers*, London: Cassell

Joyce, B., Calhoun, E. and Hopkins, D. (1997) *Models of Learning – Tools for Teaching*, Buckingham: Open University Press.

Kempa, R. (1992) 'Research in chemical education: its role and potential', in M. Atlay, S. Bennet, S. Dutch, R. Levinson, P. Taylor and D. West (eds) *Open Chemistry*, London: Hodder & Stoughton: 45–67.

King, C. (2000) 'The Earth's mantle is solid: teachers' misconceptions about the Earth and plate tectonics', *School Science Review*, **82** (298, September), 57–64.

Koufetta-Menicou, C. and Scaife, J. (2000) 'Teacher's questions – types and significance in science education', *School Science Review*, **81** (296, March) 79–84.

Kuhn, T. S. (1970) *The Structure of Scientific Revolutions*, 2nd edn, Chicago: University of Chicago Press.

Latour, B. and Woolgar, S. (1979) *Laboratory Life: The Social Construction of Scientific Facts*, London: Sage.

Leach, J. (2002) 'Teachers' views on the future of the secondary science curriculum', *School Science Review*, **83** (304, March), 43–50.

Leask, M. and Pachler, N. (1999) *Learning to Teach Using ICT in the Secondary School*, London: RoutledgeFalmer.

Lock, R. and Tilling, S. (2002) 'Ecology fieldwork in 16–19 biology', *School Science Review*, **84** (307, December), 79–88.

Louie, J. (2001) Plate tectonics: the cause of earthquakes. Online. Available HTTP: http://www.seismo.unr.edu/ftp/pub/louie/class/100/plate-tectonics.html (accessed 12 February 2004).

Lubben, F., Campbell, B. and Hogarth, S. (2001) 'Assessment through reports of "physics-in-action" visits', *School Science Review*, **82** (301, June), 47–53.

Marland, M. (1993) *The Craft of the Classroom: A Survival Guide to Classroom Management*, 2nd edn, London: Heinemann (see also 3rd edn, 2003, Oxford: Heinemann.)

Matthews, B. (1996) 'Drawing scientists', *Gender and Education*, **8**, 231–43.

McDuell, B. (2000) (ed.) *Teaching Secondary Chemistry*, London: John Murray for the Association for Science Education.

McKeon, F. (2001) 'Enhancing museum visits through web page development', *School Science Review*, **83** (303, December), 85–9.

Merton, R. K. (1973) *The Sociology of Science: Theoretical and Empirical Investigations*, Chicago: University of Chicago Press.

Millar, R. (2000) 'Science for public understanding: developing a new course for 16–18 year old pupils', *Melbourne Studies in Education* **41** (2), 201–14.

Millar, R. and Osborne, J. (eds) (1998) *Beyond 2000: Science Education for the Future: A Report with Ten Recommendations*, London: King's College London.

Monk, M. and Dillon, J. (eds) (1995) *Learning to Teach Science: Activities for Student Teachers and Mentors*, London: The Falmer Press.

Murphy, P. (1991) 'Gender differences in pupils' reactions to practical work', in B. E. Woolnough (ed.) *Practical Science*, Milton Keynes: Open University Press.

Murphy, P. J. and Murphy, E. (2002a) 'Urban geological trails', *School Science Review*, **83** (305, June), 140–3.

—— (2002b) 'A time line for geological time', *School Science Review*, **84** (306, September), 125–6.

NCC (National Curriculum Council) (1990) *Curriculum Guidance 5: Health Education*, York: NCC.

Newton, L. D. and Newton, D. P. (1998) 'Primary children's conceptions of science and the scientist: is the impact of a National Curriculum breaking down the stereotype?', *International Journal of Science Education*, **20**, 1137–49.

Nicolson, P. and Holman, J. (2003) 'National Curriculum for science: looking back and looking forward', *School Science Review*, **85** (311), 21–7.

Nott, M. and Wellington, J. (1993) 'Your nature of science profile: an activity for science teachers', *School Science Review*, **75** (270), 109–12.

—— (1999) 'The state we're in: issues in Key Stage 3 and 4 science', *School Science Review*, **81** (294) 13–18.

—— (2002) ' Using critical incidents in the science laboratory to teach and learn about the nature of science', in S. Amos and R. Boohan (eds) *Aspects of Secondary Science: Perspectives on Practice*, London and New York: RoutledgeFalmer for the Open University.

OFSTED (1995) *Science, a Review of Inspection Findings 1993/94*, London: HMSO.

—— (2000) *Progress in Key Stage 3 Science*, London: HMSO (HMI Report 221, January). Online. Available HTTP: http://www.ofsted.gov.uk/publications/ (accessed 12 February 2004).

—— (2001) *Standards and Quality in Education 1991/2000: The Annual Report of Her Majesty's Chief Inspector of Schools*, London: The Stationery Office.

—— (2002) *Standards and Quality in Education 2000/2001: The Annual Report of Her Majesty's Chief Inspector of Schools*, London: The Stationery Office.

—— (2003) *The Key Stage 3 strategy: evaluation of the second year*, London: OFSTED (March).

Ogborn, J., Kouladis, V. and Papadotretrakis, E. (1996a) 'We measured the Earth by telephone', *School Science Review*, **77** (281, June), 88–90.

Ogborn, J., Kress, K., Martins, I. and McGillicuddy, K. (1996b) *Explaining Science in the Classroom*, Buckingham: Open University Press.

Oldham, V. (2003) 'Effective use of ICT in secondary science: guidelines and case studies' *School Science Review*, **84** (309, June), 53–60.

Osborne, J. and Collins, S. (2000) *Pupils' and Parents' Views of the School Science Curriculum*, London: King's College London. Online. Available HTTP http://www.kcl.ac.uk/education/research/Public%20Understand.html (accessed 13 February 2004).

Osborne, J., Erduran, S., Simon, S. and Monk, M. (2001) 'Enhancing the quality of argument in school science' *School Science Review*, **82** (301), 63–70.

Osborne, J., Simon, S, and Erduran, S. (2004) *Ideas and Evidence – an INSET pack with video*, London: King's College.

Osborne, R. and Freyberg, P. (1985) *Learning in Science*, Auckland: Heinemann

Oulton, C. (1998) 'Science and environmental education', in M. Ratcliffe (ed.) *ASE Guide to Secondary Science Education*, Cheltenham: Stanley Thornes.

Oxlade, C. (1996) *Bridges*, London: Belitha Press.

QCA (Qualifications and Curriculum Authority) (1998) *Education for Citizenship and the Teaching of Democracy in Schools: Final Report* (The Crick Report), London: QCA.

Pappademos, J. (1983) 'An outline of Africa's role in the history of physics', in I. Van Sertima (ed.) *Blacks in Science: Ancient and Modern*, USA: Transaction Books based on articles in *Journal of African Civilisations*.

Parkinson, J. (2004) *Improving Secondary Science Teaching*, London: RoutledgeFalmer.

Peterson, S., Williams, J. and Sorensen, P. (2000) 'Science for all: the challenge of inclusion', in J. Sears and P. Sorensen (eds) *Issues in Science Teaching*, London: RoutledgeFalmer.

Popper, K. R. (1934/1972) *The Logic of Scientific Discovery*, London: Hutchinson.

Posner, G., Strike, K., Hewson, P. and Gerzog, W. (1982) 'Accommodation of a scientific conception: toward a theory of conceptual change', *Science Education*, **66** (2), 211–27.

Reiss, M. (1993) *Science Education for a Pluralist Society*, Buckingham: Open University Press.

—— (ed.) (1999) *Teaching Secondary Biology*, London: John Murray for the ASE.

—— (2000) 'Sex Education', in J. Beck and M. Earl (eds) *Key Issues in Secondary Education*, London: Casell.

Rogers, E. and Wenham, E. J. (eds)(1977) *Revised Nuffield Physics, Teachers' Guide 3*, London: The Longman Group. See also companion book *Pupils' Text Year 3* (1976).

—— (eds) (1978) *Revised Nuffield Physics, Teachers' Guide 1 and 2*, London: The Longman Group.

Rogers, L. and Finlayson, H. (2003) 'Does ICT in science really work in the classroom? Part 1: the individual teacher experience', *School Science Review*, **84** (309, June), 105–11.

Rowe, M. B. (1974) 'Wait time and rewards as instructional variables, their influence on language, logic and fate control', *Journal of Research in Science Teaching*, **11**, 81–94.

Rowell, R. and Herbert, S. (1987) *Physics: A Course for GCSE*, London: Cambridge.

Sadler, R. (1989) 'Formative assessment and the design of instructional systems', *Instructional Science*, **18**, 119–44.

Sang, D. (ed.) (2000) *Teaching Secondary Physics*, London: John Murray for ASE.

Sang, D. and Wood-Robinson, V. (eds) (2002) *Teaching Secondary Scientific Enquiry*, London: John Murray for the ASE.

Shayer, M. (1996) *Long Term Effects of 'Cognitive Acceleration through Science Education' on Achievement*, London: King's College London: Centre for the Advancement of Thinking.

Shayer, M. (2002) *GCSE 1999: Added-value from Schools Adopting the CASE Intervention*, London: King's College London. Online. Available HTTP: http://www.kcl.ac.uk/about/news/ni/3005200001.html (accessed 10 February 2004).

Shayer, M. and Adey, P. (eds) (2002) *Learning Intelligence*, Buckingham: Open University Press.

Shayer, M. and Gamble, R. (2001) *Bridging: from CASE to Core Science*, Hatfield: ASE.

Simon, S., Jones, A., Black, P., Fairbrother, R. W. and Watson, J. R. (1992) *Open-ended Work in Science: A Review of Existing Practice*, London: King's College London.

Smith, A. (1996) *Accelerated Learning in the Classroom*, Stafford: Network Educational Press.

Sobel, D. (1996) *Longitude: The True Story of a Lone Genius who Solved the Greatest Scientific Problem of his Time*, London: Fourth Estate.

Solomon, J. (1991) *Exploring the Nature of Science (Key Stage 3)*, London: Nelson Blackie

—— (1993) *Teaching science, Technology and Society*, Buckingham: Open University Press.

Staples, R. and Heselden, R. (2001) 'Science teaching and literacy, part 1: writing', *School Science Review*, **83** (303), 35–46.

Stoll, L. and Fink, D. (1996) *Changing our Schools: Linking School Effectiveness and School Improvement*, Buckingham: Open University Press.

Sutton, C. (1992) *Words, Science and Learning*, Buckingham: Open University Press.

TTA (Teacher Training Agency) (1998) *National Standards for Subject Leaders*, London: Teacher Training Agency.

—— (2002) *Qualifying to Teach: Standards for the Award of Qualified Teacher Status*. Online. Available HTTP: http://www.tta.gov.uk/php/read.php?articleid=462& sectionid= 111 (accessed 12 February 2004).

Tuke, M. (1991) *Earth Science: Activities and Demonstrations*, London: John Murray.

Turner, S. (2000) 'Health education is unavoidable', in J. Sears and P. Sorensen (eds) *Issues in Science Teaching*, London: RoutledgeFalmer.

Vygotsky, L. (1978) *Mind in Society*, Cambridge, MA: Harvard University Press.

Watkins, C. (1998) *Learning about Learning*, Coventry: National Association for Pastoral Care.

Watson, J. D. (1968) *The Double Helix*, New York: Atheneum.

Watson, R., Wood-Robinson, V. and Goldsworthy, A. (1999) 'What is not fair with investigations?', *School Science Review*, **80** (292), 101–6.

Watson, R., Wood-Robinson, V. and Goldsworthy, A. (2000) *Targeted Learning: Using Classroom Assessment for Learning,* Hatfield: ASE.

Webster, D. (1987) *Understanding Geology*, Harlow: Oliver & Boyd.

Wellington J. (2000) *Teaching and Learning Secondary Science; Contemporary Issues and Practical Approaches*, London: Routledge.

—— (ed.) (2003) ICT in science education special issue *School Science Review*, **84** (309).

Wellington, J. and Osborne, J. (2001) *Language and Literacy in Science Education*, Buckingham: The Open University.

Windale, M., Hodson, T. and Smith, R. (1995) 'Teaching and learning approaches in science education: what has been the effect of the National Curriculum?', *Journal of Biological Education*, **29**, 235–6.

Woolnough, B. (1994) *Effective Science Teaching*, Buckingham: The Open University Press.

Woolnough, B. and Allsop, T. (1985) *Practical Work in Science*, Cambridge: Cambridge University Press.

Wright, M. and Patel, M. (eds) (2000) *Scientific American: How Things Work Today*, London: Marshall Publishing.

Websites of interest

21st Century Science, Nuffield Curriculum Centre. Online. Available HTTP: http://www.21stcenturyscience.org/home/ (accessed 11 February 2004).

ACCAC (Qualification and Curriculum and Assessment Authority for Wales). Online. Available HTTP: http://www.accac.org.uk (accessed 12 February 2004).

AQA Awarding Body. Online. Available HTTP: http://www.aqa.org.uk/ (accessed 12 February 2004).

ASE (Association for Science Education) (2002) Materials for science and citizenship. http://www.ase.org.uk/htm/ase_global/index1.php (accessed 19 August 2004).

—— Online. Available HTTP: http://www.ase.org.uk/ (accessed 12 February 2004).

BBC Education – GCSE BITESIZE revision and tests. Online. Available HTTP: http://ww.bbc.co.uk/education/gcsebitesize/ (accessed 12 February 2004).

BBC Online – Education. Online. Available HTTP: http://www.bbc.co.uk/learning/ (accessed 19 August 2004).

—— Local Heroes. Online. Available HTTP: http://http://www.bbc.co.uk/history/programmes/local_heroes (accessed 12 February 2004).

—— Science. Online. Available HTTP: http://www.bbc.co.uk/science/ (accessed 12 February 2004).

BBC2 and Open University. Online. Available HTTP: http://www.open2.net/science/ (accessed 12 February 2004).

BECTa (British Educational Technology and Communications Agency). Ideas for use of ICT across the curriculum and within subjects. Online. Available HTTP: http://www.becta.org.uk. (accessed 12 February 2004).

Brain, M. *How Stuff works: Carbon dating.* Online. Available HTTP: http://www.howstuffworks.com/carbon-14.htm. (accessed 11 February 2004).

Buckyball, Diamond, and Graphite. Online. Available HTTP: http://www.chem.wisc.edu/~newtrad/CurrRef/BDGTopic/BDGtext/BDGBucky.html (accessed 11 February 2004).

CCEA (Council for Curriculum Examinations and Assessment). Online. Available HTTP: http://www.ccea.org.uk (accessed 12 February 2004).

Cells, about cells. Online. Available HTTP: http://www.cellsalive.com (accessed 11 February 2004).

CLEAPSS School Science service. Online. Available HTTP: http://www.cleapss.org.uk/ secpbfr.htm (accessed 12 February 2004).

Crosswords and Puzzles: to create crosswords and other puzzles. Online. Available HTTP: http:/ /www.discoveryschool.com(accessed 12 February 2004).

DfES (Department for Education and Skills) *National Vocation Qualifications.* Online. Available HTTP: http://www.dfes.gov.uk/nvq (accessed 12 February 2004).

—— Online. Available HTTP http://www.dfes.gov.uk (accessed 13 February 2004).

Dinosaur Footprints and Eggs. Online. Available HTTP http://www.shef.ac.uk/~es/dino.html (accessed 13 February 2004).

DOH (Department of Health) Online. Available HTTP: http:// www.doh.gov.uk.

Earth Science Teachers Association (ESTA), Burlington House, Piccadilly, London WIV OBN. Online. Available HTTP: http://www.esta-uk.org/ (accessed 12 February 2004).

Earthquake Activity. Online. Available HTTP http://neic.usgs.gov/neis/current/world.html (accessed 13 February 2004).

Edexcel Awarding Body (Now London Partnership). Online. Available HTTP: http:// www.edexcel.org.uk (accessed 12 February 2004).

Exploring science for teachers (resources for teachers including classroom activities). Online. Available HTTP: http://www.explorelearning.com/ (accessed 12 February 2004). See also ASE.

Field Studies Council (2002) *Save our Biology Fieldwork.* Online. Available HTTP: http:// www.field-studies-council.org/pr/index.asp?prid=45 (accessed 12 February 2004).

—— Online. Available HTTP: http://www.field-studies-council.org/outdoorclassroom/ index.asp (accessed 12 February 2004).

General Teaching Council. Online. Available HTTP: http://www.gtce.org.uk (accessed 16 February 2004).

Google search engine www.google.com.

Health and Safety Executive. Online. Available HTTP: http:/www.hse.gov.uk/asp/ search.asp?qu=publications+and+education (accessed 12 February 2004).

How Things Work. Online. Available HTTP: http://www.howstuffworks.com (accessed 12 February 2004).

Iceland's Island of Fire. Online. Available HTTP http://www.explorenorth.com/library/ weekly/aa042601a.htm (accessed 13 February 2004).

Induction standards for Newly Qualified Teachers in England. Online. Available HTTP: http:/ / www.tta.gov.uk/php/read.php?sectionid=96&articleid=479 accessed 16 February 2004).

Inspiration. Online. Available HTTP: http:// www.inspiration.com (accessed 15 February).

Institute of Biology. Guidelines for fieldwork. Online. Available HTTP: http://www.iob.org/ (accessed 12 February 2004). Go to 'Education and Training', then 'Schools and Colleges'.

—— Online. Available HTTP: http://www.iob.org (accessed 12 February 2004).

Institute of Physics. Online. Available HTTP: http://www.iop.org (accessed 12 February 2004).

Joint Earth Science Education Initiative. Resources for teaching Earth science. Online. Available HTTP: http:// www.jesei.org (accessed 16 February 2004).

NASA (North American Space Agency). Good pictures and up-to-date detailed information. Online. Available HTTP: http://www.nasa.gov (accessed 12 February 2004).

National Grid for Learning. Information and links. Online. Available HTTP: http://ngfl.gov.uk (accessed 12 February 2004).

National Vocation Qualifications. Online. Available HTTP www.dfes.gov.uk/nvq (accessed 13 February 2004).

Nevada Seismic Laboratory *About Earthquakes.* Online. Available HTTP: http:// www.seismo.unr.edu/htdocs/abouteq.html (accessed 12 February 2004).

New Scientist Questions and answers on everyday scientific phenomena. Online. Available HTTP www.newscientist.com/lastword (accessed 13 February 2004).

NFER. Cognitive Abilities Test (CAT). Online. Available HTTP: http://www.nfer-nelson.co.uk/secondary/secondary.asp (accessed 10 February 2004).

OCR Awarding Body. Online. Available HTTP: http://www.ocr.org.uk (accessed 12 February 2004).

Office for National Statistics. Online Available HTTP: http://www..statistics.gov.uk

Planet Science. Resources for teachers. Online. Available HTTP: http://www.planet-science.com (accessed 12 February 2004).

QCA (Qualifications and Curriculum Authority) *Planning, Teaching and Assessing the Curriculum for Pupils with Learning Difficulties: Science.* Online. Available HTTP: http://www.nc.uk.net/ld (accessed 12 February 2004).

—— Schemes of work. Online. Available HTTP: http://www.standards.dfes.gov.uk/schemes2/secondary_science/ (accessed 12 February 2004).

—— *Changes to the Key Stage 4 Curriculum: Guidance for Implementation from September 2004,* London: QCA. Online. Available HTTP http://www.qca.org.uk (accessed 13 February 2004).

—— Online. Available HTTP: http://www.qca.org.uk (accessed 12 February 2004).

Questions and answers in science. Online. Available HTTP http://www.sciencenet.org.uk (accessed 13 February 2004).

Quill Graphics. Cells alive. Online. Available HTTP www.cellsalive.com (accessed 13 February 2004).

Roger Frost's website. Online Available HTTP: www.rogerfrost.com (accessed 16 February 2004).

Royal Society of Chemistry. Online. Available HTTP: http://www.rsc.org (accessed 12 February 2004).

Salters-Horner Advanced Physics (SHAP), The visit. Online. Available HTTP: http://www.york.ac.uk/org/seg/salters/physics/assessment/coursework_assessment.html (accessed 12 February 2004).

Science Learning Centres. Online. Available HTTP: http://www.sciencelearningcentres.org.uk (accessed 16 February 2004).

Science Learning Network. Online. Available HTTP: http://www.sln.org (accessed 12 February 2004).

Science Online. Resources for teachers. Online. Available HTTP: http://www.scienceonline.co.uk (accessed 12 February 2004).

Scifun (2003) *Chemical of the week.* Online. Available HTTP: http://scifun.chem.wisc.edu/chemweek/chlrphyl/chlrphyl.html (accessed 11 February 2004).

Selected Classic Papers from the History of Chemistry. Online. Available HTTP: http://webserver.lemoyne.edu/faculty/giunta/papers1.html#elem (accessed 11 February 2004).

SQA (Scottish Qualifications Authority). Online. Available HTTP: http://www.sqa.org.uk (accessed 12 February 2004).

TTA (Teacher Training Agency) *Qualifying to Teach: Professional Standards for the Award of Qualified Teacher Status and Requirements for Initial Teacher Training,* London: TTA. Online. Available HTTP: http://www.useyourheadteach.gov.uk/being_a_teacher/qualified_teacher_status.html (accessed 11 February 2004).

UK's small-scale tremors (2003). Online. Available HTTP http://news.bbc.co.uk/1/hi/sci/tech/2275751.stm#map (accessed 13 February 2004).

Wellcome Trust. Online http://www.wellcome.ac.uk.

Ytouring. Online. Available HTTP: http://ytouring.org.uk.

Name index

Subject index